3 WKS 82

CITY AND ISLINGTON
SIXTH FORM COLLEGE
283-309 GOSWELL ROAD
LONDON
EC1

TEL 020 75200

A01618

THE ARDEN SHAKESPEARE

GENERAL EDITORS: RICHARD PROUDFOOT, ANN THOMPSON AND DAVID SCOTT KASTAN

THE TEMPEST

THE ARDEN SHAKESPEARE

All's Well That Ends Well: edited by G. K. Hunter
Antony and Cleopatra: edited by John Wilders*
As You Like It: edited by Agnes Latham
The Comedy of Errors: edited by R. A. Foakes
Coriolanus: edited by Philip Brockbank
Cymbeline: edited by J. M. Nosworthy
Hamlet: edited by Harold Jenkins
Julius Caesar: edited by T. S. Dorsch
King Henry IV, Parts 1 & 2: edited by A. R. Humphreys
King Henry V: edited by T. W. Craik*
King Henry VI, Parts 1, 2 & 3: edited by Andrew S. Cairncross
King Henry VIII: edited by R. A. Foakes
King John: edited by E. A. J. Honigmann
King Lear: edited by R. A. Foakes*
King Richard II: edited by Peter Ure
King Richard III: edited by Anthony Hammond
Love's Labour's Lost: edited by Richard David
Macbeth: edited by Kenneth Muir
Measure for Measure: edited by J. W. Lever
The Merchant of Venice: edited by John Russell Brown
The Merry Wives of Windsor: edited by H. J. Oliver
A Midsummer Night's Dream: edited by Harold F. Brooks
Much Ado About Nothing: edited by A. R. Humphreys
Othello: edited by E. A. J. Honigmann*
Pericles: edited by F. D. Hoeniger
The Poems: edited by F. T. Prince
Romeo and Juliet: edited by Brian Gibbons
Shakespeare's Sonnets: edited by Katherine Duncan-Jones*
The Taming of the Shrew: edited by Brian Morris
The Tempest: edited by Frank Kermode
Timon of Athens: edited by H. J. Oliver
Titus Andronicus: edited by Jonathan Bate*
Troilus and Cressida: edited by K. J. Palmer
Twelfth Night: edited by J. M. Lothian and T. W. Craik
The Two Gentlemen of Verona: edited by Clifford Leech
The Two Noble Kinsmen: edited by Lois Potter*
The Winter's Tale: edited by J. H. P. Pafford

* Third Series

THE ARDEN EDITION OF THE
WORKS OF WILLIAM SHAKESPEARE

THE TEMPEST

Edited by
FRANK KERMODE

The general editors of the Arden Shakespeare have been
W. J. Craig and R. H. Case (first series 1899-1944)
Una Ellis-Fermor, Harold F. Brooks, Harold Jenkins
and Brian Morris (second series 1946-1982)

Present general editors (third series)
Richard Proudfoot, Ann Thompson and David Scott Kastan

This edition of *The Tempest*, by Frank Kermode,
first published in 1954 by Methuen & Co. Ltd
Reprinted 29 times

Reprinted 1998 by Thomas Nelson & Sons Ltd

Thomas Nelson & Sons Ltd
Nelson House Mayfield Road
Walton-on-Thames Surrey
KT12 5PL UK

I⊤P® Thomas Nelson is an International
Thomson Publishing Company
I⊤P® is used under licence

Editorial matter © 1954 Methuen & Co. Ltd

Printed in Italy

ISBN 0-17-443578-9 (hardback)
ISBN 0-17-443478-2 (paperback)
NPN 9 8 7 6 5 4 3

CONTENTS

PREFACE

THIS work is based upon the original Arden edition of Morton Luce, of which the latest revision was published in 1938. My debt to the older work is considerable, but it is confined to the Commentary, where I have declared my obligation whenever I was able to take over its notes unchanged; there are a good number of places, however, where I have made little substantial alteration. Luce's Appendix on the Bermuda pamphlets, a most valuable contribution, has long since passed into general currency; it has also been developed by later scholars; and it is therefore not reprinted here, though I am, of course, indebted to it, like any other student who may now pick his way with little difficulty through what was a maze of pamphlets.

The text of this edition is based on that of the First Folio of 1623; it differs from that of the original edition in many small details, and in one or two which are not so small. The primary object of the textual notes is the usual one of enabling the reader to reconstruct the text of the Folio wherever the present text incorporates a significant departure from it (*i.e.* a change of a different order from simple modernization of spelling). Secondly, it aims to record variants proposed by other editors when these appear to deserve consideration as useful attempts to mend what is, or what may be, corrupt; or when the proposed readings seem to have some historical interest. The variants of the three later Folios are fully recorded; not of course because they have such contact with the copy as might give them authority (for they are no more than the earliest edited texts) but because they illustrate the mechanical progress of that corruption which vitiated the copy of the early eighteenth-century editors, and the first rather undiscriminating attempts to castigate the text of errors surviving from manuscript as well as errors acquired in the process of transmission. These readings are, I think, of interest to anyone who wishes to familiarize himself with the antecedents of modern textual criticism. Variations arising from abnormalities of lineation in the Folio are among the most interesting of the problems presented by this play to the expert textual critic, but they seem to me to be different in kind from verbal variants. Whoever studies them will wish to study them all, as a single problem or set of related problems, and I have therefore placed all the notes recording variants of lineation in Appendix G, where they will be conveniently assembled for those who are interested, and conveniently out of the way of those who are not. The bibliographical issues involved in these variants are extremely technical and also extremely speculative; and since so little is known of many factors which certainly affect the issue, I have not attempted a general explanation of the disturbances; and certain theories which depend upon arguments from them I do not accept.

My Introduction owes practically nothing to that of my predecessor, not because I do not understand the high opinion which many respected critics still have of it, but because there seemed to be no way of doing what, in my view, was necessary, while remaining on the path beaten out by Luce. This part of the work raised many problems; its scope does not allow for extensive treatment of all the problems of interpretation in *The Tempest*. Sections 3–6 in particular have been very heavily curtailed. In dealing with these and all other difficulties I have had good cause to be thankful for the unfailingly generous scholarship and tact of the General Editor.

I am indebted also to Mr John Munro, who allowed me to cite his private correspondence, and to see his exhaustive study of the sources of the play—this, unfortunately, when my Introduction was no longer in my hands; to Professor D. J. Gordon, who read an early draft, and provided me with a detailed and valuable critical commentary on my work; to Mr H. F. Brooks, Dr D. P. Walker, Mr J. B. Trapp, and to many patient colleagues at Reading; and to the staffs of the libraries of Reading University, the Warburg Institute, and the British Museum.

My greatest debt is to my wife, and to her I dedicate the book.

F. K.

PREFACE TO THE SIXTH EDITION

I HAVE to thank Mr E. Schanzer for valuable comments on my first edition (the fifth according to the publisher's reckoning); and Mr J. C. Maxwell, whose invaluable observations included a conjectural emendation which I have accepted into the text at I. i. 22. Dr H. F. Brooks has again given me the benefit of his rich and subtle scholarship. I have taken the opportunity to correct one or two infelicities in the Introduction, and some misprints, four of them in the text (IV. i. 124, 202, 215, 249). These corrections apart, the text has been altered in seventeen places: I. i. 22; I. ii. 248, 249, 271, 329; II. i. 35–6, 90, 247; III. i. 15; IV. i. 68, 231; V. i. 15; III. i. 82, 83; III. ii. 44; III. iii. 50; V. i. 145. In the last five only the punctuation is affected. The stage directions have been brought into conformity with the conventions established for more recent volumes in the Arden series. I have added a few pages, dealing mostly with Ralph Crane and the copy, to the Introduction. The Commentary I have altered in many places where alteration was feasible; where it was not, and some change seemed nevertheless necessary, I have written additional notes which appear on pp. 166–71. Wherever possible I have indicated the existence of these notes at the proper place in the Commentary.

F. K.

September 1957

ABBREVIATIONS

The following abbreviations are used in the Introduction and Commentary:

(1) *Works of reference*

Abbott	Abbott, *Shakespearian Grammar* (1886).
Eliz. Stage	E. K. Chambers, *The Elizabethan Stage* (4 vols.), 1923.
N.S.	The New (Cambridge) Shakespeare; *The Tempest*, ed. Sir Arthur Quiller-Couch and J. D. Wilson, 1921.
O.E.D.	*The Oxford English Dictionary.*
Onions	C. T. Onions, *Shakespeare Glossary* (1911 . . . 1951).
Schmidt	*Shakespeare-Lexicon* (1902).
Tilley	M. P. Tilley, *A Dictionary of the Proverbs in England in the Sixteenth and Seventeenth Centuries* (1950).*

(2) *Periodicals*

J.E.G.P.	*Journal of English and Germanic Philology.*
M.L.N.	*Modern Language Notes.*
M.L.R.	*Modern Language Review.*
M.P.	*Modern Philology.*
N. & Q.	*Notes & Queries.*
P.M.L.A.	*Publications of the Modern Language Association of America.*
P.Q.	*Philological Quarterly.*
R.E.S.	*Review of English Studies.*
S.A.B.	*Shakespeare Association Bulletin.*
S.P.	*Studies in Philology.*
T.L.S.	*Times Literary Supplement.*
Trans. Royal Soc. Lit.	*Transactions of the Royal Society of Literature.*

(3) *The Folios*

F	First Folio (1623).
F2	Second Folio (1632).
F3	Third Folio (1663).
F4	Fourth Folio (1685).
Ff	All Folios except the First.

The abbreviations of the titles of Shakespeare's plays and poems follow C. T. Onions, *Shakespeare Glossary*, p. x.

* The references are to the items as alphabetically arranged according to the initial letters of significant words.

INTRODUCTION

1. TEXT—DATE—INTEGRITY

1. *The First Folio. The Tempest* was first printed in the Folio of Heminge and Condell in 1623. It is the first play in the volume, and occupies nineteen of its pages. The text printed below is based upon that of 1623, and departs from it in only a very few readings. This close adherence is, of course, the result of a conservative policy; but it is also a consequence of the exceptionally "clean" character of the substantive text, which is generally agreed to be one of the most careful in the Folio.

Although there are certain physical characteristics in the Folio text which lend colour to suggestions that the play has been cut or revised, *The Tempest* seems to have been set up not from a theatrical prompt-copy but from a transcript which could have been made for any of a number of purposes before it was so used; but there are other features which suggest that it was specially made for the edition of 1623. These are its unusually elaborate stage directions, which have no parallel save perhaps in the later play, *Henry VIII*; and its rather careful punctuation.

There have been several attempts to explain the lavishness of the stage directions. It has been suggested that Shakespeare composed the play, as we have it, in retirement at Stratford, and was therefore obliged to write in various instructions which would have been unnecessary had he been at the playhouse;[1] that they were not Shakespeare's work, but that of the "incompetent coadjutor" who is alleged to have inserted the "dream-masque" in *Cymbeline*;[2] that they provide a literary equivalent for the original theatrical directions, which would, for example, read "Thunder" rather than "A tempestuous

1. *The Tempest*, ed. Sir Arthur Quiller-Couch and J. D. Wilson (*New Shakespeare*) (1921), p. 80. Henceforth referred to as N.S.
2. R. Crompton Rhodes, *Shakespeare's First Folio* (1923), pp. 140–1.

THE TEMPEST

xii

noise of Thunder and Lightning heard."[1] In the published versions of contemporary masques and entertainments at Court, with which *The Tempest* has some connexions, there were generally provided elaborate accounts of the scenes, machines, and dances exhibited at the performance; but the descriptions given in the Folio text of quaint device and mock and mow differ from those of the masques in that they are given in the present and not in the past tense. One essential difference between play and masque is that the latter is usually performed only once, and is therefore a past glory to be preserved inadequately in a lavish description, whereas the play can be more or less exactly repeated at will. The editors of 1623 may have imitated the masque convention, retaining the theatrical present from habit; or they may have had this difference in mind. Crompton Rhodes thought these masque-like stage directions supported the theory that the text in F is set up from a version of the play different from any performed in the popular theatres.[2] Sir Walter Greg regards them as a mark of careful preparation by the scrivener Ralph Crane, supposing that this servant of Shakespeare's company was commissioned to make a copy of the playhouse manuscript in all respects ready for publication "as a model for the editing of the volume".[3]

There is some other evidence that *The Tempest* was, more than most of the other plays, the object of editorial care. Its division into Acts and Scenes is accurate and thorough; it has the unusual distinction of bearing an indication of locality ("An un-inhabited Island"); it is one of the four plays equipped with a *Dramatis Personae*. There is certainly a presumption that it was, as the first play in the collection, quite attentively prepared. "Whatever you do, buy," said Heminge and Condell in their Preface; *The Tempest*, which the customer came upon first, gave him assurance that he would have his money's worth. For us, a more important consequence of this policy is the excellent punctuation of this text. It is not absolutely consistent,[4] but it is none the less above the battle which still rages

1. R. Crompton Rhodes, *Shakespeare's First Folio* (1923), pp. 140–1.
2. *ibid.* p. 101. For the relationship of *The Tempest* with the masque, see also below, pp. lxxi ff.
3. *The Editorial Problem in Shakespeare* (1942), p. 152.
4. For an account of the factors which militate against its being so, see McKerrow's *Prolegomena to the Oxford Shakespeare* (1938), pp. 40 ff.

round other Shakespearian texts, and it exemplifies in its course most of Mr Simpson's rules.[1] This quality of the text is unfortunately lost in modernization, though it has been necessary occasionally to discuss the pointing in notes. It may owe more to Ralph Crane than to Shakespeare, as Crane is known to have been fond of brackets, which are relatively frequent in this text.

In view of these marks of editorial care, we may be reasonably certain that internal inconsistencies are not the direct responsibility of the 1623 editors. There is some mislineation in the text, which is perhaps of little importance; but there are also several passages in which rhythmical speeches are set up as prose, and prose is chopped up into verse-lengths.[2] For the first of these peculiarities there are various bibliographical explanations designed to meet the more extravagant instances found in, for example, *King Lear*, and surviving manuscripts provide evidence that the author might, if pressed for space, write several lines of verse continuously as prose, or overflow into the margins. The question is discussed at length, and with reference to the theory of Professor Dover Wilson, in Sir Edmund Chambers' *William Shakespeare* (1930) I. 182, 258, and 403–4 (where a similar problem in *As You Like It* is discussed); in McKerrow's *Prolegomena*, pp. 46 ff; and in Greg's *Editorial Problem*, pp. 95 ff. But none of the explanations with which I am familiar seems to account for the comparative regularity with which certain of Caliban's speeches, particularly in II. ii, are printed as prose, though they seem to have the rhythm of verse. Stephano and Trinculo are treated likewise, though compensated by a tendency to divide their prose as verse. Many familiar expositions of the character of Caliban depend to some extent upon the assumption that the author intended him to speak verse, but as a matter of fact his prose speeches rarely convert to pentameter verse without some adjustment—the omission of a word, or the perhaps overfrequent licensing of a hemistich—and a plausible explanation of this and other features of the comic scenes is that the scribe copied from a manuscript in which an editorial hand had already participated; that the rhythmical elements in Cali-

1. P. Simpson, *Shakespearian Punctuation*, Oxford (1911).
2. Some of it is certainly the work of the compositors.

ban's language are "verse-fossils". Here we must pause, as this raises the whole question of the "integrity" of the play as it survives.

The details of the relevant passages will be found in the commentary and in Appendix G. Although we should not overstate their importance, it is evident that Caliban's language is differentiated from that of the Europeans, and it is also evident that some of his lines would normally be written as verse. (Most editors rightly so print them.) I do not think we know enough about the principles which underlie Shakespeare's choice between verse and prose to dogmatize, but this choice is certainly related to the rhetorical issue of decorum—the style must be appropriate to the speaker and the context. On this score alone an unimaginative editor might revise Caliban's verse (and possibly, though one ought not to make a point of it, the prose of Stephano and Trinculo). But it would be curious to find an editor so precise in his principles and yet so perfunctory in his practice, and certainly none of the poets suspected by one critic or another of interference (*e.g.* Chapman, Massinger, Beaumont) would normally have behaved so. It is on the whole more likely that Shakespeare himself rewrote some of Caliban's speeches, and that the prose-as-verse of the others is the work of the printer.[1] The revision is perfectly intelligible in view of the extreme audacity and complexity of the figure of Caliban, and could, if Crane was working from Shakespeare's autograph (which is not impossible), have been made in the course of the first composition. The new version would be cramped into the margins, and it is conceivable that this fact alone could account for the appearance of the revised passages in the Folio. The rhythmical element *may* be a fossil; if so, it is a remnant of an earlier draft rather than of a complete version.[2]

1. There is a possibility that a compositor may need to "lose space" in order to end his "stint" at the proper place. He breaks down speeches into phrases, as elsewhere, for the opposite reason, he crushes speeches together. It may be that p. 4 and p. 9 of F (*Temp.* I. ii. 233–346; II. i. 298–II. ii. 89) illustrate such processes. Mr H. F. Brooks proposes to publish a full study of this problem.

2. But Chambers, *Shakespearean Gleanings* (1944), pp. 81–2, shows that much of I. i can reasonably be recast as verse. Since the reasons offered above do not apply to this case, the fact that the verse is printed as prose may be without significance outside pure bibliography.

II. *Theories of Earlier Versions.* The view that there must have
been an earlier version of *The Tempest* different from that
published in 1623 is widely held. There are two classes of
evidence, the first purporting to show that the play existed
many years before 1611 (the accepted date of its first production in something like its present form), and the second to
show that it was modified, probably after 1611, for performance on a special occasion, and that the extant version incorporates the modifications. These categories are not mutually
exclusive but they make it easier to examine the issue.

i. The opinion that *The Tempest* as it stands is an early play
of Shakespeare's commands little orthodox support. It was
unavailingly proposed by Joseph Hunter in 1839 and 1845.[1]
More recently it has been suggested by Miss Janet Spens that
Pericles, Cymbeline, The Winter's Tale, and *The Tempest* were
originally short pieces presented as a sequence, in the earliest
part of Shakespeare's career. The resemblances to *Mucedorus,*
to which I refer below, seem to her to indicate a date in the
early 'nineties, and Prospero's long expository conversation
with Miranda she connects with a similar plot-device in
Lyly's *Galathea.*[2] But *Mucedorus* appears to have been as popular in 1611 as at any previous time, and there are other explanations of the resemblance. It would probably be rash to deny
any Lylyan influence on the unusual *protasis,* but it is ultimately of little significance.[3]

More frequently stated at present is the view that the extant
Tempest is a late reworking of an earlier play by Shakespeare.

---

1. Hunter posited purely literary sources for the storm (a denial of Malone's
thesis concerning the Bermuda pamphlets which is still occasionally repeated)
and thereby removed the necessity of regarding 1610 as the *terminus a quo.* He
found stylistic evidence to support his contention that the play belonged to the
early phase of romantic comedy, in which he also placed *The Winter's Tale.*
Although a reminder that Shakespeare was an old hand at romantic comedy
still does not come amiss, none of Hunter's arguments amounts to much, and
that which contends that Jonson alludes to *The Tempest* in the Prologue to
Every Man in His Humour amounts to nothing at all, since the Prologue first
appeared in the Folio of 1616, cannot have been written before 1606, and may
be as late as 1612. (Cf. *Works of Jonson,* ed. Herford and Simpson, I. 333.) After
this we need not delay over Hunter's more plausible ingenuity in disposing of
the admitted debt to the Florio translation of Montaigne (1603).

2. *Elizabethan Drama* (1922), pp. 87–8.

3. The structure of the play is discussed *infra,* pp. lxxi ff.

There are two main arguments here, both of which are pro-
pounded in the N.S. edition.

The first theory assumes that the plot-resemblances between *The Tempest* and the German *Die Schöne Sidea* are strong
enough to suggest that the two plays are materially connected
and not merely analogous. Jakob Ayrer of Nuremburg, the
author of the German play, died in 1605. In his *Opus Theatri-
cum*, published in 1618, there are several adaptations of English
plays which he must have seen in Germany when some English
company was touring there. The suggestion is that *Die Schöne
Sidea* is a German version of an *ur-Tempest* played by English
comedians before 1605.

Ever since Tieck made the preliminary observation in 1817,
serious study of *The Tempest* has been bedevilled by Ayrer. The
belief that his play is important as a close reflection of an
earlier version has brought chaos into source-study and also
into more general criticism. Such discussion as Ayrer deserves
may be postponed; it is enough to say now that the hypothetical English *Fair Sidea* could have had little more to do with *The
Tempest* than *Mucedorus*, and that the prominence of Ayrer's
play in *Tempest* studies is a tribute to the persistence of German
scholarship rather than a measure of its real importance.

But it is none the less held—and this is the second argument
for the theory that *The Tempest* is a reworking of an early play
—that the extant text contains "fossils" of the lost version. The
N.S. editors believed that *The Tempest* had originally an extensive plot like that of *The Winter's Tale*, and that in resuming
action as exposition in I. ii, Shakespeare did not quite succeed
in concealing signs that this scene does the work of several acts,
which, formerly, exhibited the expulsion of Prospero from
Milan, and everything else that we are now merely told about
as having happened twelve years earlier. The "fossils" are
half a dozen hidden rhymes in the play,[1] which are held to
indicate an earlier version with much rhyming. When these
rhymes were first noticed (by Brinsley Nicholson, who missed
some of them) it was claimed that there were too many such
rhymes to be accountable as the work of chance, since the

1. N.S., p. 79. Trinculo's doggerel couplet at III. ii. 76–8 is used in support of
the argument.

phenomenon occurs nowhere else in the canon. I do not know whether this is true, and I have not heard of any investigation having been made to ascertain it, though such research would certainly be a necessary preliminary to confident handling of the statistics. As it is, *The Tempest* examples vary in value, and one or two are nugatory. We may also reflect that Shakespeare grew increasingly fond of the pentameter which spreads itself over two half-lines, and the heavy pause in the middle of the "straddled" line tends to remove emphasis from the true sense-ending; hence the unobtrusiveness of such rhymes.[1] The possibility that not all rhymes occurring even at the ends of lines are deliberate should not be forgotten.[2]

The theory that *The Tempest* is a new version of a very early play seems, in fact, to have very little to support it. Prospero's *protasis* is far from unique in character, and we know that Shakespeare was early familiar with the neo-Terentian structural pattern.[3] It is not impossible that a romance of the *Mucedorus* type figured insignificantly in the prehistory of the play, but it cannot be deduced from the German analogue. The textual evidence for the existence of such a play is meagre and inconclusive.

ii. The theory that the play was altered in various ways after Shakespeare completed it is more formidable. Here we shall have to consider textual evidence of cuts as well as suggestions that the play bears marks of structural modification and interference by other hands.

The purely textual evidence is presented at length in the N.S. edition, and it has been examined in great detail by Chambers.[4] It seems to me that the N.S. editors, having com-

---

1. Mr John Munro, from whose private communications I borrow the term "straddled line", which seems self-explanatory, argues for the incidence of such lines as a test of Shakespearian authorship, e.g. in *Henry VIII. The Tempest* abounds in them. See II. i. 241–2; 244–5 "till new-born chins be rough and razorable"; 247–8; 256–7; 262–3; 272–3. They are of course less frequent in the earlier plays, since they can only occur where there are "run-on lines". It may be worth adding that *Paradise Lost* contains quite a number of "hidden rhymes".

2. See Chambers, *William Shakespeare*, I. 258. Chambers and Greg (*M.L.R.* XVII, 177) regard the hidden rhymes as accidental. They are susceptible to so many interpretations that they cannot, alone, support a theory.

3. *infra*, p. lxxiv. 4. *R.E.S.* I (1925), 129; *Shakespearean Gleanings*, pp. 76–97.

mitted themselves to a hypothesis which assumes a great
amount of interference, accepted as evidence much that was
very slight, and Chambers has little difficulty in disposing of a
great deal of it. For example, the failure of Prospero to answer
Miranda's question at I. ii. 158–60 is only apparent; he does
explain how they managed to survive the voyage, which is
what Miranda wanted to know. Chambers explains the half-
line, "By Providence divine", as doing "double duty as a
member of two successive metrical lines", but one could just
as easily defend it as a dramatic or rhetorical effect; the N.S.
editors do not deny that hemistichs are sometimes so caused.
The providential nature of his exile is fundamental to Prospero's view of the total situation; like Adam in Paradise, he
offered ineffective resistance to evil and was expelled; but
after this he was, like Adam with the world before him,
"blessedly holp". The first statement of an extremely important theme is differentiated by an emphatic short line. Other
broken lines are less certainly rhetorical than this—I. ii. 188,
318, 322—but in every instance here the difficulty of inferring
any omission in the sense tells against the supposition of cuts.
F generally starts new speeches at the beginning of the line,
and shows none of the eighteenth-century concern for dividing
the text throughout as pentameters. One must also consider
that Shakespeare seems to have developed a tendency to
neglect this formal division of his verse, as the F texts of *Timon
of Athens* and *Coriolanus* confirm. Odd half-lines would easily
result from these factors. It is unlikely that this problem, which
involves in unpredictable combinations the chances of every
variety of cause from bibliographical to rhetorical, will ever
be fully solved;[1] the puzzle of Virgil's hemistichs is an ancient
memento mori for all such speculations. Chambers allows the
possibility that of the forty half-lines in the play two might
indicate slight cuts (I. ii. 235, 253) but even these, on which no
hypothesis could reasonably be founded, seem to me very
improbable.

At I. ii. 301 Prospero gives Ariel the purposeless order to
dress up as a nymph of the sea, and this has been cited as

---

1. For a recent theory that such "irregularities" are deliberate, and essentially part of the Elizabethan acting text, see R. Flatter, *Shakespeare's Producing
Hand* (1948).

evidence of "botchery". But here the criterion is literary rather than bibliographical; and if we find this passage distracting we might recall the large spectacular element which is a precondition of this kind of play, or even call it a "theatrical sophistication" like Ariel's slightly inconsistent song at II. i. 295–300. Inconsistencies we should surely always expect. Shakespeare did not tidy his most careful plots, and neither the famous howler where Ferdinand speaks of Antonio's son (I. ii. 440–1) nor the curious half-life of Adrian and Francisco should disturb us unduly if we remember, say, *Othello* or *The Merchant of Venice*. Of course, there are points at which the bibliographical and the literary criteria merge; such is the passage on Sycorax (I. ii. 258–67). Certainly Prospero seems about to correct or amplify Ariel's "Sir, in Argier," and it may be that Shakespeare had it in mind to say more about Sycorax; but it is the spate of Prospero's hasty and eccentric utterance that whirls us away from the subject of the witch's birthplace, and not a cut. Chambers is obviously right when he finds in the attempt to convert the expository matter into a plausible conversation the reason for this and other obscurities in I. ii, where most of the disputed passages are found. I should have thought there was more chance of a theatrical cut being the explanation at V. i. 129, where Prospero's "No" is hard to understand. But as Chambers says, the word is not, as Dover Wilson thought, unmetrical, and we should prefer some other explanation of the difficulty.

The case for limited and local abridgement seems weak. The evidence for abridgement on a larger scale must now be considered.

N.S. argues that there must have been a longish scene between IV. i. and V. i, which was completely removed during the process of abridgement, since "this is the only occasion . . . in the canon where speakers who have concluded one scene appear at the opening of the next."[1] Greg in his review[2] mentioned the well-known episode in *Midsummer Night's Dream* when, between Acts III and IV, Hermia and Helena "sleep all the Act" (*i.e.* the interval between the acts). The drama of the period provides other examples.[3] The practice is certainly

1. p. 85. 2. *M.L.R.* XVII. And see note on p. 111.
3. *e.g.* Chapman, *Bussy d'Ambois*, II. ii–III. i.

rare in Shakespeare, and one can understand that students have speculated as to what might have been the substance of the "lost" scene.

The most ingenious attempt to foist new material into *The Tempest* is that of H. D. Gray,[1] though his concern is to fill up Act IV after removing the masque from it. He thinks that for the second court performance, given during the stay in England of the Elector Palatine, who had come to marry Elizabeth, the daughter of James I, the play was cut and altered to admit the inclusion of more spectacular elements than the first version contained.[2] These new elements were the "masque" in IV. i, the "antimasque" of dogs and so forth in v. i, and also the banquet-scene in III. iii, which needs fairly elaborate machinery. The great hole left in the play when these are removed is filled with various hypothetical developments of the action that remains. The ordeal by logs, he suggests, must have cost Ferdinand much more pain in the original; the plot against Alonso might have got as far as a second attempt on him; and above all, the conspiracy of Caliban against Prospero, which agitates the mage unreasonably in the extant text, must have gone much further. The source of this last action, argues Gray, may be traced in the *scenario* of an Italian *commedia dell'arte* called *Li Tre Satiri*. In this, a native islander conspires with two Europeans in a plot to steal a magician's book and gain power over his spirits. The plot is temporarily successful, but eventually it is thwarted by the superior powers of the magician, who conducts the plot to a happy ending in some respects resembling that of *The Tempest*. Between III. iii and v. i, therefore, we should have had a second attempt on Alonso, the capture of Miranda by spirits under the control of Stephano, now in possession of Prospero's books, an attempt to murder Prospero, and then of course the final overthrow of sedition and the reunion of children and parents.

If Gray is right, the technical objection made by Wilson about the need for another scene at the end of IV is not only met, but reduced to insignificance. But aside from the question

1. *Studies in Philology*, XVIII (1921), p. 129.

2. Somewhat similar suggestions had been made by Luce and Verplanck; this one was adumbrated by Quiller-Couch in *Shakespeare's Workmanship* (1918) and Robertson in *Shakespeare and Chapman* (1911). See also p. 171.

of Shakespeare's indebtedness to the Italian *scenario*, which must be taken up later, it is a fact that, as Chambers says, neither intrigue "is demonstrably incomplete", and it seems unlikely that the last Act could have been freed of all reference to such exciting and extensive happenings without any trace more convincing than those indicated by Gray. To remove III. iii is to cut out one of the play's vital organs. Gray does not appreciate that the extant text could well have been performed everywhere the King's Men were likely to want to perform it,[1] that "masques" of the sort we find here were not exceptional, that the play is not so remarkably short that it could not have passed without much notice being taken of its brevity. In any case, Caliban insists that the object of the attempt is to burn, not to steal, Prospero's books, and none of the conspirators suggests that anything more than temporal dominion is coveted. Common sense suggests that only complete rewriting of the hypothetical 1611 text could result in such a clean sweep of its hypothetical plot; and it also suggests that the multiplication of shadow-*Tempests* which exhibited an exact conformity with some determinable pattern is a barren occupation.

Gray treats the "masque" as a late addition; and this brings us to the last body of disintegrative theory, which takes the "masque" to be occasional, or spurious, or both. But this cannot be treated until something has been said about dates.

Although a vast amount has been written about the *termini* of *The Tempest*, it is one of the plays whose early stage history is relatively simple, and supported by external testimony. Since the authenticity of the Revels Accounts which Cunningham claimed to have found in 1842 is no longer seriously in doubt,[2] we can be certain that it was presented at Court in 1611 by Shakespeare's company. "Hallomas nyght was presented att Whithall before ye Kings Matie, a play Called the Tempest."[3] This was doubtless an early performance, though

1. See Appendix F.
2. Cunningham's vindication by Law in 1911 was later challenged by S. A. Tannenbaum in 1928. This provoked the careful inquiry of A. E. Stamp (*The Disputed Revels Accounts*, 1930), after which most scholars agreed that the case for forgery had become quite incredible in its complexity; meanwhile corroborative evidence had accumulated to Cunningham's defence.
3. See Chambers, *William Shakespeare*, II. 342.

there is little reason to suppose it was the first. The play uses material not available until the latter part of 1610, and Simon Forman, who saw, among other plays at the Globe, *Cymbeline* and *The Winter's Tale*, apparently did not see *The Tempest* there. This was during the summer of 1611.[1] *The Tempest* was again played at Court during the winter of 1612–13, as part of the astonishing round of entertainment provided during the period of the Elector's visit, particularly between the betrothal and the marriage. A record of the payment made to Heminge in May 1613 for the services of the King's Men survives in the Vertue MSS, and reads as follows:[2]

Item paid to John Heminges upon the Cowncells warrant . . . for presentinge before the Princes Highnes the Lady Elizabeth and the Prince Pallatyne Elector fowerteene severall playes, viz: one play called Filaster, One called the Knott of Fooles, One other Much Adoe abowte Nothinge, The Mayeds Tragedy, The Merye Dyvell of Edmonton, The Tempest. . .

The wedding took place on 14 February 1613 (new style). There is no evidence that *The Tempest* was regarded as any more important or appropriate than the other plays performed during the season of expensive celebrations, and none that it was used to signalize some specific event. Nevertheless, there is much modern support for the view that Shakespeare's play was altered for this performance, the "masque" being an addition to the original version. The list of scholars who have subscribed to some variety of this opinion is a formidable one; it includes Fleay and the old Cambridge editors, Robertson, Lawrence, Law, Dover Wilson, and Greg. Lawrence's variant is of some interest: he argued that the play was more suitable to the betrothal (27 December 1612) than the marriage, and tries to show a probability that *The Tempest* was performed on the earlier occasion.[3]

1. Forman's *Bocke of Plaies*, which Tannenbaum argued to be a Collier forgery, is now fully vindicated; see the article by Dover Wilson and R. W. Hunt in *R.E.S.* xxiii (1947), 193–200

2. Chambers, *ibid.* ii. 343.

3. *Fortnightly Review*, cxvii (1920), 941. (The reference in Chambers, *Gleanings*, is wrong.) Although Lawrence is right in saying that the masque is not appropriate to a wedding, that it should have been performed on the actual day of the betrothal is, as Chambers says, "a rather arbitrary conjecture". For

If one assumes that the "masque" must have some special relevance to courtly affairs it is difficult to explain its presence in the version played at court in 1611, at a time when no marriages or betrothals were being celebrated. So Chambers, who deals very thoroughly with attempts to show that the structure of the play has been interfered with,[1] believes that the "masque" was always in the play, and that there may have been a wedding in 1611 of which we know nothing. But there is surely no need to imagine such a wedding. Entertainments of this kind were not uncommon in professional plays of the period; indeed they are a fairly regular feature of the Blackfriars type of play. The "masque" is a betrothal-"masque", of course, and Ferdinand and Miranda are the contractors celebrated. The spirits in the course of their entertainment remind us of several important themes of the play as a whole—they insist on chastity, they advert to the theme of the Golden Age and its natural fertility, and they do so in language which is probably a deliberate *pastiche* of the fashionable diction of the masque proper. This last point reminds us that Shakespeare obviously valued the device of serious parody as a mode for the play within the play, and it disposes of Robertson's proof by vocabulary that the "masque" is by Chapman,[2] and of Fleay's, that it is by Beaumont.[3]

All the evidence so far brought—whether external, or from structure, or from style—to show that the masque in Act IV is an occasional addition to the play performed in 1611, fails of

his theory that the performance took place at the Cockpit, see Appendix F. Much is made to depend upon the interpretation of one passage: "Spring come to you at the farthest In the very end of harvest" (IV. i. 114–15). This is taken, by others as well as Lawrence, to be an expression of the hope that the marriage will soon bear fruit, but in view of the date of the ceremony the end of harvest is too soon for legitimate expectations of this sort. Lawrence and Dover Wilson believe the lines were once more explicit than this. The marriage was delayed by the death of the Prince of Wales; perhaps, they say, the masque was written before this event, and with the lines as follows: "Offspring come to you at farthest In etc." "The delay warned him of the inappropriateness of the sentiment, and made him write feebly in alteration: Spring come to you etc." This seems to need no comment. These lines defeat all attempts to make them apply *specifically* to human fertility and to lovers outside the play.

1. "The Integrity of *The Tempest*" (*Gleanings*).

2. *Shakespeare and Chapman* (1911).

3. See Hardin Craig's "Shakespeare's Bad Poetry", *Shakespeare Survey*, 1 (1948), 51–6.

its purpose. Whether or no we share the opinion that it is unworthy of Shakespeare, we have no right to treat it as anything but an integral part of the play as Shakespeare wrote it. And, briefly to sum up this whole section on the hypothetical pre-history of the Folio text of *The Tempest*, we have no need to invoke the arguments of Abercrombie[1] to establish the right to interpret the play exactly as it stands, for no one has even half succeeded in disintegrating it.

2. THEMES OF THE PLAY

The main purpose of what follows is to sketch the themes of *The Tempest*. It has rarely seemed sufficient to discuss the play at the level of plot alone, and there are many allegorical interpretations, some of them assuming a political, some an autobiographical, and some a religious purpose and key. These somewhat desperate expedients are unnecessary, for *The Tempest*, though exceptionally subtle in its structure of ideas, and unique in its development of them, can be understood as a play of an established kind dealing with situations appropriate to that kind.

The Tempest is a pastoral drama; it belongs to that literary kind which includes certain earlier English plays, but also, and more significantly, *Comus*; it is concerned with the opposition of Nature and Art, as serious pastoral poetry always is, and it shares this concern with the other late comedies, and with the Sixth Book of the *Faerie Queene*, to which it is possibly directly indebted.

The main opposition is between the worlds of Prospero's Art, and Caliban's Nature. Caliban is the core of the play; like the shepherd in formal pastoral, he is the natural man against whom the cultivated man is measured. But we are not offered a comparison between a primitive innocence in nature and a sophisticated decadence, any more than we are in *Comus*. Caliban represents (at present we must over-simplify) nature without benefit of nurture; Nature, opposed to an Art which is man's power over the created world and over himself;

---

1. Lascelles Abercrombie, "A Plea for the Liberty of Interpreting", *Proceedings of the British Academy*, xvi (1930), 137–64.

nature divorced from grace, or the senses without the mind. He differs from Iago and Edmund in that he is a "naturalist" by nature, without access to the art that makes love out of lust; the restraints of temperance he cannot, in his bestiality, know; to the beauty of the nurtured he opposes a monstrous ugliness; ignorant of gentleness and humanity, he is a savage and capable of all ill; he is born to slavery, not to freedom, of a vile and not of a noble union; and his parents represent an evil natural magic which is the antithesis of Prospero's benevolent Art.

This is a simple diagram of an exquisitely complex structure, but it may be useful as a guide. Caliban is the ground of the play. His function is to illuminate by contrast the world of art, nurture, civility; the world which none the less nourishes the malice of Antonio and the guilt of Alonso, and stains a divine beauty with the crimes of ambition and lust. There is the possibility of purgation; and the tragicomic theme of the play, the happy shipwreck—"that which we accompt a punishment against evill is but a medicine against evill"— is the means to this end.

The events of 1609 in Bermuda must have seemed to contain the whole situation in little. There a group of men were, as they themselves said, providentially cast away into a region of delicate and temperate fruitfulness, where Nature provided abundantly; brought out of the threatening but merciful sea into that New World where, said the voyagers, men lived in a state of nature. Ancient problems of poetry and philosophy were given an extraordinary actuality. The Bermuda pamphlets seem to have precipitated, in this play, most of the major themes of Shakespeare's last years; indeed, that is their whole importance.

3. THE NEW WORLD

It is as well to be clear that there is nothing in *The Tempest* fundamental to its structure of ideas which could not have existed had America remained undiscovered, and the Bermuda voyage never taken place. The New World stimulated interest in the great and perennial problem of the nature of Nature; but the fact that Shakespeare is at pains to establish his island in the Old World may be taken to indicate his rejection of the merely topical. When this is said, the relations of the play to the literature of voyaging remain of the greatest interest and usefulness.

1. *The Bermuda Pamphlets*. Malone[1] first suggested a connexion between *The Tempest* and certain pamphlets describing a wreck on the Bermudas in 1609. Since then much research has been done to develop his discovery, and the facts, if not the inferences that may be drawn from them, are now reasonably clear.

In May 1609[2] a fleet of nine ships with five hundred colonists under Sir Thomas Gates and Sir George Summers set out to strengthen John Smith's Virginia colony; but on 25 July the *Sea-Adventure*, which carried both Gates and Summers, was separated from the rest of the fleet by a storm. Being driven towards the coast of the Bermudas, the crew were forced to run their ship ashore; and when "neere land" she "fell in between two rockes, where she was fast lodged and locked for further budging"; but all on board got safely to the beach, and also managed to save a good part of the ship's fittings and stores. The other ships, with one exception, reached the mainland of America. Ultimately Gates and Summers again set out for Virginia in May 1610; they arrived safely, and the story of their adventures was carried to England in the autumn of the same year. But news of the storm had reached England before the end of 1609; and as it was supposed that the *Sea-Adventure* had foundered, the tidings of the safety of the crew and of their strange experiences must have made a deep impression in England, and many narratives of the wreck were published.

That Shakespeare knew these narratives is now generally agreed, though there are still dissident voices.[3] Scholars eager

---

1. *Account of The Incidents from which The Title and Part of the Story of Shakespeare's Tempest were derived* (1808).

2. The following paragraph is taken over from the Introduction of Morton Luce to the original "Arden" edition, pp. xii–xiii. Luce's investigations into the pamphlets on Bermuda, and the Somers expedition clarified an obscure and complex problem; they were the longest stride forward since Malone.

3. *e.g*, E. E. Stoll (*S.P.* xxiv [1927]. 485 ff): "There is not a word in *The*

to press home the resemblances of language have sometimes committed errors of excess which exposed them to the mockery of sceptics, but it is none the less clear that the industry of Luce, Lee, Gayley, Cawley, and Hotson has put the issue beyond reasonable doubt. There was for long considerable confusion about the bibliography of the narratives, but this was for the most part cleared up by Luce in the former Arden edition, and it is no longer necessary to establish that, out of all the real and fictitious works formerly canvassed, only three are directly relevant to *The Tempest*. These are Sylvester Jourdain's *Discovery of the Barmudas* (1610),[1] the Council of Virginia's apologetic *True Declaration of the state of the Colonie in Virginia, with a confutation of such scandalous reports as have tended to the disgrace of so worthy an enterprise* (1610),[2] and a letter by William Strachey, known as the *True Reportory of the Wrack*, dated 15 July 1610 but published for the first time in *Purchas His Pilgrimes* (1625).[3] Shakespeare's knowledge of this unpublished work makes it probable that he was deeply interested in the story. He was certainly acquainted with members of the Virginia Company, which is to say, with men who had to give serious consideration to the whole problem, practical and ethical, of the American colonies. Among these were Southampton and Pembroke, both of them financially interested in the plantation, and Shakespeare had friends in common with

---

Tempest about America... Nothing but the Bermudas, once barely mentioned as faraway places, like Tokio or Mandalay." Stoll denies that the storm in i. i. derives from the narratives. But nobody who impartially surveys the evidence here set out will deny that Shakespeare was interested in the Gates expedition, and in the New World generally. J. D. Rea (*M.P.* XXII (1919), 279 ff) found a source for the storm in the *Naufragium* of Erasmus, but he exaggerates similarities and it is not easy to see how he can regard the quarrelsome courtier of Erasmus as the progenitor of Gonzalo. We may concede, with T. W. Baldwin (*Shakspere's Small Latine and Less Greek* (1944), I. 742), a general similarity of treatment caused by Shakespeare's probable knowledge of the dialogue; *Naufragium* is one representative of a long line of literary storms which lies behind the play. It does not supplant the narratives. Hunter, who of course could not allow the *terminus* of 1610, argued similarly for Harington's translation of *Orlando Furioso* (1591), and traced the "New World" references to Ralegh's account of Guiana, published in 1596. It is not unlikely that Shakespeare knew this work, but in fact he had read widely in the voyagers.

1. There is a facsimile ed. by J. Q. Adams (New York, 1940).

2. Reprinted in *Tracts and Other Papers* ... collected by Peter Force, Washington 1844 (Volume III).

3. Part II, Book X (in Glasgow ed. of 1906, XIX. 5).

others of the Essex group similarly interested—Sir Robert Sidney, Sir Henry Nevile, and Lord De La Warr, who was to be a governor of the colony. He also knew friends of Gates, who could have enabled him to meet Strachey, and almost certainly Sir Dudley Digges, ardent in the Virginian cause, whose brother Leonard contributed memorial verses to the First Folio, and whose mother married Thomas Russell, the "overseer" of Shakespeare's will. Both Dudley Digges and William Strachey contributed laudatory verses to Jonson's *Sejanus* in 1605, and Shakespeare had acted in the play. Shakespeare's friend Heminge was at Digges's wedding, and signed as a witness. It seems likely, then, that Shakespeare knew Digges, who may have procured Strachey's appointment as Secretary in 1609, when Donne was a rival applicant. Leslie Hotson conjectures that Digges may have edited Strachey's confidential report on the state of Virginia, and produced the more cheerful *True Declaration*. There seems to have been opportunity for Shakespeare to see the unpublished report, or even to have met Strachey.[1]

Luce, Gayley, and Cawley[2] agree that Strachey's exceeds the other works in importance. In Appendix B I have therefore reprinted portions of his letter, together with a short extract from Jourdain, and the reader may judge of the verbal parallels for himself. I expect it will be agreed that they justify the assumption that Shakespeare has these documents in mind. This interest is most obviously expressed in the first scene of the play, in Ariel's description of his electric display during the storm (I. ii. 196 ff), and in the long and curious conversation in II. i; it recurs in III. iii when the banquet appears, and in other scattered passages such as those in which Stephano and Trinculo describe to each other the manner of their preservation. Fewer verbal parallels have been noted in Jourdain and in *The True Declaration*, but they are nevertheless involved in the play. It has been observed that *The True Declaration* is very

1. These facts are derived from C. M. Gayley's *Shakespeare and the Founders of Liberty in America* (1917) and Hotson's *I, William Shakespeare . . .* (1937), especially pp. 203–36. See also A. W. Ward's British Academy Lecture of 1919 on "Shakespeare and the Makers of Virginia", and for evidence of Strachey's familiarity with e.g. Jonson and Marston, the Hakluyt Society's *The Historie of Travell into Virginia Britania* (1612), ed. L. B. Wright and Virginia Freund (1954).

2. "Shakespeare's use of the Voyagers", *P.M.L.A.* XLI (1926), pp. 688–726.

near the mark with "the heavens were obscured, and made an Egyptian night of three daies perpetuall horror. . . The Islands on which they fell were the *Bermudos*, a place hardly accessable, through the environing rocks and dangers; notwithstanding they were forced to runne their ship on shoare, which through Gods providence fell betwixt two rockes, that caused her to stand firme, and not immediately to be broken."[1]

Issued as propaganda, the *Declaration* dismisses lightly the Fairies and Devils of the island; it rather emphasizes the excellent food supply, and suggests the Augustinian moral of the whole story: "*Nimium timet qui Deo non credit*, he is too impiously fearefull, that will not trust in God so powerfull." This moralizing of the event is of greater interest than has been supposed. "What is there in all this tragicall comaedie that should discourage us with impossibilitie of the enterprise? When of all the Fleete, one onely ship, by a secret leake was indangered and yet in the gulfe of Despair was so graciously preserved. *Quae videtur paena, est medicina*, that which we accompt a punishment against evill is but a medicine against evill." Later, discussing the quarrels and mutinies in Virginia, which were in progress when the *Sea-Adventurer's* party belatedly arrived, the writer says "*Omnis inordinatus animus sibi ipsi fit paena*, every inordinate soule becomes his own punishment." Strachey also is given to moralizing. *The True Declaration* spoke of "these infortunate (yet fortunate) Ilands"; Strachey wrote "Yet it pleased our mercifull God, to make even this hideous and hated place, both the place of our safetie, and the meanes of our deliverance."

All these exclamations remind us of the action of providence in Shakespeare's play. *Quae videtur paena est medicina*—why else should Ferdinand labour? And why else should so many noblemen suffer shipwreck? In the words of Hermione, "This action I now go on, Is for my better grace" (*Wint.*, ii. i. 121–2). *Omnis inordinatus animus. . .* ; Gonzalo remembers the inward corrosion of guilt when he comments upon the demoralized courtiers in iii. iii—

> All three of them are desperate; their great guilt,
> Like poison given to work a great time after,
> Now 'gins to bite the spirits. (104–6)

1. Force, *ed. cit.* p. 10.

The appeal for confidence in the mercy of God—through whom the "infortunate" becomes "fortunate"[1]—must, particularly as Strachey phrases it, recall Gonzalo's almost liturgical joy in v. i. 206 ff.[2] By this mercy we are shipwrecked, as the colonists were shipwrecked into a temperate climate, and Shakespeare's princes into health again. The qualities of the poor isle which gave their natures a new birth, which purged Alonso's guilt and taught Prospero the princely skill to submit his fury to his reason, are a main theme of the play. Shakespeare had already reflected upon the action of providence; here was a typical display of its power, a "blessed tempest"[3] which drove men into new health and knowledge.

II. *News from the New World.* The natural life, the Golden Age, and related themes, giving rise as they do to considerations of justice and mercy, man fallen and redeemed, the reclamation of nature by the ministers of grace—these themes are constantly heard in *The Tempest*; but although the complex in which they occur is peculiar to the play, they were not novel to the contemporary reader of travel literature.

Long and dangerous voyages to a new world, not to speak of happy shipwrecks, were bound to seem emblematic of man's life and of providence. The central figure of Jacobean travel-literature, Samuel Purchas, perceived the need for presenting the new facts about foreign lands with full reference to classical voyages, and to the theological and moral implications of voyaging and colonizing.[4] Long before him the translators had made available to the ordinary reader the classical works

1. Strachey writes: "The ground of all those miseries [Gonzalo is keenly aware of the miseries of the island] was the permissive Providence of God," and the word-play of "those infortunate (yet fortunate) Ilands" would perhaps also have theological connotations, suggesting the paradox, celebrated in literature from medieval hymn to *Paradise Lost*, of the unfortunate but fortunate Fall of Adam, which made possible the Redemption. This idea is present in Gonzalo's doxology. Of course the first point of the word-play concerns the legendary Fortunate Islands.

2. Cawley (*loc. cit.*) observed these passages, but associated them, less plausibly I think, with I. ii. 33–8.

3. Marlowe, *Dido*(1586?), IV. iv. 93–4, "Speaks not Aeneas like a conqueror? O blessed tempests that did drive him in!" For another resemblance between the plays see note on I. ii. 424.

4. *Purchas his Pilgrimage* (1613); *Purchas his Pilgrimes* (1625) especially the opening chapters.

on geography.[1] Many books, and many sermons, effected a characteristic Renaissance union between moral and political implications, and concerned themselves with the task of persuading the public that exploration was an honourable and indeed a sanctified activity. Drake was compared with Moses;[2] Purchas begins his last work with a long study of the allegory of voyaging, and combines with his mystagogy a practical justification of "the lawfulnesse of Discoveries", a somewhat sophistical argument for the propriety of usurping the rights of native populations, and an insistence, half-mystagogic, half-propagandist, on the temperate, fruitful nature of the New World, and the unspoilt purity of its inhabitants. The *True Declaration* defends colonizing, on the ground that it diffuses the true religion and has authority from Solomon's trade to Ophir (whether it lay in the East or, as Columbus thought,[3] in the West Indies). There is room for all; and in any case the natives cannot be regarded as civilized people. "There is no trust in the fidelitie of human beasts." But these are the inhabitants of a golden-age society, with no *meum* and *tuum*; and this is our first glimpse of a paradox in the Renaissance attitude to natural man which is examined in the play.

The confusion of interests characteristic of the subject is harmoniously reflected in Shakespeare's play; in some measure it is present throughout the record of Elizabethan travel and drama.[4] Plantation raised urgent practical problems, but they

1. See L. B. Wright, *Middle-Class Culture in Elizabethan England* (1936), p. 533. Geographical discoveries were greeted "paradoxically enough, by a deepening of interest in the classical rather than the contemporary world". G. H. T. Kimble, *Geography in the Middle Ages* (1938), p. 208.

2. Wright, *op. cit.* p. 519.

3. Columbus at Hispaniola "affirmed that he had found the island of *Ophir*" (Peter Martyr, *De Nouo Orbe*, trans. R. Eden [ed. of 1612, 9ᵛ]). He also appears to have thought he had discovered the terrestrial paradise; see Cawley, *The Voyagers and Elizabethan Drama* (1938), p. 290, n. 85. Purchas, with a parade of scholarship, is still arguing these points in 1625 (*Pilgrimes* [1906], I. 35, 66).

4. For instance, in R. Harcourt's *A Relation of a Voyage to Guiana* (Hakluyt Soc., 2nd Series, LX [1926]) published in 1613, and presumably independent of *The Tempest*, there are volleys of Shakespearian echoes, as in this passage: "Notwithstanding it bee scituate under the Equinoctiall, by ancient Philosophers called the burning *Zone*; yet such are the wonderfull works of God for the benefit of man, that contrary to their opinion, we find ... that those Regions which were in time past by them accounted uninhabitable ... are now found out to be inhabited, temperate, and healthfull Countries ... the climate ... pleasant, and agreeable to our constitutions, and the soile fruitfull ... whatso-

were almost always coloured by biblical, classical, and even medieval, or Mandevillian connotations,[1] which offered rich possibilities to the poet; and these were fortified by the voyagers' habit of seeing what they expected to see.

Shakespeare's knowledge of the field certainly goes beyond the Bermudan narratives. The name "Setebos", as is well known, is borrowed from Robert Eden's *History of Travaile* (1577), in which the Patagonians, as observed during Magellan's voyage, "roared lyke bulles and cryed uppon theyr great devill Setebos, to helpe them".[2] I believe Shakespeare also knew Eden's version of Peter Martyr, though much that might seem relevant in the work was repeated countless times elsewhere—the identification of the West Indies with Atlantis; the belief of the natives that the voyagers had descended from heaven; the elaborate description of "the golden worlde",

---

ever is necessary for the reliefe of man: eyther for food, Phisicke, or Chirurgery, or for clothing and architecture is here . . . in plentifull store even naturally provided" (p. 130). But such language is commonplace, and it is the whole complex of ideas of which this is a part, rather than any single passage, that Shakespeare uses. For the same reason we ought to reject suggestions that *The Tempest* unambiguously refers to the crisis in Virginia in 1610, described by Strachey. Gayley makes this suggestion, and Cawley only partly corrects a defect of vision which, by distorting Gonzalo's "commonwealth" speech, seriously impairs the effect of the whole play. I have no space to discuss the theory, though I should not deny that it contains a germ of truth; but nothing could be less Shakespearian than to halt in mid-career to express vehement agreement with the truism that "Adam himselfe might not live in Paridice without dressing the garden" (*True Dec., ed. cit.* p. 15).

1. The wonders referred to in III. iii are Mandevillian; perhaps the genuine wonders reported revived the virtue of credibility in these old stories, as they do for Antonio and Sebastian. Mandeville was still read (see L. B. Wright, *op. cit.* p. 508) and maps still gave pictorial versions of his curiosities (see J. M. French, "Othello Among the Anthropophagi," *P.M.L.A.* XLIX [1934], 807–9.) The medieval encyclopaedias still provided information of this kind. And travellers were willing to find such things in the new world; the Spanish letters which, according to Ralegh, were intercepted at sea, spoke of men who "had the points of their shoulders higher than the Crownes of their heads" (*The discoverie of . . . Guiana* [1595], in Hakluyt, *The Principall Navigations*, ed. of 1927, VII. 355) and we find in Laurence Keymis's sequel, *A Relation of the second Voyage to Guiana* (1596) "He certified mee of the headlesse men, and that their mouthes in their breastes are exceeding wide" (*ibid.* VII. 372). The earlier voyagers sometimes drew the long bow, feeling secure from detection, but they also saw what they felt they should see. Columbus, noting some expectations not realized, was confident that they would be fulfilled on other voyages.

2. 434ᵛ; also 435ᵛ.

with land "as common as sunne and water", and the natives knowing no difference between "Mine" and "Thine"; the "horrible roringes of the wild beastes in the woodes". But he could also have found here pugnacious and terrible bats, compared to "ravenous Harpies"; the Spanish custom of hunting natives with dogs; a Carthage in the New World to remind him of older colonial adventures; and an account of the manner in which natives "were wonderfully astonied at the sweete harmony" of music.[1] If Shakespeare also knew the part of the work which Lok translated, he had also read of "certayne wild men ... without any certaine language", and of a number of Indians who, after being educated as Christians, became the treacherous enemies of "the Monastery where they had been brought up with fatherly charity", and of territory abounding in "wild Boares, thorny Hedghogges, and Porkepennes"; of attacks by apes, and of "a Monster of the Sea like a Man".[2] It is very likely that he knew the accounts of Ralegh's voyages, and in his hints of a cannibal theology he may owe something to Hariot's report on the religion of Virginia—"Some religion they have already, which although it be far from the truth, yet being as it is, there is hope it may be the sooner and easier reformed."[3] The curious burthen of Ariel's first song (*bowgh wawgh* in F) may derive from James Rosier's account of a ceremonial Virginian dance.[4] And finally, as Lee showed, Caliban in some lights seems to be a representative Indian, and Pros-

1. *De Nouo Orbe.* Eden's trans. was of the first 3 decades only. Lok translated the remaining 5, and they were published together in 1612. References above are: 5^r, 9^v, 15^r, 24^v, 44^v, 55^r, 96^r, 120^r, 34^r.

2. 140^r, 258^v, 299^v, 202^v, 300^r. With this last, *cf. infra* p. **xl**.

3. Hakluyt, VI. 187. For more links with Hariot, see Cawley, *P.M.L.A.* XLI. 709.

4. "One among them, the eldest as he is iudged, riseth right up, the others sitting still: and looking about, suddenly cries with a loud voice, *Baugh, Waugh* ... the men altogether answering the same, fall a stamping round about the fire ... with sundrie out-cries" (*Purchas His Pilgrimage* [1613], p. 637). R. M. Kelsey refers to another version of this in *Pilgrims*, XVIII. 344 (*J.E.G.P.* XIII [1914], 98–104). Dancing Indians are similarly described by Peter Martyr, and Cartier (G. Chinard, *L'Exotisme americain dans la littérature française au XVIe siècle* [1911], p. 42). Kelsey also holds that the "living drollery" of III. ii derives from a long description by Strachey in a report of 1612 of an Indian dance and feast (*Pilgrims*, XVIII. 496). A different explanation of "living drollery" is given by M. A. Shaaber, who takes it to mean "an animated grotesque picture" and not an animated puppet-show (*M.L.N.* LX [1945], 387–91).

pero a planter;[1] but this is merely an example of a character-istically ethical attitude to politics; if the principles are worth anything, they are naturally exhibited in practice.

The Tempest also bears the marks of the application of an old learning to a new world. Its strong echoes of the *Aeneid*;[2] its references to Medea,[3] and to the voyage of Hanno;[4] its hints of the fabulous holy voyages of *The Golden Legend*, all these reflect the philosophical attitude of the Old World to the New, the attempt to read the natural life of the New World, and the morality of voyaging, in the light of all that the past had recorded concerning the strange or the paradisial nature of islands, men without civility, and providential voyages.

4. NATURE

1. *Natural Men.* The only undisputed source for any part of *The Tempest* is Montaigne's essay "Of Cannibals"; there are unmistakeable traces of Florio's translation in the text. It has been argued, most recently by A. Lovejoy,[5] that Shakespeare intends a satirical comment upon Montaigne's apparent ac-ceptance of the primitivistic view that a natural society, with-out the civilized accretions of law, custom, and other artificial restraints, would be a happy one.

Montaigne's essay as a whole is relevant to the play, and it would appear that critical comment has been hampered by a failure to understand this. The essay, like the play, is concerned

1. "The American Indian in Elizabethan England", *Scribner's*, XLII (1907), 313–30, substantially repeated in "Caliban's Visits to England", *Cornhill*, N.S., XXXIV (1913), 333–45.

2. See notes on I. ii. 421 ff, IV. i. 102, and III. iii. 52 (S.D.) and 60; J. M. Nosworthy's paper "The Narrative Sources of *The Tempest*" (*R.E.S.* XXIV [1948], 281–4), which supports my own feeling that Shakespeare has Virgil in mind, though I cannot agree with its main argument; and the occasionally suggestive remarks of C. Still in his *Shakespeare's Mystery Play* (1921) and *The Timeless Theme* (1936). Gonzalo insists (wrongly) that Tunis and Carthage are the same place; the voyage of Alonso's party was, like that of Aeneas, from Tunis to Naples, with a purgatorial interruption.

3. See Appendix D and *infra*.

4. See J. D. Rea, *M.L.N.* XXXV (1920), 313, and Florio's *Montaigne* (Tudor Translations, 1892), I. 220.

5. *Essays in the History of Ideas* (1948), p. 238. Lovejoy calls Shakespeare's source "the locus classicus of primitivism in modern literature". See also M. T. Hodgen, "Montaigne and Shakespeare again", *Huntington Library Quarterly*, XVI (1952–3), 23–42.

with the general contrast between natural and artificial socie-
ties and men, though Montaigne assumes, in his "naturalist"
way, that the New World offers an example of naturally virtuous life uncorrupted by civilization, whereas Shakespeare
obviously does not. Montaigne's general position is stated
thus:

They [the Indians] are even savage, as we call those fruits wilde,
which nature of her selfe . . . hath produced: whereas indeed . . .
those which our selves have altered by our artificiall devices, and
diverted from their common order, we should rather terme savage.
In those are the true and most profitable vertues, and naturall properties most lively and vigorous, which in these we have bastardized, applying them to the pleasure of our corrupted taste. And if
notwithstanding, in divers fruits of those countries that were never
tilled, we shall finde, that in respect of ours they are most excellent, and as delicate unto our taste; there is no reason, art should
gaine the point of honour of our great and puissant mother
Nature. . .[1]

This is a simple "primitivism", and it uses the traditional
horticultural analogy, equally available to those who held that
the gardener's art corrupted and those who believed it improved the stock.[2] The dispute is central to *The Winter's Tale*,
and is debated by Polixenes, who takes the view that Art acts
to the improvement of Nature;[3] Perdita, who disagrees, is
herself the product of careful breeding, of virtuous stock, which
can no more be concealed by her rustic milieu than can the
nobility of the salvage man and Pastorella in *The Faerie
Queene*, Book vi, or of the King's sons in *Cymbeline*.

These apparently antithetical views on the natural life to
some extent controlled the reports of the voyagers upon whom
Montaigne and Shakespeare both depend. They tended to

1. *Montaigne's Essays*, translated by John Florio, ed. of 1892, i. 219.

2. For the early history of the idea, see A. Lovejoy and G. Boas, *Primitivism
in Antiquity* (1935); Democritus alludes to it (*ibid.* pp. 207–8) and it is commonplace in Renaissance literary criticism (*e.g.*, *The Arte of English Poesie*, ed.
Willcock and Walker (1936), p. 304—the gardener does what "nature of her
selfe would never have done: as to make the single gillifloure double"). One
view, that Art is an agent of Nature, and necessary to the development of
created nature—the view of Polixenes—is set over against the other, that Art
(meaning anything that interferes with Nature) can only corrupt, which is the
view of Perdita, of the Mower in Marvell's "Mower against Gardens" and of
Montaigne in this essay.

3. iv. iv. Nature transcends Art when the statue of Hermione moves.

describe the natives as purely virtuous or purely vicious. From Eden to Harcourt they repeat the theme of Montaigne's commonwealth; and yet they also speak of the brutality of the natives, of their treachery, ugliness, and infidelity. The *True Declaration* called them "human beasts" and the experienced Captain John Smith "perfidious, inhuman, all Savage".[1] Literary men saw in the favourable reports a rich affirmation of a traditional theme of poetry; hence the enthusiasm of Drayton, the talk of "sun-burnt Indians, That know no other wealth but Peace and Pleasure";[2] but a more central humanism expressed the other view, as did Sandys in his comparison of the Indians with the Cyclops, with its emphasis on the social achievement of Art:

... The *Cyclops* were a salvage people ... unsociable amongst themselves, & inhumane to strangers: And no marvaile, when lawlesse, and subject to no government, the bond of society; which gives to every man his owne, suppressing vice, and advancing vertue, the two maine columnes of a Common-wealth. . . Man is a politicall and sociable creature: they therefore are to be numbred among beasts who renounce society, whereby they are destitute of lawes, the ordination of civility. Hence it ensues, that man, in creation the best, when averse to justice, is the worst of all creatures. Such *Polyphemus*; ... more salvage ... are the *West-Indians* at this day.[3]

Both these attitudes to primitive man are deeply rooted in the past; and both found some support in the behaviour of the natives, which was, as a rule, very amiable at first—as Caliban's was with Prospero and Stephano—but under provocation, and sometimes spontaneously, treacherous later. Behind all these observations are the two opposing versions of the natural; on the one hand, that which man corrupts, and on the other that which is defective, and must be mended by cultivation—the less than human, which calls forth man's authoritative power to correct and rule. This latter is the view which suits best the conscience of the colonist. In practice everybody except a few missionaries treated the savages literally as lesser breeds without the law; sun- and devil-worshippers, often

1. Cawley, *The Voyagers*, pp. 346 ff.
2. Beaumont and Fletcher, *Four Plays in One*, Cambridge ed., x. 360.
3. *Ovids Metamorphoses Englished* (1632), p. 477.

cannibals, they were also in occupation of fertile territory, and it was at once virtuous and expedient to convert and exploit them. In 1493, for example, the Spanish Ambassador at the Papal Court announced the discoveries of Columbus on behalf of his sovereigns; "Christ," he said, "has placed under their rule the Fortunate Isles."[1] Prospero's assumption of his right to rule the island, "to be the lord on't", is the natural assumption of a European prince, as Purchas on "The Lawfulness of Discoveries" demonstrates.[2] The natives were worth some trouble; although they had no rational language, they did not lack certain mechanic arts, like the building of dams for fish, upon which the European settler long remained dependent. Many stratagems were devised to expedite the subjection of the natives. Stephano's claim to be descended from the moon was commonly made by unscrupulous voyagers who seized the chance of turning to account the polytheism of the Indians.[3] There is ample testimony to the corrupting effect upon natives of contact with dissolute Europeans—Christian savages sent to convert heathen savages, as Fuller put it.[4] Ronsard seems to have been the first to voice this complaint,[5] and of course it is another element in the situation which interested both Montaigne and Shakespeare. Reports of such barbarism would tend to reinforce the nostalgic primitivism of the literary men, and lead them once more to reflect upon an ancient theme:

<blockquote>
not all
That beare the name of men . . .
. . . Are for to be accounted men: but such as under awe
Of reasons rule continually doo live in vertues law;
And that the rest doo differ nought from beasts, but rather
bee
Much woorse than beasts, bicause they do abace theyr owne
degree.[6]
</blockquote>

Gonzalo's half-serious talk about his commonwealth serves

1. Chinard, *op. cit.* p. 4.　　2. *op. cit.* Vol. I.

3. Cawley, *P.M.L.A.* XLI. 714 ff.

4. Cawley, *Voyagers*, p. 193. See also Jonson's *Staple of News* in *Works, ed. cit.* V. 245.

5. Chinard, *op. cit.* p. 118.

6. Golding, *The XV Bookes of P. Ovidius Naso, entytuled Metamorphosis* (1567), *Epistle*, ll. 55–62. See Appendix D.

to introduce into the play the theme of the natural life in a
guise more appropriate to pastoral poetry which takes a
"soft" view of Nature. It is over-simple to assume that this
perennial theme is destroyed by the cheap jeers of Antonio
and Sebastian. There are points in the play at which Shakespeare uses Caliban to indicate how much baser the corruption
of the civilized can be than the bestiality of the natural, and in
these places he is using his natural man as a criterion of civilized corruption, as Montaigne had done. At the end of the
play we learn Gonzalo's stature; he is not only the good-
natured calm old man of the wreck, the cheerful courtier of
the second act, and the pure soul of the third; he pronounces
the benediction, and we see that he was all the time as right
as it was human to be, even when to the common sense of the
corrupt he was transparently wrong—wrong about the loca-
tion of Tunis, wrong about the commonwealth, wrong about
the survival of Ferdinand. And we see that Nature is not, in
The Tempest, defined with the single-minded clarity of a philosophic proposition.[1] Shakespeare's treatment of the theme has
what all his mature poetry has, a richly analytical approach
to ideas, which never reaches after a naked opinion of true or
false.

The poetic definition of Nature in the play is achieved largely by a series of antitheses with Caliban constantly recurring
as one term. He represents the natural man. This figure is not,
as in pastoral generally, a virtuous shepherd, but a salvage
and deformed slave.

II. *A Salvage and Deformed Slave.* Caliban's name is usually
regarded as a development of some form of the word "Carib",
meaning a savage inhabitant of the New World; "cannibal"
derives from this, and "Caliban" is possibly a simple anagram
of that word.[2] But though he is thus connected with the Indian
savage, he is also associated, as were the uncivilized inhabit-

---

1. E. C. Knowlton in his "Nature and Shakespeare" (*P.M.L.A.* LI [1936],
719 ff), argues that Shakespeare attributes to Perdita in *The Winter's Tale* "a
kind of rightness", but that his own view was probably that of Polixenes.

2. E. K. Chambers favours the derivation from *cauliban*, a Romany word
meaning "blackness" (*William Shakespeare*, I. 494). There are also the Chaly-
beates, savage cannibals of the ancient world, whom Virgil mentions twice, and
whom Pliny situates near the Coraxi.

ants of the Indies, with the wild or salvage man of Europe, formerly the most familiar image of mankind without the ordination of civility.

The origins of this type are obscure,[1] but the wild man was a familiar figure in painting, heraldry, pageant, and drama.[2] Several varieties are distinguished; the kind which survived in the drama was a satyr-type, like Bremo in the old play *Mucedorus*, which was revived by Shakespeare's company in 1610. Bremo abducts a virgin; unchastity was a conventional attribute of salvage men, which Shakespeare skilfully exploits. These creatures were believed to occupy an "intermediate position in the moral scale, below man, just as the angels were above him ... they are the link between ... the settled and the wild, the moral and the unmoral".[3] The term "salvage", used of Caliban in the Folio "Names of the Actors", has thus a restricted meaning, as it has in Spenser. Caliban is a salvage man, and the West Indians were salvage men of a topical kind; hence the Indian element in this natural man.

The next thing the "Names of the Actors" says about Caliban is that he is deformed. He is what Thersites called Ajax, "a very land-fish, languageless, a monster".[4] There were reports from the Indies of curious specimens, and these reports may have influenced some of the things that are said about Caliban

1. It is discussed by R. Withington, *English Pageantry* (1918), 1. 72 ff, and by E. Welsford, *The Court Masque* (1927), p. 6. Possibly the practice of abandoning children in forests had something to do with it; some of the survivors, perhaps subnormal to begin with, might have led a bestial life in the woods. Linnaeus classified such survivors as a distinct species, *homo ferus*. Conceivably the Γορίλλα observed by Hanno the Carthaginian has some part in the tradition.

2. Pictorially the wodehouse, or wodewose, flourished in the thirteenth and fourteenth centuries (R. van Marle, *Iconographie de l'Art Profane* (1931), 1. 183–91). The earliest recorded dramatic specimen is in a Paduan entertainment of 1208—*magnus Ludus de quodam homine salvatico* (P. Neri, in *Giornale Storico della Letteratura Italiana*, 1. ix. 49; cited by L. Edwards, "The Historical and Legendary Background of the Wodehouse and Peacock Feast Motif in the Walsokne and Braunche Brasses", *Monumental Brass Society Transactions*, VIII. Pt. vii, 300–11). Then they occur with great frequency. In England, there is a wild man in the Christmas entertainment of Edward III in 1347, and they are common in Tudor entertainments, such as the progresses and receptions of Elizabeth. (See Nichol's *Royal Progresses, passim*.) See also p. 172.

3. L. Edwards, *loc. cit.* This idea persisted into the eighteenth century; Lovejoy quotes a poem which includes the lines, "De l'homme aux animaux rapprochant la distance, Voyez l'Homme des Bois lier leur existence" (*The Great Chain of Being* [1936], p. 236).

4. *Troilus and Cressida*, III. iii. 265. See note on II. ii. 36.

in the play;[1] but his deformity is visualized in terms of Old World monsters. Caliban's birth, as Prospero insists, was inhuman; he was "a born devil", "got by the devil himself upon thy wicked dam". He was the product of sexual union between a witch and an incubus, and this would account for his deformity, whether the devil-lover was Setebos (all pagan gods were classified as devils) or, as W. C. Curry infers, some aquatic demon.[2]

Caliban's mother, though associated with reports of devil-worship and witchcraft in the New World, belongs to the Old.[3] She is a powerful witch, deliberately endowed with many of the qualities of classical witches,[4] but also possessing a clearly defined place in the contemporary demonological scheme. She is a practitioner of "natural" magic, a goetist who exploited the universal sympathies, but whose power is limited by the fact that she could command, as a rule, only devils and the lowest orders of spirits. Prospero, on the other hand, is a theurgist, whose Art is to achieve supremacy over the natural world by holy magic. The Neo-Platonic mage studies the harmonic relationship of the elementary, celestial, and intellectual worlds,[5] and conceives it

no way irrational that it should be possible for us to ascend by the same degrees through each World to the same very original world itself, the Maker of all things, and First Cause, from whence all things are, and proceed. . .[6]

1. The closest resemblance is in a beast reported by dos Sanctos in 1597, which had the "eares of a Dog, armes like a Man without haire, and at the elbows great Finnes like a fish", which the native assistants had believed to be "the sonne of the Devill". (Quoted by J. E. Hankins, "Caliban the Bestial Man", *P.M.L.A.* LXII [1947], 794.)

2. W. C. Curry, *Shakespeare's Philosophical Patterns* (1936), pp. 148–55.

3. See note on I. ii. 261.

4. Some of the classical *loci* are: Virgil, *Eclogue* VIII, Horace, *Epode* V, Lucan, *Pharsalia*, 1; Ovid, *Met.* VII. 199–207; Seneca, *Medea*, 755–66. These witches had a share in the development of the witches of Renaissance literature. Lyly's *Endimion* has a witch, Dipsa, who says she can "darken the Sunne by my skil, and remoove the Moone out of her course". This traditional power is mentioned in the Faust books, and by Reginald Scot.

5. For detailed discussion of these topics, see R. H. West's invaluable *The Invisible World* (1939), the fullest treatment of the supernatural in Elizabethan drama; and Hardin Craig, *The Enchanted Glass* (1936), Cap. I.

6. Cornelius Agrippa, *Occult Philosophy*, translated by J. F. (1651), I. i.

His object is to "walk to the skie", as Vaughan put it, before death, by ascending through the created worlds to the condition of the angels. His Art is supernatural; the spirits he commands are the dæmons of Neo-Platonism, the criterion of whose goodness is not the Christian one of adherence to, or defection from, God, but of immateriality or submersion in matter. He deals with spirits high in the scale of goodness, and if lesser spirits ("weak masters") are required, the superior dæmon controls them on his behalf.[1] He is *"divinorum cultor & interpres*, a studious observer and expounder of divine things", and his Art is "the absolute perfection of Natural Philosophy".[2] Natural Philosophy includes the arts of astrology, alchemy, and ceremonial magic, to all of which Prospero alludes.[3]

We shall return to the special powers and the learning of the mage Prospero; the point here is that his Art,[4] being the Art of supernatural virtue which belongs to the redeemed world of civility and learning, is the antithesis of the black magic of Sycorax.[5] Caliban's deformity is the result of evil natural magic, and it stands as a natural criterion by which we measure the world of Art, represented by Prospero's divine magic and the supernaturally sanctioned beauty of Miranda and Ferdinand.

The last thing the "Names of the Actors" says about Caliban

1. For more detail about Ariel, see App. B.   2. Agrippa, *op. cit.* III. xl.

3. *e.g.*, I. ii. 181–4; v. i. 1, and the many allusions to ceremonial magic—book, rod, cloak of invisibility, which are the instruments of the "rougher magic" which the mage at a later stage renounces, as Prospero does before confronting Alonso.

4. Always spelled with the capital in F. This is a recognized method of indicating that it is a technical usage.

5. This highly important distinction is lost if Prospero is called a black magician, as he often is. The arguments against this view are conclusive but there is no space for them here; they can be deduced from the works of West and Curry. It has been objected that Shakespeare could not have presented at the Court of James I a play openly alluding to a system of magic to which the King was notoriously opposed. But James was well accustomed to such treatment; he himself was often presented as a beneficent magician, and he took pleasure in Jonson's *Masque of Queens*, a brilliant iceberg whose hidden part is a craggy mass of occult learning. He no more took exception to this than he did to the presentation of pagan gods whom he theoretically regarded as devils, because he understood the equation between a fiction of beneficent magic and the sacred power he himself professed as an actual king. See also p. 172.

is that he is a slave. We have seen the readiness with which the white man took charge of the New World; Prospero arrived on his island "to be the lord on 't". If Aristotle was right in arguing that "men . . . who are as much inferior to others as the body is to the soul . . . are slaves by nature, and it is advantageous for them always to be under government", and that "to find our governor we should . . . examine into a man who is most perfectly formed in soul and body . . . for in the depraved and vicious the body seems to rule rather than the soul, on account of their being corrupt and contrary to nature",[1] then the black and mutilated cannibal must be the natural slave of the European gentleman, and, *a fortiori*, the salvage and deformed Caliban of the learned Prospero.

Caliban is, therefore, accurately described in the Folio "Names of the Actors". His origins and character are natural in the sense that they do not partake of grace, civility, and art; he is ugly in body, associated with an evil natural magic, and unqualified for rule or nurture. He exists at the simplest level of sensual pain and pleasure fit for lechery because love is beyond his nature, and a natural slave of demons. He hears music with pleasure, as music can appeal to the beast who lacks reason;[2] and indeed he resembles Aristotle's bestial man. He is a measure of the incredible superiority of the world of Art, but also a measure of its corruption. For the courtiers and their servants include the incontinent Stephano and the malicious Antonio. Caliban scorns the infirmity of purpose exhibited by the first, and knows better than Antonio that it is imprudent to resist grace, for which, he says, he will henceforth seek. Unlike the incontinent man, whose appetites subdue his will, and the malicious man, whose will is perverted to evil ends, "the bestial man has no sense of right and wrong, and therefore sees no difference between good and evil. His state is less guilty but more hopeless than those of incontinence and malice, since he cannot be improved."[3] Men can abase their degree below the bestial; and there is possibly a hint, for which there is no support in Aristotle, that the bestial Caliban

---

1. *Politics*, 1254 a–b.
2. Cf. Horace, *De Arte Poetica*, ll. 391–2: Silvestres homines sacer interpresque deorum/caedibus et victu foedo deterruit Orpheus.
3. See the valuable essay of J. E. Hankins, *P.M.L.A.* LXII.

gains a new spiritual dimension from his glimpse of the "brave spirits". Whether or no this is true, he is an extraordinarily powerful and comprehensive type of Nature; an inverted pastoral hero, against whom civility and the Art which improves Nature may be measured.

5. ART

1. *Buds of Nobler Race.* The civilized castaways of *The Tempest* are brought into close contact with a representative of Nature uncontrolled by Art. How do they differ from Caliban, and how is this difference expressed?

It is useful to compare Spenser's treatment of two salvage men in *The Faerie Queene.*[1] The one who carries off Amoret in Book IV is an unamiable personification of greedy lust—"For he liv'd all on ravin and on rape" (IV. vii. 5). The full description leaves no doubt that this is the wild man of the entertainments, and that his are the "natural" activities of lust and cannibalism. The salvage man who treats Serena so gently in the sixth book is quite different; though he cannot speak he shows a tenderness which is, apparently, against his nature. The reason is, that "he was borne of noble blood" (VI. v. 2); we do not hear how he came to be languageless and salvage, but we know he owes his gentleness to his gentle birth.

> O what an easie thing is to descry
> The gentle bloud, how ever it be wrapt
> In sad misfortunes foule deformity
> And wretched sorrowes, which have often hapt!
> For howsoever it may grow mis-shapt,
> Like this wyld man being undisciplynd,
> That to all virtue it may seeme unapt,
> Yet will it shew some sparkes of gentle mynd,
> And at the last breake forth in his owne proper kynd.
>
> (VI. v. I.)

That gentle birth predisposed a man to virtue, even if it was not absolutely necessary to virtue, was part of the lore of

1. The Nature-Art debate is a leading motive in Spenser; the most complete study in that of R. H. Pierce, *J.E.G.P.* XLIV. A. Thaler (*S.A.B.* x) compares with Caliban the son of the Hag (*F.Q.* III. vii) who lusts after Florimell. J. A. S. McPeek (*P.Q.* xxv) adds that the beast sent after Florimell is freckled and doglike.

courtesy. *Fortes creantur fortibus . . .*—argument as to the mode of inheriting, and of cultivating, *nobilitas*, runs through the history of moral philosophy from Aristotle through Dante to the Renaissance. It is true that, with evidence to the contrary continually before their eyes, philosophers could not uniformly maintain that where there was high birth there was virtue, taking nobility to mean the *non vile*, "the perfection of its own nature in each thing";[1] and in Italy there was a growing tendency to judge of nobility by actual manners and merit, rather than by family. As early as the *Convito* the conditions of its development are described as much more complex than the racial theory of its provenance allows,[2] but more common-place thought constantly recurs to the biological analogy; *est in juvencis, est in equis, patrum Virtus*—as Polixenes conceived that there were "buds of nobler race".

The question is debated in the first book of Castiglione's *Courtier* by Canossa and Pallavicino.[3] The arguments are conventional, but they serve to illustrate the theory of natural nobility which animates Spenser's portrait of the salvage man. Nature makes the work of greatness easier, and the penalties of failure heavier, for the high-born; "because nature in every thing hath deeply sowed that privie seed, which giveth a certaine force and propertie of her beginning, unto whatsoever springeth of it, and maketh it like unto herselfe. As we see by example . . . in trees, whose slippes and grafts alwaies for the most part are like unto the stock of the tree they cam from: and if at any time they grow out of kinde, the fault is in the husbandman";[4] which is to say, in the individual nobleman—a

1. *Il Convito. The Banquet* of Dante Alighieri, trans. E. P. Sayer (1887), p. 226. See the curtain-lecture in Chaucer's *Wife of Bath's Tale*.

2. *ibid.*, see *e.g.* p. 241. Dante devotes the fourth and last extant section of the work to this subject. In the earlier *De Monarchia* he allowed more force to heredity. For a short survey of the changing theory see Burckhardt, *The Civilization of the Renaissance in Italy* (English ed. of 1944), pp. 217 ff.

3. The same theme, with many variations, is regularly treated in later works on courtesy and the education of princes and nobles. See e.g. ΗΡΩ-ΠΑΙΔΕΙΑ, or *The Institution of a Young Noble Man*, by James Cleland (1607), esp. IV. 7. Peacham (*Compleat Gentleman*, 1622+) defines nobility as "the Honour of blood", "it selfe essential and absolute". He treats also of the loss of it through vice, and of the irrepressible appearance of nobility in children (ed. Gordon, 1906, pp. 2, 3, 9, 14).

4. *The Courtier* (1528), trans. Hoby (1561), ed. of 1928 (Everyman), p. 31.

fault of nurture, not of nature. Thus Canossa, though not to the satisfaction of Pallavicino, accounts also for the Antonios of the world. He allows an important place to education, believing, with Prospero and against Socrates, that pedagogues could be found capable of nursing the seed:[1]

Therefore even as in the other artes, so also in the vertues, it is behofefull to have a teacher, that with lessons and good exhortations may stirre up and quicken in us those moral vertues whereof wee have the seede inclosed and buried in the soule.[2]

If the seed is not there (and here Prospero's experience confirms him) the husbandman loses his labour, and brings forth only "the briers and darnell of appetites" which he had desired to restrain. Canossa omits all the other factors which might be brought into consideration—"the complex nature of the seed", "the disposition of the dominant Heaven"—which Dante two centuries before had attempted to calculate, and takes account only of nature and of nurture. This leaves an opening for Pallavicino's reply, and Castiglione had, of course, to arrange matters to suit his dialectic scheme. But for Spenser moral virtues inhabit the simpler, the ideal, world of romance, and his salvage man differs from his kind in that he has the seed implanted by nature, though not husbanded by nurture.

There is a striking version of the theory by Edward Phillips, the nephew of Milton. Phillips, in a passage so much above his usual manner that critics have seen in it the hand of his uncle, identifies two forces which distinguish the better part of mankind from the more brutish:

. . . the first is that *Melior natura* which the Poet speaks of, with which whoever is amply indued, take that Man from his Infancy, throw him into the Desarts of *Arabia*, there let him converse some years with Tygers and Leopards, and at last bring him where civil society & conversation abides, and ye shall see how on a sudden, the scales and dross of his barbarity purging off by degrees, he will start up a Prince or Legislator, or some such illustrious Person: the

1. This expression occurs so frequently in discussions of this sort that it will perhaps be useful to remind the reader that it had far more force than the modern idea of analogy would allow it, and also that the word "seed" was also used as symbolizing the element of divine law implanted at birth in the human breast. This connotation is present in *Convito*, IV.

2. Castiglione, *ibid.*

other is that noble thing call'd *Education*, this is, that Harp of
Orpheus, that lute of *Amphion*, so elegantly figur'd by the Poets to
have wrought such Miracles among irrational and insensible
Creatures, which raiseth beauty even out of deformity, order and
regularity out of Chaos and confusion, and which, if throughly and
rightly prosecuted, would be able to civilize the most savage
natures, & root out barbarism and ignorance from off the face of
the Earth: those who have either of these qualifications singly may
justly be term'd *Men*; those who have both united in a happy conjunction, *more* than *Men*; those who have neither of them in any
competent measure . . . *less* than *Men*. . .[1]

Phillips here takes the view expressed by Dante, Pallavicino,
and many others, that the want of nature can be partially supplied by Education, and in this respect differs from those who,
like Canossa and, as we shall see, the romance-writers, held
more rigidly to the notion of the seed without which all hus-
bandry is not only wasted but even harmful, since it promotes
the growth of undesirable weed-like qualities. The unknown
poet's *melior natura* provides an excellent label for all the ideas
associated with "buds of nobler race", and his "Education"
enables us to see Prospero's "nurture" in its proper context.
Miranda, as Prospero early informs us, is endowed not only
with the *melior natura*, but with education:

> here
> Have I, thy schoolmaster, made thee more profit
> Than other princess' can, that have more time
> For vainer hours, and tutors not so careful. (I. ii. 171-4.)

She has both these qualities of nobility "united in a happy
conjunction". Caliban has neither, and there is in the structure of the play a carefully prepared parallel between the two
characters to illustrate this point; Caliban's education was not
only useless—on *his* nature, which is nature *tout court*, nurture
would never stick—but harmful. He can only abuse the gift of
speech; and by cultivating him Prospero brings forth in him

---

1. Preface to *Theatrum Poetarum* (1675); in *Critical Essays of the Seventeenth
Century*, ed. J. E. Spingarn (1908), III. 257. See also Peacham, *op. cit.*, where
learning is treated as an essential adjunct to birth—the gentleman is to be not
merely εὐγενής but also πολυμαθής. De la Primaudaye, *Academie Francoise*,
(1585+), a widely read book, has a chapter on the subject (XVI) called *De la
nature et de la Nourriture*. Bacon uses the phrase *melior natura* in "Of Atheism".

"the briers and darnell of appetites"—lust for Miranda, discontent at his inferior position, ambition, intemperance of all kinds, including a disposition to enslave himself to the bottle of Stephano. And there is in his "vile race" that "which *good* natures Could not abide to be with";[1] in other words there is a repugnance between the raw, unreclaimed nature which he represents, and the courtier-stock with which he has to deal, endowed as it is with grace, and nurtured in refinement through the centuries, in the world of Art.[2]

II. *Prospero's Art.* At the risk of introducing "distincts" where there is no "division" it may be said that Prospero's Art has two functions in *The Tempest*. The first is simple; as a mage he exercises the supernatural powers of the holy adept. His Art is here the disciplined exercise of virtuous knowledge, a "translation of merit into power",[3] the achievement of "an intellect pure and conjoined with the powers of the gods, without which

1. I. ii. 361-2. My italics.
2. "Nature" and its compounds are used in a wide range of meanings in *The Tempest*, as they always are in literature. I have shown how it is used in connexion with Caliban (his "vile race" opposed to the race *non vile*—the stock etymology of *nobile*) and there is also some play on the idea that this nature is "monstrous"—*i.e.* un-natural—a paradox which involves the concept of another and higher nature. "Lord, that a monster should be such a natural" (III. ii. 30-1) where the pun depends upon the colloquial "natural" (="idiot"). Miranda puts the paradox the other way round when she sees Ferdinand, and thinks he is a spirit, "For nothing natural I ever saw so *noble*" (I. ii. 421-2), where the *Melior natura* is contrasted with the *vile* she recognized in Caliban. There is here of course a strong admixture of "natural" meaning "not supernatural". This meaning recurs in the last Act, when Alonso, hearing that the ship is safe, says, "These are not natural events" (v. i. 227) where we think at once that they are due to Prospero's Art. In v. i. 157 "natural breath" is of courses imply "human" breath, though the reading "These words Are natural breath" (N.S.) modifies it slightly. There are three other meanings (though it should be pointed out that this schematization inevitably entails over-simplification): Antonio, who is of noble race, and should have the better nature, exhibits "an evil nature" (I. ii. 93) in his ambition. This is a disposition to do evil which can inhere in good stock for reasons given below. He is called "unnatural" (v. i. 79) by Prospero as he forgives him; the primary meaning here is "unfraternal, neglecting the ties of blood", but there is also the sense of "degenerate, a betrayer of his race and of the better nature". See also v. i. 78-9. Finally, *natura naturans* occurs in a form we have learned to recognize, in Gonzalo's "all things in common nature should produce" and "nature should bring forth of it own kind. . ." (*i.e.* without culture) II. i. 155, 158-9.
3. West, *op. cit.* pp. 41-5.

we shall never happily ascend to the scrutiny of secret things, and to the power of wonderfull workings".[1] This Art is contrasted with the natural power of Sycorax to exploit for evil purposes the universal sympathies.[2] It is a technique for liberating the soul from the passions, from nature; the practical application of a discipline of which the primary requirements are learning and temperance, and of which the mode is contemplation. When Prospero achieves this necessary control over himself and nature he achieves his ends (reflected in the restoration of harmony at the human and political levels) and has no more need of the instrument, "rough magic".[3]

The second function is symbolic. Prospero's Art controls Nature; it requires of the artist virtue and temperance if his experiment is to succeed; and it thus stands for the world of the better natures and its qualities. This is the world which is closed to Caliban (and Comus); the world of mind and the possibilities of liberating the soul, not the world of sense, whether that be represented as coarsely natural or charmingly voluptuous.[4] Art is not only a beneficent magic in contrast to an evil one; it is the ordination of civility, the control of appetite, the transformation of nature by breeding and learning; it is even, in a sense, the means of Grace.

Prospero is, therefore, the representative of Art, as Caliban is of Nature. As a mage he controls nature; as a prince he conquers the passions which had excluded him from his kingdom and overthrown law; as a scholar he repairs his loss of Eden; as a man he learns to temper his passions, an achievement essential to success in any of the other activities.

Prospero describes his efforts to control his own passion in v. i. 25–7 —

1. Agrippa, *op. cit.* III. iii.   2. *supra.* p. xl.

3. *The Tempest*, severe and refined as it is, is still a development of folk-tales in which magicians and their agents have not a precise status in academic demonology. Hence Prospero shows certain unschematic resemblances to the simple magicians of Italian popular comedy and Ayrer's *Die Schöne Sidea*, and Ariel (see Appendix B) is not the unalloyed Platonic dæmon of *Comus*. Nice distinctions are, however, impossible here.

4. Despite the attention given to verbal echoes of *The Tempest* in *Comus*, the deep indebtedness of Milton to the play has not been understood. Shakespeare is of course less formally allegorical, but the play is almost as important to Milton as *The Faerie Queene*.

> Though with their high wrongs I am struck to th' quick,
> Yet with my nobler reason 'gainst my fury
> Do I take part.

In an age when "natural" conduct was fashionably associated with sexual promiscuity, chastity alone could stand as the chief function of temperance, and there is considerable emphasis on this particular restraint in *The Tempest*. The practice of good magic required it;[1] but in this it is again merely the practical application of civility. Prospero twice, and Juno again, warn Ferdinand of the absolute necessity for it, and Ferdinand's ability to make pure beauty "abate the ardour of his liver"[2] is in the strongest possible contrast to Caliban's straightforward natural lust for it. The unchaste designs of Stephano arouse Prospero's anger also; it is as if he were conducting, with magically purified book and rod,[3] the kind of experiment which depended for its success on the absolute purity of all concerned; and indeed, in so far as his aims were a dynastic marriage and the regeneration of the noble, this was so.

This is characteristic of the way in which the magic of Prospero translates into more general terms. The self-discipline of the magician is the self-discipline of the prince. It was the object of the good ruler to make his people good by his own efforts; and that he might do so it was considered necessary for him to acquire learning, and to rid himself "of those troublous affections that untemperate mindes feele".[4] The personal requirements of mage and prince are the same, and Prospero labours to regain a worldly as well as a heavenly power. Like James I in the flattering description, he "standeth invested with that triplicitie which in great veneration was ascribed to the ancient *Hermes*, the power and fortune of a

---

1. Cf. Jonson's comic use of this law in *The Alchemist*.

2. IV. i. 56. C. Leech, in his *Shakespeare's Tragedies* (1950) finds the repetition of Prospero's warning "impertinent" and thinks it "cannot be understood other than pathologically"; this is the starting-point, as I understand it, of his demonstration that "*The Tempest* gave the fullest and most ordered expression of the Puritan impulse in Shakespeare."

3. The book, so highly valued by Prospero and Caliban, as well as the rod, occur in all demonology, popular and learned; they were required to be of virginal purity.

4. Castiglione, *op. cit.* p. 277.

King, the knowledge and illumination of a Priest, and the Learning and universalitie of a Philosopher".[1]

Learning is a major theme in the play; we learn that Miranda is capable of it and Caliban not, and why this should be so; but we are also given a plan of the place of learning in the dispositions of providence. Prospero, like Adam, fell from his kingdom by an inordinate thirst for knowledge; but learning is a great aid to virtue, the road by which we may love and imitate God, and "repair the ruins of our first parents",[2] and by its means he is enabled to return. The solicitude which accompanied Adam and Eve when "the world was all before them" went also with Prospero and Miranda when they set out in their "rotten carcass of a butt".

> By foul play, as thou say'st, were we heav'd thence,
> But blessedly holp hither. (i. ii. 62–3.)

They came ashore "by Providence divine"; and Gonzalo leaves us in no doubt that Prospero's fault, like Adam's, was a happy one:

> Was Milan thrust from Milan, that his issue
> Should become kings of Naples? O rejoice
> Beyond a common joy! ... (v. i. 205–7.)

He had achieved the great object of Learning, and regained a richer heritage.[3] But he is not learned in only this rather abstract sense; he is the learned prince. Like Boethius, he had been a natural philosopher, and had learnt from Philosophy that "to hate the wicked were against reason." He clearly shared the view that "no wise man had rather live in banishment, poverty, and ignominy, than prosper in his own country. . . For in this manner is the office of wisdom performed with more credit and renown, where the governors' happiness is participated by the people about them." And Philosophy, though ambiguously, taught both Boethius and Prospero "the way by which thou mayest return to thy country".[4]

---

1. Cleland, *The Institution of a Young Noble Man*, ii. i.

2. Milton, *Of Education*, in *Prose Works*, ed. Hughes, p. 31.

3. For a somewhat similar reading, though different in detail, see N. Coghill, "The Basis of Shakespearian Comedy", *Essays and Studies* (1950), pp. 1–28.

4. The *Consolation of Philosophy*, iv Prose 5, v Prose 1 (Loeb edition, pp. 335, 365).

There is nothing remarkable about Prospero's ambition to regain his own kingdom and strengthen his house by a royal marriage. To be studious and contemplative, but also to be able to translate knowledge into power in the active life, was the object of his discipline; the Renaissance venerated Scipio for his demonstration of this truth, and Marvell's Horatian Ode speaks of Cromwell in the same terms.

> The chiefe Use then in man of that he knowes,
> Is his paines taking for the good of all. . .
> Yet *Some seeke knowledge, merely but to know,*
> And idle Curiositie that is. . .[1]

Prospero is not at all paradoxical in presenting himself at the climax as he was "sometime Milan". Yet he does not intend merely to look after his worldly affairs; every third thought is to be his grave. "The end of the active or doing life ought to be the beholding; as of war, peace, and as of paines, rest."[2] The active and contemplative lives are complementary.

In all respects, then, Prospero expresses the qualities of the world of Art, of the *non vile*. These qualities become evident in the organized contrasts between his world and the world of the vile; between the worlds of Art and Nature.

6. ART AND NATURE

1. *The Vigour of Vice.* We can now see the force and purpose of the plot-devices by which Shakespeare compares the education of Miranda with that of Caliban, the love of Ferdinand with the lust of Caliban, the magic of Prospero with that of the parents of Caliban; but there are other contrasts also, which are equally clear, and in which Caliban serves as a criterion, not of the beauty and civility, but of the corruption, of the nobly born. The intemperance and folly of Stephano and Trinculo are easy enough to explain, but how are we to account for the guilt already borne and the new evils planned by men of princely stock, endowed with the "seed", and higher in the scale of life than Caliban?

1. Fulke Greville, *A Treatie of Humane Learning* (1603–5), St. 144–5; ed. G. Bullough (1938), i. 190.

2. Castiglione, *op. cit.* p. 280. See also Bacon, *Advancement of Learning*, World's Classics ed., pp. 11–12, 15–16, 42. The theme is a humanist commonplace.

Antonio is a degenerate nobleman; of such the opinion of the civilized aristocrat may be summed up in the words of Owen Felltham:

Earth hath not any thing more glorious than ancient nobility, when it is found with virtue. What barbarous mind will not reverence that blood, which hath untainted run through so large a succession of generations? Besides, virtue adds a new splendour, which together with the honour of his house, challengeth a respect from all. But bad greatness is nothing but the vigour of vice, having both mind and means to be uncontrollably lewd. A debauched son of a noble family is one of the intolerable burdens of the earth, and as hateful a thing as hell; for all know he hath had both example and precept flowing in his education; both which are powerful enough to obliterate a native illness: yet these in him are but auxiliaries to his shame, that, with the brightness of his ancestors, make his own darkness more palpable.[1]

"Good wombs", says Miranda, "have borne bad sons"—in the realm of the better nature there are "unnatural" men. Cordelia had Regan for a sister, and Edmund was Gloucester's "natural" son and Edgar's brother.[2] Pallavicino reminds the company, who have just listened to Canossa's clear-cut theory of nobility, of the many "who for all they were borne of the most noble bloud, yet have they been heaped full of vices".[3] Obviously among the better natures there were those upon whom some encounter or accident might beget an evil nature; that from the seed could grow degenerate plants. Many reasons were alleged to explain this, some astrological, some theological; and ultimately noblemen do ill because, being sons of Adam, they are free to choose. The fact of degeneracy offers little difficulty to those who, with Dante, make nobility dependent upon virtue, shunning the magical view which accepts *melior natura* as distinguished from *natura* essentially, and not merely in respect of good or bad conduct in individual cases. On this magical view, it remains troublesome to account for the fact that vileness of conduct and nobility of birth are found together. Thus Prospero finds it difficult to accept the

---

1. *Resolves Divine Moral and Political*, cxciii (1623?), ed. of 1840, p. 305.
2. On this, see G. C. Taylor, "Shakespeare's Idea of the Beast in Man", *S.P.* xlii (1945), 530–43.
3. Castiglione, *op. cit.* p. 33. Cf. *Henry VIII*, i. ii. 114 ff.

fact. Caliban has no choice but to be vile; but in Antonio there was surely a predisposition to virtuous conduct; and it could not be easy to think of one who, in the eyes of Caliban, was a "brave spirit", as the betrayer of the fulness of his own more perfect nature, as a man so unnatural as to be impervious to the action of grace, a Macbeth of comedy. We see in Antonio the operation of sin in a world magically purified but still allowing freedom to the will; inhabitants of this world can abase themselves below those who live unaided at the level of nature. And it is as a comment upon his unnatural behaviour that we are offered a close structural parallel between Antonio's corrupt and Caliban's natural behaviour in the two plots against Alonso and Prospero. Are we given any notion of the manner of this degeneracy? What has become of Antonio's nobility, his predisposition to virtue?

There is a hint to the answer in the treatment in the play of the word "virtue", which is, as I have suggested, closely related to the nature of the noble. The noble are virtuous, as was Miranda's mother (I. ii. 56)—her virtue expresses itself as chastity; this is always so in noble women. Miranda has "the very virtue of compassion" (I. ii. 27), the noble essence of it. Ferdinand has admired several women for "several virtues", which he paraphrases as "noble graces" (III. i. 42 ff). He admires Miranda because she has all these qualities without their defects, being purely noble, the perfection of her own nature. Prospero, with true princely magnanimity, decides that the act of revenge, when at his mercy lie all his enemies, must remain undone, since "virtue" is nobler than vengeance (v. i. 27–8). This is virtue in a Christian sense; specifically, the virtue of forgiveness; and it supplants revenge as the duty of the courtier. But it *had* been virtuous in a courtier to seek vengeance—it had been *of the essence* of nobility to do so;[1] the conflict between these two concepts of virtuous action in a certain situation had for long been a feature of the Elizabethan drama. For the virtue which is the essence of a magical nobility

1. Cf. *Othello*, I. iii, where Iago and Roderigo use "virtue" to mean "predisposition", with Iago ridiculing the idea. Like Edmund and Antonio, he represents that scepticism, declining into "naturalism" and "atheism", which was a strong Renaissance undercurrent, particularly strong at the turn of the century. Shakespeare always treats it as degenerate.

is not necessarily a Christian or a stoic virtue; it can be, and very generally is, *virtù*. This paradox is most clearly seen in Machiavelli, with whom *virtù* is a favourite word, and means the proper action of a prince on the political level, whether it is "virtuous" in the ethical sense or not. Thus Machiavelli commends the *virtù* of Agathocles, who, though of infamous life, understood so well the need for prudent cruelty in a usurper, that he established his *virtù* by luring his enemies to a banquet and assassinating them all.[1] The proposal Antonio makes to Sebastian in the second Act is that Sebastian should secure his accession to the throne of Naples by the murder of all the opposition, that is of Alonso and Gonzalo; he would include the rest were he not sure of their support. Indeed, throughout the scene, Antonio's conduct is perfectly "virtuous" in a Machiavellian sense, and this radical perversion of virtue represents the extent of his degeneracy, and the degree to which he is alienated from the redemptive scheme of which Prospero is the agent. The moral pervert sinks below the brute in his desire for "good mischief". "The rarer action is In virtue than in vengeance" would be to Antonio an utterly meaningless phrase. In so far as Caliban is his measure, the natural man functions like the virtuous shepherd of normal pastoral, to indicate corruption and degeneracy in the civilized world; if the natural man is a brute, so much the more terrible is the sin of the nobleman who abases himself below the natural.

II. *The Magic of Nobility.* Romance could be defined as a mode of exhibiting the action of magical and moral laws in a version of human life so selective as to obscure, for the special purpose of concentrating attention on these laws, the fact that in reality their force is intermittent and only fitfully glimpsed. Thus, although we may believe that in the end the forces of fertility, or of plenty, triumph, and that it is a law of human life that they should do so, we would not hold it as a rational conviction that this must be so in every single case, of every individual; yet comedy by a formal law, proved by a few exceptions, ends in a feast or a wedding. In the same way we

1. *Il Principe*, VIII.

accept even more arbitrary devices, such as that of the crucial "recognition" of tragedy and comedy, as formal laws corresponding to, and in some valuable way illuminating, diurnal forces which are intermittent and rarely visible. In the realm of what we agree to call romance these conventions are both more frequent and more arbitrary.

The Tempest has always been recognized as a romance; it so clearly belongs to this world that some critics, misguided by the resemblances between this play and *The Winter's Tale*, have supposed that at some stage in its history it must also have been analogous in structure. But there is no equation between romance and unclassical form; one need not look further than Sidney's *Arcadia* to establish that, though it is perhaps also relevant to look in the direction of Italian pastoral tragicomedy.

It is therefore easy enough to describe the factors which, in *The Tempest*, depend upon the ideal structure of moral and magical law in romantic thought. Miranda introduces the Platonic theme in her initial comments on Ferdinand. "There's nothing ill can dwell in such a temple. . ." (I. ii. 461) —and throughout the play the noble (and therefore virtuous) are beautiful, the vile ugly. Sycorax was an envious hoop, Caliban's mind cankers "as with age his body uglier grows" (IV. i. 191–2); even the wicked courtiers appear as brave spirits, much as the fallen angels retained something of their original brightness, and conversely, as Duessa, stripped of her evil power, became

> A loathly, wrinckled hag, ill favoured, old,
> Whose secret filth good manners biddeth not be told.
>> (*F.Q.* I. viii. 46.)

This is a law which operates imperfectly in the world of actuality.[1] Thus voyagers expressed some surprise that the natives of the new world, though they lived in sin, were not unspeakably hideous; they looked for the actual operation of

---

1. See Spenser, *An Hymne in Honour of Beautie*; Milton, *Comus*, 453 ff; and for the quasi-scientific justification of it, despite its apparent imperfection, Felltham, *Resolves*, xxx—"Philosophy tells us, though the soul be not caused by the body, yet in the general, it follows the temperament of it; so the comeliest outsides are naturally (for the most part) most virtuous within" (*ed. cit.* p. 74).

this law. In the same way the Courtier held that "as there can be no circle without a centre, no more can beautie be without goodnesse."[1] But in romance the law operates without interference, and the physical appearance of the characters becomes an index of their nobility or vileness, their virtue or depravity. In romance there survives that system of ideal correspondencies and magic patterns which in actuality could not survive the scrutiny of an informed and modern eye. It thrives upon the myth of the indefeasible magnanimity of royal children as it does upon the myth of the magical connexion between the fertility of a king and of his lands and subjects. Hence it is the only atmosphere in which extended consideration may plausibly be given to such explorations of nature as Shakespeare attempted in the group of plays known as the romances; for in actuality the issue is always obscured, but in art the ideas can develop as it were of themselves, with ideal clarity, as if to show us that a formal and ordered paradigm of these forces is possible when life is purged of accident, and upon the assumption that since we are all willy-nilly platonists we are perfectly able to understand the relevance of such a paradigm.

Thus, in Shakespeare's romances, the virtue of royal children is *given*; it controls their behaviour, and cannot be mistaken; they have it by nature. Thus the concealed children of Cymbeline, despite the advice of Belarius that the life of nature (rough, simple, uncultivated) is "nobler" than "the city's usuries", cannot suppress their better natures.

> How hard it is to hide the sparks of nature!
> ... though train'd up thus meanly
> I' the cave, wherein they bow, their thoughts do hit
> The roofs of palaces; and nature prompts them
> In simple and low things, to prince it much ...
> (*Cymb.*, iii. iii. 79–85.)

Their virtue includes *virtù*, and as Belarius says when Guiderius enters with the head of Cloten:

> O thou goddess,
> Thou divine Nature, how thyself thou blazon'st

1. Castiglione, *op. cit.* p. 309. See also note on i. ii. 460.

In these two princely boys!...
                    ... 'Tis wonder
That an invisible instinct should frame them
To royalty unlearn'd; honour untaught;
Civility not seen from other; valour
That wildly grows in them, but yields a crop
As if it had been sow'd! (IV. ii. 169 ff)

These boys might be the very examples Phillips had in mind when he spoke of his hypothetical lost prince.

In Imogen herself the virtue of noble stock is primarily figured forth in her chastity; as she is the only married woman among these last heroines, and as married chastity is a less dramatic quality than virginity, this resulted in some difficulties of expression, as in that speech of Posthumus concerning her sexual fastidiousness which has sometimes given offence to readers (II. v). There is less difficulty with the other heroines, who are all virgins. In all of them virtue is expressed as chastity, dramatically so in *Pericles*, where Marina's virtue shines forth so evidently that it abashed the brothel lechers. As for Perdita, Polixenes recognized her as "too noble" for the Shepherd's house (IV. iv. 159). She is devoted to her contract with Florizel, but it is a condition of that contract that his "lusts" should not "burn hotter than" his "faith". Similarly Miranda, like her sisters in the *Tempest*-analogues, is remarkably frank in her offers of love, and Ferdinand equally insistent that his desires are under control, that her beauty abates the ardour of his liver. Nature is always fertile; the better nature, however, is under a magical restraint; and virginity is immemorially associated with magic power, witness the *Golden Legend*, *The Old Wives' Tale*, and *Comus*. *The Tempest* makes much of this, and also of the contrast between the unchastity of the natural man, in whom cultivation has brought forth only "the briers and darnell of appetites" and the man of better nature, represented under this aspect by Ferdinand; the comparison at the level of ideas is expressed in their attitudes to Miranda, and at the level of narrative in their reactions to the duty of log-bearing which Prospero enforces upon them severally; to Ferdinand it is a sanctified labour, it physics pain with delight; it is the restraint—horticulturally one might say, the cutting-back—from which the fruit of good develops: but to Caliban it is a discipline of fear.[1] Ferdinand is not lacking in the *virtù* which makes him try to draw on Prospero (to be thwarted by the magic or divine power that hedges a prince) but he quickly understands the purpose of his suffering because he has the power properly to estimate the value of the reward; he has already taken Miranda for a goddess.

The virtue of these romantic heroines so illuminates their physical bodies that, like Pastorella their Spenserian proto-type, they could be mistaken for goddesses. (Pastorella is also the cause of a contrast between nobility and vileness, with Calidore as the knight of courtesy filling Ferdinand's place and Coridon as the boor deficient in virtue (all definitions) and courtesy filling Caliban's. This is a hint as to the extent to which Shakespeare's is a "stock" situation.) Marina's specially efficacious virtue transforms her into a splendid apparition which the vexed Pericles can scarcely accept as human; Perdita appears as Flora;

> This your sheep-shearing
> Is as a meeting of the petty gods,
> And you the queen on 't.
>
> (*Wint.*, IV. iii. 3–5.)

Ferdinand's greeting of Miranda (which his father's, later, substantiates) glances back through the earlier romantic drama to Virgil, to the hero's interview with Venus;[2] estab-lishing at one stroke the typical qualities of Ferdinand's sea-adventure (later reinforced by further significant allusions to the *Aeneid*) and the divine quality of Miranda's nobility, ex-pressed as both virtue and beauty. There is no need to labour the connexion between this romantic convention and the fitful divinization of beauty in the actual world. It corresponds to the extension of Prospero's princely powers into the realm of magic.

The romantic story is, then, the mode in which Shakespeare made his last poetic investigation into the supernatural ele-ments in the human soul and in human society. His thinking

---

1. I am here and elsewhere indebted to one of the most valuable studies of this play, A. H. Gilbert's "The *Tempest* Parallelism in Characters and Situa-tions", *J.E.G.P.* XIV (1915), 63–74, though my conclusions differ rather from Gilbert's.

2. See note on I. ii. 424.

is Platonic, though never schematic; and he had deliberately chosen the pastoral tragicomedy as the genre in which this inquiry is best pursued. The pastoral romance gave him the opportunity for a very complex comparison between the worlds of Art and Nature; and the tragicomic form enabled him to concentrate the whole story of apparent disaster, penitence, and forgiveness into one happy misfortune, controlled by a divine Art.

7. PASTORAL TRAGICOMEDY

It is well known that romantic comedy was unfashionable during the opening years of the seventeenth century, and that it was rather suddenly restored to favour towards the end of the first decade. At this time Beaumont and Fletcher were becoming established, and Shakespeare seemingly changed his general direction to produce his part in *Pericles*, and the other three romances which are his last plays except for *Henry VIII*, in which he collaborated with Fletcher. About this time (1610) the King's Men revived the old romance *Mucedorus*, and it is by no means impossible that Bremo, the wild man in that play, contributed to the emotional situation which was realized in Caliban. It seems most likely that *Mucedorus* was dug out *because* of the new demand for romantic comedy, though evidently there were differences between the old and new types. One can scarcely believe that *Mucedorus* was responsible for the vogue, even though it was somewhat refurbished. In addition to this, it has long been known that an old play of an academic type called *The Rare Triumphs of Love and Fortune* has some curious resemblances to *Cymbeline*, and also, though in lesser degree, to *The Tempest*.[1] I do not know that the full extent of the latter resemblance has been recognized;[2] but in any case it is not of much importance, except as an additional token that *The Tempest*, like its fellows, has native progenitors. Nor

1. R. W. Boodle, "The Original of *Cymbeline* and possibly of *The Tempest*", *N. & Q*. 19 Nov. 1887.
2. The hermit Bomelio calls his unwilling servant Lentulo much as Prospero calls Caliban, and with a similar result (Dodsley, VI. 175–6). Hermione, Bomelio's son, finds and destroys his father's magic books (218). Lentulo is accused of stealing the hermit's "suit of apparel" (219).

is this native line merely dramatic, for its most impressive
product before *The Tempest* is the Sixth Book of *The Faerie
Queene* (itself connected, like Sidney's *Arcadia*, with the Greek
romances) which exploits the pastoral situation for comment
upon the theme of the contrast between nature and nurture.
It might be possible to argue that Spenser alone is sufficient to
account for the pastoral situation in *The Tempest*; but there is
a fairly strong suspicion that this play and the other romances
excluding *Pericles*, being perhaps designed for a more sophisticated audience, show some marks of influence from Italian
pastoral drama.

This is a problem which demands elaborate treatment and
it is beyond the scope of the present work. It is clear that
Fletcher was familiar with the new pastoral tragicomedy of
which the laws had been promulgated and defended during
an extensive controversy by Guarini,[1] and it is conceivable
that *Philaster* was an attempt, after the failure of the more
formal *Faithful Shepherdess*, to adapt the genre to the stage of
the private theatre. It is also conceivable that Shakespeare
may have taken advice from Fletcher at the time of the company's commencing to play at the Blackfriars,[2] so that in one
way or another the fashion for Guarini may have affected
Shakespeare.

Daniel's *Queenes Arcadia*, "a Pastorall Trage-Comedie", was
performed in 1605; Fletcher's *Faithful Shepherdess* probably
in 1608. By this time the theories of Guarini were common
literary intelligence, and the Preface to the published version
of Fletcher's play gives a straightforward account of some of
them. It has been shown that Fletcher was familiar not only

1. The controversy lasted from 1587 (two years before the publication of *Il
Pastor Fido*) until the 1620s. Guarini claimed that pastoral was a moral and
socially valuable genre (his opponent De Nores had questioned this) and that
tragicomedy was critically acceptable provided it was not a clumsy intrusion of
comedy into tragedy but a third kind, such as Aristotle allows for (*Poetics*, XIII),
a harmonious mixture of comedy and tragedy and not a composite. "From the
one it takes the noble characters, not the action; the fable . . . the emotions,
aroused but tempered; the delight, not the sadness; the danger, not the death;
from the other, the sober gentleness, the invented plot, the happy 'change', and
above all the comic order " (Translation of F. H. Ristine, *English Tragicomedy*
[1910], p. 37, with some modification.)

2. See G. E. Bentley, "Shakespeare and the Blackfriars Theatre", *Shakespeare
Survey*, 1 (1948), pp. 38–50.

with Guarini but with lesser playwrights in the same tradition,[1] and it is very unfortunate that so little is at present known about the details of this indebtedness. One finds in Guarini and Fletcher the "Shakespearian" themes of royal birth, the sacrifice for love, and resurrection from death or seeming death. Fletcher gave these elements of Italian pastoral a place in the context of English popular drama; though neither he nor his Italian master so much as attempt to use the themes in a Shakespearian way. Guarini is not a great poet; indeed, with all his weight of theory, he is a pretentious poet. Fletcher is remarkably like him in so far as they both denied a predominant moral function to poetry and trifled with the genre in which they experimented. Nevertheless the tradition in which they worked may have blended with the native tradition in which *Pericles* was written to give *The Tempest* a certain resemblance to the Italian form and its popular descendant, the Commedia dell' Arte.

Even if we cannot ascertain its antecedents, there can be no question that the tragicomic form of the last plays was dictated by the nature of the fables treated, and that these were chosen because they lent themselves to the formulation of poetic propositions concerning the status of human life in relation to nature, and the mercy of a providence which gives new life when the old is scarred by sin or lost in folly. The themes are thus pastoral and tragicomic.[2] Prospero pitches his countrymen into a sea that threatens but is merciful, and does not so much as stain their clothes; into a penitence which washes away old guilt and brings new life. This is the tragicomic shipwreck of which the Bermudan castaways spoke; the apparent disaster which was a means of grace; the gods "chalk'd forth the way" for every man to find himself "when no man was his own" (v. i. 203, 212–13).

This is the great achievement of Prospero, and Gonzalo sums it up for him: self-conquest, followed by the redemption

1. See V. M. Jeffery, "Italian Influence in Fletcher's *Faithful Shepherdess*", *M.L.R.* xxi (1926), 147 ff.
2. Ristine wisely remarks: "The ruling spirit of romance is the very essence of tragicomedy . . . *Cymbeline, Winter's Tale* and the *Tempest*, whatever the inspiration, are closely identified with the new drama of tragicomic romance" (*op. cit.* pp. 73, 114).

of the noble, their liberation from the sense of loss and impurity which haunts them as they wander exhausted in search of Ferdinand and themselves. Even Antonio has not lost all his original brightness; he is part of Miranda's brave new world, and one of those brave spirits which give the natural slave the insight to "be wise hereafter And seek for grace" (v. i. 294–5). (The reactions of Caliban and Miranda to the sight of the castaways are carefully compared both at the beginning and at the end of the play, just as their reaction to the same education is compared.) But Antonio is, none the less, one of Prospero's failures; as far as can be deduced from the closing passages, in which Antonio is silent, he will not choose the good; unlike Sebastian he is unimpressed by it, and refuses to close the circuit of noble virtue which excludes only Caliban. Prospero must acknowledge another thing of darkness. In his fantasia on *The Tempest* Mr Auden, with an admirable imaginative exactitude, gives Antonio as chorus the last ironic word to each dream of the good or new life:

> Your all is partial, Prospero;
> My will is all my own:
> Your need to love shall never know
> Me: I am I, Antonio,
> By choice myself alone.[1]

A world without Antonio is a world without freedom; Prospero's shipwreck cannot restore him if he desires not to be restored, to life. The gods chalk out a tragicomic way, but enforce only disaster. The rest is voluntary.

Note. When this edition was in proof there appeared R. Bernheimer's *Wild Men in the Middle Ages* (Harvard, 1952). This excellent work contains a mass of evidence substantiating the interpretation of Caliban put forward in my Introduction, and providing much material for further development of it. The Wild Man, for example, was regarded as being unable to control his sexual instincts. He was an emblem of primitive sexuality explicitly contrasted with the values of courtly love,

1. *The Sea and the Mirror*, in *For the Time Being* (1945), p. 18. This poem provides some brilliant insights into the play although it is not in the ordinary sense a commentary. Caliban goes remarkably well as a personification of the It (as good a modern pastoral hero as could be found).

and utterly opposed to "that humble adulation and worship which the Middle Ages demanded from the well-trained knight, for this attitude implied the ability to restrain appetite for the sake of a civilized ideal" (pp. 121–2). The bearing of this on the Caliban-Ferdinand situation is clear; and Mr Bernheimer's book includes much else that is equally revealing.

8. ANALOGOUS LITERATURE

There is usually something to be learned about Shakespeare's fables and his use of them from the treatment by lesser artists of analogous themes. Romantic tragicomedy draws its stories from a vast reservoir of primitive fiction; there are not only many stories but many versions of the same story. Ultimately the source of *The Tempest* is an ancient *motif*, of almost universal occurrence, in saga, ballad, fairy tale and folk tale. The existence of this story accounts for the many analogues to *The Tempest*. That both Prospero and the father of Ayrer's Sidea are irascible is, in the last analysis, explained by the fact that they descend from a bad-tempered giant-magician. It is likewise a feature of the archetype that the princess, like Miranda and Sidea, should aid the captive prince in his task and frankly own her love. The log-bearing is also a very ancient feature, and appears in the story at a primitive stage when the task was to chop down the wood as a preparation for the second task, which was to plough the ground; later the prince had to reap the harvest, and all these tasks were to be accomplished in one day. The Jason story suggests itself as an early analogue, and the ramifications of the fable have been traced throughout Europe and the Orient. Miranda and Sidea are related to each other, but also to a host of others, and even to Medea. The presence of primitive elements in the deeply considered structure of *The Tempest* need not surprise us; they are a normal Shakespearian phenomenon, as the "source" study of *Hamlet, All's Well That Ends Well*, and *The Merchant of Venice* has proved.[1]

Scholars have not, on the whole, been satisfied with this

---

1. See W. W. Newell, "The Sources of Shakespeare's *Tempest*", *Journal of American Folklore*, XVI (1913), 234–57.

explanation of the similarity between Shakespeare's play and
Die Schöne Sidea, and it has been suggested that Ayrer, who was
a translator and adaptor, had worked on an *ur-Tempest*, as he
did on other English plays, which he may have seen during a
tour of Germany by an English troupe. Since Ayrer died in
1605 he could not have seen *The Tempest* in its extant form.
Chambers records that in 1604 and 1613 English comedians
acted an otherwise unknown play called *Celinde and Sidea* in
Germany, but Ayrer's play has no Celinde.[1] The similarities
between the two plays are not as striking as their advocates
have suggested, though it is not absolutely impossible that
Shakespeare may have known some old play on the lines of
Mucedorus which may have contributed something to the total
pattern of *The Tempest*. Even if this is so it matters very little,
since Shakespeare can scarcely have taken more from it than
he could have done from any other version of the basic story.
Little remains save the general situation: there is a displaced
ruler-magician; a captive, log-bearing prince, supervised by
the magician's daughter (though in Ayrer's play she is far
from Miranda-like in temperament); the bewitching of the
prince's sword; and the happy ending. There is also the coincidence, on which much has been based, of the words
"mountain" and "silver" in the English and German plays.
They are the names of two of Prospero's dogs (IV. i. 255 ff);
and they occur also in the part of Julia, who in the German
play is a rival of Sidea, when she is referring to the gain she
may count upon even if she misses marriage with Prince Engel-
brecht. It seems extraordinary that this has been regarded as
evidence. There is no Caliban in the German play; no shipwreck; no significant system of magic. There are plot-elements
which have nothing in common with *The Tempest*; and the
whole play is so naif and buffoonish as to be beyond the possibility of serious consideration as the reflection of an important
source. The mind of Shakespeare was, as we have seen, working along quite other lines than these.

Since Ayrer failed to give complete satisfaction, rival
sources were bound to be proposed, and for a while there was
keen interest in two Spanish works. These are Antonio de

---

1. *Elizabethan Stage*, II. 284, 289; *William Shakespeare*, I. 493.

Eslava's *Noches de Invierno* (1609), in the fourth chapter of which there is a tale resembling the plot of *The Tempest*; and Diego Ortuñez de Calahorra's *Espejo de Príncipes y Caballeros* (1562 ... English translation, 1578 ... 1601). The case for the second of these was the special interest of J. de Perott, who first stated it in 1905.[1] The book has the following ingredients: a King of England who compelled his daughter to marry the Prince of Portugal against her will (this king had a grudge against an emperor who had been responsible for his son's death, and de Perott conjectures a connexion between this story and the vestigial son of Antonio in *Tempest* [1. ii. 440–1]); a magician withdraws with his two children and his suite to devote himself to study, incidentally kidnapping a lover for his daughter; a magic island, ruled by a vicious witch who had a son by the devil; a log-bearing prince; magic storms; magic books; and invisible sages. There are also some slight verbal parallels, which are of no importance, and the names Claribel and Claribella, which Shakespeare could have found nearer to hand in Spenser. This view has won little support, and even if we forget that scholars inevitably make selections from narratives which offer far more convincing resemblances than the originals themselves, there is nothing here to suggest that Calahorra's tale is anything more than another analogue. There is not a single feature of the Spanish story that has a unique similarity to *The Tempest*.[2]

More attention has been paid to Eslava's story, which has found supporters from Garnett to Hardin Craig. This tale has no magic island, but it has a dethroned king, skilled in magic, who is forced to sail away from his kingdom, taking with him his daughter; he builds himself a palace under the sea, and eventually leads to it the disinherited son of his enemy, as a husband for his daughter. He then raises a tempest to destroy at sea the usurping son, now reigning in succession to his old enemy; whereupon his daughter's husband is established on his hereditary throne, and the magician himself returns to his own realm in retirement, having united the two rival kingdoms. "This Spanish tale," says Hardin Craig,

---

1. *The Probable Sources of Shakespeare's Tempest.*

2. De Perott, incidentally, thinks that the name "Sycorax" derives from "Iscariot".

who gives a fuller account of it, "in its political intrigue, its adventures, and its use of tempest and sea, has much in common with *The Tempest*."[1] On the other hand, Morton Luce, in the original Arden edition, could "attach but little importance" to it, and I agree with him. There are analogous elements, certainly; so there were in Calahorra. But this tale has not even an island to recommend it. However, this theory has been supported by evidence of a more historical sort. The kingdoms united in Eslava's story are those of Bulgaria and Byzantium. It appears that this union actually occurred in the eleventh century, and M. Henri Grégoire[2] has made it clear that Eslava's ultimate source was Diocleas Presbyter's *Regnum Slavorum*. There is an Italian version of 1601 by Mauro Orbini called *Il Regno degli Slavi*, and no doubt this would have been defensible as a common source for Eslava and Shakespeare (not to mention Ayrer) were it not that Orbini omits relevant portions of Diocleas, who cannot himself be seriously regarded as a likely source. Grégoire supposes that some lost Italian *novella*, based on Orbini, was the common source. Here again *Hamlet* could help, by reminding us of the way in which elements of folk tale are assimilated into historical narratives. This weird structure of Bulgarian, Byzantine, Latin, Italian, Spanish, and German testimony is a prize mare's nest, and it is politic to avoid stirring it any further.[3]

At present the most interesting reputed source is the Italian *Commedia dell'Arte*. It was first suggested by the Italian scholar F. Neri[4] that the resemblances between certain surviving *scenari* of the Italian popular comedy and the plot of *The Tempest* are too striking to be accounted for as a coincidence. The theme was taken up in English by several writers, in particular Miss K. M. Lea in her book on *Italian Popular Comedy* (1934). We know that the *Commedia dell'Arte* had been seen by

1. *Interpretation of Shakespeare* (1948), p. 345.

2. "The Bulgarian Origins of *The Tempest*", *S.P.* xxxvii (1940), 236–56.

3. Mr Robert Graves, in his study of "The Sources of *The Tempest*" (1925, reprinted in *The Common Asphodel*, 1949), accepts Ayrer and Calahorra as sources, together with Jourdain, Isaiah, and (later) a lost variant of a Welsh folk tale (*The White Goddess*, 1948, p. 113; *Asphodel*, p. 43). On the basis of these sources he erects a compound allegorical interpretation involving concealed comment upon Shakespeare's private life and upon contemporary French politics.

4. *Scenari delle Maschere in Arcadia* (1913); Lea, *op. cit.* ii. 444.

English audiences. Italian comedians were in England in the sixteenth century and, possibly, in 1610;[1] and travellers brought back accounts of it from Italy. Jonson uses some of its conventional tricks, and the names of its masks passed into English. Elements of its idiosyncratic design and characterization have been traced, by O. J. Campbell and others, in plays as diverse as *The Comedy of Errors, Love's Labour's Lost, The Merry Wives of Windsor*, and *The Tempest*.

I cannot here relate at length the characteristics of the Italian form. The *Commedia dell'Arte* came into being in the sixteenth century as a form of drama professional and popular, with typed and masked characters who improvised their parts from skeleton plots, which are called *scenari*, though the sixteenth-century word was *soggetti*. These *scenari* contain everything the trained extemporizer needed to get the plot along; and among those which are extant there are a few which are reminiscent of *The Tempest*. All of these belong to a species of *Commedia dell'Arte* which was known as pastoral tragicomedy.[2]

A large number of problems concerning these *scenari* remain to be solved by investigators competent in a specialized field of study. There is still room for very serious doubt concerning the relevance of these plays to Shakespearian source-study; the extant *scenari* post-date Shakespeare, and their own provenance is very dubious. Miss Lea contends that "if we were to insert a summary of the action of *The Tempest* . . . among the scenari . . . the resemblance would be remarkable", and believes that this resemblance may be accounted for as due to direct borrowing "taking place most probably at a pre-Shakespearian stage of development".[3] She also constructs a "normal" *scenario* which is indeed startlingly like *The Tempest*,[4] but inevitably her preoccupation with *The Tempest* has affected her choice of incidents from the corpus. Professor Baldwin, who is disinclined to credit the theory of such a relationship as far as any other play is concerned, seems half-ready to make an

---

1. Chambers, *William Shakespeare*, I. 494. The fact that there is no certain reference to the presence of these comedians in England after 1578 is, despite efforts to minimize it, a serious objection to the theory.

2. Miss Lea thinks that tragicomedy was discovered by the popular comedians in their attempt to improvise tragedy. But Fletcherian tragicomedy is primarily Guarinian.

3. *ibid.* II. 434.   4. *ibid.* I. 201-3.

exception of *The Tempest*,[1] but nevertheless a great deal needs
to be done before any such relationship can be assumed. Jacobean pastoral tragicomedy, despite certain resemblances
which can scarcely in the last analysis be completely without
cause, is very unlike the popular comedy, though it has something in common with its forebear, the *commedia erudita*. And
if we accept the very large supposition that a comedy exactly
like Miss Lea's norm was available to Shakespeare in 1610,
we have still to consider that such a source would be only a
degree more significant than the hypothetical romance under-
lying *Die Schöne Sidea*; it could have supplied, in addition to
cruder materials elsewhere available, the idea of a shipwreck
and of a wild man, and some hints concerning the intercourse
between savage and civilized boors. But even so, it could only
have acted, so to speak, as a detonator to the main charge. As
to shipwreck, the natural man, and the new situation created
by the intrusion of a new order of human life into the traditional scheme, and as to tragicomedy too, Shakespeare had
other and more suggestive materials for speculation. He did not
need a jocose pantomime to teach him how to think about it.

   Miss Lea makes much of the presence in *The Tempest* of
stage-tricks and plot-devices resembling the Italian form; but
the transformations wrought by Prospero and Ariel are of the
common stock of magic lore; and echo-poetry was a pastoral
device popularized by Guarini. The evidence is strongest in
the sub-plot, where the antics of Stephano and Trinculo certainly recall some of the *lazzi*, or tricks, of the shipwrecked
sailors in the Italian popular comedies. Hence there may be
something in Croce's conjecture that "Trinculo" is an "echo
of Neapolitan slang", and that Stephano's "O touch me not,
I am not Stephano but a cramp" (v. i. 286) contains a pun on
the Neapolitan *stefano*, a slang word for "stomach",[2] though
this latter seems unduly speculative, since Stephano's remark

1. See *Shakspere's Five-Act Structure* (1947), pp. 800-1 and 796. His pupil, Miss
Olive Henneberger, believes that if we find out more about *The Tempest* we
shall probably discover that the Italian *scenari* are merely plot-analogues, as
they are in the case of *The Comedy of Errors* and *The Two Gentlemen of Verona*.
(*Proximate Sources for the Italianate Elements in Shakespeare*, 1937. I have seen only
the published abstract of this thesis, which, with some modifications, Baldwin
resumes in his *Five-Act Structure*.)

2. Cited in Lea, *op. cit.* ii. 448-9.

is self-explanatory. Mr Gray, in studies already referred to, emphasizes the importance of *Arcadia Enchanted* and *The Three Satyrs*. He mentions also *Pantaloncino*, in which the magician throws away his staff and book (but it was usual for magicians to do so in fact and fiction alike); and *The Strangers*, in which the shipwrecked clowns get drunk and carry a bottle. In *Pazzia*, Gratiano has a passage resembling that of Trinculo when he finds Caliban under the gaberdine.[1] Some of these isolated coincidences are rather striking; for example, in *Il Capriccio* there is "a banquet which rises from the ground and is snatched away as suddenly by spirits" (Lea, I. 209). But despite the tempting nature of these similarities, it is rash at this stage to commit oneself to any explanation of them, and safe only to say that no matter what is proved in the end, it is very unlikely that the interpretation of *The Tempest* will be seriously affected.

There is one other reputed source of *The Tempest*, which, though it is not a romance, may be treated here for the sake of completeness. This is Thomas's *History of Italy* (1549). In this work, as Halliwell pointed out, certain names are mentioned, and certain events described, which somewhat resemble those of Shakespeare's play.

Thomas's account is by no means easy to follow, and as it has been inaccurately rendered, I quote it here, using the edition of 1561. He first mentions Prospero Adorno as being for a brief period Duke of Genoa in 1460 (f 180ʳ). He was deposed by the rival family of Fregosi. Once more in 1477 Prospero Adorno became ruler of Genoa, as lieutenant of the Duke of Milan. "But he continued scarcely one yeare, tyl by meane of new practises, that he held with Ferdinando Kyng of Naples, he was had in suspicion to the Milanese, who willynge to depose hym, raysed a new commocion of the people, so that where he was before the Dukes lieutenante, now he was made governoure absolutely of the common wealth" (f 181ᵛ). I suppose this means that the "commocion" was engineered to put Prospero in the position of an usurper, and then to overthrow him. If so, the plan did not work; for the Milanese army which marched against him was defeated,

---

1. But see note on II. ii.

and Prospero continued to rule until, in what seems to have
been the normal rhythm of events, the Fregosi once more
deposed him. Tired of this primitive system of succession, the
Genoese re-submitted themselves to Milan in 1488, when
Antony Adorno was made governor. Thus summarized, the
story still has points of contact with *The Tempest*, but it might
be remembered that Antony is no usurper, and in fact has a
better sanction for ruling Genoa than Prospero. The attention
devoted to Thomas has been excessive, partly because critics
have, perhaps, relied upon very biased paraphrases supplied
by anxious source-hunters. Thomas cannot even certainly
claim the names of the characters. More of these names are
found in Eden's *History of Travel*;[1] Prospero and Stephano
have parts in Jonson's *Every Man in His Humour*, a play in
which Shakespeare acted, and which perhaps taught him the
correct pronunciation of Stephano, which he got wrong in
The Merchant of Venice. It is possible that Shakespeare knew
Thomas, but it matters little either way.[2]

Analogues of the *Tempest* fable are, inevitably, quite plenti-
ful, and some of them are already tragicomic in form, as might
be expected from the affinity of romance for tragicomedy.
Whether or no there exists between them and Shakespeare's
play that direct contact which would raise them to the status
of sources is largely a matter of antiquarian interest, since at
no point could they seriously affect the account of the intellectual process which has been deduced above from the play
as it survives. These analogues and pseudo-sources could help
us only by providing information about the laws and conditions of romance as they operate within a specified area; they
may provide information as to how Shakespeare was likely
to assent to such themes as those of the lost maiden of high
birth, of the deposed magician-king, of the salvage man, or of
the shipwrecked court-party. They are more useful than, say,
Dryden, only because they are likely to be, for historical

1. *supra*, p. xxxii.
2. Hunter supplemented the debt to Thomas by claiming that Shakespeare
also referred to an historical Alonso, King of Naples, and he contrives a version
of Thomas's account which makes this seem plausible. But Thomas's character
is called Alfonso, and the resemblance is very faint. Hunter added that he had
seen a work on witchcraft, printed at Milan in 1490 and dedicated to a Duke of
Milan called Francis; its author was Jerome Visconti.

reasons, less alien to Shakespeare's way of thinking, and not because they are earlier than he. For the same reason they are more valuable than Apollonius Rhodius, who also has an analogous theme. All these works, and many others, treat at some level of seriousness fabulous elements, which are to some degree conventionally associated, and they can help us to get the feel of the specified area of the world of the *non vile* in which the plot of *The Tempest* has its being. Here and there they themselves inevitably suggest the very pattern of events in Shakespeare. They begin to tell us why Shakespeare would use a similar pattern, and they show us, in their very dulness, what it was that Shakespeare habitually did—he accepted the curious fable, not for its merely entertaining qualities, but because, passed through his fire, it had significance in terms "of man, of nature, and of human life". (See also p. 172.)

9. STRUCTURE—MASQUE ELEMENTS

Commentators have often expressed surprise that *The Tempest*, written at the end of a career devoted to the writing of plays which appear to ignore neo-classical prescription, should observe the unities of time and place. Johnson concluded that it was accidental. Other suggestions have, however, been made. Shakespeare may have been imitating a *scenario*; he may have allowed the court masque to affect the pattern of the whole play and not merely the fourth act; or he may have been demonstrating his ability to observe the classical law, despite his many infringements of it. On the other hand, it has been suggested that, for considerations which can be deduced from the play as it stands, Shakespeare chose to treat this theme in an intensive, rather than in his more usual extensive, way.

I have already commented upon the relationship of the play with the *scenari*, and it is unlikely that many will find this explanation satisfactory. Nor will most people be content to think that *The Tempest* is formally an erudite joke, or an exercise in a form which Shakespeare had sufficiently examined much earlier in his career. But the view that the structure of the play generally is conditioned by the masque must be briefly considered.

Thorndike first proposed this view. He argued that there was intimate contact between the professional and the court stages; for example, the actors who took the antic parts in antimasques were drawn from the professional companies, and occasionally traces of this interest in the antimasque appear in popular drama—thus the antimasque of Jonson's *Oberon* turns up as the dance of the satyrs in *The Winter's Tale*, and that of Beaumont's *Masque of the Inner Temple and Gray's Inn* in *Two Noble Kinsmen*. Furthermore, it had become fashionable to include some masque-like entertainment in Blackfriars and Globe plays in order to satisfy the growing desire of the audience for novelty and spectacle. Eighteen of Beaumont's and Fletcher's plays, Thorndike argued, contain masque elements derived from the elaborate Jacobean masque, not from the simpler Elizabethan form occasionally found in earlier drama. He went so far as to regard the whole of *The Tempest* as a kind of adapted masque whose chief interest resided in the opportunities it gave for music and dancing and the lavish use of scenic and mechanical display. Important as these were, it seems incredible that anyone could regard *The Tempest* as a vehicle for display and nothing more.[1] It is also a strain on one's credulity to be asked to see, in the hunting of the conspirators by Prospero and Ariel, a formal antimasque—that would convict Shakespeare of adding the philosophic refinement of an antimasque to an entertainment which, in the absence of any revelation of the masquers and of dances involving the spectators, is not really a masque at all. The theme is taken up with more subtlety by Miss Welsford, who suggests that *The Tempest* was influenced by certain particular masques, including Jonson's *Hymenaei*, *The Masque of Blackness* and *The Masque of Beauty*. The dances and music she takes to be reflections of masque influence, and the Caliban-plot a Jonsonian antimasque translated into dramatic terms. In fact the whole plot of *The Tempest* is based upon two motifs used by Jonson in *The Masque of Beauty*—the motifs of wandering and of disenchantment. It was the custom for the masquers to appear suddenly, having been hidden "as a result of adverse spells"

1. Such opinions also ignore the nature of Renaissance "Shows", which derived their structure and vitality from their allegorical content.

and then "freed from enchantment by the beneficent powers of the sovereign". Prospero plays the part of a masque presenter, and the second scene of the play is like a masque induction. The characters are throughout manipulated by the presenter, and the play takes up the narrative of event not like a classical drama during "the last few hours of uncertainty which must soon be terminated by irrevocable choice and decisive action" but like a masque, which deals with a moment of transformation: "It expresses, not uncertainty, ended by final success or failure, but expectancy crowned by sudden revelation... The plot of *The Tempest* leads up, without hesitation or uncertainty, to that moment when Prospero gathers his forgiven enemies around him, draws back the curtain from before the inner stage, and 'discovers Ferdinand and Miranda playing at chess'."[1]

This theory of an intimate connexion between the play and contemporary masques is reinforced by the claim, made originally by Whiter and elaborated in the course of time, that Prospero's speech after his sudden dismissal of the revelling spirits makes allusion to masque scenes and properties. First, the word "rack" is supposed to apply specially to stage-clouds, sometimes used to "dissolve", as we might now say, a scene. This is an attractive idea, but the word was also used of natural cloud.[2] Other speculations of this sort are recorded by Allardyce Nicoll; they include the suggestion that *The Tempest's* towers, palaces, and temples are those of *Tethys' Festival* and *Oberon*, and "the great globe itself" that much-admired stage-globe of Jonson's *Hymenaei*.[3] An older suggestion is that Prospero's speech alludes to the coronation festivities of James I.[4] These conjectures may be attractive, but they are scarcely convincing. What may be accepted is the view that Prospero's speech, in its lamentation for the transience of mortal splendour, significantly resembles Jonson's lament for the ephemeral beauty of his masque; for, as Miss Welsford says, "many

1. *The Court Masque*, pp. 335 ff.

2. *e.g.* "We see the Rack carried one way and the wind blowing right against it" (Sandys, *op. cit.* p. 394). See also *O.E.D. s.v.* "rack" (sb. 1, 3b *obs.*).

3. *Stuart Masques and the Renaissance Stage* (1937), pp. 19–21.

4. See Welsford, *op. cit.* p. 342, and Nichol, *The Progresses of King James the First* (1828), I. 339 ff.

masques end with the thought not of eternity but of the swift
flight of time and of the inevitable end of beauty and delight."[1]
This vanity of Prospero's art, like the flush of youthful love,
and the wonder—broken knowledge, as Bacon called it—of
Miranda at the brave new world, is subject to mutability like
everything else under the moon. And to broaden the field of
reference, we need only recall the resemblance between
Prospero's speech and these lines of Sir William Alexander:

> Let greatnesse of her glascie scepters vaunt;
> > Not scepters, no, but reeds, soone bruis'd, soone broken:
> And let this worldlie pomp our wits inchant,
> > All fades, and scarcelie leaves behind a token.
> Those golden pallaces, those gorgeous halles,
> > With fourniture superfluouslie faire:
> Those statelie courts, those sky-encountring walles
> > Evanish all like vapours in the aire. (*Darius*, 1603.)

Miss Welsford's theory, that the play is more a dramatized
masque than a venture into classical dramatic structure, takes
insufficient account of the fact that the play is divided into five
acts in accordance with contemporary theory, and that its
action proceeds in accordance with the scheme of classical
development which the Renaissance commentators worked
out in the tradition of Donatus and the later editors of Terence.
No one would deny a general influence from the court
masque,[2] but it should not be allowed to obscure the fact that
Shakespeare in this play reverts to something like the formal
structure which he used with varying degrees of success in
his earlier attempts at romantic comedy. In *The Comedy of
Errors* he had incorporated in his Plautine scheme a romance
plot, and in most of the other early comedies he experimented
with the five-act structure.[3] *The Tempest* insists on its observance of the unity of time (much as the academic dramatists
like Alexander might) but less obtrusive is its conformity with

---

1. Welsford, *op. cit.* p. 274. See note on IV. i. 148.
2. Prof. D. J. Gordon makes the interesting suggestion that at the climax of
each plot there is a spectacular contrivance borrowed from the masque: thus
the rapacity of the "men of sin" is confronted with its own image in the Harpy;
the disorderly desires of Caliban and the rest are chastised by hounds who, in
the Actæon story, typify such desires; and the betrothal of Miranda is conventionally signalized by a courtly mythological entertainment.
3. See Baldwin's *Five-Act Structure.*

the academic theory of structure. The first scene is like a prologue, and with the second we are plunged straight into a
protasis which conceals its studious origin by an extraordinary
though not perhaps completely successful attempt to provide a
natural motivation and a naturalistic dialogue. The present-
ment of the actors, one of the functions of the first part of a
play, is accomplished in the first act, save for Trinculo and
Stephano, who appear in II. ii, as authority permitted. All that
is relevant of what happened "in the dark backward and
abysm of time" has been related before the end of the first
act, and we are completely instructed by the end of Act II
as to the nature of the final and typical disturbance which
must be resolved by the end of the play—Ferdinand has met
Miranda, Antonio has resolved upon, and already set afoot,
another usurper's plot, the low characters are shaping their
attempt on Prospero and Miranda. In the third act the turbulence is intensified, according to the formula for the *epitasis*;
the fourth act continues the *epitasis*, with the direct threat of
intervention from Caliban, but also prepares for the comic
catastrophe, by the union of Ferdinand and Miranda. The
apparently unnecessary perturbation of Prospero at the
thought of Caliban may be a point at which an oddly pedantic
concern for classical structure causes it to force its way through
the surface of the play. This fourth act exhibits the full vigour
and crisis of the design—"Lies at my mercy all mine enemies"
—and the exode or catastrophe is finally prepared by the
persona ad catastropham machinata, who is Ariel. He is technically
responsible for the comic nature of the catastrophe, since
he makes Prospero say he will offer his enemies forgiveness
rather than revenge. Otherwise, of course, the catastrophe
would be tragic. But Ariel's act is so unnecessary in view of
the already existing comic motive—the betrothal of Ferdinand
and Miranda—that it is once more hard to avoid seeing his
persuasion of Prospero as a point at which the classical structure tears through the texture of the play. On the other hand,
the conversation about forgiveness, unlike Prospero's agitation at the prospect of Caliban's rebellion, has some motivation in the structure of the play's ideas, since it was necessary
for the prince to overcome the turbulence of his own passions.
It seems likely that Shakespeare deliberately constructed

his play in accordance with the neo-Terentian regulations.

It still remains to be asked, why did Shakespeare choose to treat this theme intensively? The play seems to follow *The Winter's Tale*, which is so deeply committed to its extensive presentation that it is difficult to conceive of its being handled in any other way. And yet there are strong affinities between the two plays. But if we see Caliban as the focus of the play's ideas, the difficulty vanishes, for it is essential to the whole system of contrasts based upon him that he should be adult. As Perdita knew, nurture will not stick on nature *tout court*; and Caliban, as we have seen, illustrates that point, but serves a double function as a criterion. He cannot serve as this criterion until *after* the attempt to educate him, and after his just enslavement when Prospero's experiment had shown that his cultivation produced only "the briers and darnell of appetites". In so far as the passions of twelve years previously are relevant, they are treated in little in the action of the play, as other critics have pointed out.

The material sought an intensive form, and with the completed product before us we can see that nothing else would have done—at any rate, that the action could not have started before the arrival of the courtiers on the island. The very complexity of the triple exposition—all of it absolutely necessary to the play's ideas—is proof that *The Tempest* could not have been expounded as *The Winter's Tale* had been, for by common admission that play already staggers under the weight of diffuse but necessary incident, as *Cymbeline* does under the burden of its complex plot. As it is, *The Tempest* is one of the most economically constructed of all Shakespeare's plays. He was able to present the redemptive achievement of Prospero as a single magical operation in five phases, and to give maximum import, by the concentration of his method, to the interrelationship of event and character. Since an intensive form was needed, Shakespeare returned, naturally, to the five-act structure which he had learnt in his youth; and as in the past he had manipulated it to serve special purposes without abandoning its basic pattern, so now he was able to incorporate into it the spectacular elements of the third act, and the atmosphere of the new tragicomedy.

10. VERSE—IMAGERY

By all known statistical tests, *The Tempest* is a late play, exhibiting great licence in the use of run-on lines, of hypermetrism, and of deficient lines. If we did not know, on the more reliable evidence of external documents, that it belonged to the end of Shakespeare's working life, we should still be able to guess it from the versification.

In the course of a lifetime's application a poet may acquire new insight into the nature of the things he is disposed to talk about, and also of the means at his command. It is generally possible to study this new insight in poets who leave a published record of a long working life; for example, Drayton, Milton, Yeats, and Shakespeare. When Shakespeare wrote *The Tempest* he would not see quite as he had seen when he wrote *Love's Labour's Lost.* He might have held, as his critical contemporaries did, a view that poetry resembled painting, understanding that the painter's art was to show in the outward form an inner quality; thus his verse and his imagery alter as the inwardness of that quality becomes more apparent to him. Also, he might have thought of himself as a craftsman—and whether or no this is, philosophically, fallacious, it has generally been the opinion of poets—and we can say that he would gain an increasing command over the materials of his craft, and progressively narrow the gap between the qualities and the equivalents by which he stated them. As a Renaissance playwright he would strive for, and achieve, a deeper understanding of decorum, which in dramatic literature meant the propriety of what was said to the speaker, to his hearers, to the situation, to the speaker's purpose, and to the function of the passage in the play as a whole. No matter how the jealousy of Leontes may have been explained, he is presented as a man saying the things a man mad with jealousy would say to such auditors, in such a situation, and in view of the long purgation which his crime must entail. He must say violent things in language and imagery of abnormal pressure and incoherence. Of course there is nothing in *The Tempest* resembling this decorous hysteria, but there are long passages which are to be explained in terms of decorum, sometimes recognizably employing the formal tropes of Renaissance poetic. The elaborate amplification of Antonio, in his speech on the remoteness of Claribel, is a neat example of the use of a rhetoric devoted to the end of "speaking well" to illustrate the improper use of a rhetoric which, ruthlessly, exercised all the available means of persuasion; for a moment the poet's rhetoric becomes the vehicle of the machiavel's, and both use the same figure. The anacolutha and general agitation of Prospero's speech in the second scene are further examples of dramatic decorum, as is the change to an artificial mode in the passage describing the wonderful voyage of Prospero and Miranda to their island. This latter is of special interest, as it blends the more natural-istic verse-movement of these late plays with deliberately archaic imagery, in order to make that imagery do the struc-tural work of introducing the romance theme and the struc-turally important idea of the providential voyage. Imagery of this sort was mocked in *Love's Labour's Lost* and used for broad-ly comic effects by Launce in *The Two Gentlemen of Verona*. It is now subserving more fully dramatic decorum. "The poet who imitates not the visible world but the intelligible as manifested in the visible will not consider that the use of artifice to em-phasize form makes imagery less 'true to Nature'."[1] Shake-speare could never again see things as he did when he wrote *Love's Labour's Lost*, but he could still recognize the value of this language in a wider and more controlled context.

The living proof of Shakespeare's study of decorum is *Coriolanus*, in which the devotedness of the language to the inwardness of the theme is as uncompromising as it is in cer-tain bitterly inhospitable and mature passages, products of a lifetime's application, in the last works of Beethoven. After this devoted experiment in the decorously clanking and grace-less, that decorum which it is the grand masterpiece to observe will never be out of Shakespeare's power. In other words, the last plays might be expected to, and do, exhibit a control of language and imagery formerly unequalled. There is little of the kind of language which extensively examines the simili-tudes by which its ideas are decorated, but a great deal of the kind which simulates the language of men in a state of pro-found sensation, progressing from idea to idea by means of

1. Rosemond Tuve, *Elizabethan and Metaphysical Imagery* (1947), p. 36.

pun, or by associations more or less consciously relevant. Thus:

> having both the key
> Of officer and office, set all hearts i' th' state
> To what tune pleas'd his ear; (i. ii. 83–5.)

and

> she that from whom
> We all were sea-swallow'd, though some cast again,
> And by that destiny to perform an act
> Whereof what's past is prologue; what to come,
> In yours and my discharge. (ii. i. 245–9.)

Metaphor gleams momentarily, and is rarely extensive enough to be catalogued and analysed. In the same way the basic rhythm of the iambic pentameters becomes more ghostly, a burthen heard faintly through the flux of thought. Shakespeare is still interested in the formal figures and tropes, but, like the beat of the pentameter, they are swamped by the involutions of a language which is artificially natural, and denied the auditor's attention, which is directed to the relationship between the characters' interests and the developing situation. Meanwhile the general complex of events within the play is more and more, and more and more deliberately, typical of larger movements of thought and image outside the play-world. Thus one can, indeed must, trespass on moral theology in discussing *The Tempest*, whereas one would not wish to in discussing *The Comedy of Errors*. This new interest in the typical qualities of narrative and character and language replaces the old one, with its concern for the mere relatedness of dissimilar objects, be they words or ideas—the former producing puns and the latter formal disquisitions of the sort found in *The Two Gentlemen of Verona*—although much emphasis was placed upon this question of relatedness in sixteenth-century thought, and particularly in the poetics when they are prescribing for metaphor. The great change in Shakespeare is the result of a deepening understanding of the object, and also of the means at the disposal of the poet.

This is one way of accounting for the later manner of Shakespeare's verse. It is not the only way, and it is, taken alone, inadequate in many respects; but of its soundness as far as it goes the proof may be found in the work of Shakespeare's imitators. In them the fluid metre and attempts at language which moves with the movement of thought are not the product of a lifetime's concentration on the object, but are taken over ready-made. In the same way, the values of Beaumont's and Fletcher's narratives are nearly always merely dramaturgical and not typical in the sense in which Shakespeare's are. Hence the legitimate association of this type of verse, as in Massinger, and this type of plotting, as in Fletcher, with the beginnings of a decadence.

The paucity of imagery in *The Tempest* has often been remarked. It has been replaced by a more decorous control of event, which gives the event itself primary significance, and requires that verse and image shall not be such as to distract the attention from it. The language of the play is chiefly notable for its insistence on the complexity of certain concepts essential to the structure of ideas and events; hence the interest, already discussed, in the words "nature", "noble", "vile", and "virtue", and in the ideas of beauty and nobility. The most remarkable changes are rung on the word "sea" and its compounds. The sea, the voyages it supports, and the wrecks it causes, are types of the action of grace and providence. Hence the "sea-change", and "sea-sorrow". Hence the description of the sea as never surfeited, as incensed, as invulnerable, as apparently cruel, as revealing guilt, as a force which swallows but casts again, which threatens but is merciful. This example alone serves to show how the imagery of *The Tempest* is determined structurally.[1]

It is not surprising that *The Tempest* has sent people whoring after strange gods of allegory, any more than it is surprising that *Coriolanus* and *Timon of Athens* are the least loved of the mature plays. They represent a maturity of conception, a control of the medium, both linguistic and dramatic, which we scarcely know how to begin to understand. We may prefer the rich thematic texture of Lear, or the haze which still gives the edges of *Twelfth Night* a romantic glow, but in its uncompromising victory over the means to truth, its control over vision and expression, and its refusal to be seduced by any

1. For a valuable comment, see Ellis-Fermor, *The Jacobean Drama* (1936), p. 269.

temptation to betray the principles of *architectonicé*, the last
period represents the summit of Shakespeare's achievement.

11. "TEMPEST" CRITICISM

There is disappointingly little memorable criticism of *The
Tempest*, although the play has always been held in high
esteem. The neo-classical critics admired it on the grounds
that it observed the unities, and that Caliban was a new character with a new language to match. Most modern attitudes
to the play are largely the product of romantic criticism with
its hazardous and licentious enthusiasms.

For Coleridge, possibly the best of all critics on this play,
The Tempest was an "almost miraculous" drama; and he introduces a new kind of criticism which, to adapt his own words,
is organic rather than mechanical. The appeal of *The Tempest*,
says Coleridge, is to the imagination; and however this be
interpreted, it serves as a kind of licence for subsequent
criticism.

This was increasingly fantastic. The observations of Schle-
gel, who first identified Ariel and Caliban with the elements
Air and Earth, seem to have been influential. When Campbell,
availing himself of the now roughly established chronology of
the corpus, found in it "a sacredness as the last work of a
mighty workman", and an allegory of the poet's farewell to
the stage, all was prepared for the kind of criticism normally
associated with this play. It varies between the allegorical
and the apocalyptic, and has not fundamentally changed
since the days when Lowell worked out his scheme (Caliban
= brute understanding, Ariel = fancy, Prospero = imagination, etc.) Nineteenth century allegorical criticism of *The
Tempest* was rooted in the romantic simplification of the relationship between pre-romantic artists and their work, which
is exemplified in Keats's remarks on Shakespeare and allegory.[1] Although allegorical readings differ in detail,[2] it may
be said that by the time Saintsbury wrote his chapter in the
Cambridge History it had been accepted that *The Tempest* was

---

1. See *e.g. Letters*, ed. M. Buxton Forman (1947), p. 305.
2. Dowden's *Shakspere: His Mind and Art* (1875), p. 424, gives an account of
the current varieties.

a personal farewell and a personal allegory. In the meantime
the concept of the "final period" had gained universal support,
and the authoritative view of this final stage of Shakespeare's
development was given by Dowden, who described this period
as being the result of Shakespeare's emergence from the depths
of despair, the work of a mature and calm artist "On the
Heights".[1] Morton Luce, in the original Arden edition, gave
what may be the best account of the autobiographical interpretation, as of so much else; it is my loss that I find his
approach incompatible with my own.

To see all Shakespeare's plays as a whole needs a vast critical
effort, and the need for it has been restated acceptably by Mr
Eliot; but in the days of Furnivall and Dowden it led even
scholars into the wilderness of undisciplined allegory. (Granted the near-infallibility of the text, interpretations of this
sort naturally multiply; Shakespeare idolatry, an eighteenth-
century phenomenon, made inevitable the normal Victorian
exegesis.) Dowden constructed the most influential system of
what Arnold would call extra-belief;[2] evidently the spear of
Ithuriel would sooner or later touch it, but in the meantime
the most widely read of all books on Shakespeare spread the
doctrine that the last plays proceed from an elderly serenity, a
marvellous rural detachment, a hard-won peace.[3]

It was against Dowden that Lytton Strachey directed his
famous attack in 1906;[4] and soon afterwards Professor Stoll,
though he did not for some years consider *The Tempest* at any
length, undermined Dowden with his demand for the objec-
tive consideration of Shakespeare's plays as artefacts obeying
certain conventional laws and wearing their meanings in
their faces. These attacks have been constantly repeated, and
although Shakespeare's development is still frequently ex-

1. Dowden, *loc. cit.*

2. Arnold himself believed that Shakespeare was a dangerous element in the
English tradition, since he distracted the attention of later poets from the para-
mount need for "design" of the Sophoclean sort. His comments on *The Tempest*
are found in a letter to A. H. Clough, dated 3 Aug. [1853]. *Letters to Clough*, ed.
Lowry (1932), p. 139.

3. Although Dowden offers, not over-seriously, an allegorical reading (Ferdinand = Fletcher, Miranda = Art, Ariel = "the imaginative genius of poetry
but recently delivered in England from long slavery to Sycorax", Prospero =
Shakespeare), he treats other allegories to a kindly but firm dismissal.

4. *Books and Characters*, p. 45.

plained in terms of hypothetical changes in his personality, most students are now aware of the arguments against such explanations.

The vein of free allegory is by no means worked out, and we still get interpretations as fantastic as that which calls the play an allegory of the history of the Church,[1] and as improbable as Colin Still's. Mr Still[2] develops a parallel between the action of *The Tempest* and the initiation ceremonies of the Eleusinian adepts. His books fascinate; but anyone who does not share Still's own view that the author's responsibility for very detailed allegorical statement may be merely subliminal, will ask for some better account of the provenance of these ritual patterns which might explain their presence in Shakespeare. I believe that Shakespeare offers an exposition of the themes of Fall and Redemption by means of analogous narrative; but there is no need to seek so far for the original form of the analogue. Such resemblances to initiation rites as can be substantiated may possibly be accounted for in a more historical way. It has, for example, been argued that the ceremonial magic of the Neo-Platonic tradition incorporates elements of the Mysteries,[3] and the traditional acts of the mage also stem from this source.[4]

Despite a surviving tendency to interpret the play as a schematic allegory, it may be said that the general interpretation of *The Tempest* now current originated with Wilson Knight. Already, critics had insisted upon Shakespeare's preoccupation in these last plays with the theme of reconciliation, and the survival into a new world of the children of those who had quarrelled.[5] Wilson Knight makes the last plays central to his interpretation of Shakespeare, and regards them as

1. E. B. Wagner, *Shakespeare's Tempest: An Allegorical Interpretation* (1935).

2. *The Timeless Theme* (1936). The theory was first stated in *Shakespeare's Mystery Play* (1921).

3. See C. G. Jung, *The Integration of the Personality* (1940), pp. 107 ff. Any reader who comes to this work with *The Tempest* in mind will see how rich it is in material for a Jungian interpretation, not only of the narrative part of the play, but also of the element of magic. But Shakespeare's is the High Dream of Dante, and not the psychic residua of the consulting room. (See T. S. Eliot, *Selected Essays* [1932], p. 243.)

4. See E. M. Butler, *The Myth of the Magus* (1948), p. 5.

5. *e.g.* A. Quiller-Couch, *Shakespeare's Workmanship* (1918); see also J. Dover Wilson's published lecture, "The Meaning of *The Tempest*" (1936).

"myths of immortality." His exposition of this view has had an extraordinary, and for the most part a beneficial, influence over modern criticism.[1]

In *Myth and Miracle* (1929), Knight indicated the strong thematic resemblances between *Pericles* and *The Winter's Tale* —the hero's loss of wife and daughter, the helplessness of a child synchronized with a sea-storm, the miraculous restoration of wife and child, and the revival from death, real or apparent, of the wife. "A reader sensitive to poetic atmosphere must necessarily feel the awakening light of some religious or metaphysical truth symbolized in the plot and attendant machinery of the two plays."[2] They are concerned with immortality, metaphorically expressed in terms of victorious love, *Cymbeline*, with differences of machinery and stress, is concerned with the same theme, but by introducing an anthropomorphic god it endangers the metaphor. *The Tempest* was a necessary development. "A prophetic criticism could, if *The Tempest* had been lost, have nevertheless indicated what must be its essential nature, and might have hazarded its name."[3] Tempest is Shakespeare's poetic symbol for high tragedy; music, for the quality of immortality. *The Tempest* is a great symbol of the progression from one to the other. It "repeats ... in miniature, the separate themes of Shakespeare's greater plays ... it distils the poetic essence of the whole Shakespearian universe".[4] It ends and transcends the great series of Shakespeare's plays.

The last of Wilson Knight's studies in the final plays (*The Crown of Life*) sums up and develops his theory. It is not his fault if we do not see that certain romance-themes acquired special values for Shakespeare before he wrote *The Tempest*— that, for instance, the equation sea = fortune, long implicit, becomes emphatic in *Pericles* and *The Tempest*; that there is a special significance in the habit of treating voyages as "all but

1. Even Miss Spurgeon's *Shakespeare's Imagery* (1935), though in its own way almost as influential, affected criticism of *The Tempest* much less than Knight's books. Miss Spurgeon found little of real interest from her point of view in the imagery of *The Tempest*. Knight gives an interesting explanation of this, at first sight rather odd, fact, in *The Crown of Life* (1947), p. 224. See also p. lxxx *supra*.

2. *The Crown of Life*, p. 14.　　3. *ibid.* p. 23.

4. *The Shakespearian Tempest* (1932), p. 247.

suicidal"; in the association of children, and birth, with tempests; in the symbolism of feasts, especially broken feasts (*Macbeth, Timon, Tempest*); in the myth of gentleness and royal blood; in the tempest-music complex as finally expressed in Prospero's dismissal of the spirits; and in the constant reiteration in *The Tempest* of themes earlier explored in the tragedies. We may complain that the last attempt occasionally sinks to the level of that kind of allegorical interpretation Dr Knight made obsolete; that the attempt to make of Prospero an historical symbol is injudicious, and involves an unfortunate confusion of critical genres. But the reader who does not know Dr Knight's work should not neglect it on that account.[1]

In D. G. James's *Scepticism and Poetry* (1937), a book better known for its critique of Coleridge's theory of imagination and of the early aesthetic of I. A. Richards, there is another remarkable examination of the last plays as myths. Unlike Knight, James is concerned with Shakespeare's intention. "Shakespeare, having failed to see human life as a neat, orderly, and satisfying unity, had resort to myth for conveyance of his new imaginative apprehension of life."[2] In this attempt he failed, because he could not allow Christian symbolism to direct his expression, or to have his symbols "contaminated by assertion". Indeed, Shakespeare is of that class of poets, to which James has later added Wordsworth, Keats and Shelley,[3] the solution to whose problems lies in Christian dogma, though its acceptance means the end of their autonomous art. The alternative mythology must fail, since "the making of a mythology is too great a work for one mind."[4] James holds that the essential myth of the romances is the finding of what is lost; other aspects of it are the recurring theme of resurrection (Thaisa, Imogen, Hermione, Ferdinand); the recovery of lost royalty by a royal personage; and the placing of lost royalty in situations of great danger. The myth is used to express the theme of deliverance from tragic existence into a new dispensation of mercy; it is found in a

---

1. For a specimen of *Tempest* criticism using Knight's method, but with more interest in the text than in general symbolism, see D. Traversi, "*The Tempest*", *Scrutiny*, XVI (1949), 127–57.

2. p. 210.   3. *The Romantic Comedy* (1948).

4. *Scepticism and Poetry*. p. 211.

very pure form in *Pericles*, but in the later plays the myth is tortured by conflict among the symbols. The plot pulls one way, the theme another. Thus, only Thaisa is really dead, and after her resurrection even she behaves with incredible stupidity; the others are not dead, and the theme "takes on something of absurdity, and is introduced with a strange arbitrariness. . ." This made "his work silly to a degree it never had before been".[1] Similarly, the royalty-symbol breaks down in narrative. The progress from *Pericles* to *The Tempest* consists of an attempt to solve these and related problems. Shakespeare casts off the more explicit elements of his symbolism; there is less religious language, and less suffering, and the symbolism becomes on the whole less evident. But the vigour of the myth is consequently enfeebled. A defence can be made of *The Tempest* as in some respects transcending these limitations . . . but we are disappointed to find that it depends on a variety of the old-style allegorical reading (Prospero = Poet, Ariel = Imagination), devised in order to diminish the symbolic confusions. James's view is original, not in substance so much as in its working out of the implications; and he undertook the heavy task of trying to see the "myths of immortality" as they manifested themselves in romance-plots. In doing so, he assumed a degree of parabolic intention in the plays which Knight would probably repudiate; and possibly we should conclude that it is dangerous both to expect plausibility of romance-narratives, and to take liberties with words like "myth"; and that, if we are concerned at all with Shakespeare's intentions, we should try to define historically the area in which they can be usefully sought and studied.[2]

There remain to be considered in this brief survey two influential books: E. M. W. Tillyard's *Shakespeare's Last Plays* (1938) and the late Theodore Spencer's *Shakespeare and the Nature of Man* (1942). Tillyard examines the relationship of the romances to "the whole world of Elizabethan romance", and his main argument is that the romances complete the pattern of tragedy, which always suggests rebirth, and which is most clearly seen in the Aeschylean trilogy. This pattern is

---

1. *op. cit.* pp. 232–3.
2. There is a fairly extensive critique of James's theory in S. L. Bethell, *The Winter's Tale* (1947), pp. 71–6.

extensively displayed in *The Winter's Tale*; *The Tempest* merely suggests the destructive part of the pattern by explanation and re-enactment of the past. Tillyard expounds this and related ideas with charm and conviction. Similar views are more suggestively, though perhaps more wildly, expressed in an essay by Northrop Frye, which only glances at *The Tempest*, but which might prompt some other writer to give a new turn to the criticism of the romances. This might be the text for a salutary sermon, and the epigraph for a long book: "The spirit of reconciliation which pervades the comedies of Shakespeare is not to be ascribed to a personal attitude of his own, about which we know nothing whatever, but to his impersonal concentration on the laws of comic form."[1]

Theodore Spencer discusses *The Tempest* "in terms of the difference between appearance and reality, but also in terms of the three levels in Nature's hierarchy—the animal, the human, and the intellectual—which were the bases of Shakespeare's view of man".[2] The conclusion is, that *The Tempest* shows us evil redeemed; "there is a re-birth, a return to life, a heightened, almost symbolic awareness of the beauty of normal humanity after it has been purged of evil—a blessed reality under the evil appearance." This statement of *The Tempest* theme differs only in emphasis from many others, and in that Spencer relates to it its intellectual potential, whereas some others do not. Nevertheless, Spencer's book confirms that there is a basic modern version of *The Tempest*, which is to be found in many books and papers apart from the handful I have space to name. It cannot be hoped that we shall for long be content to go on saying the same things about the play. Although some critics profess indifference to scholarly investigations, they are generally much more moved by them than it appears, and there is yet much to be *known* about the romances. The time is perhaps near when some critic will radically alter the assumptions upon which criticism of *The Tempest* is at present founded.

The Tempest is the last of the completely Shakespearian plays, and it is unquestionably the most sophisticated comedy

1. "The Argument of Comedy" in *English Institute Essays*, 1948 (1949), pp. 58–73.
2. p. 195.

of a poet whose work in comedy is misunderstood to a quite astonishing degree. To think of Shakespeare as a natural poet, above, or at any rate without, art, is a habit transmitted to us by many generations of criticism; but it is a bad habit in so far as it makes us neglect the conscious philosophic structure of his plays, and particularly of his comedies. For my part, I speak unrepentantly of his *intentions*, though I am aware of the dangers of "intentionalism". But what has that criticism achieved which neglects or despises the kind of idea I have here tried to uncover? It cannot give a convincing account of a relatively simple play like *The Merchant of Venice*. It has certainly failed with *The Tempest*, which, like its descendant *Comus*, is deeply concerned with difficult ideas, and with the philosophic genres of masque and pastoral. Any one who refuses to care about these things will not begin to understand why the play is as it is; and so it is described as a weary pantomime, or an obscure autobiography, or a comment on French politics. But poetry has a history; ideas-in-poetry (which are not the same as ideas) have a history too; and the historian's task is a delicate and creative one.

I cannot claim to have performed this task for the complex of ideas concerning Art and Nature in *The Tempest*; apart from any other limitations, I had not the space in an Introduction which has other duties to perform. I have one dominant fear; that in abstracting elements of the pattern of ideas in order to illustrate them—indeed, in order to show they were there—I may have left an impression that this pattern is commonplace. That would be criminal, for the truth is that the complex in which they occur is unique, that they derive from each other meanings which are beyond the last analysis of criticism. But it is a mad critical pride which holds that we need not bother our heads about them.

NOTE ADDITIONAL TO INTRODUCTION

Ralph Crane and the copy for The Tempest

It has lately been suggested that the evidence for attributing to the scrivener Ralph Crane transcripts which served as Jaggard's copy for *The Tempest* and other plays needs re-examination in the light of what is now known about the habits of his compositors. It is true that there can be no absolute certainty here; most of the difficulties outlined by Professor Wilson in his early paper on Crane[1] persist, and whatever we may say about compositors will have to be reconsidered when Mr Hinman's full analysis of the printing of F finally appears. But I can find no reason to alter the attribution, at any rate of *The Tempest* copy, to Crane's hand. The chief differentia of this hand, as is well known, is the lavish use of brackets; and although it may be true that the compositors were prone to sophisticate the pointing of the copy, it remains probable that the very curious and persistent use of brackets in *The Tempest* goes beyond what was normal for scribes, and far beyond what might be expected of compositors. I have carried out a rough test to try this latter contention, and here are the results, for what they are worth. The frequency of brackets in *The Tempest* is almost the same in the work of each compositor,[2] being about 5 per page set by B, and 5·3 per page in A's much longer portion. The inference is that the compositors are reproducing copy, especially in view of the eccentricity of most of these parentheses. The circumstances do not vary, and brackets are particularly heavy in S.D.s and vocatives. In *As You Like It*, one of the six other comedies divided into acts and scenes, the frequency of brackets is very low by comparison—something under one per page for either compositor. *The Tempest* belongs therefore to a different class of text from *As You Like It*, and the compositors appear to have reproduced this scribal eccentricity of punctuation. Another indication that the scribe was Crane is the promiscuous use of

---

1. "Ralph Crane, Scrivener to the King's Players", *The Library* (4th Series), VII (1926), 194–215, esp. 215.

2. I used E. E. Willoughby's allocation (*The Printing of the First Folio of Shakespeare*, 1932, p. 58). It is not incontestable, but serves for this purpose.

hyphens, as described by Greg;[1] and another, perhaps, is the
very unusual "Jonsonian elision", as Greg calls it,[2] on the first
page (i. i. 54—"I'am out of patience").

The question of the occasion and the date of the transcript
remains, and the indications are that it was made especially
for the Folio, probably in 1621. In that year Crane wrote of his
employment by the King's Men;[3] and there is extant the
prompt-copy of *Barnavelt*, almost certainly written by him in
1619. But, though he was an old man and a scribe of many
years' standing, this is the earliest of his extant dramatic
manuscripts. Whatever may be said about *The Tempest* copy,
it was clearly not for prompt. On the other hand, it is probably
too early to be one of those transcripts, intended for a patron's
reading (like *The Witch* and *Demetrius and Enanthe*), which
Crane seems to have begun about 1624 or 1625; though the
descriptive S.D.s and division into Acts and Scenes make it
more like these than like *Barnavelt*.[4] The probability then is

1. "Some Notes on Crane's Manuscript of *The Witch*", *The Library* (4th
Series), XXLI (1942), 208–22, esp. 215–16. See also Middleton, *The Witch*, ed.
Greg and Wilson, Malone Soc. Reprints, 1948 (1950), Introduction; and
Fletcher, *Demetrius and Enanthe*, ed. M. M. Cook and F. P. Wilson, Malone Soc.
Reprints, 1950 (1951), Introduction.

2. *Library*, XXII, 216–18.

3. In the biographical preface to his poem *The Workes of Mercy*, Crane says that
his "usefull Pen" had been employed by actors in the "*Kingly Seruice*" (Wilson,
Library, VII. 197). Incidentally, it is a little misleading to say, as I have done on
p. xii above, that Crane was a "servant of Shakespeare's company", since we do
not know that he ever worked for the King's Men in Shakespeare's lifetime; and
in any case his employment was more casual than my phrase suggests. See Sir
W. Greg, *Shakespeare's First Folio* (1955), p. 418.

4. Here are two S.D.s selected by Professor Wilson (*Library*, VII. 213) as being
descriptive and having "a literary flavour":
Enter a Magitian wth a Bowle in his hand. He seemes to Coniure: sweete
Musique is heard, and an Antick of little Fayeries enter, & dance about ye
Bowle, and fling in things, & Ex^t.   (*Demetrius and Enanthe*, IV. iii)
Enter ye Black Q^s. Pawne (wth a Tapo^r in her hand) and Conducts the White
Q^s. Pawne (in her Night Attire) into one Chamber: And then Conuaies the
Black B^s. Pawne (in his Night habit) into an other Chamber: So putts out the
Light, and followes him.   (*A Game at Chesse*, Lansdowne 690, IV. iii)
The resemblance to the elaborate S.D.s of *The Tempest* extends, in the second
example, to the use of brackets. *Barnavelt*, transcribed for use in the theatre, has
not these descriptive S.D.s but the brief and necessary notes of the prompter.
There is a similar distinction in the use of brackets; Crane seems to have thought
of them as a literary flourish, and they are accordingly most frequent in the MS.
of *Demetrius and Enanthe*, which was written for presentation to Sir Kenelm
Digby, and least common in *Barnavelt*. Once more *The Tempest* is closer to
Crane's non-theatrical MSS. It is also, of course, to be distinguished from the

that the transcript was commissioned for the Folio, like those of the three succeeding plays.

What are the textual implications of Crane's intervention in the transmission? Much more needs to be known about him (particularly as his manner varies considerably between one MS. and another) before this question can be answered. Though an excellent scribe, he was certainly not immune from error, and on the whole it is likely that mistakes occur more frequently in his transcription than in the compositors' interpretation of his hand (for example, it would be virtually impossible to confuse "d" and "e" in Crane, so errors like that at v. i. 75 are presumably Crane's own). The lack of theatrical directions, and the abundance of elaborately descriptive S.D.s, both features of *The Tempest*, are noted in other Crane MSS. and may have been his own work. He sometimes marked entrances early, even in transcribing author's autograph,[1] though the early entrance at iv. i. 72 (S.D.) may survive from some theatrical direction.[2] It is also conceivable that Crane's difficulties with his copy are responsible for some mislineation.

Much more of the responsibility for mislining, apparently representing prose as verse, and so forth, lies with the compositors, and especially with B,[3] who had the habit of losing space where necessary by breaking up prose into irregular line-lengths.[4] Yet there is evidence that the copy was treated with unusual respect; Jaggard and his men handled it, or so it would appear, in a careful, gingerly, experimental way.[5] Some

plays of F which, though having indications of Crane's hand in the copy, are deficient in S.D.s, e.g. *Two Gentlemen of Verona, Merry Wives.*

1. In the B.M. MS. of Middleton's *Game at Chesse.*

2. See additional note on this passage on p. 170.

3. It is perhaps worth saying that Crane's spelling, so far as it can be known from his transcripts and original writings, seems to be more like B's than A's, though there is nothing decisive about this.

4. It seems possible that B set the end of p. 15b, though Willoughby attributes the whole page to A. Whether this is so or not, it must mean something that the disturbance ceases at the foot of p. 15b, and does not recur in p. 16, which was set by A.

5. The notation of entrances and exits is very thorough throughout. There may be further evidence of care (see p. xii above) in the provision of a *Dramatis Personae*; the other three examples were perhaps added only to fill up space, but here the list is certainly included from choice (see Greg, *Shakespeare's First Folio*, p. 418).

aspects of this, such as proof-reading, it will be possible to pronounce upon when the Folger collations are published; but the following considerations suggest that the copy was handled in an especially tentative way:

I. The text was not set by the compositors in an economical manner (e.g., by commencing with A3ᵛ and A4ʳ). Although there are strong indications that the copy was "cast off",[1] it is also clear that p. 1 was set first. Its roman "Scena Secunda" is completely anomalous, and is immediately replaced by the italic *Scæna Secunda* of Act III (A5ʳ, p. 9), which serves again, in the same "box", for Act III[2] (A6ʳ, p. 11), and again in *The Two Gentlemen of Verona*. The casting-off is indeed difficult to interpret; but obvious space-saving on p. 7 (A4ʳ), where B is also running out of type for "w", seems inconsistent with any hypothesis of economical compositor-printer relations. The printer normally needed 3ᵛ and 4ʳ first, and there was no need in that case to cast off 4ʳ at all; and it happens that the compositors are lavish of space in 9, 10, and 12 (A6ᵛ), the point at which adjustments for 4ʳ–6ᵛ might be expected.

II. Furthermore, the evidence of headlines suggests a slow and tentative process of composition. The running-title with the "curious and damaged *T*" observed by Willoughby, occurs only in pages set by A (i.e. A2ʳ, A5ʳ, B1ʳ, B1ᵛ, B2ʳ, B2ᵛ[3]

---

1. See C. Hinman, "Cast-off Copy for the First Folio of Shakespeare", *Shakespeare Quarterly* VI (1955), 259 ff. The purpose is to prevent delays between composition and printing by eliminating the printer's long wait for 3ᵛ and 4ʳ, with which he normally began. So 3ᵛ–1ʳ could be set "backwards", and often were. I do not, however, understand why, in ordinary circumstances, it should ever have been necessary to cast off 3ʳ–6ʳ, unless more than one compositor was working on it. All adjustments might be left to 6ᵛ, and only the last line of that folio need be predicted. It may be objected that in order to predict that line one would have had to cast off the intervening folios anyway; but since the need for accuracy was so much smaller than in the first half of the gathering, a little practice might have ensured a sufficiently accurate guess about how much copy went into six folios. Certainly one cannot imagine any caster-off making a break in the middle of a hyphenated word like "loue-prate" in *AYL.* (sig. R5ʳ, p. 201). Another objection is that the copy for 6ᵛ might allow inadequate scope for the necessary adjustment, for example, if it lacked act- or scene-headings, entrances, exits, and so forth, and was lacking in prose also. But there is no example throughout the Comedies of this actually happening, and the three cases that occur in the plays I have here mentioned, *Temp.* and *AYL.*, are all distinguished by space-losing on so large a scale that it is hard to see how the caster-off could have misjudged it so badly had he cast off every page in the gathering.

2. Willoughby, *op. cit.*, p. 21.

3. *ibid.* Willoughby says it occurs in recto headlines; but see also B1ᵛ and B2ᵛ.

B3^r, B4^r). It seems safe to deduce that neither composition (B was hardly, if-at all, employed on quire B) nor press-work proceeded in any regular manner. It all sounds experimental. The casting-off may also have been experimental; possibly it was guessed that a play would normally fill twenty-four pages: hence sig. A was expected to be filled by 2½ acts of *The Tempest*, and so the compositor had to lose space on p. 12 to end it with the close of III. ii; but of course III. iii–v. i is much less than half of *The Tempest*, and if this was the scheme it did not work. *Measure for Measure* is the first play in the Folio to occupy twenty-four pages, and it exactly fills sigs. F and G.

All these remarks are made in a spirit as tentative as that I attribute to Jaggard. I do believe, however, that Crane made a transcript especially for the Folio, and that it was respectfully handled in a printing-house which had not yet, for this book, got into its full stride. Some of the time-saving methods later employed were apparently not used here, and the casting-off of the copy was not as accurate and efficient as it later became. One might guess that Jaggard took *The Tempest* very slowly; he presumably had no experience of this kind of job, so different, for instance, from that of the printers of the 1616 Jonson Folio. The material was both copious and heterogeneous, the author dead, the printer's own skill much inferior; Heminge and Condell may well, in these circumstances, have wanted to see specimen sheets.

THE TEMPEST

The Scene, an uninhabited Island

Names of the Actors.

Alonso, K. of Naples.
Sebastian his brother.
Prospero, the right Duke of Milan.   5
Antonio his brother, the usurping Duke of Milan.
Ferdinand, Son to the King of Naples.
Gonzalo, an honest old Councellor.
Adrian & Francisco, Lords.
Caliban, a salvage and deformed slave.   10
Trinculo, a jester.
Stephano, a drunken butler.
Master of a ship.
Boatswain.
Mariners.   15
Miranda, daughter to Prospero.
Ariel, an airy spirit.
Iris ⎫
Ceres ⎪
Juno ⎬ Spirits   20
Nymphs ⎪
Reapers ⎭

---

5. *Milan*] *Millaine* F (throughout; *e.g.* l. 6).   6. *Antonio*] *Anthonio* F (throughout).   8. *Councellor*] F (it includes meanings differentiated by modern spellings).   17. *Ariel*] *Ariell* F (almost throughout).

THE TEMPEST

ACT I

SCENE I.—[*On a ship at sea*]: *a tempestuous noise of thunder and lightning heard.*

Enter a Ship-Master and a Boatswain.

Mast. Boatswain!

Boats. Here, master: what cheer?

Mast. Good: speak to th' mariners: fall to 't, yarely, or we run ourselves aground: bestir, bestir.   *Exit.*

Enter Mariners.

Boats. Heigh, my hearts! cheerly, cheerly, my hearts!   5

ACT I

Scene I

Act I . . . On a ship at sea:] Pope; Actus Primus, Scena Prima. F.   3. *Good:*] *Good*, Rowe.   *to 't,*] Pope; *too't*, F, Ff; *to 't* Theobald.   5. *cheerly, cheerly*] *cheerly* F4.

The Tempest is divided into Acts and Scenes in F.

3. *Good:*] The Master is simply acknowledging the Boatswain's reply. Some editors alter the colon to a comma; *good* then means "good man!"

yarely] Smartly, briskly. In v. i. 224 "yare" is an adjective.

4. *aground:*] F has *a ground,*; the comma perhaps indicates rapid delivery. The following lines are lightly punctuated in F for the same reason.

5–50. Elementary instruction on seamanship is offered by Captain John Smith in his *Sea Grammar* (1627), an enlarged edition of his *An Accidence, or the Path-way to Experience* (1626). The following passage shows how close Shakespeare came to reproducing in this scene the prescribed behaviour of

seamen in a storm. Line references to the text of the scene are in square brackets.

How to handle a ship in a storme.	It over casts we shall have wind, fowle weather, settell your top sailes [6], take in the spret-saile, in with your top sailes, lower the fore-saile . . . strike your top-masts to the cap [34], make it sure with your sheeps feet. A storme,
Try.	let us lie at Trie with our maine course, that is, to hale the tacke aboord, the sheat close aft, the boling set up, and the helme tide close aboord [35]. When that will not serve, then Try the mizen [*i.e.* use it to support the mainsail] if

3

yare, yare! Take in the topsail. Tend to th' master's
whistle. Blow till thou burst thy wind, if room
enough!

Enter ALONSO, SEBASTIAN, ANTONIO, FERDINAND,
GONZALO, *and others.*

Alon. Good boatswain, have care. Where's the master?
Play the men.   10

Boats. I pray now, keep below.

Ant. Where is the master, boatswain?

Boats. Do you not hear him? You mar our labour: keep
your cabins: you do assist the storm.

Gon. Nay, good, be patient.   15

Boats. When the sea is. Hence! What cares these roarers

---

8. S.D. Ferdinand] Ferdinando F, Ff.   9. *have care*] *have a care* Dryden.
10. *Play*] *ply* Upton conj.   12. *boatswain*] Rowe (ed. 3), Camb.; *Boson* F, Ff,
Rowe (ed. 1).   14. *do assist*] *assist* Pope.   16. *Hence!*] Johnson; *hence,* F.
cares] *care* Rowe.

Hull.

that split, or the storme
grow so great she cannot
beare it; then hull, which
is to beare no saile, but to
strike a hull is when they
would lie obscurely in the
Sea [49? cf. *H 8*, II. iv.
199], or stay for some
confort, lash sure the
helm a lee ... (p. 40).

If *a-hold* is the same thing as "a hull"
Shakespeare has described in proper
sequence four of the things one was
recommended to do in a gale at
sea.

6. *Tend*] Attend.

7. *whistle*] The perquisite of the
Master, who was in command of navi-
gation. See Smith, *The Sea-man's
Grammar*, p. 34, and Cawley, *Unpathed
Waters*, pp. 185 ff, for details of the
use of the instrument.

Blow] Addressed to the storm. Cf.
Per., III. i. 44, "Blow, and split thyself."
There is the same anxiety for sea-
room in the storm scene of *Per.*

10. *Play*] Upton remarked (*Critical
Observations on Shakespeare*, 1746,

p. 241), "It should be *ply* the men:
keep them to their business." As the
text stands, Alonso implies a needless
and inopportune reproof. N.S. version (="pipe all hands") is attractive, but its support from *O.E.D.* is
quite illusory. Upton may be right;
O.E.D. (*s.v. ply*) *does* support this
usage. In Elizabethan pronunciation,
ply and *play* differed less than they do
now. See K. Muir's *Macbeth* (*Intro.*,
p. xvi) for an interesting comment on
such mistakes.

11–19.] This passage can be rearranged as verse, though with one or
two rough lines. The lines would end:
*boatswain, labour, storm, Hence, King, not,
aboard.* Cf. ll. 36–41, and see Chambers, "The Integrity of *The Tempest*"
(*Shakespearean Gleanings*).

14. Cf. *Per.*, III. i. 19, "Patience,
good sir; do not assist the storm."

15. Cf. *Wint.*, v. i. 19.

16. *cares*] Cf. *Per.*, IV. i. 60, "Never
was waves nor wind so violent";
this use of the singular form of the
verb with a plural subject is extremely common, and occurs frequently

for the name of King? To cabin: silence! trouble
us not.

Gon. Good, yet remember whom thou hast aboard.

Boats. None that I more love than myself. You are a   20
counsellor; if you can command these elements to
silence, and work the peace of the presence, we will
not hand a rope more; use your authority: if you
cannot, give thanks you have lived so long, and
make yourself ready in your cabin for the mischance   25
of the hour, if it so hap. Cheerly, good hearts! Out
of our way, I say.   *Exit.*

Gon. I have great comfort from this fellow: methinks he
hath no drowning mark upon him; his complexion
is perfect gallows. Stand fast, good Fate, to his   30

---

22. *presence*] J. C. Maxwell conj.; *present* F.   23. *hand*] *handle* Johnson.

---

in this play (*e.g.* I. ii. 481, IV. i. 262,
v. i. 7, v. i. 216). See Abbott,
Shakespearian Grammar ¶¶ 332, 333,
335; this usage should not be attributed to carelessness or ignorance,
and Abbott would have called *cares*
a "quasi-plural verb". Verbs are
sometimes attracted into the number of a false subject, *e.g. bones* in
"Of his bones are coral made" (I. ii.
400).

roarers] Noisy and unruly waves;
the "ruffian billows" of *2 H 4*, III. i. 22.
With an allusion to the sense "bully",
"roisterer"—"A lady to turn roarer,
and break glasses" (Massinger, *The
Renegado*, I. 3); "roaring boys" was a
slang expression for "roughs", and for
young men whose pride it was to
break the peace. See Middleton, *The
Fair Quarrel*, IV. i. Webster uses the
phrase metaphorically of naval guns
in *Cure for a Cuckold*, II. iv. 151.

17. *To cabin*] See Abbott ¶ 90.

20. *than*] *then* F. "Then" is a common form of "than", as "least" is of
"lest".

21. *counsellor*] N.S. suggests, I think
rightly, that "councillor" is meant
here. Shakespeare did not differenti-
ate the forms orthographically. The

Boatswain refers to Gonzalo's function as "a member of the King's
Council, whose business it was to
quell riots"—and "roarers".

22. *work . . . presence*] See note on 21.
I find no parallel for this phrase;
see Additional Notes, p.166.

29–30.] Cf. l. 46 and v. i. 217–18.
The proverb was "He that is born to
be hanged will never be drowned."
Cf. *Gent.*, I. i. 156 ff. The "mark"
would be a mole; it was super-
stitiously held that the position of a
mole on the body indicated the manner of a person's death (Hazlitt,
Popular Antiquities, III. 224 ff).

complexion] Meant external appearance, much as it does still, though it
retained something of a technical
meaning, so that here one might gloss
it "physical appearance as an index of
temperament". "Complexion" means
"temperament" alone, without reference to the appearance, in several
places in Shakespeare, *e.g. Ado*, II. i.
305. Originally it was a technical
word referring to the physiological
constitution of the four humours in a
man, which determined, broadly
speaking, his character or disposition.

hanging: make the rope of his destiny our cable, for
our own doth little advantage. If he be not born
to be hanged, our case is miserable.   *Exeunt.*

Re-enter Boatswain.

Boats. Down with the topmast! yare! lower, lower!
Bring her to try with main-course. *A cry within.* A   35
plague upon this howling! they are louder than the
weather or our office.

[*Re-*]*enter* SEBASTIAN, ANTONIO, *and* GONZALO.

Yet again! what do you here? Shall we give o'er,
and drown? Have you a mind to sink?
Seb. A pox o' your throat, you bawling, blasphemous,   40
incharitable dog!
Boats. Work you, then.
Ant. Hang, cur! hang, you whoreson, insolent noise-

---

33. Exeunt] Theobald; Exit F.   S.D. Re-enter] Pope; Enter F.   35. *her to
try*] F4, Camb.; *her to Try* F, F2, F3; *her to; try* Grant White.   *try with main-
course*] F4, Camb.; *Try with Maine-course* F, F2, F3; *try wi' th' main-course* Grant
White, Alexander.   A cry, *etc.*] Camb.; in F follows *A plague.*   37, 38.
office. Yet again!] Rowe, Camb.; *office: yet againe?* F.   37. S.D. Re-enter . . .
GONZALO] Enter . . . Gonzalo F, following A cry within.   41. *incharitable*]
uncharitable Rowe.

---

31. *cable*] Gonzalo's jocular nautical
analogy is not very sound, as in the
circumstances there was nothing to be
gained from using the anchor.

32. *little advantage*] Helps us little.

34. *Down with the topmast*] Whall
(*Shakespeare's Sea-terms Explained*, 1911)
says that the topmast capable of being
struck was an invention of Hawkins.
See note below.

35. *Bring . . . main-course*] F, like
Smith (see note on l. 6), spells *Try*
with the capital. Whall says *Try with
main-course* means to lie hove-to, or
nearly stationary, with the aid of a
"try-sail" (in this case the main course
or sail). *Bring her to* can stand alone,
meaning much the same thing, but

Smith's testimony makes this unlikely.

35-6. *A plague*] Followed in F by a
long dash, perhaps signifying the
oaths referred to by Sebastian as
"blasphemous"; cf. v. i. 218. An *Act
to Restraine Abuses of Players* (1606—
Chambers, *Elizabethan Stage*, IV.
338) prohibited certain oaths on the
stage. Hence some changes in the
later texts of plays existing in early
quartos (Chambers, *Wm Shakespeare*,
I. 238 ff).

36. *they are louder*] These passengers
make more noise than the storm, or
than we do at our work. Cf. *Wint.*,
III. iii. 103-4, "Both roaring louder
than the sea or weather".

maker. We are less afraid to be drowned than thou
art.   45

Gon. I'll warrant him for drowning, though the ship
were no stronger than a nutshell, and as leaky as an
unstanched wench.

Boats. Lay her a-hold, a-hold! set her two courses; off to
sea again; lay her off.   50

Enter Mariners wet.

Mariners. All lost, to prayers, to prayers! all lost!
Boats. What, must our mouths be cold?
Gon. The King and Prince at prayers, let's assist them,
    For our case is as theirs.
Seb.   I'm out of patience.
Ant. We are merely cheated of our lives by drunkards: 55

46. *for*] *from* Theobald.   49. *courses; off*] Steevens (Holt conj.); *courses off* F.
53. *Prince at prayers,*] F4; *Prince, at prayers,* F; *prince are at prayers,* Rowe; *prince at prayers!* Pope.   54. *I'm*] F3, F4, Rowe; *I'am* F, F2; *I am* Steevens.

46. *for drowning*] "for" is equivalent
to either "against" or "for what concerns" (Abbott ¶154).

47–8. *as leaky . . .*] Cf. Middleton,
Phoenix, I. ii. 29–31.

49. *Lay her a-hold*] This should probably be *a-hull*, which is equivalent to
the modern "hove-to". (The bosun
reverses this order and puts on sail
immediately he sees that there is not
in fact enough room to drift; *set her
two courses* is an unavailing attempt to
clear the lee shore.) *A-hull, a-hulling,
at hull* etc. were the usual words for
this; *a-hold* is nowhere found. The
question is discussed in detail by H. B.
Allen, *M.L.N.* LII (1937), 96–100; he
makes *a-hull* fairly secure. See *H 8*,
II. iv. 199; *Tw.N.*, I. v. 191; and p. 166.

two courses] Foresail and mainsail.
"The main-sail and the fore-sail is
called the fore-course and the main-
course, or a pair of courses" (Smith).

Note the change to blank verse. The
basic tragi-comic theme is now introduced.

52. *must our mouths be cold*] In Jour-

dain's narrative, the crew, "drunke
one to the other, taking their last
leave". Cf. also ll. 54–6. Others interpret "be cold in death", citing *The
Scornful Lady*, II. i, "Would I had been
cold i' the mouth before this day." But
Cawley (*Unpathed Waters*, p. 188) says
that sailors were reputed to take to the
bottle when in difficulties, and some
wrecks may have been caused by this
habit.

53. *Prince at prayers,*] The sense is
given by Rowe's emendation, but F is
already adequate. *The King, and
Prince, at prayers*, might be an absolute
construction (= "being at prayers");
or, *them* might be in redundant apposition to *King* and *Prince*. Both constructions are strained, but scarcely
more so than v. i. 247–50 and other
passages in this play, *e.g.* "The master
and the boatswain / Being awake, enforce them to this place" (v. i. 99–
100).

55. *merely*] Utterly. Cf. "Possess it
merely", *Ham.*, I. ii. 137. Queen Elizabeth was thus "mere English".

This wide-chapp'd rascal,—would thou mightst lie
   drowning
The washing of ten tides!

Gon.   He'll be hang'd yet,
Though every drop of water swear against it,
And gape at wid'st to glut him.
      A confused noise within: "Mercy on us!"—
"We split, we split!"—"Farewell, my wife and
   children!"—   60
"Farewell, brother!"—"We split, we split, we split!"

Ant. Let's all sink wi' th' King.

Seb. Let's take leave of him.   *Exeunt* [*Ant. and Seb.*].

Gon. Now would I give a thousand furlongs of sea for an
   acre of barren ground, long heath, broom, furze,   65

---

56. *This wide-chapp'd rascal,—*] Camb.; *This wide-chopt-rascall*, F; *This wide-chopt rascal*, F4.   61. *Farewell, brother*] *Brother, farewell* Pope.   62. *wi' th' king*] Grant White; *with' King* F, F2; *with King* F3, F4; *with the king* Rowe; *wi' the king* Capell.   63. S.D. Exeunt Ant. and Seb.] Exit F.
65. *long heath, broom, furze*] Tannenbaum conj.; *Long heath, Browne firrs* F, F2, F3 (*firs* F4); *long heath, brown furze* Rowe; *ling, heath, broom, furze* Hanmer.

---

57. *The washing of ten tides*] An ex-aggerated form of the sentence passed upon pirates by the English court of Admiralty, which was that they should be hanged on the shore at low water mark and remain there until three tides had flowed and ebbed. See p. 166.

59. *at wid'st*] A construction analo-gous to the extant "at least".

glut] Swallow. Cf. Spenser, *Shep-heards Calendar,* September, l. 185.

59–61.] The arrangement of the "confused noise" as a series of inde-pendent exclamations was first made by Capell.

61. *split*] Break up. The usual word; for examples see *O.E.D.*

62. *wi' th' King*] Grant White's emendation. The F reading probably indicates that the author, followed exactly by the printer, wrote with his mind on the words as they would be spoken in haste.

65. *long heath, broom, furze*] Much debated, with strong support for Han-

mer's reading; Farmer found in Harrison's geographical essay prefixed to Holinshed, "Brome, heth, firze, brakes, whinnes, ling", which an-swered the objection that "ling" and "heath" are the same plant. "Long heath" is a specific shrub, described in Lyte's *Herbal* (1576), but "brown furze" is not, and even if we disregard Lyte and interpret "long heath" as meaning "barren ground" (N.S.) we are faced with a certain ineptitude in the expression. Tannenbaum (*S.A.B.* VI) keeps "long heath" and produces strong support for Hanmer's "broom". *The Marriage of Wit and Wisdom* (1570) has a misprint *broume* for *browne*, and this is the same error in reverse. This is cogent; and it is supported by the fact that, as Mr J. Munro informs me, it had long been customary in land documents to particularize "broom" in citation of properties. (Cf. *O.E.D. s. vv. gorse* [1485] and *furze* [1523].) Many more examples, supplied to Mr

anything. The wills above be done! but I would fain
die a dry death.　　　　　　　　　　　　　　　*Exeunt.*

SCENE II.—[*The Island. Before Prospero's Cell.*]

Enter PROSPERO *and* MIRANDA.

Mir. If by your Art, my dearest father, you have
　　Put the wild waters in this roar, allay them.
　　The sky, it seems, would pour down stinking pitch,
　　But that the sea, mounting to th' welkin's cheek,
　　Dashes the fire out. O, I have suffered　　　　5
　　With those that I saw suffer! a brave vessel,
　　(Who had, no doubt, some noble creature in her,)

67. S.D. Exeunt] Exit F; omitted Ff.

Scene II

S.D. Scene II . . . Cell] Capell; Scena Secunda F.　　2. *roar,*] Camb.; *Rore;* F
rore, F4.　　7. *creature*] *creatures* Theobald.

Munro by Sir William Craigie, make
it fairly certain that Tannenbaum's
conjecture is right, and that Gonzalo
has here slipped into the familiar
language of estate business.

Scene II

For the place of this scene in the
structural pattern of the play, see
Intro., p. lxxv.

　1. *by your Art*] Prospero's magic is
already known to Miranda. As usual,
F gives Prospero's Art a capital A.
Miranda addresses him with the
deferential "you"; he generally uses
"thou".

　you have] A "weak" ending, found
only in late Shakespearian verse.

　2. *roar,*] F has semi-colon for emphasis. Cf. "No ceremony that to
great ones longs, / Not the Kings
Crowne; nor the deputed sword . . . /
Becomes them with one halfe so good
a grace / As mercie does" (*Meas.*,
II. ii. 59–63).

　3. *stinking pitch*] For the "savour of
. . . pitch" cf. II. ii. 53. For the dark-

ness and horror of the storm as
Miranda describes it, cf. Strachey's
account (Appendix A, *ab init.*) and
Per., III. i. 1–2, 45.

　4. *welkin's cheek*] Cf. *Wint.*, III. iii.
85 ff, where the sea "is now the sky:
betwixt the firmament and it you
cannot thrust a bodkin's point"; and
Tp., v. i. 43–4. For this use of *cheek* see
R 2, III. iii. 57, "the cloudy cheeks of
heaven", and *Cor.*, v. iii. 151, "the
wide cheeks o' the air"; also *Sonn.*,
cxxxii. 6, and *Rom.*, I. v. 47. N.S. suggests that a secondary meaning of
"cheek"—"the side of a grate"—is
also implied. (Cf. *Oth.*, IV. ii. 74.)

　7. Coleridge suggests that "no
doubt" could be said only by Miranda, obviously taking "noble" to
mean more than merely "of high
rank". We might well admit this
insight, which allows us to conceive of
the extended investigation of the
meaning of nobility, which pervades
the play, as beginning at this early
stage.

　creature] The old emendation, *crea-*

Dash'd all to pieces. O, the cry did knock
Against my very heart! Poor souls, they perish'd!
Had I been any god of power, I would   10
Have sunk the sea within the earth, or ere
It should the good ship so have swallow'd, and
The fraughting souls within her.

Pros.   Be collected:
No more amazement: tell your piteous heart
There's no harm done.

Mir.   O, woe the day!

Pros.   No harm.   15
I have done nothing but in care of thee,
Of thee, my dear one; thee, my daughter, who
Art ignorant of what thou art; nought knowing
Of whence I am, nor that I am more better
Than Prospero, master of a full poor cell,   20
And thy no greater father.

Mir.   More to know
Did never meddle with my thoughts.

Pros.   'Tis time
I should inform thee farther. Lend thy hand,
And pluck my magic garment from me.—So:

                              [*Lays down his mantle.*]

---

13. *fraughting*] *fraighted* Pope; *fraighting* Theobald; *freighting* Steevens.
19. *I am more better*] *I am more, or better* Rowe; *I'm more, or better* Pope.   20. *full poor*] *full-poor* Theobald.   22. *time*] *true* F4.   24 S.D. Lays down his mantle] Pope.

---

tures, is defended by Tannenbaum, *S.A.B.* VI. 148–60, on the ground that it is an *es : e* misprint.

10. *god of power*] Cf. "prince of power", l. 55.

13. *fraughting*] "forming the cargo" (Onions). Cf. *Mer.V.*, II. viii. 30.

14. *amazement*] Bewilderment, distraction, terror. Cf. *Ham.*, II. iv. 112, "amazement on thy mother sits", and *infra*, I. ii. 198, V. i. 104, V. i. 215 S.D.

piteous] Full of pity; the usual meaning in Shakespeare.

19. *more better*] Double comparative, common in Elizabethan English; cf.

I. ii. 442 and see Abbott ¶ 11. *better*—of higher rank.

21. *no greater*] than is implied by "a full poor cell".

22. *meddle with*] "mingle with" (Onions, who records this as a late example of the sense). Possibly there is also present a sense in which *meddle*, in a more modern signification, has *thoughts* as its subject, and *more to know* as its object.

23. *I should inform thee*] This transition from discussion of the shipwreck to recollection of relevant past events is managed with great skill and plausibility.

Lie there, my Art. Wipe thou thine eyes; have
　　comfort.   25
The direful spectacle of the wrack, which touch'd
The very virtue of compassion in thee,
I have with such provision in mine Art
So safely ordered, that there is no soul—
No, not so much perdition as an hair   30
Betid to any creature in the vessel
Which thou heard'st cry, which thou saw'st sink.
　　Sit down;
For thou must now know farther.
Mir.　　　　　　　　　　　　　　You have often
Begun to tell me what I am, but stopp'd,
And left me to a bootless inquisition,   35
Concluding "Stay: not yet."
Pros.　　　　　　　　　　　The hour's now come;
The very minute bids thee ope thine ear;
Obey, and be attentive. Canst thou remember
A time before we came unto this cell?
I do not think thou canst, for then thou wast not   40
Out three years old.

---

28. *provision*] *compassion* Ff; *prevision* Dyce, Tannenbaum conj.　29. *ordered*]
order'd Rowe.　*there is no soul*—] Steevens; *there is no soule* F; *there's no soul
lost* Pope; *there is no foyle* Theobald; *there is no soil* Johnson, N.S.　30. *an
hair*] *an hair's* Capell conj.; *a hair* Singer.　31. *betid*] *betide* Ff.　33. *often*]
oft Staunton conj.　35. *a*] *the* Ff.　37. *ear*] *ears* Tannenbaum conj.

25. *my Art*] *i.e.* "the symbol of my
Art". Prospero resumes his robe at
169, when he needs it again.

27. *virtue*] Here "essence". See
Intro., p. liii.

28. *provision*] Foresight. The *compassion* of Ff is a compositor's error, explained by preceding line.

29. *no soul*] Supply "lost"; an anacoluthon. Such constructions are
common in the later plays, but N.S.
supports Johnson's emendation on the
grounds that the punctuation does not
support the hypothesis of an anacoluthon, and that clothes without "soil"
recur later in the play. But the punc-

tuation, though careful, is not absolutely dependable; and the second
point is dealt with in a general way in
the lines following.

30. *perdition*] Loss. See l. 217.

32. Cf. *Wint.*, III. iii. 89 ff.

35. *bootless inquisition*] Profitless inquiry.

36. *The hour's now come*] See note on
l. 23.

38. *Canst*] Pope omits *thou* to regu-
larize the metre; this was his constant
practice. See Textual Notes *passim*.

41. *Out*] Fully. Cf. "And be a boy
right *out*", IV. i. 101; also "out twelve
several times" (*Cor.*, IV. v. 127–8).

Mir.   Certainly, sir, I can.

Pros. By what? by any other house or person?
    Of any thing the image tell me, that
    Hath kept with thy remembrance.

Mir.   'Tis far off,
    And rather like a dream than an assurance   45
    That my remembrance warrants. Had I not
    Four or five women once that tended me?

Pros. Thou hadst, and more, Miranda. But how is it
    That this lives in thy mind? What seest thou else
    In the dark backward and abysm of time?   50
    If thou remembrest aught ere thou cam'st here,
    How thou cam'st here thou mayst.

Mir.   But that I do not.

Pros. Twelve year since, Miranda, twelve year since,
    Thy father was the Duke of Milan, and
    A prince of power.

Mir.   Sir, are not you my father?   55

Pros. Thy mother was a piece of virtue, and
    She said thou wast my daughter; and thy father
    Was Duke of Milan; and his only heir
    And princess, no worse issued.

---

44. *with*] *in* Pope.   50. *dark backward*] F3, F4; *dark-backward* F.   53. *Twelve
year . . . year*] *'Tis twelve years . . . years* Pope.   58. *and his*] *thou his* Hanmer;
and thou his Johnson conj.   59. *And princess*] *A princess* Pope, N.S.

43.] Tell me what you can recollect
of anything else within your memory.
Such inverted sentences are frequent
in the play; cf. ll. 204, 224. (Luce.)

45. *an assurance*] A certainty that
my memory guarantees.

50. *backward and abysm*] = past and
abyss; "abysm" paraphrases "backward"; this paraphrasing frequently
occurs in Shakespeare, especially if
the first figurative expression is a little
uncommon. Cf. "transported and
rapt", ll. 76–7. Also cf. "the tender
inward of thy hand" (*Sonn.*, cxxviii. 6).
(Luce.)

53. *year*] Prospero is speaking
weightily, and says the first "Twelve
year" slowly and with emphasis, so
that "year", whether or no it is pro-

nounced dissyllabically, has the value
of a dissyllable in the prolongation of
the diphthong. If the opening words
are weighted, no sense of irregularity
remains. The scansion of some com-
mentators: "Twelve | year since |
Miran | da twelve | year since," will
not do. Cf., for change in value of
"year", "As *fire* drives out *fire*, so pity
pity" (*Caes.*, III. i. 171). Cf. Abbott
¶¶ 475, 479.

56. *piece of virtue*] "Thou art a piece
of virtue" (*Per.*, IV. vi. 118). "Piece"
means "perfect specimen", "masterpiece". "Virtue" here, of course, is
"chastity", a more central and permanent signification. See *Intro.*, p. liii.

59. *And princess*] This is possibly a
compositor's error; there are other

Mir.　　　　　　　　　　O the heavens!
　　What foul play had we, that we came from thence?　60
　　Or blessed was't we did?
Pros.　　　　　　　　　　Both, both, my girl:
　　By foul play, as thou say'st, were we heav'd thence,
　　But blessedly holp hither.
Mir.　　　　　　　　　　O, my heart bleeds
　　To think o' th' teen that I have turn'd you to,
　　Which is from my remembrance! Please you, farther.　65
Pros.　My brother, and thy uncle, call'd Antonio,—
　　I pray thee, mark me, that a brother should
　　Be so perfidious!—he whom next thyself
　　Of all the world I lov'd, and to him put
　　The manage of my state; as at that time　　　70
　　Through all the signories it was the first,

---

62. *foul play*] F3, F4; *fowle play* F; *fowleplay* F2.　*heav'd*] *heaved* Ff.　63. *O, my*] Camb.; *O my* F; *My* Pope.　71. *Through*] *Though* F2; *Though of* Hunter conj.

examples of *and* for *a*. But despite the clumsiness of so many *ands*, F makes sense, and should stand. The F colon after *princesse* is for emphasis—Prospero is giving Miranda the remarkable facts for the first time. "Thy father was a duke; and *thou* [art] no less in blood."

63. *blessedly*] See l. 159 and *Intro.*, p. xviii.

holp] Past tense of "help".

64. *teen*] Trouble, pain, anxiety.

65. *from*] Away from, out of; has no place in my memory. See Abbott ¶ 158.

66. *My brother*] Anacolutha are frequent in the play; here the broken sentences signify Prospero's actual excitement at the immediate relevance of the story he is telling.

67–8.] Take particular notice of this striking and unnatural perfidy. The parenthesizing of *that . . . perfidious* creates an awkward sentence, with two discontinuous parenthetical exclamations, and achieves only the unnecessary result of adding one more to Prospero's admonitions to Miranda to pay attention.

67–78.] The sense of this difficult passage is perhaps most easily understood if in l. 69 one temporarily substitutes "to him I" for "and to him"; insert a period after "state" in l. 70; paraphrase "as at . . . parallel" (74) as a complete sentence meaning "At that time Milan was the chief signory, and Prospero the most eminent of the dukes, being generally held to be first in dignity, and without parallel in his knowledge of the liberal arts." Here another period. A last sentence runs from "Those" to "studies" (77). This falsifies the text only in l. 69. Prospero, having some difficulty with this exposition, forgets that he has left a relative clause in the air, and becomes involved in a digression about the primacy of his dukedom, which eventually leads him to restate the theme of the transfer of government in a direct way. See note on l. 66. [The whole passage is ingeniously re-punctuated by P. Alexander in his *Tudor Shakespeare* (1951).]

71. *signories*] States of N. Italy subject to a signior, or lord. The more usual meaning is simply "domains".

And Prospero the prime duke, being so reputed
In dignity, and for the liberal Arts
Without a parallel; those being all my study,
The government I cast upon my brother,   75
And to my state grew stranger, being transported
And rapt in secret studies. Thy false uncle—
Dost thou attend me?

Mir.   Sir, most heedfully.

Pros. Being once perfected how to grant suits,
How to deny them, who t' advance, and who   80
To trash for over-topping, new created ·
The creatures that were mine, I say, or chang'd 'em,
Or else new form'd 'em; having both the key
Of officer and office, set all hearts i' th' state
To what tune pleas'd his ear; that now he was   85
The ivy which had hid my princely trunk,
And suck'd my verdure out on 't. Thou attend'st not?

Mir. O, good sir, I do.

Pros.   I pray thee, mark me.
I, thus neglecting worldly ends, all dedicated

---

74. *those*] *these* Tannenbaum conj.   78. *me*] omitted F3, F4, Rowe.   80. *who . . .
who*] *whom . . . whom* Ff.   82. *'em*] *them* Capell.   84. *i' th' state*] *o' th' state* F3.
F4, Rowe; *i' the state* Camb.; omitted Pope.   89. *dedicated*] *dedicate* Steevens,

76. *to . . . stranger*] Withdrew from
my position as duke.

79. *Being,* etc.] Having mastered
the art of controlling suitors—advancing some and checking others, so disposing matters that those already in
office by my favour became his depen-
dents, remodelled for his own purposes—having done all this he made
himself the dominant influence in the
state, draining away my power.

80. *who*] Abbott ¶ 274.

81. *trash for over-topping*] *Over-topping* means "exceeding their authority
or favour". *O.E.D.* has "If Kings pre-
sume to overtopp the Law" (Milton,
Eikonoklastes xxviii). To *trash* is to
check, by means of a cord, a hound
which is being trained (see *O.E.D.* for
examples). The phrase as a whole
means "to keep in check the over-

bold". *Trash,* as a noun, is involved in
a famous crux in *Oth.,* II. ii. 312.

82. *or*] Probably the first term in an
or . . . or construction, for which see
Abbott ¶ 136.

83. *key*] Suggested by the expression
"keys of office"; then, by association,
it becomes a musical figure.

87. *verdure*] Freshness, vigour, vitality; more specifically, power.

89.] See *Intro.,* p. l.

89–97.] This long and complicated
sentence has been punctuated in many
different ways by editors attempting
to make its meaning more obvious.
No paraphrase can reproduce its involved urgency, but perhaps it is in
some ways helpful to have one. "The
fact of my retirement, in which I neg-
lected worldly affairs and dedicated
myself to secret studies of a kind be-

To closeness and the bettering of my mind   90
With that which, but by being so retir'd,
O'er-priz'd all popular rate, in my false brother
Awak'd an evil nature; and my trust,
Like a good parent, did beget of him
A falsehood in its contrary, as great   95
As my trust was; which had indeed no limit,
A confidence sans bound. He being thus lorded,
Not only with what my revenue yielded,
But what my power might else exact, like one
Who having into truth, by telling of it,   100
Made such a sinner of his memory,
To credit his own lie, he did believe
He was indeed the duke; out o' th' substitution,

---

91. *so retir'd*] *retired* Ff.   95. *its*] F4; *it's* F, F2, F3.   99. *exact,*] *exact.* F, Ff.
100. *into truth*] *unto truth* Warburton; *minted truth* N.S. conj.; *acted truth* Parsons.
telling of it] *telling oft* Theobald conj., Parsons; *by-telling of it* Tannenbaum conj.
101. *sinner*] *finer* N.S. conj.

yond the understanding and esteem of the people, brought out a bad side of my brother's nature. Consequently the great, indeed boundless, trust I placed in him gave rise to a disloyalty equally great on his part, just as it sometimes happens that a father distinguished for virtue has a vicious son."

93. *evil nature*] See *Intro.*, p. xlvii.

trust] Tilley (T555) cites the proverb "Trust is the mother of deceit."

94. *Like a good parent*] Proverbial, as in l. 120. "A father above the common rate has commonly a son below it" (Johnson). See *Intro.*, p. liii.

97. *sans*] Without; common use.

lorded] Made a lord of.

98. *revenue*] Accent on 2nd syllable.

100. *into truth*, etc.] "into" in the sense of "unto". Who by often teiling a lie had made his memory such a sinner against truth (*i.e.* such a liar) that he came to believe the lie he told. N.S. says "Read *minted* for 'into'"; also that "telling" (*i.e.* counting it over), "credit his own lie", "out o' th' substitution" (*i.e.* of the baser metal), and

"executing the outward face, etc." (*i.e.* stamping the coin)—all carry on the idea of "minting". It also suggests that "sinner" is a misprint for "finer", an official of the mint. This is an ingenious emendation, but it suffers by comparison with Warburton's, by reason of its great complexity. There is another possible explanation; l. 100 was to have been followed by a line giving the sense "converted his own lie", but the sentence, like many others in the play, changed its course. Finally, Tannenbaum suggests "unto truth by-telling of it" (*i.e.* telling it incorrectly).

102. *To credit*] As to credit. Cf. *R 3*, II. iii. 26; Abbott ¶ 281.

he did believe etc.] So he did actually believe he was Duke of Milan, in consequence of having filled my place, and having assumed the appearances and exercised the functions of royalty with all its dignities and privileges. Cf. *Mer.V.*, v. i. 94 ff. (Luce.)

103. *He . . . substitution*] Tannenbaum suggests reading *the* in full, to make an alexandrine.

And executing th' outward face of royalty,
With all prerogative;—hence his ambition growing,—
Dost thou hear?

Mir.   Your tale, sir, would cure deafness.   106
Pros. To have no screen between this part he play'd
And him he play'd it for, he needs will be
Absolute Milan. Me, poor man, my library
Was dukedom large enough: of temporal royalties   110
He thinks me now incapable; confederates,
So dry he was for sway, wi' th' King of Naples
To give him annual tribute, do him homage,
Subject his coronet to his crown, and bend
The dukedom, yet unbow'd,—alas, poor Milan!—   115
To most ignoble stooping.

Mir.   O the heavens!
Pros. Mark his condition, and th' event; then tell me
If this might be a brother.

Mir.   I should sin
To think but nobly of my grandmother:
Good wombs have borne bad sons.

Pros.   Now the condition.   120
This King of Naples, being an enemy

---

105. *his*] *is* F2.   110. *enough*] *enough for* Keightley.   *royalties*] Camb.;
roalties F; *roialties* Ff.   112. *wi' th' King*] Rowe; *with King* F, Ff; *wi' the King*
Capell, Camb.; *with the King* Steevens; *with' King* N.S.   116. *most*] *much* Ff.
117. *his*] *the* Hanmer.   119. *but*] *not* Pope.   120. *Good . . . sons*] spoken by
Prospero, Theobald conj., Hanmer.

107. *To have no screen*] A metaphor
so mixed that it is difficult to extract
its constituents. Prospero begins to
say "To have no screen between the
office of dukedom and the title of duke
for himself . . ." (here the "screen" is
Prospero) but goes on, with a turn in
the sense, to make the "screen" stand
between the office of dukedom and
Prospero himself (the retiring duke
screened from the world); and now
the "screen" is Antonio. In other
words, "screen" means two quite different things: (1) the impediment to
Antonio's ambition; (2) the function
of Antonio as regent, screening Prospero from the world. See P. Alex-

ander's repunctuation of this passage
(*Tudor Shakespeare*). See p. 167.

109. *Absolute Milan*] The duke, and
not merely the wielder of the duke's
power; cf. *Cor.*, III. i. 116.

Me] Either equivalent to "for me"
or to "as for me".

110. *temporal*] As opposed to the
spiritual conquests of his studies.

112. *dry*] Thirsty, eager; a rare use.
wi' th' King] With F version, cf.
I. i. 64.

117. *his condition*] The compact he
made with Naples, and its results.

119. *but*] Otherwise than.

120. *Good* etc.] Unnecessarily given
to Prospero by some editors.

To me inveterate, hearkens my brother's suit;
Which was, that he, in lieu o' th' premises
Of homage and I know not how much tribute,
Should presently extirpate me and mine   125
Out of the dukedom, and confer fair Milan,
With all the honours, on my brother: whereon,
A treacherous army levied, one midnight
Fated to th' purpose, did Antonio open
The gates of Milan; and, i' th' dead of darkness,   130
The ministers for th' purpose hurried thence
Me and thy crying self.

Mir.   Alack, for pity!
I, not rememb'ring how I cried out then,
Will cry it o'er again: it is a hint
That wrings mine eyes to 't.

Pros.   Hear a little further,   135
And then I'll bring thee to the present business
Which now's upon 's; without the which, this story
Were most impertinent.

Mir.   Wherefore did they not

---

123. *premises*] N.S.; *premises,* F.   129. *purpose*] *practice* Collier, Dyce.   131. *ministers*] *Minister* Rowe.   133. *out*] *on't* Theobald; *it* Lettsom; *o'er't* Kinnear. 135. *to 't*] omitted Steevens.   137. *upon 's*] *upon us* Capell, N.S.   138. *Wherefore*] *Why* Pope.

---

123. *in lieu o' th' premises* etc.] In return for Antonio's undertaking to pay homage and tribute, Alonso was to extirpate Prospero.

125. *presently*] At once. (The usual meaning at this period.)

131. *The ministers*] Those who were employed.

132. *thy crying self*] "The power of poetry is, by a single word perhaps, [as opposed to an accumulation of detail] to instil that energy into the mind, which compels the imagination to produce the picture. Prospero tells Miranda [128–32] ... Here, by introducing a single happy epithet, 'crying', in the last line, a complete picture is presented to the mind, and in the production of such pictures the power of genius consists" (Coleridge,

Lectures on Shakespeare and Milton, Ninth Lecture, in *Coleridge's Shakespearean Criticism* [ed. T. M. Raysor], II. 174). The whole of this Lecture, and Coleridge's other references to the play, are worthy of the closest attention.

134. *hint*] Occasion; cf. II. i. 3, *Cor.,* III. iii. 23. The modern sense is found only once in Shakespeare, and then in a doubtful place (Onions).

135. *wrings mine eyes*] The metaphor may be suggested by the wringing of a wet cloth. (Luce.) But Shakespeare uses the word both literally and figuratively to mean "wrench", "wrestle" (*s.v. wring,* Onions).

137. *the which*] Abbott ¶ 270.

138. *impertinent*] In original sense "not to the purpose".

That hour destroy us?
Pros.   Well demanded, wench:
My tale provokes that question. Dear, they durst not,
So dear the love my people bore me; nor set   141
A mark so bloody on the business; but
With colours fairer painted their foul ends.
In few, they hurried us aboard a bark,
Bore us some leagues to sea; where they prepared   145
A rotten carcass of a butt, not rigg'd,
Nor tackle, sail, nor mast; the very rats
Instinctively have quit it: there they hoist us,
To cry to th' sea that roar'd to us; to sigh

---

140. *Dear*] omitted Hanmer.   141. *dear*] *dare* Staunton conj,   *me*] omitted
Pope.   *nor*] omitted Hudson (Wright conj.).   146. *butt*] *But* F4; *boat* Rowe.
147. *Nor tackle, sail,*] *Nor tackle, nor sail,* Ff, Rowe.   148. *have*] *had* Rowe.

---

141. *So dear*] This repetition is not a
deliberate chiming, but there is no
good reason to emend it, though it
could be argued, with Staunton, that
the printer accidentally substituted
the second "dear" for "dare". The
omission of "nor" from the line has
also been suggested, so that "durst"
can directly govern "set". But Shakespeare's language cannot be forced
into conformity with modern syntax.

142. *A mark*] Those who came in at
the death were marked with the blood
shed by the deer. These conspirators
disguised their intentions under fairer
but false appearances.

144. *In few*] (words); to be brief.

they hurried us] Milan is apparently here treated as a seaport, unless
Shakespeare is thinking of Genoa,
where Thomas's Prospero reigned; but
Gent. has a sea-route from Verona to
Milan, and Shakespeare seems to have
thought of the latter as a seaport.

146. *butt*] Contemptuously for a
"tub of a boat". Cf. It. "botto". The
butt would perhaps be towed out to
sea behind the "bark". Similar voyages
are not uncommon in the legends of
saints. J. F. Danby compares Sidney's
"They saw a sight full of piteous
strangeness: a ship, or rather the

carcase of a ship, or rather some few
bones of the carcase hulling there . . ."
(*Arcadia*, ed. Baker, p. 5; Danby,
Poets on Fortune's Hill [1952], pp. 48,
83).

148. *have quit*] Some suggest "had"
As it stands, a graphic present.

quit, hoist] Shakespeare usually
omits the inflexion of the past tense or
participle in verbs ending with *d* or *t*.
Cf. "requit", III. iii. 71.

149. *To cry*] Cf. Jourdain, who says
the crew committed themselves "to
the mercy of the sea (which is said to
be mercilesse)" [Appendix A]. One
of the objects of *Tp.* is to show that
this opinion is false (see *Intro.*, p. lxxx).
The imagery of Prospero suddenly
changes, and turns into what is almost
a parody of Elizabethan conceited
writing. The play on the sympathetic
sighing of the wind, the augmentation
of the sea with salt tears—these belong
to Italianate love poetry. Up to now
all has been recounted on the level of
the probable and natural; now the
story becomes miraculous and the
language prepares the shift from
"reality". At this time the exiles were
"blessedly holp"; here the story ad-
mits the element of supernatural
grace; all the events in the narrative

To th' winds, whose pity, sighing back again,   150
Did us but loving wrong.

Mir.   Alack, what trouble
Was I then to you!

Pros.   O, a cherubin
Thou wast that did preserve me. Thou didst smile,
Infused with a fortitude from heaven,
When I have deck'd the sea with drops full salt,   155
Under my burthen groan'd; which rais'd in me
An undergoing stomach, to bear up
Against what should ensue.

Mir.   How came we ashore?

Pros. By Providence divine.
Some food we had, and some fresh water, that   160
A noble Neapolitan, Gonzalo,
Out of his charity, who being then appointed
Master of this design, did give us, with
Rich garments, linens, stuffs and necessaries,
Which since have steaded much; so, of his
       gentleness,   165

---

152. *cherubin*] *cherubim* F4, Rowe.   155. *deck'd*] *mock'd* Warburton; *fleck'd* Johnson conj.; *degg'd* Hudson; *eked* N.S. conj.   159. *divine.*] Pope; *divine,* F, F2, F3; *divine;* F4.   162. *who*] omitted Pope; *he* Capell.

which needed "naturalistic" treatment have now been dealt with.

155. *deck'd*] Usually explained as "covered" or "sprinkled". N.S. suggests "eked" (= increased). But there is no need to shun the more obvious "adorn" as the primary meaning here. For the tears conceit, see *A.Y.L.*, II. i. 43 (and, with reference to the note on l. 149, observe particularly the context); and *3 H 6*, v. iv. 8. Only in the very early days of the last-named play could Shakespeare employ such language at its face value.

156. *which*] Miranda's smile.

157. *undergoing stomach*] A spirit of endurance. *Stomach* varies in meaning; perhaps the most usual is "temper", *e.g.* "that you might kill your stomach on your meat / And not upon your maid". *Gent.*, I. ii. 68, and *1 H 6*,

IV. i. 141. For the present sense, cf. *Troil.*, III. iii. 220.

159. *divine*] Here N.S. conjectures a cut. See *Intro.*, p. xviii.

162. *charity*] In a wider sense than "generosity"; the Christian virtue which is greater than faith and hope.

164. *Rich garments*] Possibly this aspect of Gonzalo's kindness is specified to account for the richness of the castaways' costume — Prospero's magic robe here, and his ducal garments in the last act, as well as the clothes to be stolen by Stephano and Trinculo.

165. *steaded much*] Been of much use; "stood us in good stead".

gentleness] Another key-word in the play, closely related to the ideas of nobility, vileness, and virtue. See I. ii. 471 and *Intro.*, p. xliii ff.

Knowing I lov'd my books, he furnish'd me
From mine own library with volumes that
I prize above my dukedom.

Mir.   Would I might
But ever see that man!

Pros.   Now I arise:
Sit still, and hear the last of our sea-sorrow.   170
Here in this island we arriv'd; and here
Have I, thy schoolmaster, made thee more profit
Than other princess' can, that have more time
For vainer hours, and tutors not so careful.

Mir. Heavens thank you for 't! And now, I pray you, sir, 175
For still 'tis beating in my mind, your reason

---

169. *I arise*] *Ariel* Theobald conj.   173. *princess'*] Dyce; *Princesse* F, F2, F3;
Princess F4; *princes* Rowe, N.S.; *princesses* Camb.   175. *Heavens*] *Hevens* F;
Heven F (variant); *Heaven* N.S.

---

167. *volumes*] Magical works, later
alluded to in III. i. 94, III. ii. 87, 90, 93,
v. i. 57.

169. *But ever*] Only, some day.

Now I arise] Prospero's precise
meaning here is disputed. Some take
him to mean simply that he is getting
up, in order to resume his robe, which
he needs to put Miranda to sleep, and
to call Ariel; they usually add the
Stage Direction *Resumes his mantle*.
Others say that he has reached the
climax of his narration; others that he
means to say that his misfortunes are
at an end, and that he has achieved
his "zenith". He probably does rise to
his feet at this point, and here, or at
187, he must resume his robe; but it
seems likely that the primary meaning
is, "Now my fortunes are mending."
He has described his fall; Fortune is
now his dear lady, and he will rise
again. Certainly this implication
would inescapably be present for the
Elizabethan auditor.

170. *sea-sorrow*] Other similar compounds in the play are: *sea-storm*, *sea-
swallowed*, *sea-change*, *sea-marge*.

173. *princess'*] F *Princesse*. Perhaps
the *s*-sounding noun is regarded as
sufficiently "possessive"; so *princess'* is

accounted a plural. (Luce.) Cf. II. i.
273, and Abbott ¶ 471 for suppression
of final *s*; some of Abbott's examples
are, however, doubtful. Paraphrase—
"Have given you the benefit of a
better education than is available to
other princesses who have access to
more diversions than you." Chapman
(?) rhymes "excesse . . . Princesses
. . . tresse . . . dress" (*The Amorous
Contention of Phillis and Flora, Poems*, ed.
Bartlett, p. 93). N.S. follows Rowe
and reads *princes*—"Shakespeare
would spell 'princess' as 'princes',
avoiding as was his habit final *ss* or
sse, but here the compositor has
taken 'princes' for 'princess'—
wrongly." The word must be femin-
ine, but 'princes' is none the less a
possible reading; 'prince' was applied
to princesses, *e.g.* by Peter Beverley in
The Historie of Ariodanto and Ieneura
(1566), I1ᵛ, I5ᵛ, L6ʳ, L8ʳ and elsewhere [C. T. Prouty, *The Sources of
Much Ado About Nothing* (1950), pp.
121, 124, 137, 138].

175. *Heavens*] Some copies of F read
Heaven, according to N.S.

176. *'tis beating in*] "Beating" occurs
in *Tp.* three times in this sense of
"working violently".

For raising this sea-storm?

Pros.   Know thus far forth.
By accident most strange, bountiful Fortune,
(Now my dear lady) hath mine enemies
Brought to this shore; and by my prescience   180
I find my zenith doth depend upon
A most auspicious star, whose influence
If now I court not, but omit, my fortunes
Will ever after droop. Here cease more questions:
Thou art inclin'd to sleep; 'tis a good dulness,   185
And give it way: I know thou canst not choose.

                              [*Miranda sleeps.*]
Come away, servant, come. I am ready now.
Approach, my Ariel, come.

Enter ARIEL.

Ari. All hail, great master! grave sir, hail! I come

186. S.D. Miranda sleeps] Theobald.

178. *Fortune*] Upon which, evidently, Prospero was dependent for the
delivery of the courtiers into his sphere
of influence. See note on l. 169. Great
men were particularly the toys of
Fortune.

179. *dear lady*] The usual personification of Fortune as a changeable
woman. See *Mer.V.*, IV. i. 266–7 and
Ham., II. ii. 233 ff.

181. *zenith*] The highest point of his
fortunes; with a suggestion that every
man, like every point on the earth, has
his own zenith astronomically; cf.
Jonson, *Poetaster*, I. iii. 43–4: "Would
sweare the tunefull orbes / Turn'd in
his zenith only."

182. *influence*] In the astrological
sense.

183. *omit*] Ignore, fail to take
advantage of; used in the same sense
in *Caes.*, IV. iii. 216 ff: "There is a tide
in the affairs of men, / Which, taken
at the flood, leads on to fortune; /
Omitted, all the voyage of their life /
Is bound in shallows and in miseries."

The idea was commonplace, and frequently represented by the emble-
matical figure of Occasio, a lock hanging before her face, and the back of
her head bald.

185.] The possibility that, in this
and the following scene, there is allusion to hypnotic techniques is in-
terestingly, but unconvincingly, suggested by L. H. Allen (*Australasian
Journal of Psychology and Philosophy*,
IV. 110 ff).

'tis a good dulness . . .] Your disposition to sleep is commendable
(timely?); do not resist it.

186. *And*] Almost has the force of
therefore: cf. "And do it with all thy
heart" (*Ado.*, IV. i. 283).

187. *away*] In the sense of "here".
Cf. "Come away, come away, death"
(*Tw.N.*, II. iv. 50).

189.] With this speech of Ariel, cf.
the Satyr in Fletcher's *Faithful Shepherdess:* "Tell me, sweetest, / What
new service now is meetest / For the
Satyre; shall I stray / In the middle

To answer thy best pleasure; be 't to fly,   190
To swim, to dive into the fire, to ride
On the curl'd clouds, to thy strong bidding task
Ariel and all his quality.

Pros.   Hast thou, spirit,
Perform'd to point the tempest that I bade thee?

Ari. To every article.   195
I boarded the king's ship; now on the beak,
Now in the waist, the deck, in every cabin,
I flam'd amazement: sometime I'd divide,
And burn in many places; on the topmast,
The yards and boresprit, would I flame distinctly,   200
Then meet and join. Jove's lightnings, the precursors
O' th' dreadful thunder-claps, more momentary
And sight-outrunning were not: the fire and cracks
Of sulphurous roaring the most mighty Neptune
Seem to besiege, and make his bold waves tremble,   205
Yea, his dread trident shake.

Pros.   My brave spirit!

---

190. *be 't*] *be it* Ff, Rowe.   193. *quality*] *qualities* Pope.   198. *sometime*]
sometimes Ff.   200. *boresprit*] N.S.; *Bore-spritt* F; *Bolt-sprit* Rowe; *bowsprit*
Steevens.   201. *lightnings*] Theobald; *Lightning* F, Ff, Rowe.   202. *O' th'*]
Of Pope.   203. *sight-outrunning*] Camb.; *sight out-running* F.   205. *Seem*]
Seem'd Rowe.   206. *dread*] *dead* Ff.   *My brave*] *My brave, brave* Theobald;
That's my brave Hanmer.

---

ayre, and stay / The sailing racke, or
nimbly take / Hold by the moone . . . /
Shall I dive into the sea?" (v. i.)
(Luce.)

190. *be 't* etc.*] Note all the four
"elements" ("earth" in l. 255).

193. *quality*] These are the other
spirits, the "weak masters", whom
Ariel controls on behalf of Prospero.
See *Intro.*, p. xli. Or possibly "gifts,
powers" as in *Troil.*, IV. iv. 78, "The
Grecian youths are full of quality."

194. *Perform'd to point*] Executed
correctly in every detail; cf. III. iii. 84.

195.] Here N.S. conjectures a cut.

196. *beak*] Prow. The *waist* is amid-
ships, the *deck* the poop.

198. *flam'd amazement*] Struck terror
by appearing as flames. Cf. Psalm ciii,

5, *Nuntios tuos facit ventos, et ministros
tuos ignem ardentem.*

200. *boresprit*] An unusual word, but
O.E.D. gives two other examples. Of
course, = "bowsprit".

flame distinctly] Manifest myself as
flame in these several places. Mention
of St Elmo's fire occurs twice in
Eden's *History of Travel*, near the page
which contains the allusion to Setebos.
See note I. ii. 375; also note on l. 198.
Douce has a good note on this (*Illustrations of Shakespeare*, pp. 2–3).

201. *lightnings*] *lightning* F—here, in
view of *precursors*, presumably an error.

205. *Seem*] A graphic present, or
possibly an error for "seem'd".

206.] The line must be read with a
heavy emphasis on "brave".

Who was so firm, so constant, that this coil
Would not infect his reason?

Ari.   Not a soul
But felt a fever of the mad, and play'd
Some tricks of desperation. All but mariners   210
Plung'd in the foaming brine, and quit the vessel,
Then all afire with me: the King's son, Ferdinand,
With hair up-staring,—then like reeds, not hair,—
Was the first man that leap'd; cried, "Hell is empty,
And all the devils are here."

Pros.   Why, that's my spirit!   215
But was not this nigh shore?

Ari.   Close by, my master.

Pros. But are they, Ariel, safe?

Ari.   Not a hair perish'd;

---

209. *mad*] *mind* Dryden, Rowe, N.S. conj.   210. *but*] *but the* Hunter conj.; *but*,
Philadelphia Shakespeare Soc. *apud* Camb.   211. *vessel*,] Rowe; *vessell;* F.
212. *afire with me:*] Rowe; *afire with me* F, Ff, N.S.   214–15. *empty,* | *And all*] F,
F2, F3; *empty, and* | *All* F4.

---

207. *coil*] Turmoil, uproar, confusion. Cf. *Ado.*, v. ii. 98.

209. *of the mad*] Such as madmen feel.

210. *but mariners*] *th'* has been absorbed into the *t* of *but*.

212. *me: the King's son . . .*] F has nothing to correspond to this colon; if this is not an accidental omission, the sense must be that Ferdinand, as well as the ship, is "all afire" with Ariel. N.S. prints and defends the F pointing, placing a semi-colon after "vessel". This restitution of the F reading requires serious consideration, but I think it must be rejected. Ferdinand, like the others, abandons the ship because it is apparently in the possession of devils. If the corposants had attached themselves to his person—which they sometimes, though rarely, do—the effect would have been spectacular enough for a less equivocal description. The phrase "Then all afire with me" is natural in apposition to "the vessel", which in any case we already know to be thus illuminated;

and it is perhaps somewhat strained if read as part of the next idea. The original reading survived through all the Folios, but the first editor, Rowe, emended as above, and every subsequent editor, except the N.S. editors, concurs. F punctuation, though exceptionally thorough in *Tp.*, is often obviously inaccurate, and even if it were not so, this is by no means an outrageously improbable error. However, the idea of Ferdinand leaping overboard with flaming hair and fingertips is very attractive. Perhaps there is something to be said for treating this as an ambiguous, facing-both-ways construction, of which it would be easy to cite other examples. But to punctuate at all, one must choose; and reason favours the suggestion of Rowe.

213. *up-staring*] Standing on end. "That mak'st my blood cold and my hair to *stare*" (*Caes.*, IV. iii. 280); cf. Germ. "Starr", stiff.

217. *Not a hair . . .*] In the account of St Paul's shipwreck on Malta (Acts

On their sustaining garments not a blemish,
But fresher than before: and, as thou bad'st me.
In troops I have dispers'd them 'bout the isle.   220
The King's son have I landed by himself;
Whom I left cooling of the air with sighs
In an odd angle of the isle, and sitting,
His arms in this sad knot.

Pros.   Of the King's ship,
The mariners, say how thou hast dispos'd,   225
And all the rest o' th' fleet.

Ari.   Safely in harbour
Is the King's ship; in the deep nook, where once
Thou call'dst me up at midnight to fetch dew
From the still-vex'd Bermoothes, there she's hid:
The mariners all under hatches stow'd;   230
Who, with a charm join'd to their suffer'd labour,

224–5. *ship,*] *ship* Hanmer.   229. *Bermoothes*] *Bermudas* Theobald.   231. *Who*] *Whom* Hanmer.

---

xxvii. 34), we read: "there shal not an heare of the head perish of any of you" (Rheims N.T.—Richmond Noble; first remarked by Holt White).

218. *sustaining*] Editors have discussed at length the propriety of this epithet. There is no evidence in the accounts of the survivors that they were supported in the water by their clothes, like Ophelia; but it is possible that Shakespeare, wrongly, imagined that clothes are buoyant enough to contribute to survival in the sea. In any case there is little to be said for any of the proposed emendations.

223. *odd angle*] Cf. Jonson, *Bartholomew Fair*, II. vi. 76–7, "Looke into any Angle o' the towne, (the Streights, or the Bermuda's) . . ."

224. *in this sad knot*] Folded sadly thus—Ariel suits the action to the word; cf. "Marcus, unknit that sorrow-wreathen knot" (*Tit.*, III. ii. 4).

225. *The mariners*] Parenthetic, and not part of a curious inversion, as Hanmer, followed by many others, suggested. Prospero is an impatient

speaker; he has this in common with Coriolanus and Leontes.

227. *nook*] Cf. *H 5*, III. v. 14, "nook-shotten isle".

228. *dew*] Sycorax also used dew in magic; see l. 323. Midnight was the proper time for these operations; see *Ham.*, III. ii. 268. See also *Cym.*, I. v. 1.

229. *Bermoothes*] The Bermudas were a byword for tempests and enchantments. See, *e.g.* Webster, *D. of Malfi* (c. 1613), III. iii. 307; *Anything for a Quiet Life* (1621), v. i. 355–8. "The place I speak of has bin kept with thunder, / With frightful lightnings, amazing Noises, / But now (th' inchantment broke) 'tis the Land of Peace, / Where Hogs and Tobacco yield fair increase" (ed. F. L. Lucas). The name was also given to a brothel district (see n. to l. 223). The spelling varied greatly, but here, as in Webster, it approximates to the Spanish pronunciation (after the proper name Bermudez). This is the only mention of Bermuda in the whole play.

231. *suffer'd labour*] The labour they have undergone.

I have left asleep: and for the rest o' th' fleet,
Which I dispers'd, they all have met again,
And are upon the Mediterranean flote,
Bound sadly home for Naples;　　　　　　　235
Supposing that they saw the King's ship wrack'd,
And his great person perish.

Pros.　　　　　　　　　　Ariel, thy charge
Exactly is perform'd: but there's more work.
What is the time o' th' day?

Ari.　　　　　　　　　　Past the mid season.

Pros. At least two glasses. The time 'twixt six and now　240
Must by us both be spent most preciously.

Ari. Is there more toil? Since thou dost give me pains,
Let me remember thee what thou hast promis'd,
Which is not yet perform'd me.

Pros.　　　　　　　　　　How now? moody?
What is 't thou canst demand?

Ari.　　　　　　　　　　My liberty.　　245

Pros. Before the time be out? no more!

Ari.　　　　　　　　　　I prithee,
Remember I have done thee worthy service;
Told thee no lies, made no mistakings, serv'd

---

232. *I have] I've* Pope.　240. Pros. *At least two glasses.*] Ari. *At least two glasses.*
Warburton.　244. *How now?] How now,* Dyce, Alexander.　245. *What]*
Which Ff.　248. *made . . . serv'd*] Rowe, N.S.; *made thee no mistakings* F.

---

234. *flote*] Flood, sea. Properly
"wave", "billow" (Onions). Cf. ". . .
draw to ebb / The *float* of those desires", Middleton, *The Spanish Gipsy*,
I. v. (Mermaid ed., p. 380).

235.] Effective short line; obviously
not indicating a cut.

240. *At least two glasses*] i.e. at least
two o'clock. These are hour-glasses,
as in *All's W.*, II. i. 168. Properly the
seamen, later, should reckon by half-
hour glasses (see v. i. 223 and *Shakespeare's England*, I. 163–4). Precision
in such a matter would be very
curious in Elizabethan drama. Shakespeare is, however, notoriously keen
in this play to limit the time of the
action which seems to cover from

three to four hours (between 2 and
6 p.m.).

242. *pains*] Labours. Cf. III. i. 1,
"There be some sports are painful,"
i.e. requiring effort. See also *Mac.*, II.
iii. 53, "The labour we delight in
physics pain."

244. *moody?*] The supernatural
powers of magicians were maintained
only by unremitting effort, as also was
their ascendancy over the spirits they
forced into unwilling service. Cf. "My
charms crack not; my spirits obey"
(v. i. 2). (Luce.)

248.] The redundant "thee" of F is
probably caught from *Done thee* and
Told thee, which the compositor has
just set.

Without or grudge or grumblings: thou did promise
    To bate me a full year.
Pros.   Dost thou forget   250
    From what a torment I did free thee?
Ari.   No.
Pros. Thou dost, and think'st it much to tread the ooze
    Of the salt deep,
    To run upon the sharp wind of the north,
    To do me business in the veins o' th' earth   255
    When it is bak'd with frost.
Ari.   I do not, sir.
Pros. Thou liest, malignant thing! Hast thou forgot
    The foul witch Sycorax, who with age and envy

249. *did*] F, F2; *didst* F3, F4.

250. *bate*] Let me off. Cf. *All's W.*,
II. iii. 234. Used in a different sense in
II. i. 96.

    252-3.] N.S. conjectures cut.

    254.] See note on I. ii. 198.

    255-6. *veins . . . frost*] Not meta-
phorical, but in accordance with contemporary cosmology. Swan's *Specu-
lum Mundi* (2nd ed., 1643) speaks of
subterranean waters "running through
the earth, as blood through the
bodie". See Cornford, *Plato's Cosmology* (1937), pp. 330 ff for an
account of the origins of the theory.
With "bak'd with frost" cf. Googe
(1572) "The cold of the winter doth
bake and season the ground"
(*O.E.D.*). The word can mean simply
"caked" or "hardened" as in *Rom.*,
I. iv. 90 and *Ham.*, I. v. 71 (F). Cf.
Donne: "The old dirt is still baked on
my hands" (*O.E.D.*).

    258. *Sycorax*] The name is usually
explained as derived from Greek σύς
and κόραξ (sow and raven). It has not
been found elsewhere. Some of her
attributes seem to support this conjecture, but it appears rather improbable. That "corax" is an element of
the name seems likely, but the word
has topographical significations which
may have contributed to the name
long before Shakespeare. If the name

is ever found elsewhere, the striking
resemblances between Sycorax and
Circe (derived from κίκρος, a hawk)
may be explained.

    Circe, according to the mytho-
graphers, was born in Colchis, in
the district of the Coraxi tribe. She
was expelled from her husband's
kingdom and exiled to a Mediterranean island; she figures regularly in
allegorized myth as that seductive
nature which by working on the
senses reduces men to beasts; her son
Comus in Milton likewise represents
the Nature against which Temperance
must strive if true civility is to be preserved, and the soul liberated. Sycorax
and Caliban represent a Nature antithetical to Spirit and therefore plato-
nically ugly and deformed; but they
are aspects of the same thing. Sycorax
is said to come from Argier, not Colchis; but Prospero may have been on
the point of denying this (see I. ii. 261).
Colchis was a centre of sorcery, associated with Circe (see Baschmakoff,
Synthèse des Périples Pontiques [1948])
and also with Medea (see Appendix D).
Incidentally there was a town called
Algher in Sardinia of which the ancient name was Corax (s.v. *Algaria*,
*Michælis Antonii Baudraud Parisini
Geographia* [1682]).

Was grown into a hoop? hast thou forgot her?

Ari. No, sir.

Pros.　　Thou hast. Where was she born? speak; tell me. 260

Ari. Sir, in Argier.

Pros.　　　　　O, was she so? I must
Once in a month recount what thou hast been,
Which thou forget'st. This damn'd witch Sycorax,
For mischiefs manifold, and sorceries terrible
To enter human hearing, from Argier,　　　　265
Thou know'st, was banish'd: for one thing she did
They would not take her life. Is not this true?

Ari. Ay, sir.

Pros. This blue-ey'd hag was hither brought with child,
And here was left by th' sailors. Thou, my slave,　　270
As thou report'st thyself, was then her servant;
And, for thou wast a spirit too delicate
To act her earthy and abhorr'd commands,
Refusing her grand hests, she did confine thee,
By help of her more potent ministers,　　　　275
And in her most unmitigable rage,
Into a cloven pine; within which rift
Imprison'd thou didst painfully remain
A dozen years; within which space she died,
And left thee there; where thou didst vent thy groans 280
As fast as mill-wheels strike. Then was this island—

---

262. *month*] F4; *moneth* F.　　264. *and sorceries terrible*] *and sorceries too terrible*
Rowe; *sorceries too terrible* Hanmer.　　269. *blue-ey'd*] *blew ey'd* F; *blear-eyed*
Staunton.　　271. *report'st*] *reports'* Tannenbaum conj.　　*was*] *wast* Rowe,
274. *grand*] *great* Tannenbaum conj.　　279. *within*] *in* Capell conj.

261. *Argier*] Old name for Algiers;
but see note on I. ii. 258.

O, was she so?] Sarcasm; or, "P. is
about to contradict A. but does not do
so; and the text leaves us in doubt as
to the birthplace of Sycorax" (N.S.).
See note on I. ii. 258.

269. *blue-ey'd hag*] Alluding to the
eyelid; blueness there was regarded as
a sign of pregnancy (W. A. Wright).
Cf. *D. of Malfi*, II. i. 67.

271. *was*] F has *was* rather than
wast, for the sake of euphony.

273. *earthy*] In antithesis to Ariel

himself, like Caliban ("thou earth",
l. 316).

274. *hests*] Used three times in this
play; otherwise, once only in Shakespeare.

275. *more potent ministers*] For the
goety of Sycorax see *Intro.*, p. xl.

277. *cloven pine*] Cf. the fate of
Fradubio in *F.Q.*, I. ii. 33.

279. *within*] Capell's change is made
because of the *within* of l. 277.

281. *strike*] the water. Cf. "Faster
than the wind-mill sails", *Faithful
Shepherdess*, v. i. *fin.* See p. 167.

Save for the son that she did litter here,
A freckled whelp hag-born—not honour'd with
A human shape.

Ari.   Yes, Caliban her son.

Pros. Dull thing, I say so; he, that Caliban,   285
Whom now I keep in service. Thou best know'st
What torment I did find thee in; thy groans
Did make wolves howl, and penetrate the breasts
Of ever-angry bears: it was a torment
To lay upon the damn'd, which Sycorax   290
Could not again undo: it was mine Art,
When I arriv'd and heard thee, that made gape
The pine, and let thee out.

Ari.   I thank thee, master.

Pros. If thou more murmur'st, I will rend an oak,
And peg thee in his knotty entrails, till   295
Thou hast howl'd away twelve winters.

Ari.   Pardon, master:
I will be correspondent to command,
And do my spriting gently.

Pros.   Do so; and after two days
I will discharge thee.

Ari.   That's my noble master!
What shall I do? say what; what shall I do?   300

Pros. Go make thyself like a nymph o' th' sea:

---

282. *son*] *Sunne* F2; *Sun* F3, F4.   *she*] Rowe; *he* F, Ff.   295. *peg thee*] F3, F4;
peg-thee F, F2.   298. *spriting*] *spiriting* Capell, Camb.   301. *like a*] *like to a* Ff,
Rowe.   301 -6.] See App. G.

284. *Yes, Caliban*] Ariel is probably referring to the "freckled whelp" and not denying Prospero's last remark.

288-9.] Presumably not to be taken as part of the natural history of the island.

291. *Art*] This is Prospero's "white" magic. See *Intro.*, p. xlvii ff.

295. *peg thee*] F *peg-thee*, to emphasize the verb; or perhaps a printer's error.

297. *correspondent*] Compliant, obedient.

298.] Hypermetrical lines are not infrequent in the later plays of Shakespeare, especially when shared between two speakers, *e.g. Troil.*, III. ii. 190. The metrical irregularity of this passage has been held to constitute evidence of "botchery".

gently] A recurring word; cf. I. ii. 165 and note; I. ii. 471, III. iii. 18 S.D., and III. iii. 32.

301.] Eden speaks of "fayre nimphes or fayeres of the sea" in his *Decades*, and Huloet, *Abecedarium*, 1552, corrected by John Higgins, 1572, of

Be subject to
No sight but thine and mine; invisible
To every eyeball else. Go take this shape,
And hither come in 't: go: hence   305
With diligence.   *Exit [Ariel]*.
Awake, dear heart, awake! thou hast slept well;
Awake!
Mir.   The strangeness of your story put
Heaviness in me.
Pros.   Shake it off. Come on;
We'll visit Caliban my slave, who never   310
Yields us kind answer.
Mir.   'Tis a villain, sir,
I do not love to look on.
Pros.   But, as 'tis,
We cannot miss him: he does make our fire,
Fetch in our wood, and serves in offices
That profit us. What, ho! slave! Caliban!   315
Thou earth, thou! speak.
Cal. within.   There's wood enough within.
Pros. Come forth, I say! there's other business for thee;

306–7. *diligence.* [Exit Ariel. / *Awake*] *diligence.* Exit. / Pro. *Awake* F.   309
Heaviness] *Strange heaviness* Camb. conj.; *Heart-heaviness* Bulloch; *A heaviness* Anon
conj.   314. *serves in*] *serves* Ff, Rowe.

"Nymphs of the Sea, the daughters of Nereus . . ." For latter reference see M. W. Latham, *The Elizabethan Fairies*, p. 60.

301–2.] If one were to accept the correction "like *to*", made by the anonymous editor of F2, and the omission of "thine and" in l. 303, these lines would be regular. There is obviously confusion of some sort in this passage. See Appendix G.

303. *invisible*] It need scarcely be said that Ariel is at all times visible to the audience, who merely need to know when he is supposed to be invisible. This they learn from the dialogue and action, or from some conventional "robe for to goo invisibell". See note on l. 376. There is no diffi-

culty about Ariel dressing up to show the audience, though "invisible", some appropriate change of costume.

310. *visit Caliban*] Caliban's rock-den, like Timon's cave, was probably at the back of the stage; it would be a representative structure erected in front of the "study". Prospero would therefore call to Caliban upstage.

312. *'tis*] Probably not an oversight, but an emphatic repetition of *'Tis* in the previous line.

313. *miss*] Do without. "Would miss it rather than carry" (*Cor.*, II. i. 253–4). On Caliban's indispensability see Sir S. Lee, "The American Indian in Elizabethan England", *Scribner's* XLII (1907), 313–30.

Come, thou tortoise! when?

[Re-]enter ARIEL *like a water-nymph.*

Fine apparition! My quaint Ariel,
Hark in thine ear.
Ari.   My lord, it shall be done.   *Exit.* 320
Pros. Thou poisonous slave, got by the devil himself
Upon thy wicked dam, come forth!

Enter CALIBAN.

Cal. As wicked dew as e'er my mother brush'd
With raven's feather from unwholesome fen
Drop on you both! a south-west blow on ye   325
And blister you all o'er!
Pros. For this, be sure, to-night thou shalt have cramps,
Side-stitches that shall pen thy breath up; urchins
Shall, for that vast of night that they may work,

---

318. *Come*] *Come forth* Steevens.   S.D. Re-enter] Enter F.   329. *Shall, for that vast of night that they may work,*] F (*shall for that vast of night, that they may worke*); *Shall forth at vast of night, that they may work* Thos. White conj.

318. *when?*] "This interrogation" is "indicative of impatience in the highest degree" (Steevens).

319. *quaint*] Onions remarks that it is "often difficult to determine the exact meaning" of this word. Here a mixture of "skilful", "dainty", "ingenious", and "elegant". See Onions, *s.v.* and III. iii. 52 S.D.

321-2.] Not sheer abuse, but an allusion to the unnatural birth of Caliban from the union of a devil (incubus) and witch. See *Intro.*, p. xl.

323-5.] Douce quotes from the famous encyclopædia, *Batman uppon Bartholome his booke De proprietatibus rerum*, 1582, "The raven is called corvus of CORAX . . . it is said that *ravens birdes* be fed with *deaw* of heaven all the time they have no black *feathers* by benefite of age" (xii. 10; Douce, p. 6). Douce believes that this is the origin of the name Sycorax.

323. *wicked*] Mischievous, baneful.

Probably suggested by the same word in the previous line.

325. *south-west*] Reckoned a pestilence-bearing wind. Cf. *Cor.*, I. iv. 30, "All the contagion of the south light on you..."

328. *urchins*] Hedgehogs, or goblins, or goblins in the shape of hedgehogs. Cf. *Wiv.*, IV. iv. 49, "Like urchins, ouphes, and fairies". Also Breton, *A Mad World My Masters*, ". . . such apish tricks, as come out of the land of Petito, where a Monkey and a Baboone make an Urchin Generation..." (I. 189, ed. Kentish-Wright, 1929).

329. *for that vast of night*] Dr H. F. Brooks convinces me that F is right. Its comma after *night* marks the start of an explanatory clause: "that vast of night, *viz.* that vast of night in which they may work." The absence of another comma after *work* may be explained as a characteristic laxity, mitigated by the natural line-end

All exercise on thee; thou shalt be pinch'd　　　330
As thick as honeycomb, each pinch more stinging
Than bees that made 'em.

Cal.　　　　　　　　I must eat my dinner.
This island's mine, by Sycorax my mother,
Which thou tak'st from me. When thou cam'st first,
Thou strok'st me, and made much of me; wouldst
　　　give me　　　335
Water with berries in 't; and teach me how
To name the bigger light, and how the less,
That burn by day and night: and then I lov'd thee,
And show'd thee all the qualities o' th' isle,
The fresh springs, brine-pits, barren place and fertile:
Curs'd be I that did so! All the charms　　　341
Of Sycorax, toads, beetles, bats, light on you!
For I am all the subjects that you have,
Which first was mine own King: and here you sty me
In this hard rock, whiles you do keep from me　　　345
The rest o' th' island.

---

331. *honeycomb*] *honeycombs* Pope.　　332. *that*] *had* Greg conj.　　334. *cam'st*]
cam'st here Ritson.　　335. *strok'st*] N.S.; *stroakst* F, F2; *stroak'st* F3, F4; *stroak'dst*
Rowe.　*made*] *mad'st* Rowe.　　341. *Curs'd*] *Cursed* Steevens.　*I that did so*]
I that I did so Ff, Rowe.

pause. The necessary alteration in
pointing is modernization, not emendation; and in any case F is basically
better than White's conjecture. Prospero is terrifying Caliban by emphas-
izing the length of the night. *For* =
"during", "throughout". "[Goblins],
throughout that time of darkness,
enormously long and desolate, during
which they are allowed to be active,
shall all of them exert their powers
on *thee*."

332. *'em*] The cells of the honeycomb.

333–4. *This island's mine*] See *Intro.*,
p. xxx.

355. *strok'st . . . made*] Ungramma-
tical but euphonious.

336. *with berries in 't*] Like the drink
of the Bermudan castaways (Appendix A *fin*.).

337. *bigger light . . . less*] Cf. Gen.
i. 16, "God then made two great
lightes: the greater light to rule
the day, and the lesse light to
rule the night" (Geneva—Richmond
Noble).

340. *brine-pits*] *i.e.* he showed how to
distinguish between useful and useless natural resources.

place] Possibly for *places*; Abbott
¶ 471.

341.] Editors generally fill out
Curs'd to *Cursed*; some adopt the Ff's
I that I . . . and retain *Curs'd*. Both compositors were careful about *-'d* and
-ed forms, so the Ff reading is more
likely, given an error.

344. *mine own King*] *min owne King*
(F) shows how line should be read.

sty me] *sty-me* (F). See note on
l. 295.

Pros.   Thou most lying slave,
Whom stripes may move, not kindness! I have us'd thee,
Filth as thou art, with human care; and lodg'd thee
In mine own cell, till thou didst seek to violate
The honour of my child.   350
Cal. O ho, O ho! would 't had been done!
Thou didst prevent me; I had peopled else
This isle with Calibans.
Mir.   Abhorred slave,
Which any print of goodness wilt not take,
Being capable of all ill! I pitied thee,   355
Took pains to make thee speak, taught thee each hour
One thing or other: when thou didst not, savage,
Know thine own meaning, but wouldst gabble like
A thing most brutish, I endow'd thy purposes

---

348. *human*] F4; *humane* F, F2, F3.   351. *would 't*] *I would it* Pope; *would it*
Steevens.   353. Mir.] Pros. Dryden, Theobald, Camb.   354. *wilt*] *will* Ff.
358. *Know*] *Shew* Hanmer.

348. *human*] Humane. F spells thus.
351. *O ho, O ho*] Malone cites Purchas's *Abstract of James Rosier's Account
of Captain Weymouth's Voyage* (IV. 1661)
where the natives express gratitude
"by these words—*oh, ho!* often repeated".

353. *Abhorred slave*] Theobald followed Dryden's guess, and gave these
lines to Prospero; but none of the
many editors has succeeded in justifying this interference. The arguments
for it run: it is Prospero who is be-
rating Caliban, and Miranda would
not interfere; the language is at once
too indelicate and too philosophical
for Miranda. Miranda, despite II. ii.
141 ("My mistress show'd me thee,
and thy dog, and thy bush"), could
not have had much to do with Caliban's education; she was too young on
arrival in the island. None of this
seems to take into account Shakespeare's habitual disregard of this
kind of immediate probability. Miranda is outraged, and says so. In 365-7
Caliban is addressing both father

and daughter (he calls Prospero *thou*
throughout) when he speaks of being
taught language.

354. *any print of goodness*] The education of virtue made no impression on
Caliban. Cf. IV. i. 188 ff, and *Intro.*, p.
xliii ff. Tannenbaum would read
point, but the metaphor seems to be
from printing. Cf. *F.Q.*, II. x. 7: "halfe
beastly men, / That never tasted
grace . . ."

355. *capable of*] Sensitive to, apt to
receive the impression of. See p. 167.

357. *when thou didst not*] "When you
were so savage that you could not
express your thoughts, nor even think
intelligently, and when your only language was a gabble of meaningless
sounds like those of the brutes, then I
taught you the use of language, and
enabled you to make known what was
going on in your mind." The whole
passage is merely this thought twice
repeated, viz. "You were unable to
express yourself." It may also include
Whateley's "Words are the pre-
requisites of thoughts." (Luce.)

With words that made them known. But thy vile race,
Though thou didst learn, had that in 't which good
   natures   361
Could not abide to be with; therefore wast thou
Deservedly confin'd into this rock,
Who hadst deserv'd more than a prison.

Cal. You taught me language; and my profit on 't   365
Is, I know how to curse. The red plague rid you
For learning me your language!

Pros.   Hag-seed, hence!
Fetch us in fuel; and be quick, thou 'rt best,
To answer other business. Shrug'st thou, malice?
If thou neglect'st, or dost unwillingly   370
What I command, I 'll rack thee with old cramps,
Fill all thy bones with aches, make thee roar,
That beasts shall tremble at thy din.

Cal.   No, 'pray thee.
  [Aside] I must obey: his Art is of such pow'r,
It would control my dam's god, Setebos,   375
And make a vassal of him.

Pros.   So, slave; hence! *Exit Caliban.*

---

360. *vile*] *vild* F; *wild* Daniel Wilson.
364. *hadst*] *hast* Tannenbaum conj.
Go, slave Tannenbaum conj.

363. *Deservedly*] omitted Walker.
374. Aside] Capell.   376. *So, slave*]

360. *race*] (1) species; (2) (as here), hereditary nature appertaining to the species. (Luce.) "Vile race", the opposite of "noble race". See *Intro.*, p. xlvi.

364. *deserv'd*] Following *Deservedly* may be a deliberate chiming; but *Deservedly* may be a compositor's error, which, among other things, upset the line-lengths, and has caused editors to invent new line-divisions. Tannenbaum reads *hast* for *hadst* and accepts the relineation which involves the omission of *Deservedly*, thus: *Confin'd into this rock, who hast deserv'd | More ...* This was, in essentials, first proposed by Walker.

366. *The red plague*] The three plague sores of the time were red, yellow, or black. Cf. *Cor.*, IV. i. 13.

rid] destroy; note the quibble on "red".

368. *thou 'rt best*] To (or for) thee it were best. Thou hadst best. There are many conjectures, not worth recording. "You'd do well to attend promptly to your tasks in future."

371. *old cramps*] The cramps of old people; cf. IV. i. 260. Or perhaps "familiar cramps". Less probably "fine old cramps"—"old" as in *Ado*, v. ii. 98, "Yonder's old coil at home."

372. *aches*] Pronounced "aitches", but the *ch* is hard in III. iii. 2.

375. *Setebos*] A god of the Patagonians. The name is found in Eden's account of Magellan's expedition in the *History of Travel*. See v. i. 261, and *Intro.*, p. xxxii.

Re-enter ARIEL, *invisible, playing and singing;*
[FERDINAND *following.*]

ARIEL['S] song.

Come unto these yellow sands,
 And then take hands:
Courtsied when you have and kiss'd
 The wild waves whist: 380
Foot it featly here and there,
 And sweet sprites bear
The burthen. Hark, hark.

Burthen dispersedly. *Bow-wow.*

S.D. Re-enter . . . following] Malone; Enter Ferdinand & Ariel, inuisible playing and singing F.   379. when you have and kiss'd] Camb.; when you haue, and kist F.   380. The wild waves whist] (The wild waves whist) Warburton.   381–3. Foot . . . burthen] Foot . . . there, / And, sweet sprites, the burthen bear Pope (following Dryden).

(S.D.) invisible] Probably wearing a conventional gown indicating invisibility. See l. 303. For evidence of the survival of this custom, see Wordsworth, *Prelude* (1850), VII. 285–7.

377. yellow sands] Cf. *M.ND.*, II. i. 126, and "Where all is whist and still,/ Save that the sea playing on yellow sand" (Marlowe's *Hero and Leander*, i. 346–7). A reminiscence of Virgil, *Aeneid*, VI. 643–4?

379. kiss'd] each other? ("The wild waves whist" is then an absolute construction—"being silent", or "now being silent" after the storm.) Or, "kiss'd the wild waves into silence"? To take hands and curtsy (make a reverence) were the first two steps in all dances, but the kiss normally came when the dance was finished, as in *H 8*, I. iv. 95–6 (and note in Arden ed.). See also M. Dolmetsch, *Dances of England and France 1450–1600*. Yet although this suggests that "kiss'd" must govern "waves", the notion is disagreeable, being grotesque in a context which does not require grotesquerie. The syntax should perhaps

be allowed to be ambiguous. Of course it was Ariel's music which allayed the tempest; see l. 394–6.

383. the burthen] Properly a continuous undersong of the sort perhaps most familiar to the modern reader in certain carols, like "Willy take your little drum," in which the burthen is *Patapan*. Editors have rearranged this passage in many ways, but the F version, here adopted, shows that the word *burthen* here means "refrain"; the animal- and bird-noises follow Ariel's verses. In this sense it is also used in *Wint.*, IV. iv. 195–6; the sense of "undersong" is clear in *Tp.*, III. iii. 99, where the thunder bears the burthen *Prospero* to the song of the wind. As for the arrangement of the song, and particularly of 382–3, F is perhaps not wholly satisfactory, but I cannot follow Capell and most editors in reversing the order of words. I have tried here to make sense with a minimum of tampering; but see R. Noble, *Shakespeare's Use of Song* (1923), pp. 104–6, and p. 167.

384. Bow-wow.] Probably derived from James Rosier's account of a

Ari. *The watch dogs bark:*   385

    [Burthen dispersedly.] *Bow-wow.*

Ari. *Hark, hark! I hear*
      The strain of strutting chanticleer

      Cry—[Burthen dispersedly.] *Cock a diddle dow.*

Fer. Where should this music be? i' th' air or the 'arth?   390
      It sounds no more: and, sure, it waits upon
      Some god o' th' island. Sitting on a bank,
      Weeping again the King my father's wrack,
      This music crept by me upon the waters,
      Allaying both their fury and my passion   395
      With its sweet air: thence I have follow'd it,
      Or it hath drawn me rather. But 'tis gone.
      No, it begins again.

                    ARIEL['s] song.

        Full fadom five thy father lies;
            Of his bones are coral made;   400
        Those are pearls that were his eyes:
            Nothing of him that doth fade,
        But doth suffer a sea-change

384–9. *Burthen* . . . Cock a diddle dow.] Capell, Camb.; *Burthen dispersedly.* |
Harke, harke, bowgh wawgh: the watch-Dogges barke, | bowgh-wawgh. |
Ar. Hark, hark, I heare, the straine of strutting Chanticlere / cry cockadidle-
dowe. F.   390. *i' th' air or th' earth?*] in air, or earth? Pope.   392. *island.*]
Pope; *Iland,* F.   393. *wrack,*] Rowe; *wracke.* F.

ceremonial Virginian dance (*Intro.,*
p. xxxiii).

392–3. *Sitting* . . . *Weeping*] We are
led to expect a clause such as "I
heard . . ." but after the word *wrack,*
after which F prints a fullstop to indicate a longish pause, as for grief, the
construction is inverted, and *music* becomes the subject. This is a syntactical
liberty by modern standards only; it
would be difficult to explain why the
result is so enchanting.

393. *again*] "used to indicate inten-
sity of action" (Onions, citing also
Mer.V., III. ii. 205 and *2 H 6,* IV. i. 78).

395. *passion*] Sorrow; lamentation,
as Julia in *Gent.* speaks of "Ariadne
passioning / For Theseus' perjury"
(IV. iv. 172–3).

396. *thence*] From the water's edge.

400. *are*] See note on I. i. 16.

401. Those are pearls . . .] Cf. *R 3,*
I. iii. 29–31, "in the holes / Where eyes
did once inhabit there were crept, / As
'twere in scorn of eyes, reflecting
gems."

402. Nothing *etc.*] Every part of his
body that is otherwise doomed to
decay is transformed into some rich or
rare sea-substance. (Luce.)

> *Into something rich and strange.*
> *Sea-nymphs hourly ring his knell:*   405
>
>   Burthen: *Ding-dong.*

Ari. *Hark! now I hear them,—Ding-dong, bell.*

Fer. The ditty does remember my drown'd father.
    This is no mortal business, nor no sound
    That the earth owes:—I hear it now above me.   410

Pros. The fringed curtains of thine eye advance,
    And say what thou seest yond.

Mir.   What is 't? a spirit?
    Lord, how it looks about! Believe me, sir,
    It carries a brave form. But 'tis a spirit.

Pros. No, wench; it eats and sleeps and hath such senses 415
    As we have, such. This gallant which thou seest
    Was in the wrack; and, but he's something stain'd
    With grief (that's beauty's canker) thou mightst call
        him
    A goodly person: he hath lost his fellows,
    And strays about to find 'em.

Mir.   I might call him   420
    A thing divine; for nothing natural

---

411. *eye*] *eyes* Tannenbaum conj.   412. *What is 't? a spirit?*] Capell; *What is't a Spirit?* F; *What! is't a spirit?* Daniel.

406.] Richmond Noble (*Shakespeare's Use of Song*, p. 107) reminds us that Robert Johnson, in his setting of this song, "omitted the burden before the last line. The sense of the song requires the burden of 'ding-dong' immediately after 'Sea-nymphs hourly ring his knell' and before 'Hark, now I hear them'. The effect which the burden had to convey was evidently that of a bell being rung by the waves —an effect absolutely necessary to the suggestion that the sea-nymphs were ringing a watery knell. Johnson's departure from the text would tend to dispose of any attribution to him of the original setting when the play was first produced in 1611 . . ." See Appendix F.

408. *ditty*] Words of the song, "The Ditty High and Tragicall", Bacon, *Essay* 37. (Luce.)
remember] Commemorate.
410. *owes*] Owns. Cf. 457, and III. i. 45.
411. *fringed curtains*] "Her eyelids, cases to those heavenly jewels . . . / Begin to part their fringes of bright gold" (*Per.*, III. ii. 99 ff).
advance] Raise, lift up. Cf. "advanc'd their eyelids", IV. i. 177. Note the formal language and rhythm as of a magician about to "raise" a "spirit". (Luce.)
417. *but*] Except that.
421. *natural*] In the realm of nature, as opposed to the realm of spirit. Cf. III. ii. 30, "that a monster should be

I ever saw so noble.

Pros.　　　　　[*Aside*] It goes on, I see,
As my soul prompts it. Spirit, fine spirit! I 'll free thee
Within two days for this.

Fer.　　　　　　　　Most sure the goddess
On whom these airs attend! Vouchsafe my prayer　　425
May know if you remain upon this island;
And that you will some good instruction give
How I may bear me here: my prime request,
Which I do last pronounce, is, O you wonder!
If you be maid or no?

Mir.　　　　　　　No wonder, sir;　　　430
But certainly a maid.

Fer.　　　　　　　My language! heavens!
I am the best of them that speak this speech,
Were I but where 'tis spoken.

Pros.　　　　　　How? the best?
What wert thou, if the King of Naples heard thee?

Fer. A single thing, as I am now, that wonders　　435
To hear thee speak of Naples. He does hear me;

---

422. Aside] Pope.　　*I see*] omitted Steevens.　　430. *maid*] F3; *Mayd* F; *made*
F4, Rowe, Pope, Theobald, etc.

---

such a natural"—where "natural" is
used in two senses, the above, and the
secondary "idiot". (Luce.) See *Intro.*,
p. xlvii.

422. *It goes on*] The charm works,
and my plan prospers. Cf. line 496,
"it works".

424. *goddess*] Each of the Romance
heroines is mistaken for a goddess.
The device has an interesting history;
the same formula is used in Marlowe's
Dido (I. i. 188–92) paraphrasing
Aeneid, i. 328 ff (*O dea certe* etc.), and in
Mucedorus ("Most gracious goddess,
more than mortal wight, / Your hea-
venly hue of right imparts no less"—
"No goddess, shepherd, but a mortal
wight" — *Shakespeare Apocrypha* ed.
Tucker Brooke, 1908. The reply here
corresponds to the *haud equidem tali me
dignor honore* of Venus in *Aeneid*, i. 335.
There is a similar encounter in *The
Rare Triumphs of Love and Fortune*

(Dodsley, VI. 186). See also *Faerie
Queene*, II. iii. 33, and especially III. v.
35–6; and *Comus*, 265 ff, to which T.
Warton adduces several parallels, in-
cluding Ovid, *Met.* iv. 320, calling
Homer "the original author of this
piece of gallantry" in the address of
Odysseus to Nausicaa. See p. 167.

425. *airs*] The music which Ferdinand has been following.

428. *prime*] In antithesis to *last* in the
following line. "Most important".

429. *O you wonder!*] A play on
Miranda's name, which Ferdinand
does not yet know. See III. i. 37.

435. *single*] A play on several senses
of the word: (1) left alone, solitary;
(2) one, sole; (3) sincere, single mind-
ed (? cf. v. i. 248); (4) weak, helpless
(cf. *Mac.*, I. iii. 140).

436. *He does hear me*] Because, of
course, Ferdinand is, as he thinks,
now King of Naples himself.

And that he does I weep: myself am Naples,
Who with mine eyes, never since at ebb, beheld
The King my father wrack'd.

Mir.   Alack, for mercy!

Fer. Yes, faith, and all his lords; the Duke of Milan   440
And his brave son being twain.

Pros.   . . . [*Aside*] The Duke of Milan
And his more braver daughter could control thee,
If now 'twere fit to do 't. At the first sight
They have chang'd eyes. Delicate Ariel,
I 'll set thee free for this. [*To Fer.*] A word, good sir;   445
I fear you have done yourself some wrong: a word.

Mir. Why speaks my father so ungently? This
Is the third man that e'er I saw; the first
That e'er I sigh'd for: pity move my father
To be inclin'd my way!

Fer.   O, if a virgin,   450
And your affection not gone forth, I 'll make you

---

438. *never*] ne'er Pope.   441. Aside] Dyce.   445. To Fer.] Camb.   447.
ungently] urgently Ff, Johnson.   448. *e'er*] Rowe; ere F.

438. *never*] Virtually a monosyllable.
   at ebb] Luce pointed out the persistence of sea-metaphors in the general language of *Tp*.
   441. *his brave son*] There is no further
mention of Antonio's son in the play,
and the conjecture that Francisco is
his son is clearly wrong, in view of the
way Antonio speaks of him at II. i.
282 ff. It has been suggested that this
character had existence in the
"source" of *Tp.*, and that Shakespeare began to put him in but
changed his mind. See de Perott's
theory, mentioned in *Intro.*, p. lxv.
N.S. thinks he must have been in an
earlier version of the play, which it
believes to have existed. "Prospero's
effective retort made a 'cut' difficult."
One hesitates to say so, but it looks as
though Shakespeare began writing
with a somewhat hazy understanding
of the dynastic relationships he was to
deal with, though he was certainly
clear enough about the main theme of
the play. However, Coleridge thought

that Ferdinand was assuming the loss
of Antonio's son in one of the other
ships. (*C's Shakesperean Criticism*, ed.
Raysor, i. 133n.).
   442. *control*] Contradict, confute,
prove you wrong (O.F. *Contrerôle*, a
duplicate register used to verify the
official or first roll). Cf. Donne, "The
Good-morrow", l. 10. F has *daughter*,
—a good example of the comma of
emphasis.
   444. *chang'd eyes*] Fallen in love; cf.
"mingle eyes" (*Ant.*, III. xiii. 156);
also, "he looks, methinks, / As he
would change his eyes with her,"
Beaumont and Fletcher, *A King
and No King*, III. i. (Cambridge ed.,
i. 182).
   446. *some wrong*] An ironical or
studiously polite way of saying, "You
are mistaken."
   448. *third man*] Later, Miranda excludes Caliban from her list of the
men she has seen (III. i. 50–1).
   450. *if a virgin*] For the ellipse following *if*, see Abbott ¶ 387.

The Queen of Naples.

Pros.   Soft, sir! one word more.
　　[*Aside*] They are both in either's pow'rs: but this
　　　　swift business
　　I must uneasy make, lest too light winning
　　Make the prize light. [*To Fer.*] One word more;
　　　　I charge thee   455
　　That thou attend me: thou dost here usurp
　　The name thou ow'st not; and hast put thyself
　　Upon this island as a spy, to win it
　　From me, the lord on 't.
Fer.   No, as I am a man.
Mir.　There's nothing ill can dwell in such a temple: 460
　　If the ill spirit have so fair a house,
　　Good things will strive to dwell with 't.
Pros.   Follow me.
　　Speak not you for him: he's a traitor. Come;
　　I 'll manacle thy neck and feet together:
　　Sea-water shalt thou drink; thy food shall be   465
　　The fresh-brook mussels, wither'd roots, and husks
　　Wherein the acorn cradled. Follow.
Fer.   No;
　　I will resist such entertainment till
　　Mine enemy has more pow'r.

　　　　　　　　　He draws, and is charmed from moving.

453. Aside] Johnson.　　*pow'rs*] *pow'r* Rowe.　　454. *lest*] F4; *least* F, F2, F3.
455. To Fer.] Camb.　　*One word*] *Sir, one word* Pope.　　459. *I am*] *I'm* Pope.
460. *ill*] *ill*, F.　　462-3. *me.* / *Speak*] *me.* / Pro. (catchword) / Pros. *Speake* F.
463. *traitor*] *Traitor* F.

454. *light . . .*] A quibble; here it means "easy", in the next line "little valued". For Prospero's unreasonable behaviour here see *Intro.*, p. lxiii; and see note on III. i. 1.

460. *There's nothing ill . . .*] In contrast with Miranda's speech l. 353 ff. This is conventional Renaissance Neoplatonic doctrine. Cf. *Euphues* (ed. Croll and Clemons), p. 50: "How can she be in mind any way imperfect who in body is perfect every way?" The human body is treated as a temple in 1 Cor. iii. 17, vi. 19. Amerigo Ves-

pucci noted with surprise that the women of the New World were often beautiful despite their "natural" (*i.e.* libidinous) ways. He expected this moral ugliness to be reflected in their physical features (Chinard, *L'Exotisme*, p. 13).

462. *dwell with 't*] Understand "which is absurd".

465. This diet was suggested primarily by the narratives of the mariners, though in the interests of romance its slight nutritive value is even further reduced.

Mir.   O dear father,
Make not too rash a trial of him, for   470
He's gentle, and not fearful.
Pros.   What! I say,
My foot my tutor? Put thy sword up, traitor;
Who mak'st a show, but dar'st not strike, thy conscience
Is so possess'd with guilt: come from thy ward;
For I can here disarm thee with this stick   475
And make thy weapon drop.
Mir.   Beseech you, father.
Pros. Hence! hang not on my garments.
Mir.   Sir, have pity;
I 'll be his surety.
Pros.   Silence! one word more
Shall make me chide thee, if not hate thee. What!
An advocate for an impostor! hush!   480

---

471. *and*] *tho'* Hanmer; *but* Capell conj.   473. *mak'st . . . dar'st*] *makes . . .
dar'st* Ff; *makest . . . darest* Camb.   474. *Is so*] *Is* Ff, Rowe; *Is all* Pope.   *come
from*] Ff; *Come, from* F.

471. *gentle, and not fearful*] Of
high birth and not a coward. This
passage has sometimes been otherwise
interpreted, and sometimes regarded
as deliberately ambiguous because of
the occurrence in the play of both
gentle and *fearful*, meaning almost the
opposite of what they mean here.
Thus, when Miranda accuses her
father of speaking "ungently", she
means, of course, "roughly". In v. i.
106, "fearful" means "terrible, fear-
inspiring". The emphasis laid in this
play upon the virtue of the high-born
makes it exceedingly unlikely that
Miranda means to say that Ferdinand
is inoffensive and harmless; indeed,
her remark follows his attempt to
draw his sword. Cf. the significant
punning on "Jew" and "gentle" in
Mer.V., I. iii. 172; II. vi. 52; IV. i. 34.
472. *My foot my tutor?*] Shall an
inferior object exercise authority over
me? An example of the commonplace
analogue between the physical and
social bodies—each observing "de-

gree". Cf. *Cor.*, I. i. 99 ff, and *Tim.*, I.
i. 94, "The foot above the head".
Brinsley Nicholson indicated a parallel
in the Homily Against Disobedience
and Wilful Rebellion: "What a peri-
lous thing were it to commit unto the
Subjects the judgment which Prince
is wise and godly . . . and which is
otherwise; as though the foot must
judge of the head." Shakespeare must
have known this Homily, and a strong
case has been made for his exceptional
interest in it, together with related
Homilies (A. Hart, *Shakespeare and the
Homilies*, 1934, pp. 9–76). J. C. Maxwell communicates a further parallel
from *The Batchelars Banquet*, ed. F. P.
Wilson, pp. 92–3. The general idea is
common enough. See the readings of
Q2 and Q3 in *Lr.*, IV. ii. 28—"My
foot usurps my head."
474. *come from thy ward*] Don't stand
there threatening me with your useless sword—lit. "drawn in a posture of
defence".
475. *stick*] The "staff" of v. i. 54.

Thou think'st there is no more such shapes as he,
Having seen but him and Caliban: foolish wench!
To th' most of men this is a Caliban,
And they to him are angels.

Mir.   My affections
Are then most humble; I have no ambition   485
To see a goodlier man.

Pros.   Come on; obey:
Thy nerves are in their infancy again,
And have no vigour in them.

Fer.   So they are:
My spirits, as in a dream, are all bound up.
My father's loss, the weakness which I feel,   490
The wrack of all my friends, nor this man's threats,
To whom I am subdued, are but light to me,
Might I but through my prison once a day
Behold this maid: all corners else o' th' earth
Let liberty make use of; space enough   495
Have I in such a prison.

Pros.   [*Aside*] It works. [*To Fer.*] Come on.
[*To Ariel*] Thou hast done well, fine Ariel! Follow me;
Hark what thou else shalt do me.

Mir.   Be of comfort;
My father's of a better nature, sir,
Than he appears by speech: this is unwonted   500

481. is] *are* Rowe.   491. nor] *and* Dryden, Rowe; *or* Capell; *nay* Keightley conj.
492. are] *were* Theobald, Warburton.   496. Aside] Capell.   To Fer.] Camb.
497. To Ariel] Theobald; To Fer. Camb.   500. by] *by's* Grey conj.

481. *there is*] "When the subject is as yet future and, as it were, unsettled, the third person singular might be regarded as the normal inflection. Such passages are very common, particularly in the case of 'There is', as 'There is no more such masters' (*Cym.*, IV. ii. 371)." Abbott ¶ 335.

483-4. *to*] Compared to; Onions, *s.v.* 7.

487. *nerves*] Sinews. "You are as helpless as a baby".

491. *nor*] Indicates a confusion of (1) "none of these afflictions, nor this man's threats . . . are heavy to me"; and (2) "all these afflictions and this man's threats . . . are but light to me".

494. *corners*] Cf. *John*, V. vii. 116, "Come the three corners of the world in arms" and *Cym.*, III. iv. 39, "all corners of the world". Hence Donne's "At the round earths imagin'd corners . . ." (*Holy Sonnets*, IX. 1).

495. *liberty*] "Those who are free may have all the rest of the world; my prison, with Miranda near, is all the space I need."

500. *by speech*] Grey's conjecture gives the sense.

Which now came from him.

Pros.   Thou shalt be as free
As mountain winds: but then exactly do
All points of my command.

Ari.   To th' syllable.

Pros. Come, follow. Speak not for him.   *Exeunt.*

ACT II

SCENE I.—[*Another part of the Island.*]

Enter ALONSO, SEBASTIAN, ANTONIO, GONZALO,
ADRIAN, FRANCISCO, *and others.*

Gon. Beseech you, sir, be merry; you have cause,
So have we all, of joy; for our escape
Is much beyond our loss. Our hint of woe
Is common; every day, some sailor's wife,
The masters of some merchant, and the merchant,   5
Have just our theme of woe; but for the miracle,
I mean our preservation, few in millions
Can speak like us: then wisely, good sir, weigh
Our sorrow with our comfort.

Alon.   Prithee, peace.

Seb. [*Aside to Ant.*] He receives comfort like cold porridge. 10

ACT II

Scene 1

S.D. Act II ... Island.] Pope; Actus Secundus. Scæna Prima. F.   3. *hint*] *stint*
Warburton.   5. *masters*] *master* Johnson.   10. Aside . . .] N.S.

3. *hint*] Cf. 1. ii. 134 and note.

4. *common*] This Stoic commonplace
is uttered in a slightly different way by
Gertrude in *Ham.*, 1. ii. 72–5.

5. *The masters* etc.] This means
either: the sea-officers employed by
some merchant, and the merchant
himself; or, the owners of some merchant vessel, and the merchant to
whom the cargo is consigned. The
first theory would be stronger if one
accepted Johnson's emendation. The
second means that Shakespeare used
the same word in two quite different
senses in the same line, not as a pun,
but from carelessness. Bulloch's emendation "mariners" for "masters" has

its attractiveness, and is not out of the
question paleographically.

6. *theme of woe*] A curious repetition;
cf. "hint of woe" in l. 3. Steevens may
be right in suggesting that the hypermetrical "of woe" has been slipped in
by the printer in unconscious repetition.

10. *He . . . porridge*] "He" is of course
Alonso. There is a concealed pun on
peace (9); porridge was a kind of broth
and contained "pease". N.S. is clearly
right in marking all the speeches of
Antonio and Sebastian down to and
including 15 as asides. Here Shakespeare "has . . . shown the tendency in
bad men to indulge in scorn and con-

43

Ant. [*Aside to Seb.*] The visitor will not give him o'er so.

Seb. [*Aside to Ant.*] Look, he's winding up the watch of
    his wit; by and by it will strike.

Gon. Sir,—

Seb. [*Aside to Ant.*] One: tell.   15

Gon. When every grief is entertain'd that's offer'd,
    Comes to th' entertainer—

Seb. A dollar.

Gon. Dolour comes to him, indeed: you have spoken
    truer than you purpos'd.   20

Seb. You have taken it wiselier than I meant you should.

Gon. Therefore, my lord,—

Ant. Fie, what a spendthrift is he of his tongue!

Alon. I prithee, spare.

Gon. Well, I have done: but yet,—   25

Seb. He will be talking.

Ant. Which, of he or Adrian, for a good wager, first
    begins to crow?

Seb. The old cock.

Ant. The cockerel.   30

Seb. Done. The wager?

Ant. A laughter.

Seb. A match!

Adr. Though this island seem to be desert,—

---

11. Aside . . .] N.S.   *visitor*] *adviser* Hanmer.   12. Aside . . .] N.S.   15. Aside
. . .] N.S.   *One*] *On* Ff, Rowe.   27. *Which, of he*] Camb.; *Which, of he*, F,
F2, F3; *Which of he*, F4, Rowe; *Which of them, he* Rowe (ed. 3).

temptuous expressions, as a mode of
getting rid of their own uneasy feelings of inferiority to the good, and
also, by making the good ridiculous,
of rendering the transition of others to
wickedness easy. Shakespeare never
puts habitual scorn into the mouths of
other than bad men" (Coleridge,
Shakespearean Criticism, ed. Raysor, I.
135).

11. *The visitor*] Of a parish, who
"comforts" the sick and distressed.
Cf. "comfort" in ll. 10 and 189-91.

13. *strike*] Striking or "repeating"
watches were invented about the year
1510.

15. *One: tell*] He has struck one;
keep count.

18. *A dollar*] An obvious quibble.
Cf. *Meas.*, I. ii. 50 and *Lr.*, II.
iv. 54.

27. *Which, of he*] Perhaps a confusion of "Which of the two, he
or Adrian", and "Which, he or
Adrian".

29. *old cock*] Perhaps with reference
to the proverb "As the olde cocke
crowes, so doeth the chick" (Puttenham, ed. Willcock and Walker,
p. 189).

32. *laughter*] Tilley (L93) cites "He
laughs that wins."

Ant. Ha, ha, ha!   35
Seb. So: you're paid.
Adr. Uninhabitable, and almost inaccessible,—
Seb. Yet,—
Adr. Yet,—
Ant. He could not miss 't.   40
Adr. It must needs be of subtle, tender and delicate
        temperance.
Ant. Temperance was a delicate wench.
Seb. Ay, and a subtle; as he most learnedly deliver'd.
Adr. The air breathes upon us here most sweetly.   45
Seb. As if it had lungs, and rotten ones.
Ant. Or as 'twere perfum'd by a fen.
Gon. Here is everything advantageous to life.
Ant. True; save means to live.
Seb. Of that there 's none, or little.   50
Gon. How lush and lusty the grass looks! how green!
Ant. The ground, indeed, is tawny.
Seb. With an eye of green in 't.

35–6. Ant. *Ha, ha, ha!* Seb. *So: you're paid*] Grant White, N. S. Alexander; Seb. *Ha, ha, ha!* Ant. *So: you're paid* F; Seb. *Ha, ha, ha!—So, you're paid.* Theobald, Camb.; Seb. *Ha, ha, ha!* Ant. *So you've pay'd* Capell.

35–6.] Most edd., since Sebastian lost his wager, give him 36; he has paid Antonio the laugh for which he wagered. This is plausible if *laughter* is a play on the secondary meaning "a sitting of eggs" (*O.E.D.*, N.S.) following the cock and cockerel; or if a "laughter" is also a small coin (but there is no evidence for this). Curiously, this word is also a problem in *Caes.*, I. ii. 72, where it is usually (and unsatisfactorily) read as "laugher". If F arrangement of 35–6 is retained, the reading *you've* for *you'r* makes sense; otherwise it seems most likely that the speech-headings were reversed, either by Crane or the compositor. Antonio characteristically evades payment by claiming that Sebastian already has his laugh. See p. 167.

41–2 *subtle . . . temperance*] cf. *Wint.*, III. i. 1, 2, and Isa. xlvii. 1 (Geneva): "Thou shalt no more be called, Tender and delicate" (Richmond Noble). The *True Declaration* (p. 14) speaks of the "virgin and temperat aire".

43. *Temperance*] A proper name, such as the Puritans gave their women. N.S. compares Chapman's "very indelicate 'Temperance'" in *May Day* (published 1611).

51. *lush*] Luxuriant.

52. *tawny*] Tanned by the sun to a parched brown colour.

53. *eye of green*] Sebastian may mean that the patches of green are very small, or that Gonzalo is himself the "green" spot in the grass. Steevens says *eye* is "a shade of colour", citing Sandys, *Travels*: "cloth of silver tissued with an eye of green". N.S. takes it to mean "spot". The expression "an eye of sturgeon" occurs in both the

Ant. He misses not much.

Seb. No; he doth but mistake the truth totally.　　　　55

Gon. But the rarity of it is,—which is indeed almost
　　　　beyond credit,—

Seb. As many vouch'd rarities are.

Gon. That our garments, being, as they were, drenched
　　　　in the sea, hold, notwithstanding, their freshness　60
　　　　and glosses, being rather new-dyed than stained
　　　　with salt water.

Ant. If but one of his pockets could speak, would it not
　　　　say he lies?

Seb. Ay, or very falsely pocket up his report.　　　　65

Gon. Methinks our garments are now as fresh as when
　　　　we put them on first in Afric, at the marriage of the
　　　　King's fair daughter Claribel to the King of Tunis.

Seb. 'Twas a sweet marriage, and we prosper well in our
　　　　return.　　　　70

Adr. Tunis was never grac'd before with such a paragon
　　　　to their Queen.

Gon. Not since widow Dido's time.

Ant. Widow! a pox o' that! How came that widow in?
　　　　widow Dido!　　　　75

56. *rarity*] F3, F4; *rariety* F, F2.　　　58. *rarities*] F3, F4; *rarieties* F, F2.　　　61.
glosses] *gloss* Dyce, Tannenbaum conj.; *gloss, as* N.S.

True Declaration and in Strachey's
Reportory.

55. *mistake*] A verbal play on
"misses" in the previous line.

59–62. *That our . . . water*] Colin
Still saw this as a hint that the immer-
sion in water of the King's party was
meant to represent a ceremonial
cleansing (*The Timeless Theme*, p. 143).
This has been regarded as over-
imaginative, but it may be right.
A. S. P. Woodhouse raises the question of such symbolism (without referring to this play) in an article on
Comus in the *University of Toronto
Quarterly*, xx (1950), p. 222.

61. *glosses*] Possibly should be singular; Tannenbaum explains as an *es : e*
misprint.

63. *pockets*] The idea seems to be

that Gonzalo's pockets must be stained and muddy, though his outer garments have dried clean. It has been
said that the pocket is named simply
as a mouthpiece for the whole suit of
clothes; and also, which is probably
the truth, though not the whole truth,
that the remark is made for the sake
of Sebastian's punning reply. Shakespeare used the expression "pocket
up" (= conceal or suppress) in *John*,
III. i. 200 and *1 H 4*, III. iii. 183.

72. *to their Queen*] Cf. "We have
Abraham *to* our father" (Luke iii. 8).
To=for; cf. III. iii. 54.

74. *Widow!*] This line begins a
series of apparently trivial allusions to
the theme of Dido and Aeneas which
has never been properly explained; if
they are to be taken at their face

Seb. What if he had said "widower Æneas" too? Good
    Lord, how you take it!

Adr. "Widow Dido" said you? you make me study of
    that: she was of Carthage, not of Tunis.

Gon. This Tunis, sir, was Carthage.   80

Adr. Carthage?

Gon. I assure you, Carthage.

Ant. His word is more than the miraculous harp.

Seb. He hath rais'd the wall, and houses too.

Ant. What impossible matter will he make easy next?   85

Seb. I think he will carry this island home in his pocket,
    and give it his son for an apple.

Ant. And, sowing the kernels of it in the sea, bring forth
    more islands.

Gon. Ay.   90

83-4. Ant. *His . . . harp.* Seb. *He . . . too.*] Seb. *His . . . too.* Camb.   90. Gon.]
Alon. Staunton.   *Ay.*] F (*I.*), Rowe; *Ay?* Capell; *I—* (F *I.*) Johnson.

value one must allow that Lytton
Strachey's strictures on this scene are
perfectly justified. He speaks of "the
dreary puns and interminable con-
spiracies" as an indication of Shakespeare's fatigue. But we must not take
them at their face value. *The Tempest*
is far from being a loosely built play;
and nowhere in Shakespeare, not even
in his less intensive work, is there anything resembling the apparent irrele-
vance of lines 73-97. It is a possible
inference that our frame of reference
is badly adjusted, or incomplete, and
that an understanding of this passage
will modify our image of the whole
play. See note on l. 78.

77. *how you take it!*] The sense is not
at all clear; it may be that Sebastian
takes Antonio to task ironically with,
"Why do you make such a fuss about
Gonzalo's remark?" But this would
be out of keeping with his own echo of
Antonio's comment, viz. "widower
Aeneas". (Luce.)

78. *Widow*] Dido was the widow of
Sychaeus. She was perhaps not often
thought of in this connection; hence,
presumably, the merriment. There is

some punning on Dido and Aeneas in
Middleton's *The Roaring Girl* (1607/8),
III. ii. 69 ff (ed. Bullen) which turns on
Dido—die, do; Aeneas—any ass. Possibly this was a chestnut mirthlessly
recalled in the *ennui* of the moment;
Adrian takes it seriously and induces
Gonzalo to commit another error for
the amusement of Antonio and
Sebastian. *Widow Dido* is apparently a
solecism; the emphatic statement
about the identity of Tunis and Carthage is a mistake at once pointed out;
later (152) there is the slip about
sovereignty. These certainly facilitate
the work of the wicked in "making the
good ridiculous". See *Intro.*, p. xxxviii.

84.] Only the *walls* of Thebes rose
to the music of Amphion's harp, but
Gonzalo, by identifying Carthage
with Tunis, fabricates a whole city.
Cf. Ovid, *Met.*, VI. 178; *Heroides*, XVI.
179. (Luce.)

86-9.] Cf. *Ant.*, V. ii. 91-2; the resemblance is discussed by G. Wilson
Knight in *The Crown of Life* (1947),
p. 215.

90. *Ay.*] "After a pause for deli-
beration, Gonzalo thus affirms his

Ant. Why, in good time.

Gon. Sir, we were talking that our garments seem now as
fresh as when we were at Tunis at the marriage of
your daughter, who is now Queen.

Ant. And the rarest that e'er came there.   95

Seb. Bate, I beseech you, widow Dido.

Ant. O, widow Dido! ay, widow Dido.

Gon. Is not, sir, my doublet as fresh as the first day I
wore it? I mean, in a sort.

Ant. That sort was well fish'd for.   100

Gon. When I wore it at your daughter's marriage?

Alon. You cram these words into mine ears against
The stomach of my sense. Would I had never
Married my daughter there! for, coming thence,
My son is lost, and, in my rate, she too,   105
Who is so far from Italy removed
I ne'er again shall see her. O thou mine heir
Of Naples and of Milan, what strange fish
Hath made his meal on thee?

Fran.   Sir, he may live:

---

98. *sir, my doublet*] *my doublet, Sir* Ff, Rowe.   109. Fran.] Gon. Rann conj.,
N.S. conj.

---

statement that Tunis *was* Carthage"
(Kittredge).

91.] Antonio is ironical; Kittredge
compares the French "à la bonne
heure".

95. Ant.] Tannenbaum suggests
Adrian as the speaker.

96. *Bate . . .*] Surely you should
make an exception of Dido. This sar-
castic remark is usually misunderstood by editors.

99. *in a sort*] Speaking comparatively; with quibble on "chance",
"lot".

100. *That sort was well fish'd for*]
Your qualification, viz. "speaking
comparatively", was a lucky catch
after much angling. Perhaps suggested
by the fisherman's terms "sort" and
"fresh" (Dirrell).

102. *You cram* etc.] You force these
words into my ears, although my

mind has no inclination to hear them;
just as food is sometimes forced into
the mouth of a man who has no
appetite. (Luce.)

105. *rate*] Opinion. See i. ii. 92.

109. *Sir*, etc.] This passage, which
some have thought un-Shakespearian,
is occasionally attributed to Gonzalo,
who has earlier attempted to cheer the
king up. Francisco has only three
words to speak apart from these (iii.
iii. 40), and even these are sometimes
given to Antonio. Both he and Adrian
have caused a good deal of speculation, and are regular features of arguments for a lost version. But lords
appear in couples, and the solution
may well be that they were to take a
larger part in some scene devoted to
commentary—such scenes occur in
practically all Shakespeare's plays,
but not in this one.

I saw him beat the surges under him,   110
And ride upon their backs; he trod the water,
Whose enmity he flung aside, and breasted
The surge most swoln that met him; his bold head
'Bove the contentious waves he kept, and oared
Himself with his good arms in lusty stroke   115
To th' shore, that o'er his wave-worn basis bowed,
As stooping to relieve him: I not doubt
He came alive to land.

Alon.   No, no, he's gone.

Seb. Sir, you may thank yourself for this great loss,
That would not bless our Europe with your
    daughter,   120
But rather loose her to an African;
Where she, at least, is banish'd from your eye,
Who hath cause to wet the grief on 't.

Alon.   Prithee, peace.

Seb. You were kneel'd to, and importun'd otherwise,
By all of us; and the fair soul herself   125
Weigh'd between loathness and obedience, at
Which end o' th' beam should bow. We have lost
    your son,
I fear, for ever: Milan and Naples have
Mo widows in them of this business' making
Than we bring men to comfort them: 130

---

115. *stroke*] strokes F4.   121. *loose*] lose Ff, Rowe.   123. *wet*] whet Rann conj.
126. *at*] as Collier.   127. *should*] she'd Capell.   129. *Mo*] More Rowe.

115. *in lusty stroke*] Cf. the swimming incident in *Caes.*, "We did buffet it,/ With lusty sinews", I. ii. 107–8.

116. *that* etc.] The image is of a cliff "beetling" anxiously over the shore.

121. *loose*] A normal F spelling of *lose*, but with a play on one sense of *loose*. See N.S. *Hamlet*, Intro., lvii–lviii. "Mate her with . . ."

123. *Who . . . on 't*] You who have good cause to weep over this grievous situation.

on 't] On that account.

126. *Weigh'd . . .*] The metaphor is imperfectly realized; the general idea is that Claribel was torn between unwillingness to marry, and a desire to obey her father. The "scale" of obedience came down.

129. *Mo*] The old word for "more in number", whereas "more", which now does duty for both, originally meant greater, more in quantity. (Luce.)

130. *Than we bring men*] Sebastian seems confident of the return of himself and the others of the crew, but doubtful about the rest of the fleet. (Luce.)

The fault's your own.

Alon.   So is the dear'st o' th' loss.

Gon. My lord Sebastian,
     The truth you speak doth lack some gentleness,
     And time to speak it in: you rub the sore,
     When you should bring the plaster.

Seb.   Very well.   135

Ant. And most chirurgeonly.

Gon. It is foul weather in us all, good sir,
     When you are cloudy.

Seb.   Fowl weather?

Ant.   Very foul.

Gon. Had I plantation of this isle, my lord,—

Ant. He'd sow 't with nettle-seed.

Seb.   Or docks, or mallows.   140

Gon. And were the King on 't, what would I do?

Seb. 'Scape being drunk for want of wine.

Gon. I' th' commonwealth I would by contraries
     Execute all things; for no kind of traffic
     Would I admit; no name of magistrate;   145
     Letters should not be known; riches, poverty,
     And use of service, none; contract, succession,
     Bourn, bound of land, tilth, vineyard, none;

---

138. *Fowl*] *Foul* F3, F4.   139. *plantation*] *the plantation* Rowe; *the planting* Hanmer.   148. *Bourn*] Rowe; *Borne* F.

---

131. *dear'st*] *dear* means "what
touches one most nearly", whatever
the particular emotion evoked; cf.
"His dearest need", *R 3*, v. ii. 21,
Ff; "dearest foe", *Ham.*, i. ii. 182.

134. *time*] The suitable time.

135. *Very well*] Such a rejoinder was
a trick of Iago's.

136. *chirurgeonly*] Like a (good)
surgeon.

138. *Fowl weather? Very foul*] There
is some pun here, and the change in
spelling in F (137, *foule*, 138 *Fowle* in
Sebastian's remark) may have the
clue; but no one has explained it, and
the various conjectures are not really
worth repeating.

139. *plantation*] Used by Gonzalo in

the sense of "colonization", and by
Antonio and Sebastian in the sense of
"planting".

143 ff.] This passage is based on
Montaigne's *Des Cannibales*. Montaigne's theme is resumed at l. 155. It
has often been assumed, as I think,
wrongly, that the passage is intended
primarily as an adverse comment on
Montaigne. See, *e.g.*, A. O. Lovejoy,
Essays in the History of Ideas, p. 238 n.
See *Intro.*, p. xxxiv ff and App. C.

143. *contraries*] In a manner the
opposite of what is customary.

147. *succession*] Inheritance of property.

148. *bound of land*] This phrase paraphrases *Bourn*. The line is metrically

No use of metal, corn, or wine, or oil;
No occupation; all men idle, all;   150
And women too, but innocent and pure:
No sovereignty;—

Seb.   Yet he would be King on 't.

Ant. The latter end of his commonwealth forgets the
   beginning.

Gon. All things in common Nature should produce   155
   Without sweat or endeavour: treason, felony,
   Sword, pike, knife, gun, or need of any engine,
   Would I not have; but Nature should bring forth,
   Of it own kind, all foison, all abundance,
   To feed my innocent people.   160

Seb. No marrying 'mong his subjects?

Ant. None, man; all idle; whores and knaves.

Gon. I would with such perfection govern, sir,
   T' excel the Golden Age.

Seb.   'Save his Majesty!

Ant. Long live Gonzalo!

Gon.   And,—do you mark me, sir?   165

Alon. Prithee, no more: thou dost talk nothing to me.

Gon. I do well believe your highness; and did it to minister occasion to these gentlemen, who are of such
   sensible and nimble lungs that they always use to
   laugh at nothing.   170

Ant. 'Twas you we laughed at.

---

152. *Yet*] *And yet* Pope.   159. *it*] *it's* F3; *its* F4.   164. *'Save*] *Save* F2, F4;
God save Walker.   165. *And,—do*] Dyce; *And do* F; *Do* N.S.

---

imperfect. Various attempts have been
made to amend it by the introduction
of "olives", etc.

   tilth] Tillage.

   149. *corn, or wine, or oil*] Here Isaiah
comes to the aid of Montaigne. See
Noble, *Shakespeare's Biblical Knowledge*,
p. 153; *Intro.* p. xxxv.

   150. *No occupation* etc.] "Nulles
occupations qu'oysifves" is vaguely
rendered by Florio, "no occupation
but idle". (Luce.)

   152. *No sovereignty*] See note on 78.
   156. *sweat*] Cf. Gen., iii. 19.

   157. *engine*] Of war.

   159. *it own*] Cf. *Lr.*, I. iv. 236. The
form *its*, adopted by F3 and F4, was in
use in Shakespeare's time, but the
regular genitive of "it" was "his", and
often the earlier genitive "it" was
used also. See Abbott ¶ 228.

   foison] Abundance; the paraphrase
is immediately supplied. Cf. IV. i. 110.

   164. *'Save*] God save. Perhaps omitted in deference to the statute for re-
straining oaths (see note on p. 168).

   169. *sensible*] Sensitive. Cf. *Meas.*,
III. i. 120.

Gon. Who in this kind of merry fooling am nothing to
    you: so you may continue, and laugh at nothing
    still.

Ant. What a blow was there given!   175

Seb. An it had not fallen flat-long.

Gon. You are gentlemen of brave mettle; you would lift
    the moon out of her sphere, if she would continue
    in it five weeks without changing.

Enter ARIEL [*invisible*] *playing solemn music.*

Seb. We would so, and then go a bat-fowling.   180

Ant. Nay, good my lord, be not angry.

Gon. No, I warrant you; I will not adventure my discre-
    tion so weakly. Will you laugh me asleep, for I am
    very heavy?

Ant. Go sleep, and hear us.   185
             [*All sleep except Alon., Seb., and Ant.*]

---

176. *An*] Pope; *And* F.   177. *of brave*] *of a brave* F3, F4, Rowe.   179. S.D.
Enter . . . music.] Malone; Enter Ariell playing solemne Musicke. F.
185. S.D. All . . . Ant.] Camb.

---

176. *An*] F reading is *And*, as often.
The meaning, of course, is "if", and
sometimes "if" follows "and" or "an"
in this sense.

flat-long] With the flat, not the edge.
Furness, *Variorum*, quotes from Sidney:
"The pitilesse sworde had such pittie
. . . that at first it did but hit flatlong".

178. *sphere*] The moon's sphere was
the nearest of the concentric zones
occupied by the orbits of the seven
planets which, in the Ptolemaic astro-
nomy, revolved round the earth. The
gist of Gonzalo's repartee is obvious—
"If you could get at the moon you
would remove it from its orbit." But
the force of the "five weeks without
changing" is not evident. He may be
alluding to the proverb "When the
moon's in the full then wit's in the
wane" (Denham, *Proverbs*, Percy
Society, xxv. 4) meaning that, if the
moon would stay at the full for a pro-
tracted period, they would not lack
the irreverence to take it for their own

frivolous purposes—with the secondary meaning, that their scanty wit
would be so attenuated by the phenomenon that it would not avail to prevent this misdeed. For "sphere" cf.
M.N.D., II. i. 7, II. i. 153; and *Wint.*,
I. ii. 48.

180. *bat-fowling*] With the moon for
a lantern. Bat-fowling = bird-catching with a light. The birds fly at the
light and are struck down with bats or
clubs. See Fielding, *Joseph Andrews*,
Cap. X. *O.E.D.* records a secondary
meaning for "bat-fowling", of which
Sebastian is probably conscious:
"gulling a simpleton".

182–3. *adventure my discretion*] Risk
my reputation for good sense by conduct so weak.

185. *Go sleep*] Compose yourself for
sleep, and we will do our part by
laughing. Keightley's conjecture—*us
not*—is unnecessary. N.S. suspects a
punning connection between "laugh
. . . asleep" and "luff asleep", a

Alon. What, all so soon asleep! I wish mine eyes
 Would, with themselves, shut up my thoughts: I find
 They are inclin'd to do so.
Seb.   Please you, sir,
 Do not omit the heavy offer of it:
 It seldom visits sorrow; when it doth,   190
 It is a comforter.
Ant.   We two, my lord,
 Will guard your person while you take your rest,
 And watch your safety.
Alon.   Thank you.—Wondrous heavy.
         [*Alonso sleeps. Exit Ariel.*]
Seb. What a strange drowsiness possesses them!
Ant. It is the quality o' th' climate.
Seb.   Why   195
 Doth it not then our eyelids sink? I find not
 Myself dispos'd to sleep.
Ant.   Nor I; my spirits are nimble.
 They fell together all, as by consent;
 They dropp'd, as by a thunder-stroke. What might,
 Worthy Sebastian?—O, what might?—No more:—
 And yet methinks I see it in thy face,   201
 What thou shouldst be: th' occasion speaks thee; and

187–8. *Would . . . find | They*] *Would . . . thoughts | I find* F.   190–1. *It seldom . . .
comforter*] one line in F.   193. S.D. Alonso sleeps] Capell.   Exit Ariel]
Malone.   198. *consent;*] Camb.; *consent* F.

nautical term which = "to draw into
the wind, so that the ship stops";
"heavy" would then mean "sluggish",
and is still used of a ship which is slow
to answer the helm.

187–93.] F mislineation is here explained by the compositor's lack of
space at the foot of p. 7. He had no
room to turn over *find* at the end of
the long l. 187, and his last line is
190, so that to get in what was for him
the next line (*It is a comforter.*) he had
to tack it on to l. 190. See p. 168.

189. *omit*] Neglect. See I. ii. 183; the
grave, solemn movement of these
lines comes as a shock; it introduces
the muted but sinister dialogue which
follows. See note on I. ii. 185.

202. *th' occasion speaks thee*] Speaks to
thee; calls upon you to embrace the
opportunity. Cf. I. ii. 37. "The scene
of the intended assassination of Alonzo
and Gonzalo is an exact counterpart
of the scene between Macbeth and his
lady, only pitched in a lower key
throughout, as designed to be frus-
trated and concealed, and exhibiting
the same profound management in
the manner of familiarizing a mind,
not immediately recipient, to the suggestion of guilt, by associating the
proposed crime with something ludi-
crous or out of place,—something not
habitually matter of reverence" (Coleridge, *ed. cit.*, I. 135–6). For the reminiscences of *Mac.*, I. iii, see also

My strong imagination sees a crown
Dropping upon thy head.

Seb.   What, art thou waking?

Ant. Do you not hear me speak?

Seb.   I do; and surely   205
It is a sleepy language, and thou speak'st
Out of thy sleep. What is it thou didst say?
This is a strange repose, to be asleep
With eyes wide open; standing, speaking, moving,
And yet so fast asleep.

Ant.   Noble Sebastian,   210
Thou let'st thy fortune sleep—die, rather; wink'st
Whiles thou art waking.

Seb.   Thou dost snore distinctly;
There's meaning in thy snores.

Ant. I am more serious than my custom: you
Must be so too, if heed me; which to do   215
Trebles thee o'er.

Seb.   Well, I am standing water.

Ant. I 'll teach you how to flow.

Seb.   Do so: to ebb
Hereditary sloth instructs me.

Ant.   O,

---

203. *crown*] *Crowne* F. 215. *if heed*] *if you heed* Rowe. 216. *Trebles thee o'er*]
Trebbles thee o'er F; *Troubles thee o'er* Rowe, Pope, N.S.

G. Wilson Knight, *The Crown of Life*,
p. 213.

203–4. *a crown | Dropping*] Cf. v. i.
202.

210. *Noble*] A singularly intense
irony.

211. *wink'st*] "keep'st thine eyes
shut".

212. *distinctly*] Something as in i.
ii. 200. "With separate and articulate
sounds"; but clearly paraphrased
by the remainder of the speech.
(Luce.)

216. *standing water*] Neither ebbing
nor flowing. A reference, perhaps, to
the proverb *Vitium capiunt, ni moveantur
aqua*; "L'eau dormant vaut pis que
l'eau courant".

217. *to ebb*] To neglect the offer of
fortune. Cf. *Ant.*, I. iv. 42.

218. *Hereditary sloth*] (1) Natural
laziness; (2) the fault of having been
born younger than my brother
Alonso, which has limited my freedom
of action and forced me to be retiring.
Antonio's reply dwells on the implications of (2), and ends with a reproach
aimed at the indolence confessed in
(1).

218–19. *O, If you . . .*] This extravagance of Antonio's must mean: in
describing your situation you have
suggested the remedy for it, which is
to remove the hereditary impediment
to your greatness (not sloth, but
Alonso).

If you but knew how you the purpose cherish
Whiles thus you mock it! how, in stripping it,   220
You more invest it! Ebbing men, indeed,
Most often do so near the bottom run
By their own fear or sloth.

Seb.   Prithee, say on:
The setting of thine eye and cheek proclaim
A matter from thee; and a birth, indeed,   225
Which throes thee much to yield.

Ant.   Thus, sir:
Although this lord of weak remembrance, this,
Who shall be of as little memory
When he is earth'd, hath here almost persuaded,—
For he's a spirit of persuasion, only   230
Professes to persuade,—the King his son's alive,
'Tis as impossible that he's undrown'd
As he that sleeps here swims.

Seb.   I have no hope
That he's undrown'd.

Ant.   O, out of that "no hope"
What great hope have you! no hope that way is   235
Another way so high a hope, that even
Ambition cannot pierce a wink beyond,
But doubt discovery there. Will you grant with me

236. *a hope*] *an hope* Rowe, N.S.   238. *doubt*] *doubts* Capell; *douts* Nicholson conj.,
N.S.

224. *setting*] Fixed look; cf. III. ii. 8,
and *Wint.*, v. iii. 67.

proclaim] Here a plural by attrac-
tion to "eye and cheek".

226. *throes thee*] Costs thee great pain
to utter.

227. *of weak remembrance*] "Of failing
memory"; selected not so much as a
figure for the dotage of age, as to pair
with "of as little memory". (Luce.)

227–31. *Although . . . alive*] Johnson
and others failed to understand this
passage. "Although this lord with the
bad memory [cf. l. 153] (who will himself be forgotten as soon as buried) has
almost persuaded—he's a persuasive
sort of person, in fact it's his sole job

to persuade—the King his son's
alive". Obviously it refers to Gonzalo,
and it is over-curious to protest that
Francisco makes the effort of which
Antonio complains, especially as
Alonso showed clear signs of having
heard the consoling words before.

229. *earth'd*] Laid in his grave.

235. *that way*] In regard to Ferdinand's being "undrown'd".

237. *a wink*] A glimpse.

238. *But doubt discovery there*] The
reading *douts*, supported by Furness
and adopted by N.S., is attractive.
"Even Ambition cannot look beyond
a crown, but there *puts out* her torch of
discovery." But it still means the same

That Ferdinand is drown'd?

Seb.   He's gone.

Ant.   Then tell me,
Who's the next heir of Naples?

Seb.   Claribel.   240

Ant. She that is Queen of Tunis; she that dwells
Ten leagues beyond man's life; she that from Naples
Can have no note, unless the sun were post,—
The man i' th' moon's too slow,—till new-born chins
Be rough and razorable; she that from whom   245
We all were sea-swallow'd, though some cast again,
And that by destiny, to perform an act
Whereof what's past is prologue; what to come,
In yours and my discharge.

Seb.   What stuff is this! how say you?
'Tis true, my brother's daughter 's Queen of Tunis; 250
So is she heir of Naples; 'twixt which regions
There is some space.

Ant.   A space whose ev'ry cubit

---

245. *she that from whom*] *she for whom* Pope.   246. *all were*] *were all* Steevens;
were Pope.   *cast*] *cast up* Keightley.   247. *And that by destiny*] Johnson; (*And
by that destiny*) F.   248. *is*] in F3, F4.   249. *In*] *Is* Pope; *'S in* Daniel conj.

---

thing, though it gives the idea figurative expression. Ambition cannot set its eye on a higher object (than the crown), and even there must have difficulty in discerning the goal. A pun is possible.

242. *beyond man's life*] = roughly, "it would take a lifetime to get there." The elaborate hyperbole of Antonio's language exhibits great rhetorical energy; here is the actor as orator, persuading, using the subtle devices of rhetoric. "Hyperbole" Puttenham paraphrases as "by incredible comparisons giving credit".

243. *no note*] No communication.
post] Messenger.

245. *she that*] Probably suggested by the same words in ll. 241 and 242; *that* appears redundant because the construction is not analogous to that

of the preceding phrases. *From* has the force of a verb of motion. *She that* might be paraphrased "this Claribel"; or the whole phrase as "the very person in coming from whom we, etc.".

246. *cast*] Thrown on shore. Cf. *Per.*, II. i. 56. This word introduces a series of theatrical puns: *perform, act, prologue, discharge* (= the acting of a part).

247. Strange as the use of brackets in F may be, I think *And . . . destiny* is intended as a parenthesis: "What has happened so far has been fated; the next step we may take as free agents". Compositor B is known to have transposed words, as here.

249. *What stuff . . .*] Sebastian gives the gist of Antonio's speech completely stripped of hyperbole.

Seems to cry out, "How shall that Claribel
Measure us back to Naples? Keep in Tunis,
And let Sebastian wake." Say, this were death   255
That now hath seiz'd them; why, they were no
          worse
Than now they are. There be that can rule Naples
As well as he that sleeps; lords that can prate
As amply and unnecessarily
As this Gonzalo; I myself could make   260
A chough of as deep chat. O, that you bore
The mind that I do! what a sleep were this
For your advancement! Do you understand me?
Seb. Methinks I do.
Ant.   And how does your content
Tender your own good fortune?
Seb.   I remember   265
You did supplant your brother Prospero.
Ant.   True:
And look how well my garments sit upon me;
Much feater than before: my brother's servants
Were then my fellows; now they are my men.
Seb. But for your conscience.   270
Ant. Ay, sir; where lies that? if 'twere a kibe,
'Twould put me to my slipper: but I feel not

---

253. *that*] *thou* Hanmer.   254. *to*] *by* Ff.   *Keep*] *Sleep* Johnson conj.

254. *us*] The cubits. The ancient
measure was of 18–22 inches.

Keep] Addressed to Claribel.

261. *A chough . . .*] I could teach a
chough to talk as he does. Or, I could
prate as well myself. Cf. *All's W.*, IV. i.
22, and p. 168.

265. *Tender*] Probably (1) esteem,
care for; (2) comply with. Cf. *Ham.*,
I. iii. 107 ff. The question is "How do
you like your good fortune?" (expect-
ing the answer "Very much"), and
"Will you acquiesce in this good fortune?" (*i.e.* "Take your chance").
See *O.E.D. s.v.*

267.] This use of the garment-

figure (reiterated later) recalls *Macbeth.* See Spurgeon, *Shakespeare's Imagery*, pp. 325–7, and Knight, *Crown of
Life*, p. 218.

268. *feater*] More gracefully, neatly.
Cf. I. ii. 381.

270. *But for your conscience*] Sebastian tersely answers the implied "I'm
better off than before." Editions
show unnecessary wrestlings with this,
and there are many attempts to re-
punctuate.

271. *kibe*] If it were a sore on my
heel it would compel me to wear a
slipper. (It isn't even as troublesome
as that.) Cf. *Lr.*, I. v. 9.

This deity in my bosom: twenty consciences,
That stand 'twixt me and Milan, candied be they,
And melt, ere they molest! Here lies your brother,   275
No better than the earth he lies upon,
If he were that which now he 's like, that 's dead;
Whom I, with this obedient steel, three inches of it,
Can lay to bed for ever; whiles you, doing thus,
To the perpetual wink for aye might put   280
This ancient morsel, this Sir Prudence, who
Should not upbraid our course. For all the rest,
They 'll take suggestion as a cat laps milk;
They 'll tell the clock to any business that
We say befits the hour.

Seb.   Thy case, dear friend,   285
Shall be my precedent; as thou·got'st Milan,
I 'll come by Naples. Draw thy sword: one stroke
Shall free thee from the tribute which thou payest;

---

274. *candied*] *discandy'd* Upton.   274–5. *be they, | And melt, ere they molest*] *were they, | Wou'd melt ere they molested* Hanmer.   275. *And melt*] *Would melt* Johnson conj.; *Or melt* Johnson conj.   279. *whiles*] omitted Pope.

273. *consciences*] Perhaps a dissyllable. Cf. *princess*, I. ii. 173.

274. *candied*] So powerful is the "dog-licking-candy" group of images for flattery etc. in Shakespeare (as Whiter pointed out, and as Dr Spurgeon made well-known) that it is a little surprising to find the word here in apparent isolation from associated ideas. But we may recall that the passage has many conscious or unconscious reminiscences. The situation Antonio has just described hints at fawning and flattery; 271–2 strongly recalls *Ham.*, v. i. 153, with its social implications, and the famous dog-candy group appears in that play (III. ii. 65). *Candied* (*pace* N.S.) almost certainly means "sugared" rather than "frozen" (though the latter is of course possible—cf. *Tim.*, IV. iii. 225) because it does faintly suggest the context of its usual image-group, and is followed by the normal *melt*. Anyway "frozen" somewhat enfeebles the idea.

277. *that's dead*] "If he were that

which now he's like" repeats the thought of ll. 255–6, "Say this were death, etc."

280. *wink*] This word occurs three times in the scene; see ll. 211, 237. Here "sleep" in the sinister sense of *Wint.*, I. ii. 317, "To give mine enemy a lasting wink".

281. *morsel*] Cf. *John*, IV. iii. 143, "This morsel of dead royalty".

283. *They'll take suggestion*] "They will listen to our evil promptings as eagerly as a cat laps milk." (The prevailing sense of "suggestion" at this period.—Onions.)

284. *They'll tell the clock*] The former thought expressed by a different metaphor. "Pretend that whatever we propose is opportune." From this and l. 15 one might infer some proverbial expression for sycophancy, couched in these terms; it does not seem to have survived. Cf. *All's W.*, I. ii. 38–40—"his honour, | Clock to itself, knew the true minute when | Exception bid him speak."

And I the King shall love thee.

Ant.   Draw together;
And when I rear my hand, do you the like,   290
To fall it on Gonzalo.

Seb.   O, but one word. [*They talk apart.*]

[*Re-*]*enter* ARIEL [*invisible*], *with music and song.*

Ari. My master through his Art foresees the danger
That you, his friend, are in; and sends me forth,—
For else his project dies,—to keep them living.

Sings in Gonzalo's ear.

> *While you here do snoring lie,*   295
> *Open-ey'd conspiracy*
>   *His time doth take.*
> *If of life you keep a care,*
> *Shake off slumber, and beware:*
>   *Awake, Awake!*   300

Ant. Then let us both be sudden.

Gon. [*Waking*]   Now, good angels
Preserve the King!   [*The others wake.*]

Alon. Why, how now? ho; awake?—Why are you drawn?

---

291. They talk apart.] Capell.   S.D. invisible] Capell.   293. *you, his
friend*] *these, his friends* Johnson conj.: *you, his friends* Grant White.   294. *them*]
you Hanmer; *thee* Halliwell.   301-4.] See note.   301. waking] N.S.
302. The others wake] Camb.; They wake Rowe.

---

291. *O, but one word*] "Just a
moment; one more thing".

293-4. *you . . . them*] There is some
confusion here; Ariel begins by apos-
trophizing the sleeping Gonzalo, and
then addresses the audience. But it is
scarcely worth much argument, as the
whole speech is for the benefit of the
audience—Ariel does not, presumably, wish to inform Gonzalo of Prospero's project. He explains why he has
come, and then wakes Gonzalo by
singing.

294. *project*] See v. i. 1 and note.

296. *Open-ey'd*] By contrast with
you, who are asleep.

301-4.] The rearrangement of this
passage suggested by Staunton and

improved by Dyce has won much support—(beginning l. 301):

Gon. (waking) Now, good angels /
Preserve the king! (*To Seb. and Ant.*)
Why, how now! (*To Alon.*) Ho,
awake! / [Some give this next speech
to *Alonso*]—(*To Seb. and Ant.*) Why
are you drawn? wherefore this ghastly
looking? / *Alon. (waking)* What's the
matter? /

This is attractive, but if we take it that
Gonzalo is rousing the King as he
speaks (301-2) there is no need to
change F. Alonso is surprised to find
everybody awake; and Gonzalo's
next speech is a very reasonable
"What's happened?" in support of
the King's inquiry.

Wherefore this ghastly looking?

Gon.   What's the matter?

Seb. Whiles we stood here securing your repose,   305
Even now, we heard a hollow burst of bellowing
Like bulls, or rather lions: did 't not wake you?
It struck mine ear most terribly.

Alon.   I heard nothing.

Ant. O, 'twas a din to fright a monster's ear,
To make an earthquake! sure, it was the roar   310
Of a whole herd of lions.

Alon.   Heard you this, Gonzalo?

Gon. Upon mine honour, sir, I heard a humming,
And that a strange one too, which did awake me:
I shak'd you, sir, and cried: as mine eyes open'd,
I saw their weapons drawn:—there was a noise,   315
That's verily. 'Tis best we stand upon our guard,
Or that we quit this place: let 's draw our weapons.

Alon. Lead off this ground; and let 's make further search
For my poor son.

Gon.   Heavens keep him from these beasts!
For he is, sure, i' th' island.

Alon.   Lead away.   320

Ari. Prospero my lord shall know what I have done:
So, King, go safely on to seek thy son.   *Exeunt.*

311. *Gonzalo*] omitted Pope.   316. *verily*] *verity* Pope.   *'Tis best we*] *Best we*
Steevens.   *upon our*] *on* Pope.

306–11.] Possibly in allusion to the
many accounts of terrifying noises on
unexplored islands, from Hanno up to
date.

306–7. *hollow . . . lions*] Cf. Psalm
xxii. 12–13, ". . . bulls of Basan close

me in . . . as it were a ramping and a
roaring lion."

312. *a humming*] Ariel's song. Cf.
"Will hum about mine ears" (III. ii.
136).

319. *Heavens*] As in I. ii. 175.

SCENE II.—[*Another part of the Island*].

Enter CALIBAN *with a burthen of wood. A noise of thunder heard.*

Cal. All the infections that the sun sucks up
        From bogs, fens, flats, on Prosper fall, and make him
        By inch-meal a disease! his spirits hear me,
        And yet I needs must curse. But they'll nor pinch,
        Fright me with urchin-shows, pitch me i' th' mire,   5
        Nor lead me, like a firebrand, in the dark
        Out of my way, unless he bid 'em: but
        For every trifle are they set upon me;
        Sometime like apes, that mow and chatter at me,
        And after bite me; then like hedgehogs, which   10
        Lie tumbling in my barefoot way, and mount
        Their pricks at my footfall; sometime am I
        All wound with adders, who with cloven tongues
        Do hiss me into madness.

Enter TRINCULO.

                Lo, now, lo!
        Here comes a spirit of his, and to torment me   15

Scene II

S.D. Another . . . Island] Camb.   4. *nor*] not F3, F4, Rowe.   9. *Sometime*]
Sometimes Theobald.   15. *and*] *now* Pope; *sent* Camb. conj.

It does not appear to have been observed that the main comic device of this scene seems to originate in Suetonius, *Divi Augusti Vita*, XC.

1.] Cf. *Cor.*, I. iv. 30.

3. *By inch-meal*] Cf. *Cym.*, V. v. 52. Inch by inch.

5. *urchin-shows*] Cf. Scot, *The Discovery of Witchcraft* (ed. Summers), VII. xv. 86: ". . . and they have so fraied with bull beggers, spirits, witches, urchens, elves, hags, fairies, satyrs, pans, faunes, sylens. . ." And *Comus*, l. 845.

6. *firebrand*] So Puck in *MND* would "mislead night-wanderers, laughing at their harm" (II. i. 49). This is presumably Ariel in a fairy capacity as will-o'-the-wisp. Fletcher uses the idea in *Faithful Shepherdess*; and cf. *Comus*, l. 845.

9. *mow*] moe F. Used as a verb in IV. i. 47. Here it means "make grimaces".

10–11. *hedgehogs . . . tumbling*] Douce quotes from S. Harsnet's *Declaration of Popish Impostures* (1603), which Shakespeare is known to have used in *Lear*, these words about girls possessed by demons: "They make anticke faces, girn, mow and mop like an ape, tumble like a hedge-hogge . . ." (See also l. 9.)

11. *my barefoot way*] *i.e.* the way along which I tread barefooted.

13. *wound*] Twined about with.

15. *and*] And that to; emphatic use Abbott ¶ 96.

For bringing wood in slowly. I'll fall flat;
Perchance he will not mind me.

Trin. Here's neither bush nor shrub, to bear off any
weather at all, and another storm brewing; I hear
it sing i' th' wind: yond same black cloud, yond   20
huge one, looks like a foul bombard that would
shed his liquor. If it should thunder as it did before,
I know not where to hide my head: yond same
cloud cannot choose but fall by pailfuls. What have
we here? a man or a fish? dead or alive? A fish: he   25
smells like a fish; a very ancient and fish-like smell;
a kind of, not of the newest Poor-John. A strange
fish! Were I in England now, as once I was, and
had but this fish painted, not a holiday fool there
but would give a piece of silver: there would this   30
monster make a man; any strange beast there
makes a man: when they will not give a doit to relieve a lame beggar, they will lay out ten to see a
dead Indian. Legg'd like a man! and his fins like

21. *foul*] *full* Upton.

17. *mind*] Notice.

18. *bear off*] Ward off.

21. *foul*] The bombard is "foul" because it contains bad weather. Cf. II. i.
136–7; *John*, IV. ii. 108.

bombard] Originally a siege-engine;
then a large leathern vessel to carry
liquor, possibly because of some resemblance to the former.

27. *kind of,*] The comma, which is in
F, signifies a pause during which Trinculo searches his mind for an apt
comparison.

Poor-John] Dried hake.

27–8. *A strange . . . now*] Malone
quotes a licence granted by the Master of the Revels, "To shew a strange
fish for half a year, the 3rd of Sept.
1632." This does not make Caliban a
fish. See note on l. 34.

29. *painted*] On a board hung outside some booth at a fair.

31. *monster make a man*] A pun. The
secondary sense is "make a man's fortune".

32. *doit*] Small coin; cf. *Ant.*, IV. xii.
37.

34. *dead Indian*] Many Indians were
brought to England after Frobisher's
in 1576. Such exhibitions were profitable investments, and were a regular
feature of colonial policy under James
I. The exhibits rarely survived the experience, but it is an indication of the
excitement they caused that Montaigne went out of his way to converse
with some who visited France. As
Indians became familiar they tended
to replace the traditional wild man in
pageants and masques; a further link
between the Indian and Nature.

Legg'd like a man . . .] Trinculo soon
discovers that Caliban is not a fish; he
smelt like one, and perhaps, hidden by
the gaberdine, looked like one. Although he is occasionally called a fish
(*e.g.* v. i. 266), this is largely because
of his oddity, and there should be no
fishiness about his appearance. He
might even be costumed as a conven-

arms! Warm o' my troth! I do now let loose my   35
opinion, hold it no longer: this is no fish, but an
islander, that hath lately suffered by a thunderbolt.
[*Thunder.*] Alas, the storm is come again! my best
way is to creep under his gaberdine; there is no
other shelter hereabout: misery acquaints a man   40
with strange bed-fellows. I will here shroud till the
dregs of the storm be past.

Enter STEPHANO, *singing:* [*a bottle in his hand*].

Ste.   *I shall no more to sea, to sea,*
                  Here shall I die ashore,—

This is a very scurvy tune to sing at a man's funeral;   45
well, here's my comfort.   *Drinks.*
Sings.

          The master, the swabber, the boatswain, and I,
                  The gunner, and his mate,
          Lov'd Mall, Meg, and Marian, and Margery,
                  But none of us car'd for Kate: 50
                  For she had a tongue with a tang,
                  Would cry to a sailor, Go hang!
          She lov'd not the savour of tar nor of pitch;
          Yet a tailor might scratch her where'er she did itch.
                  Then to sea, boys, and let her go hang!   55

This is a scurvy tune too: but here's my comfort.

                                        Drinks.

---

38. Thunder] Capell.   42. S.D. a bottle in his hand] Capell.   49. and
Marian] Marian Pope.

tional salvage man. Malone says that
Caliban's dress ,"which doubtless was
originally prescribed by the poet himself and has been continued, I believe,
since his time, is a large bear skin, or
the skin of some other animal; and he
is usually represented with long
shaggy hair" (*Variorum*, xv. 13).

37. *suffered*] (death). Cf. l. 109.
39. *gaberdine*] Cloak.
42. *dregs*] Cf. the "bombard", l. 21.
43-4.] There is a theory that

Shakespeare is here, and in ll. 47-55,
recording or adapting some actual
shanty. This is, on the whole, improbable, as the lines have not the marks of
the working-song. The second song is
also too sophisticated.

45. *at a man's funeral*] His own, or
Trinculo's. These lines appear, for
reasons of space-losing, as verse in F.

47. *the swabber*] Whose task "is to
wash and keepe cleane the ship".
(Smith, *Sea Grammar*, p. 31).

Cal. Do not torment me:—O!

Ste. What's the matter? Have we devils here? Do you
put tricks upon 's with salvages and men of Ind, ha?
I have not scap'd drowning, to be afeard now of   60
your four legs; for it hath been said, As proper a
man as ever went on four legs cannot make him give
ground; and it shall be said so again, while Stephano
breathes at' nostrils.

Cal. The spirit torments me:—O!   65

Ste. This is some monster of the isle with four legs, who
hath got, as I take it, an ague. Where the devil
should he learn our language? I will give him some
relief, if it be but for that. If I can recover him, and
keep him tame, and get to Naples with him, he's a   70
present for any emperor that ever trod on neat's-
leather.

Cal. Do not torment me, prithee; I'll bring my wood
home faster.

Ste. He's in his fit now, and does not talk after the   75
wisest. He shall taste of my bottle: if he have never
drunk wine afore, it will go near to remove his fit.
If I can recover him, and keep him tame, I will not
take too much for him; he shall pay for him that
hath him and that soundly.   80

59. *salvages*] *savages* Johnson.   60. *afeard*] *afraid* F4, Rowe.   64. *at' nostrils*]
at nostrils Ff; *at his nostrils* Rowe; *at's nostrils* Grant White.

58–9. *Do you put tricks upon 's, etc.*]
"Trick" may here be a conjuror's or
showman's device, cf. IV. i. 37.

59. *tricks*] Tilley (T521) cites "Do
not put tricks on travellers."

salvages] "Salvage" is a spelling
Shakespeare used only in this play;
even when the word "savage" is used
in an apparently similar sense (as in
LLL., IV. iii. 222 and *H 5*, v. ii. 59) it
is spelled in the ordinary way. For the
significance of the spelling see *Intro.*,
p. xxxix. "Man of Inde" occurs in
Jeremiah, xiii. 23 (Coverdale).

61. *As proper*] Ironically; "As fine
a fellow as ever went on crutches cannot make him yield." Or the pro-

verb—". . . as ever went on two
legs . . ." may have been modified
to suit the monster Stephano sees
before him.

64. *at' nostrils*] Cf. "He foamed . . .
at mouth" (*Caes.*, I. ii. 257); contrac-
tion of "at the". Cf. also "with' King"
I. i. 64.

68. *should he learn*] Where can he
have learned?

69. *recover*] Restore.

71–2. *neat's-leather*] *i.e.* cowhide. Cf.
Caes., I. i. 29, "As proper men as ever
trod upon neat's-leather".

79. *too much, etc.*] Meaning, as the
sequel shows, "I will take as much as
I can get for him."

Cal. Thou dost me yet but little hurt; thou wilt anon, I
know it by thy trembling: now Prosper works upon
thee.

Ste. Come on your ways; open your mouth; here is that
which will give language to you, cat: open your   85
mouth; this will shake your shaking, I can tell you,
and that soundly: you cannot tell who's your friend:
open your chaps again.

Trin. I should know that voice: it should be—but he is
drowned; and these are devils:—O defend me!   90

Ste. Four legs and two voices,—a most delicate monster! His forward voice, now, is to speak well of his
friend; his backward voice is to utter foul speeches
and to detract. If all the wine in my bottle will
recover him, I will help his ague. Come:—Amen!   95
I will pour some in thy other mouth.

Trin. Stephano!

Ste. Doth thy other mouth call me? Mercy, mercy!
This is a devil, and no monster: I will leave him; I
have no long spoon.   100

Trin. Stephano! If thou beest Stephano, touch me, and
speak to me; for I am Trinculo,—be not afeard,—
thy good friend Trinculo.

Ste. If thou beest Trinculo, come forth: I'll pull thee by
the lesser legs: if any be Trinculo's legs, these are   105
they. Thou art very Trinculo indeed! How cam'st
thou to be the siege of this moon-calf? can he vent
Trinculos?

Trin. I took him to be kill'd with a thunder-stroke. But
art thou not drown'd, Stephano? I hope, now, thou   110

89. *be*—] Ff; *be*, F.   92. *well*] omitted Ff.

82. *trembling*] The effect of being
"possessed". Cf. *Err.*, IV. iv. 54. Trinculo is trembling with fear.

85. *cat*] Tilley (A99) cites several
examples of the proverb "Ale (liquor)
will make a cat speak."

95. *help*] Cure. Cf. *Gent.*, IV. ii.
47.

Amen] That's quite enough for that
mouth.

99–100. *I have no long spoon*] Cf. *Err.*,
IV. iii. 64, "Marry, he must have a
long spoon that must eat with the
devil." A very old saying; see Chaucer, *The Squieres Tale*, l. 594.

107. *siege*] Here "excrement"; more
usually "seat", "stool".

moon-calf] Abortion, monstrosity—
formed imperfectly through the influence of the moon.

art not drown'd. Is the storm over-blown? I hid
me under the dead moon-calf's gaberdine for fear of
the storm. And art thou living, Stephano? O
Stephano, two Neapolitans scap'd!

Ste. Prithee, do not turn me about; my stomach is not   115
constant.

Cal. [*Aside.*] These be fine things, an if they be not sprites.
That's a brave god, and bears celestial liquor:
I will kneel to him.

Ste. How didst thou scape? How cam'st thou hither?   120
swear, by this bottle, how thou cam'st hither. I
escap'd upon a butt of sack, which the sailors heaved
o'erboard, by this bottle! which I made of the bark
of a tree with mine own hands, since I was cast
ashore.   125

Cal. I'll swear, upon that bottle, to be thy true subject;
for the liquor is not earthly.

Ste. Here; swear, then, how thou escap'dst.

Trin. Swum ashore, man, like a duck: I can swim like a
duck, I'll be sworn.   130

Ste. Here, kiss the book. Though thou canst swim like
a duck, thou art made like a goose.

Trin. O Stephano, hast any more of this?

Ste. The whole butt, man: my cellar is in a rock by th'
sea-side, where my wine is hid. How now, moon-   135
calf! how does thine ague?

Cal. Hast thou not dropp'd from heaven?

Ste. Out o' the moon, I do assure thee: I was the man
i' th' moon when time was.

Cal. I have seen thee in her, and I do adore thee: 140

117. S.D. Aside] Dyce.   *an if*] Pope; *and if* F.   129. *Swum*] Camb.; *Swom*
F, Ff, Rowe; *Swam* Malone.   140. *I have*] *I've* Dyce.

117. *an if*, etc.] Caliban's brave new
world, unlike Miranda's, can only be
if the people are *not* spirits.

122. *butt of sack*] Mentioned in the
Bermuda narratives.

128. *Here; swear, then*] The whole
line is probably addressed to Trinculo, but various attempts have
been made to distribute it between

Caliban and him.

131. *kiss the book*] Trinculo raises the
bottle to his lips. Tilley (C909) cites
"to kiss the cup".

138. *Out o' the moon*] Other travellers had thus beguiled natives. See
Intro., p. xxxvii.

139. *when time was*] Once upon a
time.

My mistress show'd me thee, and thy dog, and thy
    bush.

Ste. Come, swear to that; kiss the book: I will furnish
    it anon with new contents: swear.

Trin. By this good light, this is a very shallow monster;
    I afeard of him? A very weak monster! The man i' 145
    th' moon! A most poor credulous monster! Well
    drawn, monster, in good sooth!

Cal. I'll show thee every fertile inch o' th' island; and
    I will kiss thy foot: I prithee, be my god.

Trin. By this light, a most perfidious and drunken mon- 150
    ster! when 's god 's asleep, he'll rob his bottle.

Cal. I'll kiss thy foot; I'll swear myself thy subject.

Ste. Come on, then; down, and swear.

Trin. I shall laugh myself to death at this puppy-headed
    monster. A most scurvy monster! I could find in 155
    my heart to beat him,—

Ste. Come, kiss.

Trin. But that the poor monster's in drink. An abomin-
    able monster!

Cal. I'll show thee the best springs; I'll pluck thee berries;
    I'll fish for thee, and get thee wood enough.   161
    A plague upon the tyrant that I serve!
    I'll bear him no more sticks, but follow thee,
    Thou wondrous man.

---

141. *and . . . bush*] *thy dog and bush* Steevens.   143. *contents*] *new contents* Ff.
145. *weak*] *shallow* Ff, Rowe.   148. *island*] *isle* Ff, Rowe.   149. *I will*]
omitted Ritson; *I'll* Dyce.

---

141. *My mistress*] See I. ii. 353 ff.
Cf. *MND.*, v. i. 136.

142–3. *furnish it*] Perhaps both the
moon and the bottle.

146–7. *Well drawn*] A splendid
draught (of wine).

148. *every fertile inch*] Twelve years
earlier he had shown them to Prospero (I. ii. 340). The colonists were
frequently received with this kindness,
though treachery might follow. For
the bearing of this on the theme of
the noble and ignoble savage, see
Intro., p. xxxvi, and see the articles of

Cawley and Lee referred to in the
Intro.

149.] Caliban's readiness to abase
himself to the "new spirits" is in
strong contrast to Miranda's attitude.

161. *I'll fish for thee*] The colonists
were often dependent upon the natives
for the supply of water and fish.
Strachey refers to the inability of his
party to catch fish in quantity. See
p. 172.

164–5. *Thou wondrous man. . . a
wonder*] Language of this sort is significantly associated with Miranda

Trin. A most ridiculous monster, to make a wonder of a 165
  poor drunkard!

Cal. I prithee, let me bring thee where crabs grow;
  And I with my long nails will dig thee pig-nuts;
  Show thee a jay's nest, and instruct thee how
  To snare the nimble marmoset; I'll bring thee   170
  To clustering filberts, and sometimes I'll get thee
  Young scamels from the rock. Wilt thou go with me?

Ste. I prithee now, lead the way, without any more
  talking. Trinculo, the King and all our company
  else being drown'd, we will inherit here: here; bear 175
  my bottle: fellow Trinculo, we'll fill him by and by
  again.

Cal. sings drunkenly

      Farewell, master; farewell, farewell!

Trin. A howling monster; a drunken monster!

---

172. *scamels*] *shamois* Theobald; *sea-mels* Malone; *sea-mells* Steevens, N.S.;
Staniels Theobald conj.; *seamews* Jackson conj., Tannenbaum conj.   173. Ste.]
Cal. Ff.   178. Farewell ... farewell] Rowe; not italicized F.

and Prospero; this assists the irony of
the present scene.

168. *pig-nuts*] Otherwise earth-nuts,
hawk-nuts, etc. *Bunium flexuosum.*

170. *marmoset*] Harcourt names this
little monkey as "good meate" (see
reference below).

172. *scamels*] The weight of opinion
seems to be for *sea-mels*. Although *scamel* is not recorded elsewhere as a
literary word, it appears in Wright's
Dialect Dictionary, where it is described
as a "bar-tailed godwit". *O.E.D.* does
not give much credit to this entry.
W. A. Osborne (*M.L.R.*, xx. 73) says
that the variants *scameler* and *scamler*
are used in N. Ireland and Scotland of
sheldrakes and "even mergansers". It
is known that the travellers preferred
to give to foreign fauna the names of
similar species familiar at home; Harcourt does this in a list of wildfowl
which includes the godwit (*A Relation
of a Voyage to Guiana*, 1613. Hakluyt
Soc., ed. 1928, p. 97). Shakespeare

follows this custom, applying a name
perhaps in more general use then to a
foreign bird. *Sea-mell* or *sea-mel* is
plausible paleographically and yields
good sense, especially when supported
as aptly as it is by Bertram Lloyd
(*M.L.R.*, xix. 102). Nevertheless I
have retained *scamels*, since there is a
good chance that it means something.
Sea-mell is, by the way, a variant of
sea-mew, a bird mentioned by Strachey, and regarded as a delicacy. It is
not yet impossible that this tedious
argument will be settled by evidence
that *scamel* is after all a shellfish;
though the context calls to mind Strachey's description of native methods
of bird-catching on the rocks. (See
Appendix A.)

175-6. *bear my bottle*] Presumably
addressed to Trinculo as royal cup-
bearer.

178. *Sings drunkenly*] Sometimes
placed after l. 178; but Caliban must
presumably have sung the line follow-

Cal.			*No more dams I'll make for fish;*					180
				Nor fetch in firing
				At requiring;
			Nor scrape trenchering, nor wash dish:
				'Ban, 'Ban, Cacaliban
			Has a new master:—get a new man.			185

	Freedom, high-day! high-day, freedom! freedom,
	high-day, freedom!

Ste. O brave monster! lead the way.				*Exeunt.*

---

183. trenchering] trencher Pope.

ing to be called "a howling monster".

180. No more dams] See note on
l. 161.

183. *trenchering*] Almost always altered to "trencher" on insufficient
grounds; it means "trenchers" col-
lectively (Onions); cf. "clothing",
"housing".

184. Cacaliban] Possibly indicates
intoxication.

ACT III

SCENE I.—[*Before Prospero's Cell.*]

Enter FERDINAND, *bearing a log.*

Fer. There be some sports are painful, and their labour
    Delight in them sets off: some kinds of baseness
    Are nobly undergone; and most poor matters
    Point to rich ends. This my mean task
    Would be as heavy to me as odious, but   5
    The mistress which I serve quickens what's dead,
    And makes my labours pleasures: O, she is
    Ten times more gentle than her father's crabbed,
    And he's compos'd of harshness. I must remove
    Some thousands of these logs, and pile them up,   10
    Upon a sore injunction: my sweet mistress

ACT III

Scene 1

S.D. ACT III . . . Cell] Theobald; Actus Tertius. Scæna Prima. F.   1. *and*]
but Pope.   2. *sets*] Rowe; *set* F, Ff.

1–2.] In some arduous sports, our
pleasure cancels out our pains. Cf.
Mac., II. iii. 55, "The labour we delight in physics pain." See Abbott
¶ 300, for the indicative use of "be",
and ¶ 244 for the omission of the relative before "are". Another interpretation is "their arduousness increases
our delight in them." There is sufficient similarity, both here and elsewhere, with certain passages in St
Augustine's *Confessions* to make it
probable that Shakespeare is here
alluding to that book. See in particular Book VIII. 7–8. "Yea, the very
pleasures of human life men acquire
by difficulties . . . It is . . . ordered,
that the affianced bride should not at

once be given, lest as a husband he
should hold cheap whom, as betroth-
ed, he sighed not after. [Cf. I. ii. 450–
1] . . . Every where the greater joy is
ushered in by the greater pain . . ."
(translated by Pusey, Everyman edition, pp. 154–5). Steevens cites Horace, *Satires*, II. ii: "Molliter austerum
studio fallente laborem."

6. *which*] Used originally of persons,
as in the Lord's Prayer.

9–13.] Ferdinand explains that he
has to remove and make a pile of the
logs under pain of severe punishment;
Miranda weeps to see him labour in
this way, and says that no such menial
work was ever done by one so noble.

11. *sore*] Severe, harsh; cf. v. i. 288.

Weeps when she sees me work, and says, such baseness
Had never like executor. I forget:
But these sweet thoughts do even refresh my labours,
Most busilest when I do it.

14. *thoughts*] thoughts, F.   15. *busilest*] busie lest, F; *busiliest* Bulloch conj.; *busy, least* Collier, Alexander; *busiest* Spedding conj.; *busy-less* Theobald.   *I do it*] *idlest* Spedding conj.

15. *Most busilest when I do it*] It seems to be generally agreed that Spedding's conjecture (Most busiest when idlest) gives the sense required; whatever the reading accepted, most explanations tend that way, *e.g.* Capell's "I am least engag'd by my business . . . when engag'd by such thinking". My view is that this is not so, and that Spedding's conjecture gives a sense almost opposite to what is required. The arguments in favour of defensible readings may be summarized thus:

(i) The F reading repunctuated and with *lest* modernized as *least*. The assumption is that there is no corruption. P. Simpson (*R.E.S.*, July 1946) treats the comma after *lest* as emphatic, pointing up the antithesis *most . . . least*. Luce's parallel with *MND.*, v. i. 104–5 may be cited in support of this: "Love, therefore, and tongue-tied simplicity, / In least, speak most, to my capacity." C. J. Sisson (*New Readings in Shakespeare*, Cambridge, 1956) also defends F, placing the comma after *busy*; and he argues, correctly I think, that *most busy* is to be taken not with *I* but with *thoughts*. He paraphrases: "I am refreshed in my labours by these sweet thoughts, and I am kept busy and occupied by these thoughts, though I am even more busy with them when I am actually performing my labour." The trouble with *Most busy least*, as with *busiest . . . idlest*, is that it involves Ferdinand in a *non sequitur*: "these thoughts refresh my labours; I am busiest when not labouring"—although he has just been saying that his labour is a pleasure because of these thoughts. Similarly Prof. Sisson, though he

avoids the mistake entailed upon those who take *most busy* with *I*, is forced to interpret *refresh my labours* as "give me refreshment between spells of work", which is not only strained in itself but runs counter to the sense of ll. 1–6; they give him refreshment *while* he works. One doubts also whether the text can support all the meaning he gives it. I do not think the F reading can be justified.

(2) *Most busiest when idlest*, Spedding's conjecture, has recently been supported on grounds both literary and bibliographical by Mr A. S. Cairncross (*Shakespeare Quarterly*, VII (1956), 448–9). Cairncross supposes that one or more letters, "l" or "le", in "idlest", worked loose and dropped out of the compositor's stick, leaving "id est" or "id st" or eventually "id t". Replacing the letters, the compositor inserted them before the "st" of "busiest", giving "busielest when id st". Then he, or the proofreader, divided the first word and emended "id st" to read *I doe it*. (If the proofreader meddled we shall know soon enough.) As literary evidence in support of Spedding, Cairncross refers to the Ciceronian paradox I cited in the previous edition: "Publium Scipionem . . . eum qui primus Africanus appellatus est, dicere solitum scripsit Cato, qui fuit eius fere aequalis, *numquam se minus otiosum esse quam cum otiosus, nec minus solum quam cum solus esse*" (*De Officiis*, III. i). "Cato, who was virtually his contemporary, wrote of that Publius Scipio who was first given the name of Africanus, that he used to say *he was never less idle than when at leisure, and never less lonely than when alone.*"

Tilley cites the line in connexion with the proverb "never less alone than when alone"; he also refers to *Rom.*, III. i. 10 (Q): "I noting his affection by my own, / That most are busy when th'are most alone". Cairncross also alludes to this passage, saying that it "uses one member of each of Cicero's antitheses, with reference to the *affections* of the lover Romeo, escaping to solitude to think, busily, of his lady". So far I agree; but no longer think this has any relevance to the present line. The rest of Mr Cairncross's argument is invalid. "So in *The Tempest*," he says, "Ferdinand, setting to work to carry logs, is *idling* at his work, but very *busy* in his sweet thoughts; so that he is 'Most busiest when idlest'." The error is that of Spedding and Capell; *most busy* is read as referring to *I*, whereas it refers to *thoughts*; and the result is a total misunderstanding of what Ferdinand is saying. He could scarcely have so altered the relation in his mind between *sordid labour* and *that which enables him to delight in it* that a few lines later he should defend his laziness by arguing that it is really less idle to daydream than to work.

The general run of Ferdinand's meditation seems to me to go like this: "Miranda makes my labours pleasures, arduous as they are. I take the pains involved as I might the pleasant exertions of sport, not only because they may have an agreeable end, but also because the thought of her makes them light even as I do them. However, meditating thus I am foolishly forgetting to go on with such pleasant work—foolishly, because I can go on thinking these thoughts even when I am working—in fact that is when they are most active." This is to read l. 14 with a strong emphasis on *labours*; in modern usage we should say "refresh even my labours". The comma after *thoughts* in F contributes, I think, to this interpretation of l. 14.

As for l. 15, "busiest" would do well enough, so far as the sense goes, but "idlest" is the exact opposite of what is required; the thoughts are busiest when Ferdinand is busiest, not when he is idlest. And if, as I think, the copy cannot have read "idlest", there is no point at all in the Ciceronian reference, and the loose-letters-in-the-stick bibliographical explanation collapses also. There was no spare "le" to fit in, so, however the compositor got to *busie lest*, he did not do so by interpolating these letters into "busiest". And it would not be easy to explain how, at any stage of transmission, "busiest" could be so misread. In fact, "busiest" and "idlest" are alike unacceptable.

Now, we must emend; and a proposal which is open to none of the objections stated above is that Shakespeare wrote *busielest* and the compositor, or a copyist, split this into *busie lest*. This reading has the advantage that, as Dr Harold Brooks remarks, it would have been a hard one for anyone dealing with the copy, from the first transcriber up to the proofreader. It is certainly a curious formation—a superlative form of the adverb "busily"—but is paralleled by the *easilest* of *Cymb.*, IV. ii. 207. Bulloch conjectured "busiliest", and this needs only slight alteration to meet bibliographical objections and conform more closely to the example from *Cymbeline*. In one respect, it must be confessed, *busilest* is less satisfactory than "busiest": "my thoughts are then busiest" serves better than "my thoughts then most busily refresh me", because they obviously would refresh his labours most when he was labouring, not when he wasn't. But the adverb-adjective confusion is no great matter in this play; perhaps Shakespeare "should" have written "busiest", but what he probably did write was *busielest*.

There seems no sufficiently strong reason to emend *I doe it*. Obviously we must not mind that the antecedent of *it* is *labours*; this false concord could be the work of the compositor, but it could also be Shakespeare's, and

Enter MIRANDA; *and* PROSPERO [*at a distance, unseen*].

Mir.   Alas now, pray you,   15
      Work not so hard: I would the lightning had
      Burnt up those logs that you are enjoin'd to pile!
      Pray, set it down, and rest you: when this burns,
      'Twill weep for having wearied you. My father
      Is hard at study; pray, now, rest yourself: 20
      He's safe for these three hours.
Fer.   O most dear mistress,
      The sun will set before I shall discharge
      What I must strive to do.
Mir.   If you'll sit down,
      I'll bear your logs the while: pray give me that;
      I'll carry it to the pile.
Fer.   No, precious creature;   25
      I had rather crack my sinews, break my back,
      Than you should such dishonour undergo,
      While I sit lazy by.
Mir.   It would become me
      As well as it does you: and I should do it

S.D. at a distance, unseen] Rowe.   17. *you are*] *thou art* Ff; *thou'rt* Rowe;
you're Hanmer.

there is no occasion to change it. But
whether because of general puzzle-
ment, or by catching the word *doe*
from the previous line, a copyist or
compositor may here have denied us
some stronger verb than *doe*, something
on the lines of "work" or "drudge".
There is balance in the line: "*They* are
busiest when *I* am". *Doe* is certainly
weak, but it does make sense, so there
is no call to seek an alternative.

Therefore I read *Most busilest when
I do it.* Ferdinand is perfectly cheerful,
and returns to his task knowing that
his sweet thoughts, so far from being
present only when he idles, will
attend him even more assiduously
when he works. He has said much the
same thing all along. Finally, one
more slight argument in favour of this
reading—though it applies equally to
"busiest"—is that it avoids an objec-

tion that has been levelled at "Most
busy, least . . .", namely that the
rhythm is ugly.

      *Most busilest when I do't. Alas, now,
            pray you*

can certainly stand in a passage
which is notable, even in *The Tempest*,
for its metrical licence.

18–19.] This conceit refers to the
resinous drops which issue from burning wood.

23–5.] If you'll sit down, I'll bear
your logs the while; / Pray give me
that, I'll carry it to the pile. For
other "concealed couplets" see *Intro.*,
p. xvi and ll. 29–30 below.

26. *crack*] Often used by Shakespeare in a sense apparently strained,
as here; cf. v. i. 2, "My charms crack
not"; and *Cor.*, v. iii. 9.

29–30.] Another couplet, sometimes
used in support of the argument that

       With much more ease; for my good will is to it,   30
       And yours it is against.
Pros.   Poor worm, thou art infected!
       This visitation shows it.
Mir.   You look wearily.
Fer. No, noble mistress: 'tis fresh morning with me
       When you are by at night. I do beseech you,—
       Chiefly that I might set it in my prayers,—   35
       What is your name?
Mir.   Miranda.—O my father,
       I have broke your hest to say so!
Fer.   Admir'd Miranda!
       Indeed the top of admiration! worth
       What's dearest to the world! Full many a lady
       I have ey'd with best regard, and many a time   40
       Th' harmony of their tongues hath into bondage
       Brought my too diligent ear: for several virtues
       Have I lik'd several women; never any
       With so full soul, but some defect in her
       Did quarrel with the noblest grace she ow'd,   45
       And put it to the foil: but you, O you,

this scene is based upon some scene in an old rhymed play. See note on ll. 23–5, and *Intro.*, p. xvi.

31, 32. *infected . . . visitation*] The primary sense of *visitation* is, of course, "visit"; there may be a play upon the sense in which the word was habitually used, of an epidemic of the plague. This is suggested by *infected*. Strangely enough, Shakespeare nowhere else uses the word *visitation* in its medical (and topical) signification. But cf. *Mac.*, IV. iii. 150.

37. *hest*] Cf. I. ii. 274 and IV. i. 65. Yet the word is found only twice in other plays, and one of these examples is doubtful.

37–8. *Admir'd Miranda . . .*] Here Shakespeare plays upon the name he has invented for his last heroine. Whether or no Ruskin's speculations concerning the meanings of Shakespearian names deserved the censure of Arnold, it cannot be denied that

both at the beginning and at the end of his career Shakespeare gave to certain of his characters names by which we might understand something of their situations and functions. Thus, for example, Proteus and Valentine in *Gent.*; and in the last plays Perdita, Marina, and Miranda.

46. *foil*] Ferdinand is using at least two senses of this word. (1) The defect rendered the virtue liable to overthrow. (2) The defect was employed as a foil to set off the virtue. Or, as Luce held, the sense of *foil* may be as in Spenser, *F.Q.*, v. xi. 33, "and foyle/ In filthy durt" (cf. O. Fr. "fouler", "to trample underfoot"). Taking (1) and (2) as the foremost meanings: Miranda, being all graces, is not endangered by such defects, nor in need of such meretricious aid. There is a suggestion, in the punning, of the worldliness of Ferdinand's former mistresses, and perhaps the other mean-

So perfect and so peerless, are created
Of every creature's best!
Mir.   I do not know
One of my sex; no woman's face remember,
Save, from my glass, mine own; nor have I seen   50
More that I may call men than you, good friend,
And my dear father: how features are abroad,
I am skilless of; but, by my modesty,
The jewel in my dower, I would not wish
Any companion in the world but you;   55
Nor can imagination form a shape,
Besides yourself, to like of. But I prattle
Something too wildly, and my father's precepts
I therein do forget.
Fer.   I am, in my condition,

---

47. *peerless*] F2; *peetlesse* F.   59. *I therein do*] *I do* Pope; *Therein* Steevens.

---

ings of *foil*, here logically irrelevant—
as a term in fencing and wrestling—
support the general suggestion of
more corrupt and complex love adventures. Cf. *Cym.*, III. v. 70–4.

48. *Of every creature's best*] This
is a transmutation of a common
enough love-compliment; cf. *AYL.*,
III. ii. 157–160. The notion is ultimately Platonic; but Johnson sensibly
relates it to the story of the picture of Venus by Apelles; Steevens,
however, contested this.

49. *no woman's face remember*] It has
been objected that Miranda remembered her female attendants in I. ii.
46–7; to which it has been answered,
that she didn't claim to remember
their *faces*. Other details have been
questioned; ll. 33–4 are inappro-
priate, since the lovers have just met;
Miranda should have remembered
men as well as women, or at least
known how many men she knew (see
I. ii. 448, and ll. 50–2 below). How
did Miranda manage for clothes?
How did Caliban know what a house
was (III. ii. 95)? How many children
had Lady Macbeth?

52. *features*] Used of the body

generally. What men and women are
like (or, how people look) in the world
at large, I know not.

53. *skilless of*] Ignorant of; cf.
Tw.N., III. iii. 9.

57. *like of*] This cadence is a favourite of Shakespeare's, especially in his
later plays. Cf. *Mac.*, II. iii. 101; *Ham.*,
II. ii. 7–10; *Wint.*, II. i. 60–61, etc. Also
l. 74 below.

59–63.] Mr H. F. Brooks has suggested to me that the metrical irregularity in l. 62, considered together with
the hypermetrical nature of l. 59,
could possibly be taken to indicate a
mislineation caused by an error of the
scribal copyist. The theory is that the
scribe inverted the two opening
phrases of Ferdinand's speech, and
wrote the line-and-a-half as one
line:

I am in my condition a prince Miranda
I do think. . . .

(The Folio occasionally gives evidence
of this kind of "cramping" in the
copy.) The confusion caused by this
error was further confounded by the
attempt of the editors of the Folio to
re-divide the lines as verse, which they
were unable to do without leaving two

A prince, Miranda; I do think, a King;   60
I would not so!—and would no more endure
This wooden slavery than to suffer
The flesh-fly blow my mouth. Hear my soul speak:
The very instant that I saw you, did
My heart fly to your service; there resides,   65
To make me slave to it; and for your sake
Am I this patient log-man.

Mir.   Do you love me?
Fer. O heaven, O earth, bear witness to this sound,
And crown what I profess with kind event,
If I speak true! if hollowly, invert   70
What best is boded me to mischief! I,
Beyond all limit of what else i' th' world,
Do love, prize, honour you.

Mir.   I am a fool
To weep at what I am glad of.

Pros.   Fair encounter
Of two most rare affections! Heavens rain grace   75
On that which breeds between 'em!

Fer.   Wherefore weep you?
Mir. At mine unworthiness, that dare not offer
What I desire to give; and much less take
What I shall die to want. But this is trifling;
And all the more it seeks to hide itself,   80
The bigger bulk it shows. Hence, bashful cunning!

---

62. *wooden*] F2; *wodden* F.   *to suffer*] *I would suffer* Pope; *to suffer tamely* Dyce.
68. *O heaven, O earth*] *O heauen; O earth* F; *O heaven & earth* Tannenbaum conj.

lines imperfect. Perhaps the passage originally read:
  I therein do forget.
                    In my condition
  I am a prince, Miranda; I do think
  A King; I would not so!—and would no
    more
  Endure this wooden slavery than to
    suffer
  The flesh-fly blow my mouth.
63. *blow*] To foul, sully. Cf. v. i. 284.

69. *kind event*] A favourable result.
70. *hollowly*] Insincerely, falsely.
  invert] Turn to misfortune whatever good fortune is in store for me. Cf. *Troil.*, v. ii. 122.
72. *what else*] Whatsoever else.
74. *encounter*] Meeting. Cf. v. i. 154.
75. *Heavens rain grace*] Cf. "The heavens rain odours," *Tw.N.*, III. i. 95–6, and for variations on this theme in *Tp.*, IV. i. 18 and v. i. 201–2.
79. *to want*] Through wanting.

And prompt me plain and holy innocence!
I am your wife if you will marry me;
If not, I'll die your maid: to be your fellow
You may deny me; but I'll be your servant,   85
Whether you will or no.

Fer.   My mistress, dearest;
And I thus humble ever.

Mir.   My husband, then?

Fer. Ay, with a heart as willing
As bondage e'er of freedom: here's my hand.

Mir. And mine, with my heart in 't: and now farewell   90
Till half an hour hence.

Fer.   A thousand thousand!

                        Exeunt [Fer. and Mir. severally].

Pros. So glad of this as they I cannot be,
Who are surpris'd with all; but my rejoicing
At nothing can be more. I'll to my book;
For yet, ere supper-time, must I perform   95
Much business appertaining.   *Exit.*

---

88. *as*] *so* Ff, Rowe.   91. S.D. Exeunt . . . severally.] Capell; Exeunt F.
93. *with all*] *withal* Theobald, Camb., Alexander.

83-6.] Malone cites Catullus, *Carmen* 62; Douce "The nut-brown maid".

84. *maid*] Perhaps in two senses—(1) unmarried; (2) servant. "Wife" corresponds to "fellow" in the context, and "maid" partly to "servant". (Luce.)

fellow] Companion, equal.

87. *thus humble*] Ferdinand may kneel.

89. *As bondage*] With a heart as desirous of it as bondage is of freedom (*i.e.* as the bondman is to be free).

my hand] *i.e.*, in betrothal.

91. *thousand*] *Sc.* farewells. Cf. *Gent.*, II. i. 102 ff.

(S.D.) Exeunt Fer. and Mir. severally] Ferdinand presumably carrying his log.

93. *Who are surpris'd with all*] *surpris'd* means primarily "taken unaware". F. reading *with all* makes good sense—"with all that is going on"; Theobald's conjecture, "withal", has been very generally accepted, and may be neater, but there is no reason for interference.

94. *my book*] For Prospero's book see *Intro.*, p. xlix.

SCENE II.—[*Another part of the Island.*]

Enter CALIBAN, STEPHANO, *and* TRINCULO.

Ste. Tell not me;—when the butt is out, we will drink
water; not a drop before: therefore bear up, and
board 'em. Servant-monster, drink to me.

Trin. Servant-monster! the folly of this island! They say
there's but five upon this isle: we are three of them; 5
if th' other two be brain'd like us, the state totters.

Ste. Drink, servant-monster, when I bid thee: thy eyes
are almost set in thy head.

Trin. Where should they be set else? he were a brave
monster indeed, if they were set in his tail. 10

Ste. My man-monster hath drown'd his tongue in sack:
for my part, the sea cannot drown me; I swam, ere
I could recover the shore, five-and-thirty leagues
off and on. By this light, thou shalt be my lieutenant,
monster, or my standard. 15

Trin. Your lieutenant, if you list; he's no standard.

Ste. We'll not run, Monsieur Monster.

Scene II

S.D. SCENE II . . . Island.] Camb.; Scæna Secunda F.   3. *Servant-monster*]
Theobald; *Servant Monster* F.   4. *folly*] Sophy N.S. conj.   14. *off and on. By*]
Camb.; *off and on, by* F.   *lieutenant, monster*] *Lieutenant Monster* F; *Lieutenant-
Monster* Sutherland conj.

2–3. *bear up, and board 'em*] A term,
obviously from sea-warfare, meaning,
here, "drink up".

3. *Servant-monster*] Cf. the Induction
to Jonson's *Bartholomew Fair* (1614),
which glances at *The Tempest*: "If
there be never a servant-monster i' the
Fayre. . ." A "base and silly sneer",
says Coleridge (*C.'s Miscellaneous Criticism*, ed. Raysor, p. 59).

4. *the folly of this island*] There has
been some mystification about this.
Some accept Nicholson's suggestion
that the words are a toast. N.S. conjectures *Sophy* ("fofy", misread as *foly*).
"Sophy" means not only the Shah,
but also a mage; hence Trinculo's
talk of brains. But all this is super-
fluous. *Folly* here means "freak", as in

Evelyn (1648), "The celebrated follies of Bartholomew Fair" (*O.E.D.*,
s.v.); and this sense was current until
quite recently. Like "servant-monster", "folly" leads us back to the
great centre of freaks and monsters,
Bartholomew Fair.

7 ff.] For this joke cf. Middleton,
Women Beware Women, III. iii.

15. *standard*] Standard-bearer. A
pun; Caliban is reeling drunk and
cannot stand. N.S. suggests the further sense "conduit", in connection
with obscene double-meanings in *run*
and *lie*. Steevens said *standard* meant a
fruit-tree that grows without support.

17. *run*] i.e. from the enemy, but
with the sense, suggested by *standard*,
of "make water". See p. 168.

Trin. Nor go neither; but you'll lie, like dogs, and yet
　　say nothing neither.

Ste. Moon-calf, speak once in thy life, if thou beest a　20
　　good moon-calf.

Cal. How does thy honour? Let me lick thy shoe: I'll
　　not serve him, he is not valiant.

Trin. Thou liest, most ignorant monster: I am in case to
　　justle a constable. Why, thou debosh'd fish, thou,　25
　　was there ever man a coward that hath drunk so
　　much sack as I to-day? Wilt thou tell a monstrous
　　lie, being but half a fish and half a monster?

Cal. Lo, how he mocks me! wilt thou let him, my lord?

Trin. "Lord," quoth he? That a monster should be such　30
　　a natural!

Cal. Lo, lo, again! bite him to death, I prithee.

Ste. Trinculo, keep a good tongue in your head: if you
　　prove a mutineer,—the next tree! The poor mon-
　　ster's my subject, and he shall not suffer indignity.　35

Cal. I thank my noble lord. Wilt thou be pleas'd to
　　hearken once again to the suit I made to thee?

Ste. Marry, will I: kneel and repeat it; I will stand, and
　　so shall Trinculo.

---

25. *debosh'd*] F; *debauched* Collier.　　27. *tell a*] *tell me a* Ff, Rowe.　　29. *my lord*]
lord Grey conj.　　36–7. *to hearken once again*] F, F2; *once again to hearken* F3, F4.
37. *to . . . thee*] *the suit I made thee* Steevens.

18. *go*] Walk. "He may ill run that
cannot go" (Tilley, R208).

lie] "Recline"; "tell lies"; possibly,
N.S. suggests, a hint of the slang sense
"excrete".

24. *in case to*] In a condition to.

25. *debosh'd*] Debauched, probably
pronounced with a long *o*; Cotgrave
translates *Desbauché* as *Deboshed*.

27. *monstrous*] A great, an outrage-
ous lie, told by a sort of monster.

31. *natural*] A monster is by definition unnatural; yet this one is a
natural (an idiot).

33. *keep . . . head*] "To keep a good
tongue in one's head"—a proverbial
expression, see Tilley, T402.

36–7. *I thank my noble lord . . .*] As
often noted, little alteration is necessary to convert these lines into verse.
This is true of many of Caliban's
speeches, though occasionally they are
more stubborn, as in 40–2 below,
which is, perhaps surprisingly, cut up
into verse lengths in F; this counts
against the theory that the comic
scenes existed earlier in a different
form. Yet Caliban so often approaches
verse as to provoke the suspicion that
some passages at some stage have been
deliberately broken down from verse
to prose, as may have happened also
in *H 4*. (See N.S., *1 H 4*, p. 112.) The
Ff reading *once again to hearken*, followed by Rowe, breaks the verse rhythm.
See *Intro.*, p. xiv, and Appendix G.

Enter ARIEL, *invisible.*

Cal. As I told thee before, I am subject to a tyrant, a   40
    sorcerer, that by his cunning hath cheated me of the
    island.

Ari. Thou liest.

Cal. "Thou liest," thou jesting monkey, thou!
    I would my valiant master would destroy thee!   45
    I do not lie.

Ste. Trinculo, if you trouble him any more in 's tale, by
    this hand, I will supplant some of your teeth.

Trin. Why, I said nothing.

Ste. Mum, then, and no more. Proceed.   50

Cal. I say, by sorcery he got this isle;
    From me he got it. If thy greatness will
    Revenge it on him,—for I know thou dar'st,
    But this thing dare not,—

Ste. That's most certain.   55

Cal. Thou shalt be lord of it, and I'll serve thee.

Ste. How now shall this be compass'd? Canst thou bring
    me to the party?

Cal. Yea, yea, my lord: I'll yield him thee asleep,
    Where thou mayst knock a nail into his head.   60

Ari. Thou liest; thou canst not.

Cal. What a pied ninny's this! Thou scurvy patch!
    I do beseech thy greatness, give him blows,
    And take his bottle from him: when that's gone,
    He shall drink nought but brine; for I'll not
      show him   65

51-2. *isle; / From me*] Theobald; *Isle / From me*, F.   56. *I'll serve thee*] *I will serve thee* Walker, N.S.   57. *now*] omitted Pope.   62. Cal. *What . . . patch*] Ste. *What . . . patch* Johnson conj.

43.] Perhaps a variation on the ancient echo-scene, which was popular at this period. It is found in the *Commedia dell'arte.*

48. *supplant*] Displace, uproot. This speech as two lines of verse in F. See *Intro.*, p. xiv.

50. *Mum*] "I will say nothing but mum" (Tilley, N279).

54. *this thing*] *this Thing* F. He means Trinculo, or perhaps himself. Cf. v. i. 275.

60. *knock a nail*] As Jael did to Sisera, Judg. iv. 21.

62. *pied ninny*] Referring to the jester's motley? *Ninny* probably from "innocent". See also p. 173.

patch] Jester; so called from his patched dress. Otherwise clown, simpleton; cf. *Mer.V.*, II. v. 46.

Where the quick freshes are.

Ste. Trinculo, run into no further danger: interrupt the
 monster one word further, and, by this hand, I'll
 turn my mercy out o' doors, and make a stock-fish
 of thee.   70

Trin. Why, what did I? I did nothing. I'll go farther off.

Ste. Didst thou not say he lied?

Ari. Thou liest.

Ste. Do I so? take thou that. [*Beats him.*] As you like
 this, give me the lie another time.   75

Trin. I did not give the lie. Out o' your wits, and hearing too? A pox o' your bottle! this can sack and
 drinking do. A murrain on your monster, and the
 devil take your fingers!

Cal. Ha, ha, ha!   80

Ste. Now, forward with your tale.—Prithee, stand
 further off.

Cal. Beat him enough: after a little time,
 I'll beat him too.

Ste.   Stand farther.—Come, proceed.

Cal. Why, as I told thee, 'tis a custom with him 85
 I' th' afternoon to sleep: there thou mayst brain him,
 Having first seiz'd his books; or with a log
 Batter his skull, or paunch him with a stake,
 Or cut his wezand with thy knife. Remember

---

71. *farther*] *no further* Ff, Rowe. 74. *take thou*] *take you* F3, F4, Rowe. *Beats him*] Rowe. *As*] *An* Keightley conj. 76. *give the lie*] *give thee the lie* F4, Rowe, Tannenbaum conj. 78. *murrain*] F3, F4, Rowe; *murren* F. 86. *there*] *then* Collier, Dyce.

66. *quick freshes*] Swift-flowing springs; cf. I. ii. 338.

69. *make a stock-fish. . .*] "Beat thee as a stock-fish is beaten before it is boiled" (Dyce). (See Tilley, S867.) This speech could be divided as verse.

76–8.] In F, *I . . . too* and *A pox . . . do* form a rhyming doggerel couplet, probably fortuitously. See *Intro.*, p. xvi.

76. *give the lie*] Tannenbaum supports F4 reading; *thee* was perhaps spelt *the*, and the compositor, seeing two *the*'s, cancelled one.

78. *A murrain*] The "red plague" of I. ii. 366.

81–2. *stand further off*] Addressed to Trinculo, whose supposed fooling has held up Caliban's story. Furness and others like to think that Caliban is addressed, and that Stephano cannot stand his smell.

86. *there*] Often used with a connotation of time; it means "on that occasion", as in *Rom.*, II. iv. 193, "And there she shall at Friar Laurence' cell". Cf. the use of "where" in v. i. 236.

89. *wezand*] Wind-pipe.

First to possess his books; for without them   90
He's but a sot, as I am, nor hath not
One spirit to command: they all do hate him
As rootedly as I. Burn but his books.
He has brave utensils,—for so he calls them,—
Which, when he has a house, he'll deck withal.   95
And that most deeply to consider is
The beauty of his daughter; he himself
Calls her a nonpareil: I never saw a woman,
But only Sycorax my dam and she;
But she as far surpasseth Sycorax   100
As great'st does least.

Ste.   Is it so brave a lass?

Cal. Ay, lord; she will become thy bed, I warrant,
And bring thee forth brave brood.

Ste. Monster, I will kill this man: his daughter and I
will be king and queen,—save our graces!—and   105
Trinculo and thyself shall be viceroys. Dost thou
like the plot, Trinculo?

Trin. Excellent.

Ste. Give me thy hand: I am sorry I beat thee; but,

90. *books;*] *Bookes;* F.   93. *books.*] *Bookes,* F.   95. *deck*] *deck't* Hanmer.
99. *she*] *her* Hanmer.   101. *As great'st does least*] *As greatest does the least* Rowe.

91. *sot*] Impotent fool, rather than drunkard.

93. *Burn but*] *but* probably in two senses—(1) only be sure to burn his books; (2) burn nothing but his books. This latter meaning might explain the mention of the "brave utensils", which must not be burnt; and in F *books* is followed only by a comma.

94. *utensils*] (útensils). This pronunciation was standard until the eighteenth century—*e.g.* in Swift's *Strephon and Chloe*, "Fair útensíl, as smooth and white / As Chloe's skin". The word may mean "instruments of art"; but *O.E.D.* thinks it merely means "household goods". The parenthesis may imply, "Thus I account for the word in my vocabulary", for in line 98. "nonpareil" is accounted for

in that way. (Luce.) We are sometimes reminded that Caliban should not know what a house is.

96. *that*] "That which is".

to consider] "To be considered". Cf. "There is much to do."

98. *nonpareil*] Without equal for beauty.

I never saw a woman] Another element in the parallelism between Miranda and Caliban; cf. the accounts given of their education, and their reaction to the sight of the noblemen. See *Intro.*, p. li.

107. *plot*] In the modern sense; but with a touch of an Elizabethan usage, now extinct—the "plot" was a skeleton programme giving a synopsis of a masque or entertainment. (See *O.E.D.*, *s.v.*, II. 46.)

while thou liv'st, keep a good tongue in thy head.   110

Cal. Within this half hour will he be asleep:
Wilt thou destroy him then?

Ste.   Ay, on mine honour.

Ari. This will I tell my master.

Cal. Thou mak'st me merry; I am full of pleasure:
Let us be jocund: will you troll the catch   115
You taught me but while-ere?

Ste. At thy request, monster, I will do reason, any
reason.—Come on, Trinculo, let us sing.   *Sings.*

> *Flout 'em and cout 'em,*
> *And scout 'em and flout 'em;*   120
> *Thought is free.*

Cal. That's not the tune.

Ariel plays the tune on a tabor and pipe.

Ste. What is this same?

Trin. This is the tune of our catch, played by the picture
of Nobody.   125

---

117. *any*] *and* Ff, Rowe.   119. *cout*] *scout* Rowe.

110. *keep . . . head*] See note on l. 33.

115. *troll the catch*] troll (a derivative of "roll") was in common use for "sing (lustily)". A catch was a song for three or more voices, in which the second voice began as the first ended the opening line, and the others entered in regular sequence. "The catch was for each succeeding singer to take up or catch his part in time" (Grove).

116. *while-ere*] (F *whileare*). The only instance in Shakespeare, though the word is common in earlier verse.

119. *cout*] Generally altered to "scout", but, as N.S. points out, "cout" is a variant of "colt", "befool". This justification of F is impugned by M. Hunter in *R.E.S.*, II. 347, where it is claimed that "scout" is more suitable to a catch, and that "cout" as a variant of "colt" does not occur before the nineteenth century. Tannenbaum also takes this view; but it is still

possible that "cout" had a pre-literary history, or that it is a nonce- and nonsense-word. It may be chance, but textual difficulties are relatively frequent in the songs of this play.

121. *Thought is free*] Probably the refrain of a song, quoted by Maria in *Tw.N.*, I. iii. 73. Also proverbial, see Tilley, T244. The passage in *Tw.N.* gives a fair indication of its normal employment.

122. (S.D.) *tabor*] Small drum, worn at the side. "You shall heare in the ayre the sound of tabers and other instruments . . . by evill spirites that make these soundes" (Marco Polo, *Travels*, tr. Frampton, 1579). (Luce.)

124-5. *picture of Nobody*] Some topical allusion, possibly to the picture of a man all head and legs and arms, but no body, which appeared on the title-page of a comedy called *No-body and Some-body* (1606). John Trundle, book-

Ste. If thou beest a man, show thyself in thy likeness: if
    thou beest a devil, take 't as thou list.

Trin. O, forgive me my sins!

Ste. He that dies pays all debts: I defy thee. Mercy upon
    us!   130

Cal. Art thou afeard?

Ste. No, monster, not I.

Cal. Be not afeard; the isle is full of noises,
    Sounds and sweet airs, that give delight, and
      hurt not.
    Sometimes a thousand twangling instruments   135
    Will hum about mine ears; and sometime voices,
    That, if I then had wak'd after long sleep,
    Will make me sleep again: and then, in dreaming,
    The clouds methought would open, and show
      riches
    Ready to drop upon me; that, when I wak'd,   140
    I cried to dream again.

Ste. This will prove a brave kingdom to me, where I
    shall have my music for nothing.

Cal. When Prospero is destroy'd.

Ste. That shall be by and by: I remember the story.   145

---

135. *Sometimes*] *Sometime* Dyce.   *twangling*] *twanging* Pope.   136. *sometime*]
sometimes Ff, Rowe.   137. *had*] *have* Allen.   140. *that*] omitted Pope.

---

seller, used the sign of Nobody, and
this may have been known to the
audience. See N.S. Glossary (*s.v.* Nobody) for an interesting development
of this. See also Middleton, *Blurt,
Master-Constable*, ed. Bullen, I. 22.

    127. *take 't as thou list*] Alluding to
the saying "The devil take it."

    129. *He that dies. . .*] Proverbial; cf.
1 H 4, III. ii. 157, *2 H 4*, III. ii. 254,
Cym., v. iv. 160 ff, and Montaigne,
Essays, i. 7. Tilley, D148.

    133. *full of noises*] Montaigne, in his
essay "Of Cannibals", alludes to the
Carthaginian expedition, which, as
Purchas puts it, found "a fertile
desart Iland . . . distant many days
sailing from the African Continent. . .
This is by some interpreted of the

West-Indies, or some Iland thereof"
(*Pilgrims*, I. 163). Hanno came upon a
country "very barbarous, and full of
wilde Beasts . . . and round about the
Mountaine inhabit men of divers
shapes. . . We heard Phifes and the
noise and sound of Cimbals" (*ibid.*,
207 ff).

    135. *twangling*] Portmanteau word,
like *windring* (IV. i. 128). Also found in
Shr., II. i. 159. Pope and others here
and elsewhere select one of the meanings and emend accordingly.

    135–41.] "It will be noticed that the
illogical sequence of tenses creates a
perfect suspension of time" (Robert
Graves, *The White Goddess*, p. 374).
For Caliban and music, see *Intro.*,
p. xlii.

Trin. The sound is going away; let's follow it, and after
    do our work.
Ste. Lead, monster; we'll follow. I would I could see
    this taborer; he lays it on.
Trin. Wilt come? I'll follow, Stephano.   *Exeunt.* 150

SCENE III.—[*Another part of the Island.*]

Enter ALONSO, SEBASTIAN, ANTONIO, GONZALO,
ADRIAN, FRANCISCO, *&c.*

Gon. By 'r lakin, I can go no further, sir;
    My old bones ache: here's a maze trod, indeed,
    Through forth-rights and meanders! By your patience,
    I needs must rest me.
Alon.   Old lord, I cannot blame thee,
    Who am myself attach'd with weariness,   5
    To th' dulling of my spirits: sit down, and rest.
    Even here I will put off my hope, and keep it
    No longer for my flatterer: he is drown'd
    Whom thus we stray to find; and the sea mocks
    Our frustrate search on land. Well, let him go.   10

149. *this*] F, F2; *his* F3, F4.

Scene III

S.D. SCENE III . . . Island.] Camb.; Scena Tertia. F.   2. *ache*] Ff; *akes* F.
3. *forth-rights*] F3, F4; *fourth rights* F; *forthrights* F2.   8. *flatterer*] *flatterers* Ff.

146.] Some editors give this to
Caliban.

150.] Trinculo's "Wilt come?" may
be addressed to Caliban, and in that
case the comma after "follow" should
be omitted, as in F. Otherwise "Wilt
come?" may be given to Stephano,
and then a comma would be required
after "follow", as in the text. Or again,
Trinculo's "Wilt come?" may still be
addressed to the lingering Caliban,
and the reading of "I'll follow, Stephano," remain as in text.

Scene III

The intervention of Ariel, and the
confession of Alonso, in this scene,

recall Job xx, 23, 27: "When he is
about to fill his belly, God shall cast
the fury of his wrath upon him. . . The
heaven shall reveal his iniquity; and
the earth shall rise up against him."

1. *lakin*] Ladykin—the Virgin
Mary.

3. *forth-rights and meanders*] Paths
sometimes straight, sometimes winding (like those in an artificial maze);
cf. v. i. 242. (Luce.)

5. *attach'd*] Seized; used figuratively
in its legal sense. (Luce.)

10. *frustrate*] Participle left in Latin
form, as often in Milton; here used as
an adjective meaning "vain, doomed
to failure".

Ant. [*Aside to Seb.*] I am right glad that he's so out of hope.
    Do not, for one repulse, forego the purpose
    That you resolv'd t' effect.

Seb.   [*Aside to Ant.*] The next advantage
    Will we take throughly.

Ant.   [*Aside to Seb.*] Let it be to-night;
    For, now they are oppress'd with travel, they   15
    Will not, nor cannot, use such vigilance
    As when they are fresh.

Seb.   [*Aside to Ant.*] I say, to-night: no more.

Solemn and strange music; and PROSPER *on the top* (*invisible*).
    Enter several strange Shapes, bringing in a banquet; and dance
    about it with gentle actions of salutations; and inviting the
    King, &c., to eat, they depart.

Alon. What harmony is this? My good friends, hark!
Gon. Marvellous sweet music!
Alon. Give us kind keepers, heavens!—What were these? 20
Seb. A living drollery. Now I will believe

11. Aside to Seb.] Hanmer.   13. Aside to Ant.] Capell.   14. Aside to Seb.]
Capell.   15. *travel*] F3, F4; *trauaile* F.   17. Aside to Ant.] Capell.   17. S.D.
Solemn . . . depart.] after *fresh* F; Enter Prospero above, invisible . . . they
dance about it with gentle actions of salutation . . . depart. Camb.   on the
top] above Malone.   20. *were*] are F4.

14. *throughly*] Thoroughly. "The
next . . . throughly", one line in F.
    17. (S.D., l. 1.) on the top] This
should not be altered, as it has a precise meaning. See Appendix E for observations on the staging of this crucial
and spectacular scene.   (l. 2.) Shapes]
See note on III. ii. 144.   bringing in
a banquet] The magician was often
held to be capable of conjuring up
banquets. Illusory banquets are a
feature of the Italian pastoral *scenari*;
see *Intro.*, p. lxix. This one is conceivably related to allegorical interpretations of Scripture. Eve was tempted
with an apple, and Christ with an
illusory banquet; the former temptation successful, as with the "men of
sin", the latter a failure, as with the
pure Gonzalo. For the exegetical tra-

dition on this point, see E. M. Pope,
*Paradise Regained: The Tradition and
the Poem* (1947). It is clear that there
was an accepted allegorical reference
in banquet-scenes, such as those in
Timon, Jonson's *Poetaster*, Chapman's
Ovids Banquet of Sence and Milton's
Comus and *Paradise Regained*; but this
question has not yet been studied in
any detail. Banquets represent the
voluptuous attractions of sense which
(as in Marvell's *Dialogue*) the resolved
soul must resist.
    20. *keepers*] Guardian angels. Cf.
Ham., I. iv. 39.
    21. *A living drollery*] Perhaps a pup-
pet-show in which the figures are alive
and not merely dressed-up wood. But
see *Intro.*, p. xxxiii for two rival interpretations.

That there are unicorns; that in Arabia
There is one tree, the phoenix' throne; one phoenix
At this hour reigning there.

Ant.   I'll believe both;
And what does else want credit, come to me,   25
And I'll be sworn 'tis true: travellers ne'er did lie,
Though fools at home condemn 'em.

Gon.   If in Naples
I should report this now, would they believe me?
If I should say, I saw such islanders,—
For, certes, these are people of the island,—   30
Who, though they are of monstrous shape, yet, note,
Their manners are more gentle, kind, than of
Our human generation you shall find
Many, nay, almost any.

Pros.   [*Aside.*] Honest lord,
Thou hast said well; for some of you there present   35
Are worse than devils.

Alon.   I cannot too much muse
Such shapes, such gesture, and such sound,
       expressing—

27. 'em] *them* Malone.   29. *islanders*] Ff; *Islands* F.   32. *gentle, kind*] *gentle-kind*
Theobald.   34. Aside] Capell.   36. *muse*] *muse,* F4; *muse;* Capell.

23. *the phoenix*] Sebastian is, of course, alluding to travellers' tales, and offering examples of the two he finds least credible. It is pointless to seek specific sources for these widely current mythological allusions. The phoenix renewed itself from the ashes of its pyre, and not by generation. The unicorn was the centre of a large body of curious lore, which constantly figures in Elizabethan writing.

25. *And . . . credit*] Cf. "And what is else not to be overcome", *Par. Lost*, I. 109. "Bring me any other improbable story, and I will, etc."

26. *travellers . . . lie*] Contradicting the proverb, "A traveller may lie with authority" (Tilley, T476).

31. *Who, though,* etc.] A characteristic anacoluthon.

32. *gentle, kind*] F is quite satisfactory, with *kind* reinforcing the recurring word *gentle*. There is no warrant for the reading *gentle-kind*, although it is a plausibly Shakespearian compound. The presumably accidental and unobtrusive internal rhyme *kind/find* has been used in evidence by disintegrators. Strangely enough, this expression occurs in Peter Martyr's *De Novo Orbe* (tr. Lok): "Beyond the mountaines . . . the Inhabitauntes say, that Montanous wilde beastes inhabite, which counterfeit the shape of a man, in countenance, feete, and handes . . . [the country] nourishes also *Leopardes* and Lyons, but mild, and gentle, and not hurtfull." In the margin: "Leopards, and Lyons of a mild & gentle kind" (299 *recto*).

36. *muse*] Wonder at. Nowhere else used transitively by Shakespeare.

Although they want the use of tongue—a kind
Of excellent dumb discourse.

Pros.   [*Aside*] Praise in departing.

Fran. They vanish'd strangely.

Seb.   No matter, since   40
They have left their viands behind; for we have
    stomachs.—
Will 't please you taste of what is here?

Alon.   Not I.

Gon. Faith, sir, you need not fear. When we were boys,
Who would believe that there were mountaineers   44
Dew-lapp'd like bulls, whose throats had hanging at 'em
Wallets of flesh? or that there were such men
Whose heads stood in their breasts? which now we find
Each putter-out of five for one will bring us
Good warrant of.

---

39. *excellent dumb*] *excellent-dumb* Walker.   Aside] Capell.   40. Fran.] Ant.
Kinnear conj.; Gon. N.S. conj.   *No*] *'Tis no* Hanmer.   42. *Will 't*]
Capell; *Wilt* F.   Alon.] Ant. Hanmer.   43. Gon.] Ant. N.S. conj.   48.
five for one] *one for five* Malone; *five for ten* Thirlby conj.

39. *Praise in departing*] A proverbial
expression; "do not praise your host
or his entertainment too soon; wait to
see how all will end". Cf. *Wint.*, i. ii.
10. (Luce.) See Tilley, P 83.

40. *They . . . strangely*] The only
words given to Francisco apart from
ii. i. 109 ff, which is often given to
Gonzalo. If these words are given to
Antonio or Gonzalo, the part of
Francisco disappears.

45. *Dew-lapp'd*] Cf. *MND.*, iv. i.
126, "Dew-lapp'd like Thessalian
bulls"; and the previous line, "With
ears that sweep away the morning
dew", gives the meaning of "dew-
lap", viz. the skin pendulous from the
throats of cows, etc.

46-7. *men Whose heads stood in their
breasts*] This Mandevillian motif occurs also in *Oth.*, i. iii. 144, 145.
"The Anthropophagi, and men whose
heads / Do grow beneath their shoulders". It is discussed in *Intro.*, p.
xxxii.

46. *Wallets*] According to Skeat this

is a cognate form of "wattle", the
matted, fleshy skin that hangs from
the neck of the turkey, etc. See p.
169.

48. *Each putter-out of five for one*] It
was not unusual in this speculating
age to recover the costs of travel, and
indeed make an investment of travel,
by depositing a sum of money in London before departure, which was for-
feit if the traveller failed to return, but
which was repaid fivefold if he returned safe and fulfilled the stipulated conditions; *e.g.* produced proof of his
having reached his destination. Punt-
arvolo, in Jonson's *Every Man Out of
his Humour* (ii. iii. 244 ff) says "I doe
intend . . . to travaile: and (because
I will not altogether goe upon ex-
pence) I am determined to put forth
some five thousand pound, to be paid
me, five for one, upon the returne of
my selfe, my wife, and my dog, from
the *Turkes* court in *Constantinople*."
The *putter-out* here, if we retain F
reading, is perhaps the underwriter.

Alon.   I will stand to, and feed,
Although my last, no matter, since I feel   50
The best is past. Brother, my lord the duke,
Stand to, and do as we.

Thunder and lightning. Enter ARIEL *like a Harpy; claps his wings
upon the table; and, with a quaint device, the banquet vanishes.*

Ari. You are three men of sin, whom Destiny,—
That hath to instrument this lower world
And what is in 't,—the never-surfeited sea   55
Hath caus'd to belch up you; and on this island,
Where man doth not inhabit,—you 'mongst men
Being most unfit to live. I have made you mad;
And even with such-like valour men hang and drown
Their proper selves.

                              [*Alon., Seb., etc., draw their swords.*]
                    You fools! I and my fellows   60
Are ministers of Fate: the elements,
Of whom your swords are temper'd, may as well

52. *stand to*] F4; *stand too* F.   54–5. —*That . . . in't,*—] Pope; *That . . . in't:* F.
54. *instrument*] *instruments* F4.   56. *belch up you*] *belch you up* F4; *belch up, yea,*
Hudson.   60. Alon. . . . swords.] Camb.

50, 51. *last . . . past*] Another "concealed" rhyme. See III. i. 29, note.
    52. (S.D.) *like a Harpy*] Steevens
observed that this S.D. is virtually a
translation of *Aeneid*, III. 225–8. Cf.
"With thine angel's face . . . with
thine eagle's talons", *Per.*, IV. iii. 46–8.
Virgil's harpies are *virginei volucrum
voltus* (*Aeneid*, III. 216). This highly
theatrical "show" of a harpy is as
appropriate to the "men of sin" as the
betrothal-masque to Ferdinand and
Miranda. Cf. Milton, *P.R.*, II. 401–3.
    with a quaint device] See Appendix
E.
    53.] You (Alonso, Antonio, Sebas-
tian) are three sinful men, whom Providence, of which this world is the instrument, has caused the ever-hungry
sea to belch up. Staunton is followed
by N.S. in reading *belch up—yea*; but
the construction is Shakespearian as it

stands, with the redundant *you* induc-
ed by the parenthesis. Cf. the exactly
parallel "Whom, / Though bearing
misery, I desire my life / Once more to
look on him" (*Wint.*, v. i. 136–8). The
insistence on the world and the sea as
instruments of Providence is central
to the theme of the play. See p. 169.
    57–9.] This kind of courage was
carefully distinguished from true
valour in Elizabethan ethical thought.
It is the courage which enables the
dove to peck the estridge, and which
strengthens Macbeth when he must
fight his course.
    60. *Their proper selves*] *i.e.* themselves.
    61. *Fate: the elements*] F has comma,
and possibly the author changed
direction here, after beginning to say
"We are the elements of which your
swords are tempered; therefore they
cannot hurt us."

Wound the loud winds, or with bemock'd-at stabs
Kill the still-closing waters, as diminish
One dowle that's in my plume: my fellow-ministers   65
Are like invulnerable. If you could hurt,
Your swords are now too massy for your strengths,
And will not be uplifted. But remember,—
For that's my business to you,—that you three
From Milan did supplant good Prospero: 70
Expos'd unto the sea, which hath requit it,
Him and his innocent child: for which foul deed
The powers, delaying, not forgetting, have
Incens'd the seas and shores, yea, all the creatures,
Against your peace. Thee of thy son, Alonso,   75
They have bereft; and do pronounce by me
Ling'ring perdition—worse than any death
Can be at once—shall step by step attend
You and your ways; whose wraths to guard you
        from,—
Which here, in this most desolate isle, else falls   80

---

65. *plume*] Rowe; *plumbe* F; *plumb* F4.   67. *strengths*] *strength* F4, Rowe.
79. *wraths*] F; *wrath* Theobald.

---

64. *still-closing*] That always close
up again. Cf. "still-vex'd", I. ii.
229.

65. *dowle . . . plume*] "Dowle" is a
rare word meaning "small feather".
Cf. *Piers Plowman*, "The griffen . . .
swore . . . he wold tere him every
doule" (*O.E.D.*). Cf. also Virgil's
account of the harpy-raids: *invadunt
socii . . . obscenas pelagi ferro foedare
volucris | sed neque vim plumis ullam
nec volnera tergo | accipiunt* (*Aen.*, III.
240–2). See also p. 173.

my fellow-ministers] There is no mention of their re-entry, but it is not improbable that other spirits dressed as
harpies could have assisted Ariel in
his descent upon the men of sin at
Court, at the Blackfriars, and at the
Globe; this would enhance the already elaborate spectacle. See Appendix E.

66. *invulnerable*] Ariel and his fel-

lows, like Virgil's Harpies (*Aen.*, III.
242–3) have, like all daemonic bodies,
this indivisibility and invulnerability;
cf. the warring angels in *Par. L.*, VI.

67. *too massy*] An accomplishment of
the white magician was the power to
induce "a kind of paralysis which
seizes the agents who attempt to
oppose their wills to the saint's"
(Loomis, *White Magic*, p. 56). See
Intro., p. xli.

71. *requit it*] i.e. the deed. See p. 169.

77. *Ling'ring perdition*] Having served as the object of *pronounce*, now becomes the subject of *shall step . . .*

79. *whose*] Refers to *powers* and *they*
(73, 76); some find the antecedent in
seas (74).

80. *falls*] Once more the singular
verb with a plural subject (*wraths*); irregular by modern grammatical conventions, but frequent in the more
flexible English of Shakespeare.

Upon your heads,—is nothing but heart-sorrow
And a clear life ensuing.

He vanishes in thunder; then, to soft music, enter the Shapes again,
and dance, with mocks and mows, and carrying out the table.

Pros. Bravely the figure of this Harpy hast thou
Perform'd, my Ariel; a grace it had devouring:
Of my instruction hast thou nothing bated   85
In what thou hadst to say: so, with good life
And observation strange, my meaner ministers
Their several kinds have done. My high charms work,
And these mine enemies are all knit up
In their distractions: they now are in my power;   90
And in these fits I leave them, while I visit
Young Ferdinand,—whom they suppose is drown'd,—
And his and mine lov'd darling.   [*Exit.*]
Gon. I' th' name of something holy, sir, why stand you
In this strange stare?
Alon.   O, it is monstrous, monstrous!   95
Methought the billows spoke, and told me of it;

81. *heart-sorrow*] Camb.; *hearts-sorrow* F, Ff.   82. mocks] mopps Theobald.
90. *now*] omitted Pope.   93. *and mine*] *and my* Rowe; *admired* N.S. conj.
Exit] Exit above Camb.

81. *is nothing but*] There is no alternative but.
82. *clear*] Free from blame; "so clear
in his great office", *Mac.*, I. vii. 18.
83. *Bravely*] You have acted the
Harpy very well; your performance
had a ravishing grace. Here *devouring*
is used in the hyperbolical manner
hinted at in the paraphrase; the meaning cannot be, primarily, "as you
devoured the food". Yet there may be
a suggestion of this; the word is
specially appropriate to a Harpy, and
Ariel has just removed the food, perhaps in such a way as to suggest that
he had devoured it. See Appendix E.
N.S. conjectures *devoiring* (= waiting
at table) which is more ingenious than
credible.
85. *bated*] Deducted, omitted; cf. I.
ii. 250. Used in another sense, II. i.
96.

87. *observation*] Cf. *MND.*, IV. i. 108.
"Care; respectful attention".
strange] Wonderful; cf. IV. i. 7.
88. *Their several kinds have done*]
Have acted the parts their natures
suited them for. Cf. *Ant.*, V. ii. 264,
"The worm will do his kind."
high] Used in the same sense, V. i.
25, V. i. 177.
89. *all knit up*] Cf. "My spirits, as in
a dream, are all bound up" I. ii. 489.
See also *MND.*, V. i. 193.
92. *whom*] Abbott § 410. To the
modern eye a confusion of two constructions, "Ferdinand, who, they suppose, is drown'd", and "Ferdinand,
whom they suppose to be drown'd".
93. *his and mine*] Cf. II. i. 249 and
Cym., V. v. 186, "By hers and mine
adultery".
95. *stare*] Cf. *this roar*, I. ii. 2.
96. *of it*] Of my sin.

The winds did sing it to me; and the thunder,
That deep and dreadful organ-pipe, pronounc'd
The name of Prosper: it did bass my trespass.
Therefor my son i' th' ooze is bedded; and   100
I'll seek him deeper than e'er plummet sounded,
And with him there lie mudded.   *Exit.*

Seb.   But one fiend at a time,
I'll fight their legions o'er.

Ant.   I'll be thy second.

                          Exeunt [Seb. and Ant.].

Gon. All three of them are desperate: their great guilt,
Like poison given to work a great time after,   105
Now 'gins to bite the spirits. I do beseech you,
That are of suppler joints, follow them swiftly,
And hinder them from what this ecstasy
May now provoke them to.

Adr.   Follow, I pray you.   *Exeunt omnes.*

---

99. *Prosper*] *Prospero* Anon. conj. and Ant.] Malone; Exeunt F. *spirit* N.S.   *bass*] Johnson; *base* F.   103. Exeunt Seb. 106. *the spirits*] *their spirits* Allen conj.; *the do*] omitted Pope.

99. *bass my trespass*] Here the image is of the whole harmony of nature enforcing upon Alonso the consciousness of his guilt; the thunder supplies a pedal bass, and seems to name Prospero. The name is a "ground". Cf. *F.Q.*, II. xii. 33, "The rolling sea, resounding soft, / In his big base them fitly answered." But the basic idea is a commonplace of Renaissance literature. Note that Gonzalo did not hear the words of Ariel, and assumes (104 ff) that the guilt of the three men has begun to bite, not because of a new stimulus, but because it is the nature of guilt to work thus. The "strange stare" of the king is caused by his guilt; he himself thinks all nature informs against him; we know that these two phenomena are, for Shakespeare, aspects of the same

moral law. For a possible source (Juvenal, XIII. 217 ff) see Baldwin, *Shakspere's Small Latin*, II. 535.

100. *Therefor*] I act on Tannenbaum's suggestion in spelling the word thus, to clarify the sense. It means, "in consequence of this", a meaning somewhat blurred in modern usage.

105. *poison . . .*] Elizabethan England was credulous about poisons; the drama exhibits an extraordinary array of drugs which kill at touch, etc., generally attributed to Italy. (See F. T. Bowers, *The Elizabethan Revenge Play*, 1940, pp. 26–8.) Here Gonzalo uses the legend of the slow poison, which could be set to act at some future time. Cf. *Wint.*, I. ii. 321.

108. *ecstasy*] Madness; cf. *Mac.*, III. ii. 22, *Ham.*, III. iv. 138.

ACT IV

SCENE I.—[*Before Prospero's Cell.*]

Enter PROSPERO, FERDINAND, *and* MIRANDA.

Pros. If I have too austerely punish'd you,
    Your compensation makes amends; for I
    Have given you here a third of mine own life,
    Or that for which I live; who once again
    I tender to thy hand: all thy vexations   5
    Were but my trials of thy love, and thou
    Hast strangely stood the test: here, afore Heaven,
    I ratify this my rich gift. O Ferdinand,
    Do not smile at me that I boast her off,

ACT IV

Scene 1

ACT IV . . . Cell.] Capell; Actus Quartus. Scena Prima. F.   3. *third*] *thread*
Theobald; *thrid* Wright.   4. *who*] *whom* Pope.   7. *test*] *rest* Ff.   9. *her off*]
Ff; *her of* F; *hereof* N.S.

1. *punish'd*] Not for the sin of the
father, but as explained below: "All
thy vexations / Were but my trials of
thy love"; a parallel is found in the
story of Joseph. (Luce.)

3. *a third of mine own life*] Theobald's
fairly popular conjecture *thread* arises
from the consideration that as a
widower, Prospero would call Miranda a *half*, not a *third* of himself. (Cf.
Oth., I. i. 87.) But the change would be
reasonable only if *third* were unintel-
ligible. It is not; Capell's suggestion
that Prospero's three thirds are Miranda, Milan, and himself, is plausible,
and there are others. If Prospero is
still thinking of his dead wife, then
Miranda is still more clearly the third
for which he lives. Less probable is the
suggestion that Prospero has a third
part of his life left to live, which is of

interest only as it concerns the
daughter he is giving away. This con-
tradicts an important theme of the
play, which is Prospero's legitimate
desire to regain his secular authority.
W. A. Bacon in *N. & Q.*, 9 Aug. 1947,
defends the view that Prospero means
that Miranda's upbringing has occupied him a third of his forty-five years.

It should be added that the words
third and *thrid* were so nearly identical
in form and pronunciation that the
strongest argument for *third* is merely
that it makes better sense; possibly
thrid was present as a kind of pun.

4. *who*] When the poet begins his
clause, he does not stop to decide
whether "who" is to be a subject or an
object in the grammatical organism.

7. *strangely*] Cf. III. iii. 87.

9. *off*] Intensive; "cry up her

For thou shalt find she will outstrip all praise,   10
And make it halt behind her.

Fer.   I do believe it
Against an oracle.

Pros. Then, as my gift, and thine own acquisition
Worthily purchas'd, take my daughter: but
If thou dost break her virgin-knot before   15
All sanctimonious ceremonies may
With full and holy rite be minister'd,
No sweet aspersion shall the heavens let fall
To make this contract grow; but barren hate,
Sour-ey'd disdain and discord shall bestrew   20
The union of your bed with weeds so loathly
That you shall hate it both: therefore take heed,
As Hymen's lamps shall light you.

Fer.   As I hope

---

11. *do*] omitted Pope.   13. *gift*] Rowe; *guest* F, Ff.   14. *but*] omitted Ff.
17. *rite*] Rowe; *right* F, Ff.   18. *aspersion*] *aspersions* F4.   23. *lamps*] *lamp*
Elze conj., N.S.

---

praises". I follow F2, on the ground
that it has presumably emended the
odd F construction by adding a letter
to make a phrase which, though N.S.
dismisses it in the absence of recorded
parallels, still makes sense. N.S. reads
hereof, which refers to *rich gift*.

11. *halt*] Cf. *Mer.V.*, III. iii. 130.

12. *Against*] Though an oracle
should declare otherwise.

13. *gift*] Rowe's emendation is
beyond dispute. See p. 170.

14. *purchas'd*] Won, obtained, acquired.

15. *virgin-knot*] "*Virgineam dissoluit
zonam*, saith the Poet, conceiving out
of a thing precedent, a thing subsequent." Puttenham, *ed. cit.* p. 196.
("The Poet" is unknown.) Cf. *Per.*, IV.
ii. 160. See *Intro.*, p. xlix. For an interesting comment upon James I's attitude in these matters see K. Muir's
Macbeth, p. lxii. See p. 170.

16. *sanctimonious*] Holy; (not ironical). Compare the insistence on Ceremony in Chapman's continuation of
Hero and Leander.

18. *aspersion*] Cf. III. i. 75, 76. The
word has a strongly religious overtone
(cf. the *asperges* of the Mass). Here the
meaning is, that grace which furthers
a true marriage and which is earned
by it.

19. *grow*] Opposed to *barren* (l. 19);
so Juno later wishes "increasing".

21. *weeds*] Not the usual flowers.

23. *lamps*] The reading of Elze may
well be correct. Hymen carried a
single torch (see l. 97) and the next
word may have affected the spelling,
accidentally converting *lamp* into
lamps. There may be reference in this
passage to Catullus *Carm.* 61—*nil
potest sine te* [i.e. *Hymen*] *Venus*, / *fama
quod bona comprobet*, / *commodi capere*;
and the usual *soluere zonam* for marriage also occurs; together with a mul-
tiplicity of torches (78–9) which may
justify the F reading. For the Hymen
who recurs constantly in Renaissance
poetry, see ll. 6–15, though the
sources of such information were
not usually the classical texts themselves. See p. 170.

For quiet days, fair issue and long life,
With such love as 'tis now, the murkiest den,   25
The most opportune place, the strong'st suggestion
Our worser genius can, shall never melt
Mine honour into lust, to take away
The edge of that day's celebration
When I shall think, or Phoebus' steeds are founder'd, 30
Or Night kept chain'd below.
Pros.   Fairly spoke.
Sit, then, and talk with her; she is thine own.
What, Ariel! my industrious servant, Ariel!

Enter ARIEL.

Ari. What would my potent master? here I am.
Pros. Thou and thy meaner fellows your last service 35
Did worthily perform; and I must use you
In such another trick. Go bring the rabble,

---

25. *den*] *e'en* or *ev'n* Anon. conj.   31. *Fairly spoke*] *Most fairly spoke* Hanmer.

---

25. *den*] "even", conjectured by some, is improbable; the next phrase, as often, provides a paraphrase of the *murkiest den*. Bernhard Smith makes the imaginative suggestion that *den* has a concealed reference to *Aen.*, IV. 124: *speluncam Dido dux et Troianus eandem/devenient.* Stanyhurst (1588) translates *speluncam* as "den". But cf. *MND.*, II. i. 217–19: "To trust the opportunity of night, / And the ill counsel of a desert place, / With the rich worth of your virginity".

26. *suggestion*] Temptation, as in II. i. 283. For Ferdinand's protestation, see *Intro.*, p. lvii.

27. *genius*] Refers to the old belief that each human being has a good and a bad angel. Cf. *Ant.*, II. iii. 19, 21; *Sonn.*, CXLIV.

can] Is able to make.

27–8. *melt Mine honour*] Cf. II. i. 274.

28. *to take*] So as to take.

29. *edge*] Keen enjoyment.

30. *When I shall think*, etc.] (For such will be my longing), that either the horses of the sun have broken down,

or . . . The "foundering" of a horse is explained by Cotgrave as "heating of his feet by over much travell"; *i.e.*, *founder'd* = "gone lame". Cf. Jonson, *Cynthia's Revels*, I. i. 18. These are an anticipation of the conventional emotions of a bridegroom on his wedding-day; Shakespeare emphasizes the *coldness* of the words by the formality of the conceit.

Phoebus] The sun-god.

33. *What*] Not impatient; = "now then", "here!".

37. *trick*] This word has been overlooked by commentators. Like *subtlety* (v. i. 124) it has a technical meaning; it derives from the Fr. *truc*, which "was used to denote an elaborate device or ingenious piece of mechanism used for pageantry, etc." (E. Welsford, *Court Masque* [1927], p. 124).

rabble] Not at this stage of development contemptuous. Prospero means Ariel's meaner fellows. It has been suggested that the word refers to Caliban, Stephano and Trinculo. This view is connected with the opinion

O'er whom I give thee power, here to this place:
Incite them to quick motion; for I must
Bestow upon the eyes of this young couple   40
Some vanity of mine Art: it is my promise,
And they expect it from me.

Ari.   Presently?

Pros. Ay, with a twink.

Ari.   Before you can say, "come," and "go,"
And breathe twice, and cry, "so, so,"   45
Each one, tripping on his toe,
Will be here with mop and mow.
Do you love me, master? no?

Pros. Dearly, my delicate Ariel. Do not approach
Till thou dost hear me call.

Ari.   Well, I conceive.   *Exit.* 50

Pros. Look thou be true; do not give dalliance
Too much the rein: the strongest oaths are straw
To th' fire in' th' blood: be more abstemious,
Or else, good night your vow!

Fer.   I warrant you, sir;
The white cold virgin snow upon my heart   55
Abates the ardour of my liver.

Pros.   Well.
Now come, my Ariel! bring a corollary,

42. *from*] *jor* F4.   48. *master? no?*] *master, now?* Crosland conj.; *master? no.* Rowe.
52. *rein*] F4; *raigne* F.   53. *abstemious*] F2; *abstenious* F.   56. *ardour*] *ardours* F4.

that the masque is an interpolation,
the place of which was originally filled
by a passage in which Ariel befooled
the drunkards, as he describes in IV. i.
171 ff. See *Intro.*, p. xx.

39. *motion*] Perhaps with a trace of
the sense "puppet-show".

41. *vanity*] Trifle—"another trick".

42. *Presently*] Immediately.

43. *with a twink*] In the twinkling of
an eye.

47. *mop and mow*] See *mock and mow*,
III. iii. 82 S.D. Cf. *Lr.*, IV. i. 63–4.

50. *conceive*] Understand.

51. *Look . . .*] On Prospero's insistence see *Intro.*, p. xlix.

55. *The white cold*, etc.] Ferdinand

and Miranda may have embraced,
earning Prospero's warning; possibly
editors are right in paraphrasing "her
pure white breast on mine must subdue my passion." But Ferdinand may
mean simply that the idea of Miranda
"packed and locked within his heart"
has this salutary physiological effect.
The liver was the seat of the physical
process attending the sensation of love;
cf. *Wiv.*, II. i. 121, *Tw.N.*, II. iv. 101.

57. *corollary*] Cotgrave gives "Coro-
laire : m. A corollarie; a surplusage,
overplus, addition to, vantage above
measure". The passage means: Let us
have too many spirits rather than too
few. (Luce.)

Rather than want a spirit: appear, and pertly!
No tongue! all eyes! be silent.   *Soft music.*

Enter Iris.

Iris. *Ceres, most bounteous lady, thy rich leas*   60
  Of wheat, rye, barley, vetches, oats, and pease;
  Thy turfy mountains, where live nibbling sheep,
  And flat meads thatch'd with stover, them to keep;
  Thy banks with pioned and twilled brims,

60. thy] the Ff, Rowe.   61. vetches] Capell; fetches F.   64. pioned]
pionied Theobald, Massingham conj.; peonied Steevens.   twilled] tulip'd
Rowe; tilled Capell; lilied Rann.

58. *pertly*] Used of young people
in *MND.*, I. i. 13, and of fairies in
Comus, 118 (a passage echoing this
play). There is no pejorative implication.

59. *No tongue*] Silence was necessary
during magical operations; Agrippa
explains at the opening of the Third
Book of his *Occult Philosophy* that a
talkative companion can ruin an
experiment.

60.] The Masque is discussed in
Intro., p. lxxi ff. and Appendix E.

61. vetches] fetches F, an alternative
form in wide use.

63. stover] Winter food for cattle.
Cf. Golding, *Met.*, v. 116: "Dame
Ceres . . . made corne and stover
soft to grow upon the ground"
(*O.E.D.*).

64. pioned and twilled] The two
principal schools of thought on this
crux are (1) those who think the words
refer to flowers, and (2) those who
suspect a reference to some agricul-
tural operation. The first group must
emend. Their position is defended by
Luce, C. D. Stewart (*Some Textual Difficulties in Shakespeare*, 1914, p. 192) and
best of all by H. J. Massingham (*An
Englishman's Year*, 1948, p. 51) who
passes by the more favoured "peonied
and lilied" and claims that we should
read "pionied". "Pionies", he says, is

still in local use as the name of a certain variety of wild orchis; "twilled"
is another current dialect word for
plaited osiers used to prevent bank
erosion. The second school does not
emend. There is some variety within
the general agreement on some sort of
ditching operation. The credit for the
idea must go to Henley, but the
modern version was most completely
anticipated by an anonymous correspondent of Boswell's (see Furness
Variorum). The two explanations
which seem to me best are (*a*) that of
T. P. Harrison (*M.L.N.*, June 1943,
p. 422). Developing an idea of Kittredge, he treats "pioned" and "twilled" as meaning "dug" and "woven".
The phrase describes "the channelled
and indented appearance of the edges
of each elevated bank, worn and
carved by the current and . . . the
weather". The "pioneers" have built
embankments; these banks are fortified by layers of branches criss-cross.
The top layer shows thus, creating a
ridged, "woven" ("twilled") surface,
justifying "the happy trope, *twilled
brims*". We are referred to photo-
graphs showing similar effects in
modern embankments. (*b*) Middleton
Murry's theory (*Shakespeare*, 1937)
takes "pioned" as meaning "sloping"
(thus used of a woman's shoulders in

Which spongy April at thy hest betrims, 65
To make cold nymphs chaste crowns; and thy broom-groves,
Whose shadow the dismissed bachelor loves,
Being lass-lorn; thy poll-clipt vineyard;
And thy sea-marge, sterile and rocky-hard,
Where thou thyself dost air;—the queen o' th' sky, 70
Whose wat'ry arch and messenger am I,
Bids thee leave these; and with her sovereign grace,

JUNO *descends.*

Here, on this grass-plot, in this very place,
To come and sport:—her peacocks fly amain:
Approach, rich Ceres, her to entertain. 75

Enter CERES.

Cer. *Hail, many-colour'd messenger, that ne'er*

66. broom-groves] brown groves Hanmer, ed. conj.   68. poll-clipt] F (pole-clipt); pale-clipt Warburton.   69. rocky-hard] rocky hard Gould conj.
72. S.D. *Juno descends*] transposed to 102 Theobald, Camb.   74. her] Rowe; here F.   76. many-colour'd] Rowe; many-coloured F.

example given by *O.E.D.*) and "twilled" as meaning "tewelled" ("tewel" [obsolete] = pipe or channel). A "pioned and twilled brim" is a mill-dam or a drainage bank in flat country. If one must choose between these explanations, there is little doubt that Mr Harrison's is the most likely. See pp. 170 and 173.

65. spongy April] Cf. *Cym.*, IV. ii. 349.

66. broom-groves] Explanations offered are (1) the *genista* which shades shepherds in Virgil (*Georg.*, II. 434) (W. P. Mustard, *M.L.N.*, XXXVIII, 79); and (2) clumps of gorse (W. Taggard, *ibid.*, 375). Neither seems very convincing, and I think the copy may have had *broune-groves*. What Tannenbaum says in favour of *broom* in I. i. 62 can be urged in reverse, in favour of *broune* (*brown*). Crane often joined epithet to noun by a hyphen. But F is not so obviously corrupt that I dare print *brown*.

68. poll-clipt] This modernized spelling is explained by H. Kökeritz (*M.L.R.*, April 1944). Pole=poll; therefore "pole-clipt" = "pruned", "pollarded", here with reference to the practice of pruning grapevines in spring. "Vineyard" must be trisyllabic.

69. rocky-hard] F has "Sea-marge stirrile, and rockey-hard", which is normal pointing, even if "rocky-hard" is an epithet of "sea-marge"; but the hyphen may be Crane's and "hard" a noun, meaning "embankment" or "jetty".

72. (S.D.) *Juno descends*] See note on p. 170. Unless those who suspect serious interference with the play at this point are right, Juno must be held to start or prepare her passage earthward here; but many editors transpose the S.D. to l. 102. The reference in l. 72 suggests an appearance.

76. Ceres] Perhaps impersonated by Ariel; see l. 167 and note.

> *Dost disobey the wife of Jupiter;*
> *Who, with thy saffron wings, upon my flowers*
> *Diffusest honey-drops, refreshing showers;*
> *And with each end of thy blue bow dost crown*   80
> *My bosky acres and my unshrubb'd down,*
> *Rich scarf to my proud earth; why hath thy queen*
> *Summon'd me hither, to this short-grass'd green?*

Iris. *A contract of true love to celebrate;*
> *And some donation freely to estate*   85
> *On the blest lovers.*

Cer.   *Tell me, heavenly bow,*
> *If Venus or her son, as thou dost know,*
> *Do now attend the queen? Since they did plot*
> *The means that dusky Dis my daughter got,*
> *Her and her blind boy's scandal'd company*   90
> *I have forsworn.*

Iris.   *Of her society*
> *Be not afraid: I met her deity*
> *Cutting the clouds towards Paphos, and her son*
> *Dove-drawn with her. Here thought they to have done*
> *Some wanton charm upon this man and maid,*   95

---

83. short-grass'd] Camb.; short grass'd F3, F4; short gras'd F, F2.

---

78. saffron wings] Phaer (1588) rendered Virgil's *croceis . . . pennis* as "saffron wings" (*Aen.*, IV. 700).

81. bosky acres] The antithesis to "bosky" is "unshrubb'd" in the same line; *i.e.*, the land with bush, brake, thicket, as contrasted with the bare plain or hill.

82. Rich scarf] *i.e.*, adornment (usually of silk); cf. *Mer.V.*, III. ii. 98, *All's W.*, II. iii. 214.

83. short-grass'd green] Law suggested the green baize floor-covering of the inner stage at Court. See Appendix E.

85. estate] Bestow (cf. *MND.*, I. i. 98).

85–6.] It is upon this passage that W. J. Lawrence based his theory that the play was performed at the betrothal of the Elector Palatine and Princess Elizabeth on 27 December 1612.

See *Intro.*, p. xxii and Appendix E.

86. heavenly bow] *i.e.*, Iris.

89. that] Whereby.

dusky] Being king of the underworld. The episode alluded to is the subject of two famous passages, in *Wint.*, IV. iv. 116 ff, and *Par. L.*, IV. 268–72.

90. scandal'd] One shuns Cupid's society because he has made himself an evil reputation by his improper acts. "Scandal" as a verb is not rare. Here, simply, "touched with scandal". N.S. unnecessarily conjectures "sandalled". See under *scandal* in *O.E.D.*

93. Cutting the clouds] Cf. "Night's swift dragons cut the clouds full fast" (*MND.*, III. ii. 379).

Paphos] In Cyprus; the favourite resort of the goddess, and centre of her cult.

> *Whose vows are, that no bed-right shall be paid*
> *Till Hymen's torch be lighted: but in vain;*
> *Mars's hot minion is return'd again;*
> *Her waspish-headed son has broke his arrows,*
> *Swears he will shoot no more, but play with sparrows,*   100
> *And be a boy right out.*

Cer.   *Highest queen of state,*
> *Great Juno comes; I know her by her gait.*

Juno. *How does my bounteous sister? Go with me*
> *To bless this twain, that they may prosperous be,*
> *And honour'd in their issue.*   They sing: 105

Juno.   *Honour, riches, marriage-blessing,*
> *Long continuance, and increasing,*
> *Hourly joys be still upon you!*
> *Juno sings her blessings on you.*

Cer.   *Earth's increase, foison plenty,*   110

96. bed-right] bed-rite Steevens.   98. Mars's] F3, F4; Marses F, F2.   99.
waspish-headed] waspish-heady A. W. Reed conj. (*apud* N.S.).   101. Highest]
High'st Capell; High Pope.   102. gait] Johnson; gate F.   106. marriage-
blessing] Theobald; marriage, blessing F.   110. *Cer.*] Theobald; omitted F,
Ff.   Earth's] Earthes Wright conj.   foison] and foison Ff, Rowe.

96. bed-right] A variant of bed-
rite. Cf. the warning of Prospero,
ll. 14 ff. See note on p. 170.

98. hot minion] Hot-blooded darling, lustful mistress, *i.e.*, Venus. For
this defeat of Venus see note on l. 23.

99. waspish-headed] Not to be
taken too literally; Cupid is peevish
and stings. Cf. Jonson, *Cynthia's Revels*,
v. x. 111, where Mercury addresses
Cupid as "light hony-bee".

100. sparrows] Cf. in the song in
Lyly's *Alexander and Campaspe*, "His
Mothers doves, and teeme of sparows"
(III. v; Malone Soc. Reprint 66, 1934,
Appendix).

101. of state] Stately.

102.] Ultimately, derived from the
divom incedo regina and the *vera incessu
patuit dea* of Virgil. Sandys, in his translation of *Aen.* I, has "gait" in this
latter place. But the idea seems to
have been commonplace; Baldwin,
Shakspere's Small Latin, cites Erasmus,
Adagia (II. 481.)

103. bounteous sister] Cf. l. 60.

106.] *Juno pronuba* pronounces a
marriage-blessing on the couple; then
Ceres, the bounteous, endows them
with her abundance. Or so it is agreed.
But possibly "They sing" the whole
song together. The rough rhyming of
these lines has often been remarked
upon. They are not without parallel;
compare the octosyllabics of *Meas.*,
which some editors wish to dispose of;
and also the disastrous conclusion of
R 2, which persuaded E. M. W.
Tillyard that "he [Shakespeare] was
never very good at the couplet."
(*Shakespeare's History Plays* (1944),
p. 245.) In fact these lines are far from
being the doggerel that an unsympa-
thetic criticism has called them. Their
movement is expertly and variously
solemn. Cf. *Epil.*

110.] The need here is to give
"earth's" its full stress, and not to correct the line. F2, characteristically,
eked it out with "and"; W. A. Wright

> *Barns and garners never empty;*
> *Vines with clust'ring bunches growing;*
> *Plants with goodly burthen bowing;*
> *Spring come to you at the farthest*
> *In the very end of harvest!*   115
> *Scarcity and want shall shun you;*
> *Ceres' blessing so is on you.*

Fer. This is a most majestic vision, and
       Harmonious charmingly. May I be bold
       To think these spirits?
Pros.   Spirits, which by mine Art   120
       I have from their confines call'd to enact
       My present fancies.
Fer.   Let me live here ever;
       So rare a wonder'd father and a wise

121. *from their confines*] *from all their confines* Ff, Rowe.   123. *So . . . wise*] *So rare
a wonder, and a father wise* Staunton.   *wise*] *wife* F variant?

and N.S. more ingeniously with
"earthes". The 1609 editor of the
First Folio of *The Faerie Queene* failed
to understand Spenser's "th' Earthes
gloomy shade" (III. x. 46 in 1590 and
1596) and read "the Earthes gloomy
shade". The form introduced by W.
A. Wright was obsolete by 1609. See
J. C. Smith's Oxford edition of *The
Faerie Queene, Intro.,* pp. xvii–xviii.

    foison] Used earlier, II. i. 159.

    plenty] Plentiful; as in "If reasons
were as plenty as blackberries . . .",
1 H 4, II. iv. 264–5.

    114–15. Spring, *etc.*] Almost cer-
tainly the expression of a conventional
wish for a Golden Age of winterless
years, in which spring and autumn
are simultaneous, or consecutive. See
F.Q., III. vi. 42; *Par. L.*, IV, Bacon *Of
Gardens,* etc. Mrs Kemble rightly
draws attention to Leviticus xxvi, but
the main sources of the idea in Renaissance literature are Virgil, *Eclogue* IV,
Ovid, *Met.* I, and Boethius, *de Consola-
tione Philosophiae.* The reference, which
Gonzalo made rather differently in
II. i, is, by convention and the logic of
the *genre*, particularly to be sought in

pastoral contexts, like this one. For the
use of this passage as evidence to show
that the masque is interpolated, see
Intro., p. xxiii.

    119. *charmingly*] With a reference
to magic, and also to music. Cf. v.
i. 54.

    123. *So . . . father*] A father to be
wondered at; a father capable of producing wonders. Cf. "So fair an offer'd
chain" (*Err.*, III. ii. 186). Possibly, if
we read *wife* at the end of the line,
another play on Miranda's name.

    and a wise] We may think that, in
this Adam-like situation, Ferdinand
must have said *wife*; and the rhyme is
unexpected. It has long been on record that some copies of F read *wife*,
but no editor of the play seems to have
examined such a copy, though other
variant readings in the Folio text of
the play are amply vouched for. This
is obviously a matter for further inquiry; meanwhile one must read *wise*.
(Rowe's *wife* is almost certainly an
emendation of F4, since he did not
collate F.) In any case, ſ : f is an easy
misprint, and the true reading may be
wife after all.

Makes this place Paradise.

Juno and Ceres whisper, and send Iris on employment.

Pros.   Sweet, now, silence!
Juno and Ceres whisper seriously;   125
There's something else to do: hush, and be mute,
Or else our spell is marr'd.

Iris. You nymphs, call'd Naiads, of the windring brooks,
With your sedg'd crowns and ever-harmless looks,
Leave your crisp channels, and on this green land   130
Answer your summons; Juno does command:
Come, temperate nymphs, and help to celebrate
A contract of true love; be not too late.

Enter certain Nymphs.

You sunburn'd sicklemen, of August weary,
Come hither from the furrow, and be merry: 135
Make holiday; your rye-straw hats put on,
And these fresh nymphs encounter every one
In country footing.

---

124. *Makes*] *Make* Pope.   Juno . . . employment] Capell; following 127, F.
128. Naiads] Steevens; Nayades F.   windring] winding Rowe; wandring
Steevens.   129. sedg'd] sedge Walker.   130. green land] Theobald; greene-
Land F.   136. holiday] Camb.; holly day F; holy-day F4.

124. *Makes*] If *wife* is read in the previous line this is another example of a singular verb with a plural subject. It certainly could not be used as an argument against the reading *wife*.

Sweet, now, etc.] Wright suggests that this speech, down to *seriously*, might be given to Miranda.

125. *Ceres . . . seriously*] An Elizabethan jingle.

126–7.] See note on l. 59.

128.] Beaumont, in his *Masque of the Gentlemen of Gray's-Inn and the Inner Temple*, of 1613, has a masque of Naiads, joined later by one of Knights. This Masque was also performed during the marriage celebrations, and there are other slight points of similarity. Iris is the presenter in both; and there are two verbal parallels which

are easily explained by the occasion and the theme.

windring] See note on III. ii. 135. *O.E.D.* has only this example. Editors break it down into *winding* and *wandering*, but there is no need to choose between the two; *windring* is an easily understood portmanteau-word. W. W. Greg cites Greene's *James IV*, l. 1074, "Inconstinence"—a combination of "inconstancy" and "incontinence".

130. crisp] Covered with wavelets. So, "crisp heaven" (covered with small curled clouds), *Tim.*, IV. iii. 183.

132. temperate] This is why Naiads are summoned; they are temperate, chaste (suggested by the cool water, etc.).

138. footing] Dance, cf. I. ii. 381.

Enter certain Reapers, properly habited: they join with the Nymphs in a graceful dance; towards the end whereof PROSPERO *starts suddenly, and speaks; after which, to a strange, hollow, and confused noise, they heavily vanish.*

Pros. [*Aside*] I had forgot that foul conspiracy
        Of the beast Caliban and his confederates   140
        Against my life: the minute of their plot
        Is almost come. [*To the Spirits.*] Well done! avoid;
            no more!
Fer. This is strange: your father's in some passion
        That works him strongly.
Mir.   Never till this day
        Saw I him touch'd with anger, so distemper'd.   145
Pros. You do look, my son, in a mov'd sort,
        As if you were dismay'd: be cheerful, sir.
        Our revels now are ended. These our actors,

---

139. Aside] Johnson.   142. To the Spirits.] Johnson.   143. *strange*] *most strange* Theobald.   146. *You do look*] *Why, you do look* Hanmer; *You look* Pope.

S.D., l. 4] "heavily" means "dejectedly", "sorrowfully". For this abrupt conclusion, for which the motivation is apparently inadequate, see *Intro.*, p. lxxv. Play-"masques" could never end properly; see *Intro.*, p. lxxii.

142. *avoid*] Begone. Cf. *Wint.*, I. ii. 462.

143.] Walker seems to be right in requiring that we should read the line as if *is* were absorbed into *This*, giving the usual trisyllabic value to *passion* at the end of the line.

144. *works*] Agitates. Cf. "so strongly works 'em", v. i. 17.

145. *distemper'd*] Cf. "My pulse as yours doth *temperately* keep time" (*Ham.*, III. iv. 140). If the comma after *anger* is omitted, we have the tautology *distemper'd anger*. This is unnecessary; Miranda is describing the loss of "temperament" which is the result of anger; cf. *F.Q.*, II, *passim*.

146. *You do look*] Having wondered that Prospero should so excite himself over an easily controlled insurrection,

we are now puzzled by his turning to console Ferdinand in a distress which is far less apparent, and in language of great, though elegiac serenity. But Ferdinand is disturbed because he has seen Prospero disturbed; for the reasons of Prospero's disturbance, see note on S.D. above. This development has been much discussed by those who regard the masque as an interpolation.

mov'd sort] Troubled state. The metrical irregularity of this line persuaded the old Cambridge editors that Shakespeare could not have written it. It has been regarded as a "join", by someone who had to fit the masque into the play.

148. *revels*] The term used of the livelier dances, by masquers and audience, in masques and other courtly displays. Here used more generally (cf. "Master of the Revels"). This passage has long been recognized as owing something to a stanza in the *Tragedie of Darius*, by William Alex-

As I foretold you, were all spirits, and
Are melted into air, into thin air: 150
And, like the baseless fabric of this vision,
The cloud-capp'd towers, the gorgeous palaces,
The solemn temples, the great globe itself,
Yea, all which it inherit, shall dissolve,
And, like this insubstantial pageant faded,   155
Leave not a rack behind. We are such stuff
As dreams are made on; and our little life
Is rounded with a sleep. Sir, I am vex'd;
Bear with my weakness; my old brain is troubled:
Be not disturb'd with my infirmity: 160

151. *this vision*] *their vision* Ff, Rowe.   154. *inherit*] *inherits* Furness conj., Tannenbaum conj.   156. *rack*] F3, F4; *racke* F; *wrack* Singer; *wreck* Dyce 157. *on*] *of* Steevens.

ander, Earl of Sterline (1603). See *Intro.*, p. lxxiv. There is also a significant similarity to a passage in Daniel's masque, *Tethys' Festival*. However, Baldwin says the source is Palingenius, through Googe. The idea of comparing actors to the dissolving pageant of dreams originates in Chrysostom, and was widely known "among the learned men of the church" (*Shakspere's Small Latin*, 1. 673–5). See also Job, xx. 6–8.

149. *and*] Weak ending.

151. *like the baseless fabric*] The idea is almost repeated in l. 155.

154. *inherit*] Possess, occupy; cf. *Cym.*, III. ii. 63 and Matt. v. 5. The climax *all which it inherit* introduces *We are such stuff*; it is therefore unlikely that it should be rendered, "all things that the globe inherits", as Furness suggests.

155. *pageant*] Again a semi-technical reference; Shakespeare has perhaps in mind the elaborate but temporary structures contrived for civic pageants and royal entries at this period. See *Intro.*, p. lxxiii.

156. *rack*] Perhaps Alexander's "vapours" (*Intro.*, p. lxxiv). Rack (cf. Scots "reek", smoke) is a light cloud or bank of clouds. Cf. *Ant.*, IV. xiv. 10:

"The rack dislimns." See *Intro.*, p. lxxiii.

157. *on*] Of.

158. *rounded*] Wright's suggestion that this means "crowned" (cf. *MND.*, IV. i. 53—and he might have added *R 2*, III. ii. 161, *R 3*, IV. i. 60, *Mac.*, I. v. 29, IV. i. 88), seems good when supported by so many parallels. Usually the meaning is taken to be "rounded off". The sentiment in either case is stoical in the negative way; it does not, for instance, suggest the technical neo-Stoicism of Chapman and his "Senecal" heroes *à thèse*.

159. *my old brain*] Prospero's disturbance continues from his sudden outburst during the masque; and in the next act we find him in the grip of that righteous anger which is an attribute of the temperate man. Apart from motives already suggested, we may accept Warburton's observation that Prospero's anger at this point is quite adequately motivated by ingratitude; Caliban's ingratitude recalls that of Antonio—to the one he gave the use of reason, to the other ducal power. The conspiracy afoot reminds him of the trials of the past twelve years, which are now being rapidly re-enacted.

If you be pleas'd, retire into my cell,
And there repose: a turn or two I'll walk,
To still my beating mind.

Fer., Mir.   We wish your peace.   *Exeunt.*
Pros. Come with a thought. I thank thee. Ariel: come.

Enter ARIEL.

Ari. Thy thoughts I cleave to. What's thy pleasure?
Pros.   Spirit,   165
    We must prepare to meet with Caliban.
Ari. Ay, my commander: when I presented Ceres,
    I thought to have told thee of it; but I fear'd
    Lest I might anger thee.
Pros. Say again, where didst thou leave these varlets?   170
Ari. I told you, sir, they were red-hot with drinking;
    So full of valour that they smote the air
    For breathing in their faces; beat the ground
    For kissing of their feet; yet always bending
    Towards their project. Then I beat my tabor;   175
    At which, like unback'd colts, they prick'd their ears,
    Advanc'd their eyelids, lifted up their noses
    As they smelt music: so I charm'd their ears,

---

161. *you*] *thou* Rowe.   163. *your*] *you* F4, Rowe.   Exeunt] Theobald; Exit F.
164. *thank . . . come*] *thank thee* Ariell: *come* F; *thank you: Ariel, come.* Theobald;
think thee, Ariel: come. N.S.   169. *Lest*] F4; *Least* F.

163. *beating*] Cf. I. ii. 176, v. i.
246.
164. *I thank thee.*] Addressed, I believe, to Ferdinand and Miranda; the
thanks are for their *We wish your peace.*
This was Theobald's view; the objection to it is that one would expect *you*
rather than *thee.* Some editors have
read *you* or *ye,* but Prospero could
easily address to one person a remark
intended for both. If the F reading is
right, Prospero is presumably thank-
ing Ariel for the masque; but this
seems unlikely, since Ariel has not yet
arrived.
166. *meet with*] Encounter. Or, pay
out, be even with; or, deal with.
167. *presented*] Either, played the

part of Ceres; or, as "presenter" of the
masque, introduced her while playing
the part of Iris. Why does Ariel mention this?
170–1. *Sa again . . . I told you*] N.S.
uses these words in support of the
theory that the play has been cut; certain remarks in *Mac.* are treated
similarly. But we are not to imagine
that there is no commerce between
characters save that which is represented directly. Ariel repeats a private
message; "this time", so to speak, the
audience hears it.
176. *unback'd*] That had never been
ridden.
177. *Advanc'd*] Cf. I. ii. 411 and
note. Paraphrased by *lifted up.*

That, calf-like, they my lowing follow'd, through
Tooth'd briers, sharp furzes, pricking goss, and thorns,
Which enter'd their frail shins: at last I left them   181
I' th' filthy-mantled pool beyond your cell,
There dancing up to th' chins, that the foul lake
O'erstunk their feet.

Pros.   This was well done, my bird.
Thy shape invisible retain thou still: 185
The trumpery in my house, go bring it hither,
For stale to catch these thieves.

Ari.   I go, I go.   *Exit.*

Pros. A devil, a born devil, on whose nature
Nurture can never stick; on whom my pains,
Humanely taken, all, all lost, quite lost;   190

---

182. *filthy-mantled*] Camb.; *filthy mantled* F; *filth-ymantled* Steevens conj.   184.
feet] *fear* Spedding conj.; *sweat* N.S. conj.

179–84.] Cf. Puck's feats in *MND.*
See Appendix B.

180. *goss*] Gorse.

182. *filthy-mantled*] Covered with
filthy scum. Cf. "The green mantle of
the standing pool", *Lr.*, III. iv. 139.

183. *that*] So that—owing to the
disturbance of the water.

184. *O'erstunk their feet*] To be precise, their feet when normally exposed,
not submerged. There is no point in
trying to alter this. N.S. suggests
sweat for *feet*.

bird] Cf. "My Ariel, chick", v. i.
316.

186. *trumpery*] Hints of this plot-
device occur in the Italian *scenari*. See
Intro., p. lxviii. Holt's frequently repeated statement that it is a way of
hindering the murderers from enter-
ing the cave for an attack on Prospero
is sound as far as it goes; and Luce
was right to observe that it tells us
more about the natures of Caliban
and his confederates.

187. *stale*] Decoy; a stuffed bird of
the species the fowler wished to take,
or sometimes a live bird.

188–9. *nature Nurture*] Cf. *Euphues*:
"[he] began to bewaile his *Nurture*,

and to muse at his *Nature*." See V. M.
Jeffery's *John Lyly and the Italian Renaissance*, p. 126. *Nature* is here a complex
idea involving an opposition to Art (as
exemplified by Prospero's art) and
Grace (superadded to Nature by
divine agency); representing not only
the idea of innate character, but of
graceless and fallen life. *Nurture* is
what Miranda has been given by
Prospero—with her the operation was
successful, because her nature is differentiated from Caliban's—and it
stands for "education" in a broad
sense, taking learning to be a way of
compensating for the Fall (cf. the
myth of the learned Adam) and re-
pairing the defects of "nature". *Nurture* is often associated with high birth
(cf. *AYL.*, II. vii. 97 and the sharp
nature-nurture contrasts in Spenser;
also Imogen's brothers in *Cym.*). These
points are developed at length in the
Intro. (pp. xliii ff). See J. Middleton
Murry (*Shakespeare* [1936]) for an
interpretation of the play based on
a special reading of these lines.
Tilley cites variations on the theme
(N47).

190. *Humanely*] Cf. 1. ii. 348.

And as with age his body uglier grows,
So his mind cankers. I will plague them all,
Even to roaring.

[Re-]enter ARIEL, *loaden with glistering apparel, etc.*

Come, hang them on this line.

*[*PROSPERO *and* ARIEL *remain, invisible.]*

Enter CALIBAN, STEPHANO, *and* TRINCULO, *all wet.*

Cal. Pray you, tread softly, that the blind mole may not
　　　Hear a foot fall: we now are near his cell.　　　　195
Ste. Monster, your fairy, which you say is a harmless
　　　fairy, has done little better than played the Jack
　　　with us.
Trin. Monster, I do smell all horse-piss; at which my
　　　nose is in great indignation.　　　　200
Ste. So is mine. Do you hear, monster? If I should take
　　　a displeasure against you, look you,—
Trin. Thou wert but a lost monster.

193. S.D. Re-enter ... etc.] Capell; Enter ... etc. F (following *line.*).　　Prospero ... invisible] Capell.

191–2.] Again the Platonic equation of spirit and body.

193. *line*] There is a dispute as to
whether this means "lime-tree" (see
v. i. 10) or "clothes-line". There were
certainly trees on the stage in this, as
in many other plays, and "line" is a
variant of "lime" or "linden". The
main objection to this view is that
some of the later punning is said to be
easier to explain if *line* means a
clothes-line made of hair, as was
usual; but this does not seem to be so,
since, as Luce pointed out, there is no
unequivocal allusion to a hair-line.
Brae (*Trans. Royal Soc. Lit.*, 1873) is as
anxious to be rid of the clothes-line as
many of his predecessors were, on the
ground of decorum, and is led into
some follies as a result; but he does
make it seem more probable that the

line is a tree by an apt citation from
Holinshed. We should beware of following him on grounds of decorum (a
clothes-line would do quite well here),
but a tree nevertheless seems the probable explanation. Brae's contribution
refuted the contention that "line'
never occurred without "tree". See'
l. 235, etc., below.

194–5. *the blind mole may not Hear*]
This keen hearing of the mole is
noticed in *Euphues*, "Doth not ... the
moale heare lightlyer ..." (Luce.)

197. *played the Jack*] In two senses,
played the knave, and played the
Jack o' lantern (will-o'-the-wisp). For
the first, cf. "Do you play the flouting
Jack, to tell us Cupid is a good hare
finder?" (*Ado*, I. i. 186). For the
second, see *MND.*, II. i. 39. (Luce.)
See Tilley, J8.

Cal. Good my lord, give me thy favour still.
    Be patient, for the prize I'll bring thee to   205
    Shall hoodwink this mischance: therefore speak softly.
    All's hush'd as midnight yet.

Trin. Ay, but to lose our bottles in the pool,—

Ste. There is not only disgrace and dishonour in that,
    monster, but an infinite loss.   210

Trin. That's more to me than my wetting: yet this is
    your harmless fairy, monster.

Ste. I will fetch off my bottle, though I be o'er ears for
    my labour.

Cal. Prithee, my King, be quiet. See'st thou here,   215
    This is the mouth o' th' cell: no noise, and enter.
    Do that good mischief which may make this island
    Thine own for ever, and I, thy Caliban,
    For aye thy foot-licker.

Ste. Give me thy hand. I do begin to have bloody   220
    thoughts.

Trin. O King Stephano! O peer! O worthy Stephano!
    look what a wardrobe here is for thee!

Cal. Let it alone, thou fool; it is but trash.

Trin. O, ho, monster! we know what belongs to a frip-   225
    pery. O King Stephano!

---

204. *Good*] *Good, good* Hanmer.   207. *hush'd*] *husht* F; *hush* Tannenbaum
conj.   208. *lose*] Ff; *loose* F.

---

206. *Shall hoodwink this mischance*] In *Cym.* we may find a somewhat similar use of the figure: "For friends kill friends, and the disorder's such / As war were hoodwink'd" (v. ii. 15, 16). Here in *Tp.*, mischance is to be hoodwinked like a hawk, and so rendered incapable of further harm-doing, and also put out of sight and remembrance. (Luce.)

212. *fairy*] Note a degree of interchangeability in the expressions "spirit" and "fairy". See Appendix B for comment on the identification of native fairies with classical and Neo-Platonic daemons.

217. *good mischief*] An oxymoron; cf. "loving wrong", I. ii. 151.

222. *King Stephano*] In *Oth.*, II. iii. 92, are two stanzas of a ballad printed in Percy's *Reliques*, entitled "Take thy old cloak about thee"; one of these is as follows: "King Stephen was a worthy peere, / His breeches cost him but a crowne, / He held them sixpence all too deere; / Therefore he called the taylor Lowne." Hence Trinculo's remark, "What a wardrobe." (Luce.)

225–6. *frippery*] Old clothes shop. Old French, "Fripper", to rub up and down, wear to rags. Cotgrave gives "*Friperie*, brokers shop, street of brokers, or of Fripiers". And "*Fripier*, a mender or trimmer up of old garments, and a seller of them so mended". (Luce.)

Ste. Put off that gown, Trinculo; by this hand, I'll have
    that gown.

Trin. Thy grace shall have it.

Cal. The dropsy drown this fool! what do you mean   230
    To dote thus on such luggage? Let't alone,
    And do the murther first: if he awake,
    From toe to crown he'll fill our skins with pinches,
    Make us strange stuff.

Ste. Be you quiet, monster. Mistress line, is not this my   235
    jerkin? Now is the jerkin under the line: now,
    jerkin, you are like to lose your hair, and prove a
    bald jerkin.

Trin. Do, do; we steal by line and level, an' like your
    grace.   240

---

231. *Let't alone*] Rann; *let's alone* F; *Let's along* Theobald; *Let it alone* Hanmer;
Let's all on N.S.   239. *Do, do*] Camb.; *Doe, doe* F; *Do-de* N.S. conj.   *an't*]
Capell; *and't* F.

---

231. *luggage*] See v. i. 298. "Camp-
followers' pickings", *1 H 4*, v. iv. 160.
But also "an encumbrance"; *O.E.D.*
2a. This is probably dominant.

Let't alone] Probably a repetition of
his "Let it alone" in l. 224. Otherwise
perhaps "Let's along."

234. *stuff*] Must here refer back to
the "glistering apparel"; the line
should be read with an emphasis on
us. "If you don't leave *that* stuff alone
and do the murder, he'll make *us*
strange stuff by pinching and bruising
us."

235. *Mistress line*] Brae argues for
Stephano's knowledge of the metamorphosis of the nymph Philyra into
a linden. But these words support
neither the "tree" nor the "clothes-
line" theory, though Luce finds in
Gerarde's *Herbal* a reference to the
"female line".

236. *Now is the jerkin under the line*]
He has taken down the garment; and
it is first, under the line, or lime; and
next, by a punning transition, under
the equinoctial line (as in *H 8*, v. iv.
44); and since, as it was thought,
people often lost their hair in fevers

contracted in crossing the line or in
regions near to it, so this jerkin was
like to lose its hair, and become
threadbare. There may also be a reference to the practical joke played by
sailors crossing the line, when they
shaved the heads of passengers. There
is perhaps a further play on "line and
hair" (a building material—*O.E.D.*
3c), in which hair was mixed with
lime to bind it into a cement. But
Tilley cites the passage in connexion
with the proverb, "He has struck the
ball under the line" (B62) and Malone
records a suggestion that the jest is
less decent than any of these conjectures.

239. *Do, do*] Perhaps signifying
approval; one would expect a laugh at
Stephano's joke, and it may be a misprint for some notation of a laugh.
Perhaps there is a similarity in Thersites' use of the expression in *Troil.*,
II. i. 40 ff.

by line and level] A quibbling rejoinder; according to rule, systematic-
ally. Tilley gives several examples of
this meaning, L305.

an't like] If it please.

Ste. I thank thee for that jest; here's a garment for't:
    wit shall not go unrewarded while I am King of this
    country. "Steal by line and level" is an excellent
    pass of pate; there's another garment for't.

Trin. Monster, come, put some lime upon your fingers, 245
    and away with the rest.

Cal. I will have none on't: we shall lose our time,
    And all be turn'd to barnacles, or to apes
    With foreheads villainous low.

Ste. Monster, lay-to your fingers: help to bear this away 250
    where my hogshead of wine is, or I'll turn you out
    of my kingdom: go to, carry this.

Trin. And this.

Ste. Ay, and this.

A noise of hunters heard. Enter divers Spirits, in shape of dogs and
    hounds, hunting them about; PROSPERO *and* ARIEL *setting*
    them on.

Pros. Hey, Mountain, hey!   255

Ari. Silver! there it goes, Silver!

Pros. Fury, Fury! there, Tyrant, there! hark, hark!
                  [*Cal., Ste., and Trin. are driven out.*]
    Go charge my goblins that they grind their joints

---

247. *lose*] Ff; *loose* F.   248. *or to*] *or* Pope.   257. S.D. Cal. . . . out]
Camb.

244. *pass of pate*] Thrust of wit, witty
sally. A figure from fencing. The point
of the pass of pate is quite lost.

245. *lime*] Bird-lime—possibly carrying on the punning. A very sticky
substance; a usual periphrasis for
thieving. See Tilley, F236.

248. *barnacles*] The lore of the barna-
cle is curious and widespread. It is
found in Mandeville, Gerarde, Holinshed, and in many other places. The
notion of the metamorphosis of shellfish into goose is scarcely so relevant to
the text that we should pause longer
than to give the most attractively conceited version of it: ". . . rotten sides of
broken ships do change / To *Barnacles*;

O Transformation strange! / 'Twas
first a green Tree, then a gallant
Hull; / Lately a Mushroom, now a
flying Gull." (Sylvester's *Du Bartas*,
6th day, 1st week, ll. 1127–30.)

254. S.D.] Thorndike first suggested
that this episode corresponded to an
anti-masque. See *Intro.*, p. lxxii. Peter
Martyr, as translated by Eden, speaks
of "dogges of maruelous deformed
shape, & such as coulde not barke" as
inhabiting the New World (*De Novo
Orbe*, f22ᵛ). See *Intro.*, p. xxxiii.

256. *Silver!*] Also name of a hound
in *Shr.*, I. i. 19. For the names of these
dogs and the supposed connexion
with *The Fair Sidea*, see *Intro.*, p. lxiv.

With dry convulsions; shorten up their sinews　　259
With aged cramps; and more pinch-spotted make them
Than pard or cat o' mountain.
Ari.　　　　　　　　　　　　Hark, they roar!
Pros.　Let them be hunted soundly. At this hour
Lies at my mercy all mine enemies:
Shortly shall all my labours end, and thou
Shalt have the air at freedom: for a little　　265
Follow, and do me service.　　　　　　*Exeunt.*

---

259. *dry*] *wry* Warburton conj.　　260. *aged*] *agued* Daniel Wilson.　　263. *Lies*]
Lie Rowe.

259. *dry convulsions*] *dry* is of doubtful
meaning. Sutherland suggests that it
is as in the phrase "dry-beating"—a
beating that bruises without drawing
blood. Probably there is an allusion to
current physiology; a condition of
"dryness" resulting from a deficiency
in the bodily humours might have as
a symptom the grinding of joints, etc.

261. *cat o' mountain*] Leopard; cf.
Jer., xiii. 23, *Wiv.*, II. ii. 27.

263. *Lies at my mercy*] Another singular verb with plural subject, this time
the result of the inversion; to call it a
false concord would be to judge Elizabethan syntax by the rules of modern
grammar.

266. Exeunt] The immediate reap-
pearance of Ariel and Prospero in
v. i is "not evidence that an intervening scene has been omitted, as Dover
Wilson contends, but that the act division is original" (Greg, *The Shakespeare
First Folio* [1955], p. 418, n. 1).

ACT V

SCENE I.—[*Before the Cell of Prospero.*]

Enter PROSPERO *in his magic robes, and* ARIEL.

Pros. Now does my project gather to a head:
  My charms crack not; my spirits obey; and time
  Goes upright with his carriage. How's the day?
Ari. On the sixth hour; at which time, my lord,
  You said our work should cease.
Pros.   I did say so,   5
  When first I rais'd the tempest. Say, my spirit,
  How fares the King and 's followers?
Ari.   Confin'd together
  In the same fashion as you gave in charge,
  Just as you left them; all prisoners, sir,

ACT V

Scene 1

ACT V . . . Prospero.] Camb.; Actus quintus: Scæna Prima. F.   7. *fares*] *fare*
Capell conj.

1. *project*] Undertaking, venture; but with a hint of the alchemical "projection", the last phase of the philosopher's experiment. "Project" could be used of the experiment as a whole. The metaphor in *gather to a head* (which is not unique) is certainly of a boil; perhaps there is some analogy between the process of a boil's development and the alchemical process. Both are slow, and the latter is also expected to discharge a new substance.

2. *crack*] Furness was certainly right in suspecting an alchemical reference. "Crack" is used of the explosion of retorts, etc., which brings Mammon's venture to disaster in Jonson's *Alchemist,* IV. v. 56 (S.D.). Shakespeare, however, uses the word in a great variety of metaphors, and the whole alchemical reference here, though of high importance in setting the tone of this last stage in Prospero's long self-preparation as a mage, is not obtruded.

3. *Goes upright*] "I have almost finished my task, and Time's burden is therefore light" (N.S.).

7. *How fares*] The singular verb expects "the King" alone as subject. Note the collection of unaccented syllables. See Abbott ¶ 484; but the phenomenon is not rare in Shakespeare.

9.] This line is deficient in one syllable, perhaps indicating a pause.

In the line-grove which weather-fends your cell;   10
They cannot budge till your release. The King,
His brother, and yours, abide all three distracted,
And the remainder mourning over them,
Brimful of sorrow and dismay; but chiefly
Him you term'd, sir, "The good old lord,
       Gonzalo";   15
His tears runs down his beard, like winter's drops
From eaves of reeds. Your charm so strongly
       works 'em,
That if you now beheld them, your affections
Would become tender.
Pros.   Dost thou think so, spirit?
Ari. Mine would, sir, were I human.
Pros.   And mine shall.   20
Hast thou, which art but air, a touch, a feeling
Of their afflictions, and shall not myself,
One of their kind, that relish all as sharply
Passion as they, be kindlier mov'd than thou art?

---

10. *line-grove*] *lime-grove* Rowe.   11. *your*] *you* F3, F4, Rowe.   15. *Him you*]
Him that you F.   16. *winter's*] *winter* F4, Rowe.   17. *reeds*] *reed* Capell conj.
20. *human*] Rowe; *humane* F, Ff.   23-4. *sharply / Passion*] F3, F4, Rowe;
sharpely, / Passion F, F2; *sharply / Passion'd* Pope; *sharply, / Passion'd* Hanmer.

---

10. *line-grove*] See note on IV. i.
193.
   weather-fends] Protects from the
weather.
   11. *your release*] Till released by
you.
   15. *Him you*] Rhythm and metre
suggest the redundancy of F's *that*.
   16. *fears runs*] Singular verb with
plural subject.
   17. *works*] Cf. IV. i. 144.
   18. *affections*] Feelings. Cf. *Mer.V.*,
IV. i. 50–2.
   20.] For the place of this conversation in the structure of the play, see
Intro., p. lxxv; and for its significance
in the development of the play's ideas,
Intro., p. xlviii.
   21. *touch*] Delicate feeling. Cf.
Tw.N., II. i. 13.
   21 ff. *Hast*, etc.] The difficulty of
this passage has been much exagger-

ated. We have to choose between
making *all* an adverb, and making
passion a verb; there are plenty of pre-
cedents for either procedure. If the
former is chosen (and in this case it
seems the better) the F comma after
sharply should be deleted. The meaning is then. Have you, mere air, been
able to sympathize with them,—and
shall I then, being human, and ex-
periencing emotion quite as intensely
as they, not feel more human sympathy than you? If *passion* is a verb,
Passion as they is a paraphrase of
relish all as sharply. Have you . . . and
shall I then, being human, and ex-
periencing everything as they do, and
feeling as they do, not etc.
   24. *kindlier*] Not only "more sym-
pathetically" but also "more in accordance with my kind, which is human".
Shakespeare constantly plays upon

Though with their high wrongs I am struck to th'
            quick,   25
Yet with my nobler reason 'gainst my fury
Do I take part: the rarer action is
In virtue than in vengeance: they being penitent,
The sole drift of my purpose doth extend
Not a frown further. Go release them, Ariel: 30
My charms I'll break, their senses I'll restore,
And they shall be themselves.
Ari.   I'll fetch them, sir.   *Exit.*
Pros. Ye elves of hills, brooks, standing lakes, and groves;
And ye that on the sands with printless foot
Do chase the ebbing Neptune, and do fly him   35
When he comes back; you demi-puppets that

---

26. *'gainst*] *against* F3, F4.   27. *action*] *virtue* Daniel conj.   28. *virtue*] *pardon*
Daniel conj.

---

this word, as in Hamlet's opening speech.

25. *their high wrongs*] Cf. III. iii. 88; v. i. 177. The cruel injuries inflicted on me by them (cf. l. 11).

27–8.] Another gnomic and vital idea, like IV. i. 188–9. *Virtue* is a word under strain; "pardon", as the commentator observed, would "suit" better. But *virtue* has a curiously positive and inclusive quality, and indeed is one of the leading motifs of the play. For full discussion, see *Intro.*, p. liii. Here *virtue*, being sharply contrasted with *vengeance*, cannot be other than the Christian virtue; but there is still the unmistakeable suggestion that Prospero here transcends the typical colossi, Tamburlaine and Bussy, and in his wisdom includes their strength as well as his own superior virtue. It may be noted that the writers of revenge plays, particularly Chapman in *The Revenge of Bussy d'Ambois* and Tourneur in *The Atheist's Tragedy*, were showing some signs of a more critical attitude to the ethical issues of their theme. For the self-conquest, always required of a prince, and here achieved by Prospero, see *Intro.*, p. xlviii. The function of reason in this

predicament is clearly stated in the fairly orthodox psychology of Gianfrancesco Pico della Mirandola's *Liber de Imaginatione* (1501; ed. and trans. Caplan, 1930) in the tenth chapter. He concludes, after quoting from St Augustine the remark, *omnis inordinatus animus poena sibi*, used by the author of *The True Declaration*: "We ought, therefore, to be drawn to pity and sympathy rather than to the commission of wrong, if only because our enemy is of the same nature as we, if only because from the very origin of nature we bear engraved in us the precept to love our kind . . ." (*ed. cit.*, p. 77). Here a formal psychology takes notice of the Sermon on the Mount.

Tilley cites this passage in connection with the proverb, "To be able to do harm and not do it is noble" (H170). Cf. *Sonn.*, XCIV; and Massinger, *Bashful Lover*, III. i, "'Tis truly noble, having power to punish, / Nay, king like, to forbear it"; and the Latin proverb, *Posse et nolle, nobile.*

33. *Ye elves*, etc.] Cf. IV. i. 213 and note. See *Intro.*, p. xli and Appendix D.

36. *demi-*] Probably with the sense of *quasi*. Cf. *Ant.*, I. v. 23, "The

By moonshine do the green sour ringlets make,
Whereof the ewe not bites; and you whose pastime
Is to make midnight mushrooms, that rejoice
To hear the solemn curfew; by whose aid—   40
Weak masters though ye be—I have bedimm'd
The noontide sun, call'd forth the mutinous winds,
And 'twixt the green sea and the azur'd vault
Set roaring war: to the dread rattling thunder
Have I given fire, and rifted Jove's stout oak   45
With his own bolt; the strong-bas'd promontory
Have I made shake, and by the spurs pluck'd up
The pine and cedar: graves at my command
Have wak'd their sleepers, op'd, and let 'em forth
By my so potent Art. But this rough magic   50
I here abjure; and, when I have requir'd

---

39. *mushrooms*] Rowe; *Mushrumps* F, F2; *Mushromes* F3, F4.   41. *masters*]
min'sters Hanmer.

---

demi-Atlas of this earth". Refers to
the doll-like size of the elves. Cf.
the puppets (tree-spirits) with
which children decorated Maytide
hoops.

37. *green sour ringlets*] "Fairy rings",
variously explained in folklore, but in
fact due to the underground part
(mycelium) of a toadstool, which
affects the grass roots.

38.] Mushrooms, because they
grow overnight, are "here imagined to
be produced by the art of elves at the
witching hour of midnight". (Kittredge).

39, 40. *rejoice*, etc.] Cf. I. ii. 329; also
Lr., III. iv. 120: "This is the foul fiend
Flibbertigibbet; he begins at curfew
and walks till the first cock."

41. *Weak masters*] This has not been
satisfactorily explained. *Masters* cannot here mean "adepts", and there is
no parallel in *O.E.D.* Some explain
that the masters are weak because
their magical powers derive from Prospero; some, like N.S., follow Hanmer
in reading *ministers*. But Jonson helps
us to understand the expression. In a
note to the *Masque of Queens* he

speaks of the witches' "little masters
or martinets", "Their little Martin is
he that calls them to their conven-
ticles . . . Delrio. *Disq. Mag.* quaest.
16, lib. 2" (H. A. Evans, *English
Masques*, pp. 39-40, 36n). See also
Spenser, *F.Q.*, III. viii. 4: "She was
wont her Sprights to entertaine, / The
maisters of her art." See also p. 173.

48. *graves*, etc.] There seems to be no
occasion for this; all the other magic
feats Prospero has performed, or
could have performed, save this one.
The function of the speech is not, of
course, informative; although Prospero refers to his recent tempest, its
object is the general one of using every
possible resource to enforce the
potency of his powers, immediately
before he abjures them. See Appendix D.

50. *rough*] Expressing itself in the
manipulation of material forces; un-
subtle by comparison with the next
degree of the mage's enlighten-
ment.

51. *requir'd*] Probably in the early
sense of "asked for"—not a command.

Some heavenly music,—which even now I do,—
To work mine end upon their senses, that
This airy charm is for, I'll break my staff,
Bury it certain fadoms in the earth,   55
And deeper than did ever plummet sound
I'll drown my book.   *Solemn music.*

Here enters ARIEL *before: then* ALONSO, *with a frantic gesture,
attended by* GONZALO; SEBASTIAN *and* ANTONIO *in like
manner, attended by* ADRIAN *and* FRANCISCO: *they all enter
the circle which* PROSPERO *had made, and there stand charm'd;
which* PROSPERO *observing, speaks:*

A solemn air, and the best comforter
To an unsettled fancy, cure thy brains,
Now useless, boil'd within thy skull! There stand,   60
For you are spell-stopp'd.

58. *and*] omitted Capell.   60. *boil'd*] Rowe; *boile* F; *boil* N.S.; *toil'd* Tannenbaum conj.

53. *their senses, that*] The senses of
those for whom.

54. *airy charm*] The music. A play on
the word "charm". It is used primarily in its magical sense, secondarily in
the sense of "song"—a sense in which
it applies to birdsong, but also more
generally. Cf. Milton, *Par. L.*, IV. 643,
"charm of earliest birds". The magical sense derives from the Latin *carmen*;
for the history of the word, and its
connection with the native word
which carries the secondary meaning,
see *O.E.D.*

55. *certain*] Cf. *Caes.*, IV. iii. 70. For
the abjuration of magic, see *Intro.*,
p. xlviii.

57. (S.D., l. 4) the circle] A common feature in ceremonial magic.

58. *and the best comforter*] *and* must
here represent "which is". Cf. "and to
torment me", II. ii. 15. The speech
alludes to the widely-known Renaissance theory of the affective and thera-
peutic powers of music.

59. *unsettled fancy*] Cf. *MND.*, v. i.
25 and *Wint.*, II. iii. 119, "weak-
hinged fancy".

60. *boil'd*] F has *boile*, and I think
we must here believe in an *e : d* misprint, though Tannenbaum conjectures *toil'd*. The sense "over-excited"
"reduced by passion", is fairly common. Jonson, for instance, speaks of
lovers' marrow being boiled by their
passion (*Cynthia's Revels*, v. x. 38). See
also *Wint.*, III. iii. 64, where the sense
is slightly different. In *MND.*, lovers
have "seething" brains (v. i. 4). It is
just possible that the contemporary
slang meaning, "betrayed", affects
this context (see *O.E.D.*). F encloses
now useless in parentheses. M. R.
Ridley suggests that the F reading is
acceptable if one treats the expression
as a particularly harsh example of
the omitted relative, thus: "The
brains *which* useless boil . . ."

61.] A good example of an incontestable hemistich, which proves itself
by sheer weight. No one suggests a
cut.

you] "thy" in l. 59 was addressed to
Alonso; *you* to the whole party as soon
as they have all entered the magic
circle.

Holy Gonzalo, honourable man,
Mine eyes, ev'n sociable to the show of thine,
Fall fellowly drops. The charm dissolves apace;
And as the morning steals upon the night,   65
Melting the darkness, so their rising senses
Begin to chase the ignorant fumes that mantle
Their clearer reason. O good Gonzalo,
My true preserver, and a loyal sir
To him thou follow'st! I will pay thy graces   70
Home both in word and deed. Most cruelly
Didst thou, Alonso, use me and my daughter:
Thy brother was a furtherer in the act.
Thou art pinch'd for 't now, Sebastian. Flesh and blood,
You, brother mine, that entertain'd ambition,   75
Expell'd remorse and nature; whom, with Sebastian,—

63. *ev'n*] *ever* N.S. conj.   72. *Didst*] F (catchword), F3, F4; *Did* F.   74.
Sebastian. Flesh and blood,] Sebastian. *Flesh, and bloud,* F; *Sebastian, flesh and blood*.
Theobald.   75. *entertain'd*] Ff; *entertaine* F.   76. *whom*] *who* Rowe.

62. *Holy*] Cf. *Wint.*, v. i. 170-1,
"You have a holy father, / A graceful
gentleman ..."

63. *ev'n sociable to the show*, etc.] Full
of sympathy at the mere sight of
yours.

64. *Fall*] let fall.

66. *Melting the darkness*] As Luce
pointed out, this is the converse of
Macbeth's "Light thickens" (III. ii.
50).

67-8. *ignorant fumes . . . reason*] Cf.
l. 81. Fumes of ignorance that cover
their faculty of reason. *Clearer* may be
regarded as proleptic, having the
force of "and thus make it clearer".
There is probably a physiological element in the metaphor; the *ignorant
fumes* operate like the "animal spirits"
which rise from the heart to the brain
and, in normal cases, suffuse it with
the power to direct the movements of
the members. Tannenbaum suggests
that *ignorant* should be pronounced
"ing'rant"; see under †*Ingrant* in
O.E.D., which conjectures **ingnorant*
as a transitional form.

70. *thy graces*] Thy virtues and thy
services.

71. *Home*] To the utmost.

72. *Didst*] F reading in this case was
probably a misprint, since *didst*
appears as a catchword at the foot of
the previous page.

74, 75, 78. *Thou . . . You . . . thee*] It
is argued that these variations accord
with the system rather like that which
persists in modern French; but the
usage in Elizabethan drama is far
from consistent. R. Flatter (*Shakespeare's Producing Hand*, 1948) believes
that Shakespeare was systematic and
the others not. But this is too sweep-
ing; there are many exceptions; and
Flatter's contention must go down with
other theories of his under the fire of
Fredson Bowers (*M.P.*, XLVIII, 1950).

74. *pinch'd*] By conscience and hard-
ship. See l. 77.

74-6. *Flesh . . . nature*] A curious
construction; you, my brother, my
own flesh and blood, who entertained
ambition and expelled remorse. . . F
entertaine is another *d : e* misprint.

76. *nature*] See *Intro.*, p. xlvii.

whom] often altered to *who*, but the
construction is not extraordinary; see
Onions, *s.v.*

Whose inward pinches therefor are most strong,—
Would here have kill'd your King; I do forgive thee,
Unnatural though thou art. Their understanding
Begins to swell; and the approaching tide   80
Will shortly fill the reasonable shore,
That now lies foul and muddy. Not one of them
That yet looks on me, or would know me: Ariel,
Fetch me the hat and rapier in my cell:
I will discase me, and myself present   85
As I was sometime Milan: quickly, spirit;
Thou shalt ere long be free.

Ariel sings and helps to attire him.

Where the bee sucks, there suck I:
In a cowslip's bell I lie;
There I couch when owls do cry.   90
On the bat's back I do fly
After summer merrily.
Merrily, merrily shall I live now
Under the blossom that hangs on the bough.

Pros. Why, that's my dainty Ariel! I shall miss thee;   95

81–2. *shore . . . lies*] F3, F4; *shore . . . lie* F; *shores . . . lie* Malone.   83. *or*]
e'er Keightley, Tannenbaum conj.   88. suck] lurk Theobald.   90. couch]
crowch F3, F4, Rowe; couch: Capell; couch. Heath.   92. summer merrily.]
sunset, merrily. Theobald; summer: Merrily, Holt.

77. *therefor*] F has *therefore*, but I
adopt Tannenbaum's helpful modernization. See III. iii. 100.

80. *Begins to swell:*] the sea's rising
as the tide begins to flow.

81. *reasonable shore*] The shore of
reason—the mind, here temporarily
deprived of consciousness, and therefore *foul and muddy*, like a shore below
tide-level. Cf. the former figure, which
suggested that reason was obscured by
physiological fumes, as in drunken-
ness.

82–3. *Not one . . . know me*] They are
all dazed; this means, "None of
them can yet see me, or would know
me if he could." Tannenbaum says
yet = "now", and reads "e'er" for *or*,
which is unnecessary. The word *discase*, which, of clothing, is used by

Shakespeare, and by no one else,
occurs also in *Wint.*, IV. iv. 646.

86. *Milan*] *i.e.* Duke of Milan.

88. Where the bee sucks] There are
no real difficulties in this song, but
many have been invented. Ariel sings
entirely as a fairy diminutive (see
Appendix B). He sleeps, or shelters, in
cowslips, and pursues the summer
with the bat. Theobald prefers *sunset*
to *summer*, on the ground that bats do
not migrate, but as Luce remarks, it is
quite likely that the Elizabethans
thought they did. I record various
conjectural readings and pointings by
critics unhappy about these arguments. Colin Still remarks that Virgil
compares the blessed spirits in Ely-
sium to bees in *Aen.* VI (*Timeless Theme*,
p. 160).

But yet thou shalt have freedom: so, so, so.
To the King's ship, invisible as thou art:
There shalt thou find the mariners asleep
Under the hatches; the master and the boatswain
Being awake, enforce them to this place,   100
And presently, I prithee.

Ari. I drink the air before me, and return
Or ere your pulse twice beat.   *Exit.*

Gon. All torment, trouble, wonder and amazement
Inhabits here: some heavenly power guide us   105
Out of this fearful country!

Pros.   Behold, sir King,
The wronged Duke of Milan, Prospero:
For more assurance that a living Prince
Does now speak to thee, I embrace thy body;
And to thee and thy company I bid   110
A hearty welcome.

Alon.   Whether thou be'st he or no,
Or some enchanted trifle to abuse me,
As late I have been, I not know: thy pulse
Beats, as of flesh and blood; and, since I saw thee,
Th' affliction of my mind amends, with which,   115
I fear, a madness held me: this must crave—
An if this be at all—a most strange story.
Thy dukedom I resign, and do entreat

---

106. *Behold*] *Lo* Pope.   111. *Whether thou be'st*] Camb.; *Where thou bee'st* F,
Ff; *Whe'r thou be'st* Capell.   *or no*] omitted Jervis conj.   117. *An*] Pope;
And F.

96. *so, so, so*] Prospero perhaps
arranges his cloak: splendid, splendid.

98.] Cf. I. ii. 230.

101. *presently*] Immediately; as in
I. ii. 125. Note this trimeter line—
and l. 193—at the end of a speech.
(Luce.)

102. *drink the air*] Cf. "He seem'd in
running to devour the way", *2 H 4*,
I. i. 47. In *MND.*, Puck goes "Swifter
than arrow from the Tartar's bow"
(III. ii. 101). (Luce.)

103. *Or ere*] See I. ii. 11.

105. *Inhabits*] See note on I. i. 16.

108. *For more assurance*] In order to
make thee more sure.

111. *Whether*] Pronounce "whe'r".
Folio has "Where".

112. *trifle*] Cf. *vanity, trick*, etc. Here
a hallucinatory apparition, such as
magicians—and the devil—were capable of raising. Perhaps a glance at the
orthodox Protestant opinion on ghosts.

abuse] Deceive, delude.

117. *An if this be at all*] If this is
really happening, and not merely a
dream.

118. *Thy dukedom*] My right to
tribute; my suzerainty.

Thou pardon me my wrongs.—But how should
    Prospero
Be living and be here?

Pros.   First, noble friend,   120
Let me embrace thine age, whose honour cannot
Be measur'd or confin'd.

Gon.   Whether this be
Or be not, I'll not swear.

Pros.   You do yet taste
Some subtleties o' the isle, that will not let you
Believe things certain. Welcome, my friends all!   125
[*Aside to Seb. and Ant.*] But you, my brace of lords,
    were I so minded,
I here could pluck his highness' frown upon you,
And justify you traitors: at this time
I will tell no tales.

Seb.   [*Aside*] The devil speaks in him.
Pros.   No.
For you, most wicked sir, whom to call brother   130
Would even infect my mouth, I do forgive
Thy rankest fault,—all of them; and require
My dukedom of thee, which perforce, I know,
Thou must restore.

---

124. *not*] F3, F4; *nor* F, F2.   126. Aside . . . Ant.] Johnson.   129. Aside]
Johnson.   *No.*] omitted Hanmer.   132. *fault*] *faults* F4, Rowe.

119. *my wrongs*] The injuries inflicted on you by me. (See above,
ll. 11, 25.)

122. *Whether*] Possibly pronounced
whe'r, as in l. 111.

124. *subtleties*] This is the F spelling;
some editors prefer "subtilties" to
emphasize the limited and special
meaning of the word. They were
"curious devices of cookery and confectionery common at the banquets of
the fifteenth and sixteenth centuries"
(Nichols, *Progresses*, 1. 18). They include "allegorical figures, temples and
chariots" (Withington, *English Pageantry*, 1. 83), and were somewhat like a
formal pageant, made of sugar and
jelly. See also Welsford, *The Court*

Masque, p. 47. The normal meaning of
the word is presumably also present.

127. *pluck*] A characteristically brief
and violent metaphor.

128. *justify*] Prove, establish.

129. *The devil*] Sebastian's remark
would have been defended by many
students of supernatural phenomena,
including James I.

No] Either a contradiction of Sebastian's aside, which as a magician he has
overheard, or a confirmation of his
promise to "tell no tales". Some read
"Now", as Prospero turns to address
another of the company. N.S. suggests a cut.

130. *you*] The change to *thy* (l. 132)
is rational. See l. 74, note.

Alon.   If thou be'st Prospero,
    Give us particulars of thy preservation;   135
    How thou hast met us here, whom three hours since
    Were wrack'd upon this shore; where I have lost—
    How sharp the point of this remembrance is!—
    My dear son Ferdinand.
Pros.   I am woe for 't, sir.
Alon. Irreparable is the loss; and patience   140
    Says it is past her cure.
Pros.   I rather think
    You have not sought her help, of whose soft grace
    For the like loss I have her sovereign aid,
    And rest myself content.
Alon.   You the like loss!
Pros. As great to me, as late; and, supportable   145
    To make the dear loss, have I means much weaker
    Than you may call to comfort you, for I
    Have lost my daughter.
Alon.   A daughter?
    O heavens, that they were living both in Naples,
    The King and Queen there! that they were, I wish   150
    Myself were mudded in that oozy bed
    Where my son lies. When did you lose your daughter?

---

136. *whom*] *who* Ff.   145. *supportable*] *insupportable* F3, F4, Rowe; *portable*
Steevens.   145-6. *supportable . . . loss*] *supportable* / *To make the deere losse* F;
support, able / *To make the dere less* N.S. conj.   149. *Naples*] Ff; *Nalpes* F.

136. *whom*] This form, which may
survive from an abandoned phrase—
e.g. "whom . . . the seas cast up . . ."
was changed to *who* by the editor of
F2.

three hours] See l. 186.

139. *woe*] Sorry.

142. *of whose soft grace*] By whose
mercy.

145. *late*] As recent as yours.

supportable] If correct, this word
must be accented on the first syllable,
or the first syllable must be elided.
And may have crept in unwanted.
Portable is improbable, despite *Lr.*, III.
vi. 115. F3's emendation is possible
metrically, but Prospero's boast about

his use of patience, immediately
above, disqualifies it. For another line
which is made clumsy by a similar
word, cf. Middleton, *Women Beware
Women*, III. ii—"To flesh and blood
so strange, so insupportable".

146. *dear*] Cf. II. i. 131. N.S. conjectures "*dere*", meaning "injury".

much weaker] Possibly because Alonso
has still one child left—Claribel; or
because Miranda will live at Naples.

148. *daughter*] Some suggest that
this word should be pronounced as a
trisyllable, for the metre. But there
is often a pause in lines so divided,
and here it is justified by Alonso's
surprise.

Pros. In this last tempest. I perceive, these lords
        At this encounter do so much admire,
        That they devour their reason, and scarce think   155
        Their eyes do offices of truth, their words
        Are natural breath: but, howsoe'er you have
        Been justled from your senses, know for certain
        That I am Prospero, and that very duke   159
        Which was thrust forth of Milan; who most strangely
        Upon this shore, where you were wrack'd, was landed,
        To be the lord on 't. No more yet of this;
        For 'tis a chronicle of day by day,
        Not a relation for a breakfast, nor
        Befitting this first meeting. Welcome, sir;   165
        This cell's my court: here have I few attendants,
        And subjects none abroad: pray you, look in.
        My dukedom since you have given me again,
        I will requite you with as good a thing;
        At least bring forth a wonder, to content ye   170
        As much as me my dukedom.

Here PROSPERO *discovers* FERDINAND *and* MIRANDA
playing at chess.

156. *their*] *these* Capell, N.S.

154. *encounter . . . admire*] Both words
have already been used in this sense:
"meeting"; "are astonished", "wonder".

155. *devour their reason*] The figure
may have been suggested by open-
mouthed astonishment. (Luce.)

156. *truth, their words*] N.S. claims
respect for the F pointing (*Truth :
Their words*) and therefore emends,
following Capell, to read *truth : these
words* (i.e. the words Prospero is
speaking). But to alter the text in
order to preserve the pointing argues
a degree of confidence in the latter
which very few can pretend to.

157. *natural breath*] The ordinary
speech of human beings.

162. *To be the lord on 't*] Cf. 1. ii. 459;
see *Intro.*, p. xxxvii.

167. *abroad*] Except myself; Prospero conceals for his dramatic purposes the existence of his family. Or,
"about the island".

168. *you have*] Often printed without
mark of elision; as Jonson, normally
extremely careful in his pointing,
prints *there will* for "there'll" in *Epi-
coene*, Prol. 12.

170. *a wonder*] Meaning Miranda.

171. (S.D.) *discovers*] Displays to
view.

playing at chess] One of the relatively rare references to chess in Shakespeare. It has been suggested that it
owes something to a passage in the
popular romance *Huon de Bordeaux*, in
which the hero plays chess with the
daughter of King Ivoryn; and also
that the device of discovering the

Mir.　Sweet lord, you play me false.
Fer.　　　　　　　　　　　　No, my dearest love,
　　　I would not for the world.
Mir.　Yes, for a score of kingdoms you should wrangle,
　　　And I would call it fair play.

172. *dearest*] *dear'st* Capell; *dear* Pope.　　174. *Yes*] *Yet* Moore Smith conj.
kingdoms you] F4; *Kingdomes, you* F; *kingdoms. You* Johnson.　　*wrangle*] *wrong me*
Staunton conj.

lovers at chess derives from a scene in Barnabe Barnes's *Divils Charter* (1607) in which the two sons of Katherine, whom she had believed to be dead, are discovered "at Cardes". Neither of these conjectures is likely to be right. The reference in Huon is paralleled in many other romances, all of which refer to chess in this way because it was an essentially aristocratic game (Huon, when disguised as a churl, draws suspicion upon himself by alluding to his ability to play chess) and because it was a general and valued liberty permitted to medieval lovers. "At chess the sexes met on equal terms, and the freedom of intercourse which the game made possible was much valued. It was even permissible to visit a lady in her chamber to play chess with her. . . The *Cle*ʒ *d'amors* has much to say about the etiquette of chess from this point of view: especially how the knight will find a knowledge of chess of the greatest value in his courtship" (H. J. R. Murray, *A History of Chess*, 1913, pp. 436–7). In *Les Eschez amoureux* the lady's pieces represent the courtly virtues of the female, the knight's of the male. "The game is a parallel of the course of love between two lovers" (Murray, p. 556). Chess-games between lovers are frequently represented on wedding-chests and mirror-cases, and there is a characteristic mirror-case in the Victoria and Albert Museum which depicts a lover and a lady at play in a tent; allowing for the costume, it could be an illustration to *The Tempest*. We must suppose that

Ferdinand and Miranda are discovered in a situation which suggests the context of high-born and romantic love.

174–5.] The general idea is obvious enough, but the passage is not easy to understand in detail. Unfortunately there seems to be no warrant for interpreting *wrangle* as meaning "cheat"; it must mean "dispute". The view that Ferdinand's crime has been to sacrifice the game for love (C. D. Stewart, *Some Textual Problems in Shakespeare*, p. 125) is not supported by the evidence. *Score* means either "stake" or "twenty". The most convincing interpretation that I have seen of the text as it stands takes Miranda's *Yes* as meaning not "Yes, you do play me false, despite your denial" but "Yes, you would indeed play me false for the world." (Cf. *Oth.*, IV. iii. 64 ff, where there is more extensive play on the same lines.) "Yes, you would! And you would similarly play false, and similarly defend yourself, even if the stake were smaller than 'the world', being reckoned only in kingdoms; and such is my tenderness for you that I should still allow it to be fair play." (This version is based on a suggestion of Professor Ellis-Fermor.) If only *wrangle* could mean "play unfairly, cheat", the solution would be much neater; "Yes, you play me false over one kingdom, at chess; but even if the stake were greater, much nearer to being 'the world'—even if it were twenty kingdoms—I should still let your practices pass as fair." M. R. Ridley

Alon.   If this prove   175
　　A vision of the island, one dear son
　　Shall I twice lose.

Seb.   A most high miracle!

Fer. Though the seas threaten, they are merciful;
　　I have curs'd them without cause.

Alon.   Now all the blessings
　　Of a glad father compass thee about!   180
　　Arise, and say how thou cam'st here.

Mir.   O, wonder!
　　How many goodly creatures are there here!
　　How beauteous mankind is! O brave new world,
　　That has such people in 't!

Pros.   'Tis new to thee.

Alon. What is this maid with whom thou wast at play?   185
　　Your eld'st acquaintance cannot be three hours:
　　Is she the goddess that hath sever'd us,
　　And brought us thus together?

Fer.   Sir, she is mortal;
　　But by immortal Providence she's mine:
　　I chose her when I could not ask my father   190
　　For his advice, nor thought I had one. She
　　Is daughter to this famous Duke of Milan,
　　Of whom so often I have heard renown,
　　But never saw before; of whom I have

---

177. *lose*] F3, F4; *loose*, F, F2.   188. *thus*] omitted F4.   189. *Providence*]
Camb.; *prouidence*, F.

---

supports the meaning "cheat, deceive"
and suggests that *wrangled* with the
same sense might be read for *wrong led*
in *Ant.*, III. vi. 80: "We perceiv'd . . .
how you were wrong led." See p. 171.

176. *A vision*] Only another illusion;
cf. l. 112.

177. *high miracle*] Cf. l. 25. Notice
the speaker. For the few lines of the
recognition, the language assumes a
hieratic quality.

181. *Arise*] Ferdinand has knelt for
the paternal blessing.

182. *goodly creatures*] Miranda had
apparently not believed that Ferdinand was representative.

183. *mankind*] In general; but also,
the male sex.

184. *'Tis new to thee*] Cf. "So glad
of this as they I cannot be" (III. i.
92).

186. *three hours*] Another reminder
of the duration of the play.

187. *Is she the goddess*] Cf. I. ii. 424
and note.

189. *immortal*] Antithesis here,
rather than paronomasia. Cf. I. ii.
159. (Luce.)

Providence] Cf. I. ii. 159.

193. *renown*] Partly with the sense of
"rumour", like French *renommee* and
Latin *Fama*. (Luce.)

Receiv'd a second life; and second father   195
This lady makes him to me.

Alon.   I am hers:
But, O, how oddly will it sound that I
Must ask my child forgiveness!

Pros.   There, sir, stop:
Let us not burthen our remembrance' with
A heaviness that's gone.

Gon.   I have inly wept,   200
Or should have spoke ere this. Look down, you
    gods,
And on this couple drop a blessed crown!
For it is you that have chalk'd forth the way
Which brought us hither.

Alon.   I say, Amen, Gonzalo!

Gon. Was Milan thrust from Milan, that his issue   205
Should become Kings of Naples? O, rejoice
Beyond a common joy! and set it down
With gold on lasting pillars: in one voyage
Did Claribel her husband find at Tunis,
And Ferdinand, her brother, found a wife   210
Where he himself was lost, Prospero his dukedom
In a poor isle, and all of us ourselves
When no man was his own.

Alon.   [*To Fer. and Mir.*] Give me your hands:
Let grief and sorrow still embrace his heart
That doth not wish you joy!

Gon.   Be it so! Amen!   215

199–200. *remembrance' with* | *A*] Allen conj.; *remembrances, with* | *A* F; *remembrances with* | *An* F4; *remembrances* | *With a* Malone.   213. To Fer. and Mir.] Hanmer.

199. *remembrance'*] F's *remembrances* probably represents the pronunciation "remembrance"; *s* was occasionally absorbed from the plural inflexion by sibilant singular endings.

200. *heaviness*] Sorrow. Cf. IV. i. 138 (S.D.).

202. *crown*] Singular, because of the idea of joint sovereignty. See II. i. 203. So the spirits hold a garland over the head of Queen Katherine (*H 8*, IV. ii.

82). Cf. also *Wint.*, v. iii. 121-3. (Luce.)

203. *chalk'd*] For the metaphor cf. *H 8*, I. i. 60.

205. *Was Milan*, etc.] See *Intro.*, p. l. There is a strong hint of rejoicing at the *felix culpa* in this beautiful speech.

213. *his own*] *i.e.*, master of himself; but see *Intro.*, p. xxix.

214. *still*] Always, for ever.

[Re-]enter ARIEL, *with the Master and Boatswain
amazedly following.*

O, look, sir, look, sir! here is more of us:
I prophesied, if a gallows were on land,
This fellow could not drown. Now, blasphemy,
That swear'st grace o'erboard, not an oath on
        shore?
Hast thou no mouth by land? What is the news?   220
Boats. The best news is, that we have safely found
Our King, and company; the next, our ship—
Which, but three glasses since, we gave out split—
Is tight and yare and bravely rigg'd, as when
We first put out to sea.
Ari.   [*Aside to Pros.*] Sir, all this service   225
Have I done since I went.
Pros.   [*Aside to Ari.*] My tricksy spirit!
Alon. These are not natural events; they strengthen
From strange to stranger. Say, how came you
        hither?
Boats. If I did think, sir, I were well awake,

S.D. Re-enter] Camb.; Enter F, Ff.   216. *sir, look, sir*] *sir, look* F3, F4, Rowe.
219. *o'erboard*] Camb.; *ore-boord* F; *overboard* N.S.   221. *safely*] *safe* F3, F4.
222. *the next,*] Camb.; *The next:* F.   225. Aside to Pros.] Capell.   226. Aside
to Ari.] Capell.   227. *events*] *euens* F (variant).

(S.D.) amazedly] Cf. *MND.*, IV.
i. 150-1, "My lord, I shall reply
amazedly,/Half sleep, half waking".
Cf. I. ii. 14.

216. *here is more*] *more* perhaps functions here as a noun; see Abbott ¶ 335,
and cf. *Cym.*, IV. ii. 283, "Here's a few
flowers," and *Cym.*, IV. ii. 371, "There
is no more such masters."

218. *blasphemy*] Cf. *diligence*, l. 241,
and *malice*, I. ii. 369. See I. i. 42 and
note on I. i. 35-6 for the lack of textual evidence of the boatswain's blasphemy.

219. *grace o'erboard*] When at sea,
you blaspheme enough to cause grace
to be withdrawn from the ship. For an
interesting account of swearing at sea,
see R. R. Cawley, *Unpathed Waters*,
pp. 194-5. Ralegh ordered his cap-

tains to "take especial care that God
be not blasphemed in your ship".

221. *safely*] See note on *freshly*, l.
236; and cf. I. ii. 226.

223. *glasses*] Cf. l. 186; see note on
I. ii. 240.

gave out] Stated to be; cf. *Wint.*,
v. i. 85.

split] Broken up; cf. I. i. 61.

224. *yare*] Cf. I. i. 3.

226. *tricksy*] Cf. *Mer.V.*, III. v. 74, "a
tricksy word". Cotgrave's definition,
"Prettie and neat; minion, briske", as
Furness says, suits very well here.
There is probably also a reference to
"trick" in its conjuring sense; cf.
IV. i. 37.

227. *strengthen*] Increase in strangeness. There is verbal chiming in this
phrase.

I 'ld strive to tell you. We were dead of sleep,   230
And—how we know not—all clapp'd under hatches;
Where, but even now, with strange and several noises
Of roaring, shrieking, howling, jingling chains,
And mo diversity of sounds, all horrible,
We were awak'd; straightway, at liberty;   235
Where we, in all our trim, freshly beheld
Our royal, good, and gallant ship; our master
Cap'ring to eye her:—on a trice, so please you,
Even in a dream, were we divided from them,
And were brought moping hither.

Ari.   [*Aside to Pros.*] Was 't well done? 240
Pros. [*Aside to Ari.*] Bravely, my diligence. Thou shalt be
        free.

Alon. This is as strange a maze as e'er men trod;
        And there is in this business more than nature
        Was ever conduct of: some oracle
        Must rectify our knowledge.

Pros.   Sir, my liege,   245
        Do not infest your mind with beating on

230. *of sleep*] *a-sleep* Pope; *on sleep* Malone.   231. *under*] *under the* Hunter conj.
234. *mo*] *moe* F3, F4; *more* Rowe.   236. *Where*] *When* Dyce.   *our trim*] *her trim*
Theobald.   240. Aside to Pros.] Capell.   241. Aside to Ari.] Capell.
242. Alon.] Ari. Ff.   246. *infest*] *infect* F4, Rowe.

230. *of*] As a consequence of. Or, as
N.S. suggests, incorrectly filled out by
compositor from "a sleep".

232. *several*] Different; as specified
in the next line.

233.] This line has been criticized
as crude, "hardly to be matched even
in the earliest plays" (Luce); but
such irruptions of an earlier kind of
rhetoric occur frequently in Shakespeare—*e.g.* in *Ham.*, *Mac.*, *Wint.*,
when they are called for by the requirements of the narrative or the
characterization.

236. *Where*] Cf. III. ii. 86.

all our trim] They themselves being
unscathed, saw their ship to be equally
unharmed.

freshly beheld] Perhaps a transferred
epithet. Cf. *safely* in l. 221; also I. ii.
226 and II. i. 316.

238. *Cap'ring to eye her*] Dancing for
joy at the sight of his vessel restored to
good order.

on a trice] In an instant.

239. *them*] The rest of the crew.

240. *moping*] Either, sulking at being
separated from their companions; or,
with an older meaning, dulled, acting
without full consciousness. Cf. "Could
not so mope", *Ham.*, III. iv. 81.

242. *maze*] Cf. III. iii. 2, 3.

243. *nature*] See *Intro.*, p. xlvii.

244. *conduct*] There are other recorded uses of the word to mean what
we should call "conductor", one of
them in *Rom.*, v. iii. 116. The figure is
suggested by *maze*, above.

246. *infest*] Shakespeare's only use
of this word; Luce adds that it gives
plausibility to the reading "Against
infestion and the hand of war" (*R 2*,

The strangeness of this business; at pick'd leisure
Which shall be shortly single, I'll resolve you,
Which to you shall seem probable, of every
These happen'd accidents; till when, be cheerful,   250
And think of each thing well. [*Aside to Ari.*] Come
    hither, spirit:
Set Caliban and his companions free;
Untie the spell. [*Exit Ariel.*] How fares my gracious sir?
There are yet missing of your company
Some few odd lads that you remember not.   255

[*Re-*]enter ARIEL, *driving in* CALIBAN, STEPHANO, *and*
    TRINCULO, *in their stolen apparel.*

Ste. Every man shift for all the rest, and let no man take
    care for himself; for all is but fortune.—Coragio,
    bully-monster, coragio!

247. *leisure*] *seisure* F2; *seizure* F3, F4.   248. *shortly single,*] *shortly, single* Rowe.
251. Aside to Ari.] Capell.   253. Exit Ariel] Capell.   255. S.D. Re-enter]
Capell; Enter F, Ff.   258. *coragio*] F2; *Corasio* F.

ii. i. 44). Cotgrave has "*Infester*, to
infest, annoy, molest..."

248. *shortly single*] F, which N.S.
follows, places *which . . . single* in
brackets, and the phrase means,
"which will soon be continuous". If
Rowe and the others are right, *single*
means "privately", or "sincerely"
(cf. *H 8*, v. iii. 38, Ford, *Broken Heart*
iv. i. 14–15), or "simply", "without
ambiguity". See *O.E.D.*, *s.v.*

resolve you] Explain to you. Cf.
"Resolve me, in all modest haste"
(*Lr.*, ii. iv. 25).

249. *Which to you shall seem probable*]
F places in brackets. Perhaps *seem* =
"be seen" (*videri*), and *probable* =
"capable of proof"; "opinions not
probable by scripture" (*O.E.D.*).

249–50. *every . . . accidents*] A good
example of the syntactical tortuous-
ness of the later manner. For the two
telescoped constructions, cf. *Wint.*, ii.
iii. 35. It is of such constructions that
Abbott is thinking when he writes
of the way in which "the old versa-

tility and audacity in the arrangement of the sentence, the stern sub-
ordination of grammar to terseness
and clearness, and the consequent
directness and naturalness of expression, all conspire to give a liveliness
and wakefulness to Shakespearian
English which are wanting in the
grammatical monotony of the present
day". (*Intro.*, p. 16).

253. *Untie the spell*] Cf. i. ii. 489, iii.
iii. 89.

255. *odd*] Unreckoned; not accounted for; cf. i. ii. 223.

256. *Every man shift*, etc.] Perhaps
this means something profound, about
life (Meiklejohn) or the play (Luce)
or the Merchant Navy (N.S.). But it
could be just a drunken inversion of a
remark more in character, and then it
has no more ulterior significance than
one of Dogberry's errors. N.S. suggests a quibble on *shift*, which may
have been used in domestic service
(cf. *Rom.*, i. v. 2). Stephano was, of
course, a butler—a drunken butler.

Trin. If these be true spies which I wear in my head,
  here's a goodly sight.   260
Cal. O Setebos, these be brave spirits indeed!
  How fine my master is! I am afraid
  He will chastise me.
Seb.   Ha, ha!
  What things are these, my lord Antonio?
  Will money buy 'em?
Ant.   Very like; one of them   265
  Is a plain fish, and, no doubt, marketable.
Pros. Mark but the badges of these men, my lords,
  Then say if they be true. This mis-shapen knave,
  His mother was a witch; and one so strong
  That could control the moon, make flows and ebbs,   270
  And deal in her command, without her power.

---

259. *true spies*] Honest or trust-worthy observers. Cf. *Mer.V.*, II. vi. 54, "If that mine eyes be true." See also l. 268. (Luce.)

261. *Setebos*] See I. ii. 375.

brave spirits] The Miranda-Caliban comparison persists; it began with the accounts of their education, was continued in the linked accounts of their reactions to the first encounter with men; and ends here with the parallelism of these lines and ll. 181–4. This constitutes an extension into the structure and language of the play at large of the nature/nurture theme discussed in IV. i. 188–9 n, and *Intro.*, pp. xliii–xlvii.

262. *fine*] In his ducal costume.

263.] Some say that this and the following speech should be in prose, as a contrast to Caliban's. In fact, they are almost normal blank verse.

266. *a plain fish*] See II. ii. 36.

marketable] A quibble; as a fish may be sold at market, so this oddity has its value in a freakshow.

267–8. *badges . . . true*] "Badge"—a device worn by the servants of a nobleman. "True"—"honest", as in *1 H 4*, II. ii. 98–9, "The thieves have bound the true men." So much is clear, but it is not clear what Prospero

meant the gentlemen to learn from observing the badges. He may mean, using "badges" figuratively, "Judge by their outward appearance whether these are honest or good men." He may have meant to show the noblemen that, in stealing his finery, the conspirators, one of whom (Trinculo) might be wearing the badge of Milan as the servant of Antonio, were stealing their own master's property. This implies an ironical comment on Antonio's usurpation; but it is not easy to see how it could be acted. Perhaps, after all, Prospero means only to identify the thieves as servants of the King.

268. *This*] "As for this . . ."

270. *That*] That she. For a similar case of omission of the pronoun, see l. 315.

control the moon] *Te quoque luna, traho*, said Medea, Ovid, *Met.*, VII, 207. For this technical accomplishment of witches, and the relationship of Sycorax to classical witches, see *Intro.*, p. xl. See also App. D. Douce, *Illustrations*, pp. 16–18, cites a large number of ancient examples of this power.

flows and ebbs] Cf. *MND.*, II. i. 103.

271. *deal in her command*] Wield the moon's authority.

These three have robb'd me; and this demi-devil—
For he's a bastard one—had plotted with them
To take my life. Two of these fellows you
Must know and own; this thing of darkness I   275
Acknowledge mine.
Cal.   I shall be pinch'd to death.
Alon. Is not this Stephano, my drunken butler?
Seb. He is drunk now: where had he wine?
Alon. And Trinculo is reeling ripe: where should they
Find this grand liquor that hath gilded 'em?—   280
How cam'st thou in this pickle?
Trin. I have been in such a pickle, since I saw you last,
that, I fear me, will never out of my bones: I shall
not fear fly-blowing.
Seb. Why, how now, Stephano!   285
Ste. O, touch me not;—I am not Stephano, but a cramp.

---

280. *liquor*] *Liquor* F; *'lixir* Theobald.   285. *Why*] *Who* F (variant).

without her power] This probably means, *though* to do so was not in her own power. *Without* means "outside", cf. *MND.*, IV. i. 157. That is to say, that she was dependent upon her diabolical agents for this power; which is orthodox witch-lore. Otherwise, the passage means either (1) beyond the moon's power to control her; or (2) she could command the moon to do that which the moon, but not Sycorax herself, was capable of performing; or (3) without having the power of the moon, she could meddle in the moon's realm of sovereignty.

272. *demi-devil*] See *Intro.*, p. xl.

275. *thing of darkness*] Possibly contains an allusion to Caliban's colour. Chambers derives his name from Romany *cauliban*, which means blackness. See *Intro.*, p. xxxviii.

279. *reeling ripe*] So drunk that he was reeling. Cf. "weeping ripe", *LLL.*, v. ii. 274.

280. *grand liquor*] Perhaps, as some have pleasantly maintained, a reference to the *aurum potabile* of the alchemists—the elixir of life. But Theobald's emendation is surely improper.

The primary meaning of *gilded* in this context is certainly "flushed", as *O.E.D.* fully substantiates; *grand liquor* may be a glance at the other idea.

282. *pickle*] An obvious quibble on *pickle* = "mess" and *pickle* = preservative, usually of meat; with a reference to his having been steeped in the pond, or in liquor, like meat in pickling fluid.

284. *fly-blowing*] Being pickled, he is free from the attentions of flies which corrupt meat.

286. *I am . . . cramp*] This hyperbole can stand alone, but Warburton tried to find in it a pun on Stephano's name (*Staffilato*, "lashed or flayed"), and claimed that this, like some other features of the play, pointed to an Italian source. This guess was given little attention, but more recently the whole matter of Italian sources has been raised again in a different form, and Benedetto Croce has suggested once more that this line contains a pun on Stephano's name. (*Stefano*, a Neapolitan slang word for "stomach".) See *Intro.*, p. lxviii.

Pros. You 'ld be King o' the isle, sirrah?

Ste. I should have been a sore one, then.

Alon. This is a strange thing as e'er I look'd on.

[*Pointing to Caliban.*]

Pros. He is as disproportion'd in his manners   290
　　As in his shape. Go, sirrah, to my cell;
　　Take with you your companions; as you look
　　To have my pardon, trim it handsomely.

Cal. Ay, that I will; and I'll be wise hereafter,
　　And seek for grace. What a thrice-double ass   295
　　Was I, to take this drunkard for a god,
　　And worship this dull fool!

Pros.　　　　　　　　Go to; away!

Alon. Hence, and bestow your luggage where you found it.

Seb. Or stole it, rather.

Pros. Sir, I invite your Highness and your train   300
　　To my poor cell, where you shall take your rest
　　For this one night; which, part of it, I'll waste
　　With such discourse as, I not doubt, shall make it
　　Go quick away: the story of my life,
　　And the particular accidents gone by   305

289. *This is a strange*] *'Tis a strange* F3, F4; *This is as strange a* Capell, N.S., Alexander.

288. *a sore one*] Perhaps in three senses—(1) smarting; (2) sorry; (3) severe. See III. i. 11.

289. *a strange*] None of the passages with omitted demonstratives cited as parallels is as strained as this; it is noteworthy that F3 emends the line, though hardly helpfully. The nearest parallel is *1 H 4*, III. ii. 108.

291. *As in his shape*] The conventional (ex-Neo-Platonic) correlation of physical and moral beauty. See IV. i. 191–2.

295. *seek for grace*] For pardon, or favour. See *Intro.*, p. xlii.

298. *luggage*] As in IV. i. 231.

where you found it] *i.e.* on the "line". The tree is presumably still on the stage, and it may be that the three thieves do not go out until they have disposed of the clothing. F marks

no exit for them. But it is far more likely that they withdraw with the luggage.

302. *waste*] Cf. *MND.*, II. i. 57, "A merrier hour was never wasted there."

303. *not doubt*] Although the auxiliary "do" was in general use in Shakespeare's English, it was not employed in accordance with modern rules, such as that which requires its presence whenever *not* precedes the verb. Hence the present construction is very common in Elizabethan English; cf. l. 38 above. The Shakespearian use of the auxiliary *do* is examined by Abbott in ¶¶ 304–6.

304. *quick*] Either adverb with lost inflection, or adjective used as adverb.

305. *accidents*] Incidents; cf. V. i. 250, and *Ado*, II. i. 188, "An accident of hourly proof".

Since I came to this isle: and in the morn
I'll bring you to your ship, and so to Naples,
Where I have hope to see the nuptial
Of these our dear-belov'd solemnized;
And thence retire me to my Milan, where   310
Every third thought shall be my grave.

Alon.   I long
To hear the story of your life, which must
Take the ear strangely.

Pros.   I'll deliver all;
And promise you calm seas, auspicious gales,
And sail so expeditious, that shall catch   315
Your royal fleet far off. [*Aside to Ari.*] My Ariel, chick,
That is thy charge: then to the elements
Be free, and fare thou well! Please you, draw near.

                                    Exeunt omnes.

---

308. *nuptial*] *Nuptialls* Ff, Rowe.   309. *dear-belov'd solemnized*] *dear-beloved solemniz'd* Rowe.   315. *that shall*] *it shall* Hanmer; *that't shall* Allen conj. 316. Aside to Ari.] Camb.

308. *nuptial*] Always used in this singular form in Shakespeare, except in a Q reading in *Oth.*, and in *Per.*, v. iii. 80.

309. *solemnized*] Pronounced "solémnizéd".

311. *Every third thought*] Recalls IV. i. 3. Presumably the two others will be Miranda and Milan; or perhaps it means mearly, "I shall give much thought to death."

313. *Take*] Affect, captivate. Cf. "take / The winds of March with beauty", *Wint.*, IV. iv. 119–20.

deliver all] Tell everything.

315. *so expeditious, that*] For this construction, which is not uncommon, see Abbott § 279. The meaning is: I promise you . . . such speedy progress that it will enable you to overhaul your royal fleet. Cf. v. i. 270.

316. *far off*] Which is now far off; or: far off as it is.

chick] Cf. IV. i. 184.

317. *the elements*] Which Ariel and the class of spirits to which he belonged were free of. See Appendix B.

EPILOGUE

Spoken by PROSPERO.

Now my charms are all o'erthrown,
And what strength I have's mine own,
Which is most faint: now, 'tis true,
I must be here confin'd by you,
Or sent to Naples. Let me not, 5
Since I have my dukedom got,
And pardon'd the deceiver, dwell
In this bare island by your spell;
But release me from my bands
With the help of your good hands: 10
Gentle breath of yours my sails
Must fill, or else my project fails,
Which was to please. Now I want
Spirits to enforce, Art to enchant;
And my ending is despair, 15
Unless I be reliev'd by prayer,
Which pierces so, that it assaults
Mercy itself, and frees all faults.
 As you from crimes would pardon'd be,
 Let your indulgence set me free. Exit. 20

S.D. Prospero.] Prosper F3, F4. 1. Now] Now now F3, F4. 3. now] and now Pope. 13. Now] For now Pope. 20. *Exit*] *Exeunt Omnes* Collier.

Epilogue] These twenty lines are at the heart of the controversy concerning the interpretation of this play as a personal allegory. It is on the whole more plausible to treat them as an apology to James I "for dabbling in magic" (N.S.), if such an interpretation must be sought. The Epilogue, of course, can stand on its own feet, and be read as the conventional appeal for applause. The most immediate and commonplace play on the idea of the magician-without-magic has reference to the actor-without-part. "I am now outside the tale you have just followed; just as I surrendered my powers in that tale, so I now stand before you stripped of imaginary glamour. One might say that the success of my enterprise as an actor is parallel to the happy outcome of my stage-plot. I behaved well in my fictitious character

133

(and, I hope, acted well also); my fictitious reward is to return to Italy. To complete the parallel, *you* must release me from the bonds of failure as a performer. Just as Ariel in the fable speeds my ship, and brings my magical 'project' to a successful conclusion, so must you, to ensure the prosperity of my theatrical venture, applaud me for the pleasure I have given you. I am now stripped of my stage powers, which might have enabled me to obtain this applause by daemonic agency; and I face the despair your disapproval would bring, unless this prayer to you succeeds; for I have still the power of every man to appeal direct to the supreme mediating spirit, that of Christian mercy. I implore you to exercise mercy towards me, as you would have mercy procure forgiveness for your own trespasses." It is the weighty allusion to Christian mercy and the Lord's Prayer which lends force to some of the many allegorical interpretations. On the other hand, some critics not only deny that the Epilogue allegorizes, *e.g.*, Shakespeare's return to Stratford, but deprecate the notion that Shakespeare wrote it. "One hopes that these sorry lines are not by Shakespeare", writes E. E. Stoll, who thinks that "the Epilogue is nothing more than a series of wire-drawn conceits on the subject of pardon and indulgence, and with Shakespeare's own personality and present situation seems to have nothing to do" (*P.M.L.A.*, XLVII, 704). But we need scarcely concern ourselves with this assault on the authenticity of the lines. They are characteristic, and indeed profoundly satisfactory, Shakespearian octosyllabics. As to the allegorical interpretation of

them, such interpretation is almost inevitable; why should it not attach itself to Shakespeare as it did to Homer, Virgil, and Ovid? It is harmful in so far as it deflects attention from the structure of ideas in the play, which has to be historically ascertained; and it lacks historical warrant in itself.

10. With the help of your good hands] Cf. *MND.*, v. 444, "Give me your hands if we be friends"; and the Epilogue to *All's W.*, v. iii. 340, "Your gentle hands lend us and take our hearts." The closing request of the Latin comedians was *nunc, spectatores, valete et nobis clare applaudite.* (Luce.)

the help of] For the noise of clapping would break the charm.

16. reliev'd by prayer] Warburton's remark should be recorded: "This alludes to the old stories told of the despair of necromancers in their last moments, and of the efficacy of the prayers of their friends for them." He has in mind scenes like that in *Dr Faustus: Faustus.* Ay, pray for me, pray for me. . . *Second Scholar.* Pray thou, and we will pray that God may have mercy upon thee. (ll. 1976–9, ed. W. W. Greg, 1950). But I doubt if this reference is, so to speak, positive. Prospero is throughout presented as a theurgist, and here he refers to his renunciation of special powers over the spirit-world and his retention of the normal means of access to it. To turn him into a Faustian goetist at this point is to invite confusion.

17–18. *Which . . . itself*] Cf. the proverb, "Prayers like petards, break open heaven gate" (Tilley, P557). Herbert's "Prayer" calls it "Engine against th' Almighty".

APPENDIX A

STRACHEY, JOURDAIN, AND *THE TRUE DECLARATION*

(*a*) Extracts from Strachey's *True Reportory of the Wracke* (*Purchas His Pilgrimes*, XIX. 5–72).

... on S. James his day, July 24, being Monday (preparing for no lesse all the blacke night before) the cloudes gathering thicke upon us, and the windes singing, and whistling most unusually, which made us to cast off our Pinnace ... a dreadfull storme and hideous began to blow from out the North-east, which swelling, and roaring as it were by fits, some houres with more violence then others, at length did beate all light from heaven; which like an hell of darkenesse turned blacke upon us, so much the more fuller of horror, as in such cases horror and feare use to overrunne the troubled, and overmastered sences of all, which (taken up with amazement) the eares lay so sensible to the terrible cries, and murmurs of the windes, and distraction of our Company, as who was most armed, and best prepared, was not a little shaken. [There follows a passage of moralising.] For foure and twenty houres the storme in a restlesse tumult, had blowne so exceedingly, as we could not apprehend in our imaginations any possibility of greater violence, yet did wee still finde it, not onely more terrible, but more constant, fury added to fury, and one storme urging a second more outragious then the former; whether it so wrought upon our feares, or indeede met with new forces: Sometimes strikes [?shrieks] in our Ship amongst women, and passengers, not used to such hurly and discomforts, made us looke one upon the other with troubled hearts, and panting bosomes: our clamours dround in the windes, and the windes in thunder. Prayers might well be in the heart and lips, but drowned in the outcries of the Officers: nothing heard that could give comfort, nothing seene that might incourage hope... The Sea swelled above the Clouds, and gave battell unto Heaven. It could not be said to raine, the waters like whole Rivers did flood in the ayre. And this I did still observe, that whereas upon the Land, when a storme hath powred it selfe forth once in drifts of raine, the winde as beaten downe, and vanquished therewith, not long after indureth: here the glut of water (as if throatling the winde ere while) was no sooner a little emptied and qualified, but instantly the windes (as having gotten their mouthes now free, and at liberty) spake more loud, and grew more tumultuous, and malignant. . . Howbeit this was not all; It pleased God to bring a greater affliction yet upon us; for in the beginning of the storme we had received likewise a mighty leake. And the Ship in every joynt almost, having spued out her Okam, before we were aware (a casualty more desperate then any other that a Voyage by Sea draweth with it) was growne five foote suddenly deepe with water above her ballast, and we almost drowned within, whilest we sat looking when to perish from above. This imparting no lesse terrour than danger, ranne through the whole Ship with much fright and amazement, startled and turned the bloud, and tooke downe the braves of the most hardy Marriner of them all, insomuch as he that before happily felt not the sorrow of others, now began to sorrow for himselfe, when he saw such a pond of water so suddenly broken in, and which he knew could not (without present avoiding) but instantly sinke him. . . The Lord knoweth, I had as little hope, as desire of life in the storme, & in this, it went beyond my will; because beyond my reason, why we should labour to preserve life; yet we did, either because so deare are a few lingring houres of life in all mankinde, or that our Christian knowledges taught us, how much we owed to the rites of Nature, as bound, not to be false to our selves, or to neglect the meanes of our owne preservation; the most despairefull things amongst men, being matters of no wonder nor moment with him, who is the rich Fountaine and admirable Essence of all mercy. . .

Our Governour was at this time below at the Capstone, both by his speech and authoritie heartening every man unto his labour. It [a huge sea] strooke him from the place where hee sate, and groveled him, and all us about him on our faces, beating together with our breaths all thoughts from our bosomes, else, then that wee were now sinking. . . During all this time, the heavens look'd so blacke upon us, that it was not possible the elevation of the Pole might be observed: nor a Starre by night, nor Sunne beame by day was to be seene. Onely upon the thursday night Sir George Summers being upon the watch, had an apparition of a little round light, like a faint Starre, trembling, and streaming along with a sparkeling blaze, halfe the height upon the Maine Mast, and shooting sometimes from Shroud to Shroud, tempting to settle as it were upon any of the foure Shrouds: and for three or foure houres together, or rather more, halfe the night it kept with us; running sometimes along the Maine-yard to the very end, and then returning. At which, Sir George Summers called divers about him, and shewed them the same, who observed it with much wonder, and carefulnesse: but upon a sodaine, towards the morning watch, they lost the sight of it, and knew not what way it made. The superstitious Sea-men make many constructions of this Sea-fire, which neverthelesse is usuall in stormes: the same (it may be) which the Græcians were wont in the Mediterranean to call Castor and Pollux, of which, if one onely appeared without the other, they tooke it for an evill signe of great tempest. . .

East and by South we steered away as much as we could to beare upright, which was no small carefulnesse nor paine to doe, albeit we much unrigged our Ship, threw over-boord much luggage, many a Trunke and Chest (in which I suffered no meane losse) and staved many a Butt of Beere, Hogsheads of Oyle, Syder, Wine, and Vinegar. . . But see the goodnesse and sweet introduction of better hope, by our mercifull God given unto us. Sir George Summers, when no man dreamed of such happinesse, had discovered, and cried Land. . . We were inforced to runne her ashoare, as neere the land as we could, which brought us within three quarters of a mile of shoare. . .

We found it to be the dangerous and dreaded Iland, or rather Ilands of the Bermuda: whereof let mee give your Ladyship a briefe description, before I proceed to my narration. And that the rather, because they be so terrible to all that ever touched on them, and such tempests, thunders, and other fearefull objects are seene and heard about them, that they be called commonly, The Devils Ilands, and are feared and avoyded of all sea travellers alive, above any other place in the world. Yet it pleased our mercifull God, to make even this hideous and hated place, both the place of our safetie, and meanes of our deliverance.

And hereby also, I hope to deliver the world from a foule and generall errour: it being counted of most, that they can be no habitation for Men, but rather given over to Devils and wicked Spirits; whereas indeed wee find them now by experience, to bee as habitable and commodious as most Countries of the same climate and situation: insomuch as if the entrance into them were as easie as the place it selfe is contenting, it had long ere this beene inhabited, as well as other Ilands. Thus shall we make it appeare, That Truth is the daughter of Time, and that men ought not to deny every thing which is not subject to their owne sense. . .

Sure it is, that there are no Rivers nor running Springs of fresh water to bee found upon any of them: when wee came first wee

digged and found certaine gushings and soft bublings, which being
either in bottoms, or on the side of hanging ground, were onely fed
with raine water, which neverthelesse soone sinketh into the earth
and vanisheth away. . . A kinde of webbe-footed Fowle there is, of
the bignesse of an English greene Plover, or Sea-Meawe, which all
the Summer wee saw not. . . Their colour is inclining to Russet, with
white bellies (as are likewise the long Feathers of their wings Russet
and White) these gather themselves together and breed in those
Ilands which are high, and so farre alone into the Sea, that the
Wilde Hogges cannot swimme over them, and there in the ground
they have their Burrowes, like Conyes in a Warren, and so brought
[?wrought] in the loose Mould, though not so deepe: which Birds
with a light bough in a darke night (as in our Lowbelling) wee
caught. I have beene at the taking of three hundred in an houre,
and wee might have laden our Boates. Our men found a prettie way
to take them, which was by standing on the Rockes or Sands by the
Sea side, and hollowing, laughing, and making the strangest out-
cry that possibly they could: with the noyse whereof the Birds
would come flocking to that place, and settle upon the very armes
and head of him that so cryed, and still creepe neerer and neerer,
answering the noyse themselves: by which our men would weigh
them with their hand, and which weighed heaviest they tooke for
the best and let the others alone, and so our men would take twentie
dozen in two houres of the chiefest of them; and they were a good
and well relished Fowle, fat and full as a Partridge. . . The Tortoyse
is reasonable toothsom (some say) wholsome meate. I am sure our
Company liked the meate of them verie well, and one Tortoyse
would goe further amongst them, then three Hogs. One Turtle (for
so we called them) feasted well a dozen Messes, appointing sixe to
every Messe. It is such a kind of meat, as a man can neither absolutely call Fish nor Flesh, keeping most what in the water. . .

[Strachey goes on to describe a number of mutinies dealt with
in the course of the Bermudan occupation.] In these dangers and
divellish disquiets (whilest the almighty God wrought for us, and
sent us miraculously delivered from the calamities of the Sea, all
blessings upon the shoare, to content and binde us to gratefulnesse)
thus inraged amongst our selves, to the destruction each of other,
into what a mischiefe and misery had wee bin given up, had wee
not had a Governour with his authority, to have suppressed the
same? [Of the last of these mutinies he writes] They had now purposed to have made a surprise of the Storehouse, and to have forced
from thence, what was therein either of Meale, Cloath, Cables,
Armes, Sailes, Oares or what else it pleased God that we had re-

covered from the wracke, and was to serve our generall necessity and use, either for the reliefe of us, while wee staied here, or for the carrying of us from this place againe, when our Pinnace should have bin furnished.

But as all giddy and lawlesse attempts, have alwayes something of imperfection, and that as well by the property of the action, which holdeth of disobedience and rebellion (both full of feare) as through the ignorance of the devisers themselves; so in this (besides those defects) there were some of the association, who not strong inough fortified in their owne conceits, brake from the plot it selfe, and (before the time was ripe for the execution thereof) discovered the whole order, and every Agent, and Actor thereof, who neverthelesse were not suddenly apprehended, by reason the confederates were divided and seperated in place, some with us, and the chiefe with Sir George Summers in his Iland (and indeede all his whole company) but good watch passed upon them, every man from thenceforth commanded to weare his weapon, without which before, we freely walked from quarter to quarter, and conversed among our selves, and every man advised to stand upon his guard, his owne life not being in safety, whilest his next neighbour was not to be trusted.

[Arriving at last in Virginia Strachey found the colony in a disastrous condition and he expatiates on the reasons for the decline.] Onely let me truely acknowledge, they are not an hundred or two of deboist hands, dropt forth by yeare after yeare, with penury, and leisure, ill provided for before they come, and worse to be governed when they are here, men of such distempered bodies, and infected mindes, whom no examples daily before their eyes, either of goodnesse or punishment, can deterre from their habituall impieties, or terrifie from a shamefull death, that must be the Carpenters, and workemen in this so glorious a building.

[After the arrival of De la Warre, there was an attempt to put the colony on its feet. Strachey comments upon the attempts of the unskilled colonists to catch fish.] It pleased not God so to blesse our labours, that we did at any time take one quarter so much, as would give unto our people one pound at a meale a peece, by which we might have better husbanded our Pease and Oatemeale, notwithstanding the great store we now saw daily in our River: but let the blame of this lye where it is, both upon our Nets, and the unskilfulnesse of our men to lay them.

[On the characteristic Indian treachery described in the next extract, Purchas has a marginal comment expressing his view of the problem—"Can a Leopard change his spots? Can a Savage remayning a Savage be civill? Were not wee our selves made and not borne civill in our Progenitors dayes? and were not Caesars Britaines as brutish as Virginians? The Romane swords were best teachers of civilitie to this & other Countries neere us." Gates has sent a man to recover a longboat. His canoe being driven on to a beach occupied by Indians] certaine Indians (watching the occasion) seised the poore fellow, and led him up into the Woods, and sacrificed him. It did not a little trouble the Lieutenant Governour, who since his first landing in the Countrey (how justly soever provoked) would not be any meanes be wrought to a violent proceeding against them, for all the practises of villany, with which they daily indangered our men, thinking it possible, by a more tractable course, to winne them to a better condition: but now being startled by this, he well perceived, how little a faire and noble intreatie workes upon a barbarous disposition, and therefore in some measure purposed to be revenged.

[Strachey concludes with an extract from the *True Declaration* of which these paragraphs are relevant.] The ground of all those miseries, was the permissive Providence of God, who, in the forementioned violent storme, seperated the head from the bodie, all the vitall powers of Regiment being exiled with Sir Thomas Gates in those infortunate (yet fortunate) Ilands. The broken remainder of those supplyes made a greater shipwracke in the Continent of Virginia, by the tempest of Dissention: every man over-valuing his owne worth, would be a Commander: every man underprizing another's value, denied to be commanded.

The next Fountaine of woes was secure negligence, and improvidence, when every man sharked for his present bootie, but was altogether carelesse of succeeding penurie. Now, I demand whether Sicilia, or Sardinia (sometimes the Barnes of Rome) could hope for increase without manuring? A Colony is therefore denominated, because they should be Coloni, the Tillers of the Earth, and Stewards of fertilitie: our mutinous Loyterers would not sow with providence, and therefore they reaped the fruits of too deere bought Repentance. An incredible example of their idlenesse, is the report of Sir Thomas Gates, who affirmeth, that after his first comming thither, he hath seene some of them eat their fish raw, rather then they would goe a stones cast to fetch wood and dresse it. Dei laboribus omnia vendunt, God sels us all things for our labour, when Adam himselfe might not live in Paradice without dressing the Garden.

(*b*) Extracts from Sylvester Jourdain's *A Discovery of the Barmudas*, 1610.

... All our men, being utterly spent, tyred, and disabled for longer labour, were even resolved, without any hope of their lives, to shut up the hatches, and to have committed themselves to the mercy of the sea, (which is said to be mercilesse) or rather to the mercy of their mighty God and redeemer. . . So that some of them having some good and comfortable waters in the ship, fetcht them, and drunke the one to the other, taking their last leave one of the other, untill their more ioyfull and happy meeting, in a more blessed world; when it pleased God out of his most gracious and mercifull providence, so to direct and guide our ship . . . for her most advantage; that *Sir George Sommers* . . . most wishedly happily discryed land. . . It pleased God to send her within halfe an English mile, of that land . . . which were the Ilandes of the Barmudas. And there neither did our ship sincke, but more fortunately in so great a misfortune, fell in betweene two rockes, where shee was fast lodged and locked, for further budging. . . But our delivery was not more strange in falling so opportunely, and happily upon the land, as our feeding and preservation, was beyond our hopes, and all mens expectations most admirable. For the Ilands of the Barmudas, as every man knoweth that hath heard or read of them, were never inhabited by any Christian or heathen people, but ever esteemed, and reputed, a most prodigious and inchanted place affoording nothing but gusts, stormes, and foule weather; which made every Navigator and Mariner to avoide them, as Scylla and Charibdis, or as they would shunne the Devill himselfe; and no man was ever heard, to make for the place, but as against their wils, they have . . . suffered shipwracke; yet did we finde there the ayre so temperate and the Country so aboundantly fruitful of all fit necessaries, for the sustenation and preservation of mans life . . . [that we lived there comfortably for some nine months.] . . . Wherefore my opinion sincerely of this Iland is, that whereas it hath beene, and is still accounted, the most dangerous infortunate, and most forlorne place of the world, it is in truth the richest, healthfullest, and pleasing land . . . as ever man set foot upon . . . [Jourdain goes on to speak of the food supply, which includes tortoises and cedar-berries.]

Appendix B

ARIEL AS DÆMON AND FAIRY

The name of Ariel is ancient; it occurs in the Bible, notably in an obscure passage in Isaiah xxix. The Geneva Bible has a marginal note to the effect that "The Ebrew word Ariel signifieth the Lyon of God."[1] Richmond Noble is clearly right when he says that Shakespeare's Ariel "is independent of any Biblical model", and the source of the name is probably the magical tradition, in which it frequently recurs, though it is used of spirits who differ widely in character.[2] "Names of the Actors" calls him "an ayrie spirit", and if the description of Caliban in the same place is anything to go by, this is meant seriously, and probably indicates a spirit technically associated with the element of air. In Agrippa's systematic exposition of the dæmonic hierarchy, Ariel is not an air-spirit, but the presiding spirit of the element of earth.[3] It may be that Shakespeare had not entirely overlooked this, despite the fact that Ariel deals mostly in fire and air;[4] for Prospero does mention one of his duties as being "to do me business in the veins o' th' earth", in a speech which mentions also the spirit's duties in the air and water, and follows close upon Ariel's description of how he "flam'd amazement" (I. ii). Shakespeare has been at some pains to show Ariel as being at ease in all the elements, a privilege which he shares with the classical Hermes, the messenger, with whom he has, historically, other qualities in common.[5] There is some warrant for crediting an "ayrie" spirit with power to deal in all the elements.[6]

1. See Noble, *Shakespeare's Biblical Knowledge*, p. 251.
2. See E. M. Butler, *Ritual Magic* (1949), p. 78, and A. Koszul, "Ariel", *English Studies* XIX (1937), 200–4, for historical accounts of the name. Miss Butler says the Ariel of the Faust-books had a special dislike for pacts, and had to be coerced (p. 168).
3. *Occult Philosophy*, II. i; III. xxiv.
4. N. Coghill, "The Basis of Shakespearian Comedy", *Essays and Studies* [1950], pp. 1–28) finds allegorical significance in the Caliban-Ariel opposition, arguing that Caliban is associated with water and earth, Ariel with air and fire. This is agreeable, provided it is not made a be-all and end-all; though Ariel, even allowing that he might, as a spirit of the upper elements, control the lower, is by no means a perfect fit.
5. Butler, *op. cit.* p. 168. St Elmo's fire was sometimes, by the Italians, called St Hermes' fire.
6. The classification of dæmons by elements derives from Michael Psellos. Guazzo, after him, says of aerial spirits: "They live in the air about us, sometimes descend into hell, appear to men, raise tempests" (West, *Invisible World*, p. 23). This fits Ariel very well.

Ariel has nothing of humanity—he has only an imaginative apprehension of the pity he would feel "were he human"—being pure intelligence, "free from all gross and putrifying mass of a body, immortall, unsensible, assisting all, having Influence over all".[1] He has the qualities allowed to Intelligences in medieval theology, which include simultaneous knowledge of all that happens; understanding of the cause of things; the power to alter his position in space in no time, and to manipulate the operations of nature, so as, for example, to create tempests; the power to work upon a human being's will and imagination for good or evil ends; and total invulnerability to assault by material instruments.[2] However, by a magician in full panoply, in a state of grace, and in possession of his 'seal' (a microcosmic emblem of the spirit), he can be invoked and commanded even against his will. A spirit as remote from materiality as Ariel cannot be commanded, though he may be invoked and indeed maltreated, by a goetist, as Ariel was by Sycorax; but the theurgist commands him by "reasons of affinity".[3] By virtue of Ariel's powerful position and by "the constraint of his own worthiness," Prospero can demand the services of other and lower spirits, including evil spirits. With these demons Prospero has no direct communication, and in this respect he exactly resembles white magicians like Agrippa himself. The relationship between Prospero and Ariel is perhaps not theurgically pure, since it appears to contain elements of black magic—Ariel is bound by pact, like his namesake of the Faust-books, and it is sometimes possible to see him as a "familiar". "Come, with a thought," orders Prospero; and though this was well within Ariel's powers, as I have described them, the ability to arrive "as quick as thought" was sometimes required by goetists of their demons. These traces are no doubt due to the element of popular demonology in the play, and it would be foolish to expect absolute lucidity and consistency in the treatment of these ideas. It is surely remarkable that, in all that concerns Ariel, the underpinning of technical "natural philosophy" should be as thorough as in fact it is.

Many elements are mixed in Ariel, and his strange richness derives from the mixture. For instance, he often behaves like a native English fairy. Shakespeare was not the first to portray fairies as of less than normal human stature, but he so fixed the idea in the popular mind that we have no difficulty in thinking of fairies as being of the size of Mustardseed, or of Ariel couching in the cow-

1. Agrippa, *op. cit.* III. xvi.
2. See Curry, *Shakespeare's Philosophical Patterns*, pp. 73 ff.
3. West, *op. cit.* pp. 39–40.   4. Butler, *Ritual Magic*, p. 185.

slip's bell. This sophistication enabled him, and other poets, to achieve enchanting rhetorical and poetical effects, but it was essentially a townsman's device, impossible to anyone who took real fairies seriously. And indeed Shakespeare's fairies, particularly in *The Tempest*, are rather learned than rustic. The tiny exquisites of *A Midsummer Night's Dream* recur as demi-puppets, and as Ariel in his gossamer mood; Puck reappears as Ariel, fooling the conspirators, and leading them into the filthy-mantled pool. But how changed they are, how much more self-conscious, even if the earlier fairies are far from innocent!

There were current concerning the nature of fairies two theories which Shakespeare must have had in mind. One treated them as dæmons, or as demons—in fact, as the fallen angels.[1] The other made the identification, inevitable after a wide dissemination of Ovid, of English fairies with classical nymphs, fauns, hamadryads, and so forth. The first of these associations enabled Shakespeare to move freely, and solved the problem of presenting and, I suppose, costuming Ariel, who raises difficulties in that line which the drama, apart from the masque, had not so far encountered, except in so far as Shakespeare himself had solved them in his union of witch and demon in the hags of *Macbeth*. Even so, he takes the liberty of giving Ariel a double fairy-character. As a diminutive, he has the ready charm of the *Dream* fairies; as a puck, he conveniently bridges the gap between his demonological and his moral functions. When he leads astray the drunken Stephano and his party, he is thwarting the unchaste, whose unchastity throws into relief the absolute value as well as the expediency of chastity, which is simultaneously demonstrated by the young lovers. Fairies dislike uncleanliness, and abhor unchastity; there is no better defence against the fairy who misleads than a pure life.[2] This doctrine is alluded to in two works, both in some degree related to *The Tempest*; in Fletcher's *Faithful Shepherdess* it helps to introduce the rather itchy chastity-theme; and in *Comus* it is transfigured:

> Some say, no evil thing that walks by night
> In fog or fire, by lake or moorish fen,
> Blue meager hag, or stubborn unlaid ghost
> That breaks his magick chains at Curfeu time,
> No goblin, or swart fairy of the mine,
> Hath hurtful power o'er true Virginity. (ll. 432–7.)[3]

1. See M. W. Latham, *The Elizabethan Fairies* (1930), p. 58.
2. Based on Latham, *op. cit.*, especially p. 136.
3. The Attendant Spirit in *Comus* is, in certain respects an academically Platonic version of Ariel.

As Prospero's agent, and also in his own right as a fairy, Ariel takes a hand in the prevention of lechery. Similarly, the spirits who torment Caliban, and whom he obviously thinks of as fairies, have the traditional power of elves to pinch and inflict cramps and agues. [1] When Ariel, in a passage which has caused some comment, is sent to make himself like a nymph of the sea, he changes into a recognizable fairy costume; water-nymphs had appeared previously in English dramatic entertainments [2]—perhaps they owed their dramatic existence to another theory, that fairies were all water-devils, or that proportion of Lucifer's angels which fell into streams; or perhaps to the aforementioned links with classical mythology.

These links were forged long before Shakespeare's time; dictionaries defined elves and fairies in terms of their approximate classical equivalents and translators commonly substituted the native word for a transliteration of the Greek or Latin one in rendering classical texts. Among these translators was Golding; [3] and it is satisfying that in the great speech of renunciation, wherein Shakespeare is to some extent dependent upon Golding's version of Medea's speech in *Metamorphoses* VII, there is a final fusion of the supernatural elements in the play, classical, Neo-Platonic, and native, and a silent differentiation of the good magic of the better nature and the ill magic of the vile who are without virtue. See also p. 173.

APPENDIX C

MONTAIGNE

(*a*) Extract from Montaigne's essay "Of the Caniballes", in the translation of John Florio, published in 1603. (There is in the British Museum a copy of this work which contains what may be a genuine signature of Shakespeare.)

Now . . . I finde (as farre as I have beene informed) there is nothing in that nation, that is either barbarous or savage, unlesse men call that barbarisme which is not common to them. As indeed, we have no other ayme of truth and reason, than the example and

1. Latham, *op. cit.* p. 138.
2. *ibid.* p. 51. Burton describes water-nymphs as "water-devils" who "cause inundations, many times shipwrecks, and deceive men divers ways". Quoted *ibid.* p. 59, and by Luce in the former Arden edition.
3. See Appendix D.

Idea of the opinions and customes of the countrie we live in. There is ever perfect religion, perfect policie, perfect and compleat use of all things. They are even savage, as we call those fruits wilde, which nature of her selfe, and of her ordinarie progresse hath produced: whereas indeed, they are those which our selves have altered by our artificiall devices, and diverted from their common order, we should rather terme savage. In those are the true and most profitable vertues, and naturall properties most lively and vigorous, which in these we have bastardized, applying them to the pleasure of our corrupted taste. And if notwithstanding, in divers fruits of those countries that were never tilled, we shall finde, that in respect of ours they are most excellent, and as delicate unto our taste; there is no reason, art should gaine the point of honour of our great and puissant mother Nature. We have so much by our inventions surcharged the beauties and riches of her workes, that we have altogether overchoaked her: yet where ever her puritie shineth, she makes our vaine and frivolous enterprises wonderfully ashamed...

All our endevour or wit, cannot so much as reach to represent the nest of the least birdlet, it's contexture, beautie, profit and use, no nor the web of a seely spider. "All things" (saith Plato) "are produced, either by nature, by fortune, or by art. The greatest and fairest by one or other of the two first, the least and imperfect by the last." Those nations seeme therefore so barbarous unto me, because they have received very little fashion from humane wit, and are yet neere their originall naturalitie. The lawes of nature doe yet command them, which are but little bastardized by ours, and that with such puritie, as I am sometimes grieved the knowledge of it came no sooner to light, at what time there were men, that better than we could have judged of it. I am sorie, Lycurgus and Plato had it not: for me seemeth that what in those nations we see by experience, doth not only exceed all the pictures wherewith licentious Poesie hath proudly imbellished the golden age, and all her quaint inventions to faine a happy condition of man, but also the conception and desire of Philosophy. They could not imagine a genuitie so pure and simple, as we see it by experience; nor ever beleeve our societie might be maintained with so little art and humane combination. It is a nation, would I answer Plato, that hath no kinde of traffike, no knowledge of Letters, no intelligence of numbers, no name of magistrate, nor of politike superioritie; no use of service, of riches or of povertie; no contracts, no successions, no partitions, no occupation but idle; no respect of kindred, but common, no apparell but naturall, no manuring of lands, no use of wine, corne, or mettle. The very words that import lying, falshood, treason, dissimulations, covetousnes, envie, detraction, and pardon, were never heard of amongst them. How dissonant would hee finde his imaginarie common-wealth from this perfection? . . .

Furthermore, they live in a country of so exceeding pleasant and temperate situation, that as my testimonies have told me, it is verie rare to see a sicke body amongst them; and they have further assured me they never saw any man there, either shaking with the palsie, toothlesse, with eies dropping, or crooked and stooping through age.

[Montaigne goes on to consider cannibalism itself.] I am not sorie we note the barbarous horror of such an action, but grieved, that prying so narrowly into their faults we are so blinded in ours. I thinke there is more barbarisme in eating men alive, than to feed upon them being dead; to mangle by tortures and torments a body full of lively sense, to roast him in peeces, to make dogges and swine to gnaw and teare him in mammockes (as wee have not only read, but seene very lately, yea and in our owne memorie, not amongst ancient enemies, but our neighbours and fellow-citizens; and which is worse, under pretence of pietie and religion) than to roast and eat him after he is dead.

Appendix D

OVID AND GOLDING

Shakespeare's witch Sycorax, as Malone observed, acquired some of the characteristics of the Medea of Ovid's *Metamorphoses* VII. Yet the most resonant echo of Ovid in the whole corpus is in Prospero's valedictory invocation of the spirits in v. i. 33–50. These are Ovid's lines:

> . . . auraeque et venti montesque amnesque lacusque
> dique omnes nemorum, dique omnes noctis adeste,
> quorum ope, cum volui, ripis mirantibus amnes
> in fontes rediere suos, concussaque sisto,
> stantia concutio cantu freta, nubila pello
> nubilaque induco, ventos abigoque vocoque,
> vipereas rumpo verbis et carmine fauces,
> vivaque saxa sua convulsaque robora terra
> et silvas moveo iubeoque tremescere montis
> et mugire solum manesque exire sepulcris!
> te quoque, Luna, traho, quamvis Temesaea labores

aera tuos minuant; currus quoque carmine nostro
pallet avi, pallet nostris Aurora venenis! . . .

(*Met.*, VII. 197–209.)

It is generally held that Shakespeare used Golding's translation
(1567—*The XV Bookes of P. Ovidius Naso, entytuled Metamorphosis*. . .)
Here are Golding's lines:

Ye Ayres and windes: ye Elves of Hilles, of Bookes, of Woods
alone,
Of standing Lakes, and of the Night approche ye everychone.
Through helpe of whom (the crooked bankes much wondring at
the thing)
I have compelled streames to run cleane backward to their
spring.
By charmes I make the calme Seas rough, and make the rough
seas plain
And cover all the Skie with Cloudes, and chase them thence
againe.
By charmes I rayse and lay the windes, and burst the Vipers jaw,
And from the bowels of the Earth both stones and trees doe
drawe.
Whole woods and Forestes I remove: I make the Mountaines
shake,
And even the Earth it selfe to grone and fearfully to quake.
I call up dead men from their graves: and thee O lightsome
Moone
I darken oft, though beaten brasse abate thy perill soone.
Our Sorcerie dimmes the Morning faire, and darkes the Sun at
Noone.

Malone followed the somewhat prejudiced Farmer in attributing Shakespeare's knowledge of the passage in Ovid entirely to
Golding's loose version; but a juster analysis by Maginn arrived at
the conclusion that Shakespeare used both the original and the
translation, the former if anything more than the latter. (See Furness *Variorum*, pp. 234–5.) The latest and fullest of many examina-
tions is that of T. W. Baldwin in his *Shakspere's Small Latine and
Lesse Greeke* (1944), II. 443–52. Baldwin argues that in view of
standard instruction in the art of translation in the schools, and
the use of common works of reference, close similarities are to be
looked for in any two versions of the same original. This accounts
for many of the parallels in Golding, but not all; Shakespeare
seems, for instance, to have used Golding's version of *currus quoque
nostro carmine / pallet*—"Our Sorcerie . . . darkes the Sun at Noone"

—in his "I have bedimm'd The noontide sun." But "by whose aid" is a direct translation of *quorum ope* and not a paraphrase of "Through helpe of whom . . ." In short, Shakespeare was adapting Ovid from the Latin, with a glance at Golding here and there.[1]

This conclusion is consistent with the orthodox modern opinion on Shakespeare's learning, and Baldwin's own labours almost conclusively show that the best explanation of it is that Shakespeare had at least a partial grammar school education.

The adaptation of Medea's incantation to the needs of Prospero is very skilful. Only those elements which are consistent with "white" magic are taken over for Prospero, though some of the remnant is transferred to Sycorax. The grim *dii . . . omnes noctis* become English elves; Shakespeare consistently, and traditionally, makes this and similar changes.[2] (There are, however, some slightly sinister mushrooms in the same book of Ovid—l. 393, which may have affected the references to English fairies.)

The Ovid Shakespeare used would probably be a heavily annotated text, carrying a load of mythographical matter. Since the traditional allegorical interpretation varied little throughout the whole period, Sandys' Commentary of 1632, in his *Ovids Metamorphosis Englished*, may be regarded as typical, and more thorough than Golding's samples in his introductory Epistle, though scarcely different in kind. That Shakespeare knew Golding's prefatory matter is certain enough, and for *The Tempest* he would scarcely banish from his mind "this dark Philosophie of turned shapes". Thus when we read ll. 55–62 of Golding's prefatory statement we are forcibly reminded of the degradation of Stephano and Trinculo (see *Intro.*, p. xxxvii). For comment on the Medea passage we may look to Sandys; he allows no distinction between black and white magic, this being an issue upon which men were divided, though believers in white magic were a very small minority; there is no need to count Shakespeare among them though he left no note, as Wordsworth did, to caution us against over-literal acceptance of an occult metaphor. Sandys is orthodox: "These wonders were not effected by the vertue of words, or skill of *Medea*; but rather by wicked Angels, who seem to subject themselves, the better to delude, to the art of the Inchantresse." Drawing down the moon simply indicates that the sorceress was capitalizing a timely eclipse. "But that of *Medea's* raising the dead from their graves, is more credible; since the like was acted on the body of a

---

1. Maginn used some of the same examples, and came to the same conclusion.
2. See Appendix B.

Saint by the witch of *Endor*: although whether done by divine permission, or diabolicall illusion, as yet is in controversy."[1] It is noteworthy that the story of Medea, a witch, stood in little need of allegorizing; it was quite intelligible in the light of contemporary doctrine and controversy. Thus her methods generally resemble those of contemporary witches, and Shakespeare went to Ovid as to a *locus classicus*. I do not think there is any reason to doubt that Shakespeare's audience was quite capable of the degree of discrimination required to perceive that there were two opposed kinds of magic in *The Tempest*, and that their opposition provided an important structural tension. Those who knew Ovid would have the additional knowledge that the action of these opposites was epitomized in the imitation of his Medea passage. Finally, it may be mentioned that Middleton gives his Hecate these lines of Ovid to speak in *The Witch* (ed. Bullen, Vol. v, p. 443), using a corrupt version of the text which was, it appears, current in works on magic.

APPENDIX E

THE TEMPEST ON THE JACOBEAN STAGE

Four playing-places have been suggested for *The Tempest*. They are:

(1) The Banqueting House at Whitehall. This is quite certain, and the date of the performance, which the King attended, was 1 November 1611.

(2) The Blackfriars Playhouse. Dryden, in the Preface to his adaptation, *The Tempest, or, The Enchanted Island* (1674) wrote that "The Play . . . had formerly been acted with success in the *Black-Fryers*," and there is a strong probability that it was so.

1. pp. 254–5. Sandys here follows the famous commentary by Raphael Regius (Venice, 1497) which, after selling 50,000 copies in sixteen years, was constantly reprinted in modified forms. (See D. P. Harding, *Milton and the Renaissance Ovid* [1946], p. 18.) Baldwin suggests that Shakespeare may have relied on the notes of Regius in distinguishing the black from the white in Medea's magic, but it is unlikely that he needed such help.

A few passages from Sandys will be found in my commentary; the implication should not be forgotten, that Sandys is rarely original, and the parallels may be explained as having some common source in an earlier edition of or commentary upon Ovid.

(3) The Globe. There is no evidence for this, but it is likely enough.

(4) The Cockpit, a royal preserve off Whitehall, probably used for the less stately occasions when plays were presented by command. (See Chambers, *Eliz. Stage*, I. 216.) W. J. Lawrence conjectured, from certain aspects of the "masque", that the play was given there during the festival of 1612–13. He cites Nichol's *Royal Progresses* in support of this, saying that the Elector's first entertainment took place there. (*Fortnightly Review*, CXVII (1920), 941 ff.) On looking up his (inaccurate) reference, I find that Nichol does in fact give a letter of Finett which speaks of the Princess having "sent to invite him, as he sat at supper, to a play of her own servants in the Cock-pit" (*The Progresses of King James the First* (1828), II. 466). Her servants were, of course, The Lady Elizabeth's Men. Such a performance, almost informal, is a very different matter from those commanded in the course of official celebrations, which left their marks in various ways upon the court records.[1] In fact, there is no need to consider an extra-mural performance, even if the lack of machines in the "masque" seems to make the Banqueting House an improbable site. There were other rooms indoors which were used, as for instance when a masque was being prepared in the Banqueting House, and which were obviously not equipped as theatres. There is therefore no need to consider the Cockpit any further.

We are left with a possibility, amounting almost to a probability, that *The Tempest* was performed between 1611 and 1613 at three theatres.

The Globe was the regular playing place of Shakespeare's Company from 1599 until the opening of their venture at the Blackfriars in 1608, after which year both playhouses were used until the destruction of the Globe by fire in 1613. After 1606 the company (now the King's Men) must also have become familiar with the permanent Banqueting House and its stage, and remained so until that also was destroyed ten years later.

The Tempest has long, and for the present purpose, quite rightly, been regarded as belonging to that group of plays which, in their sophisticated design and presentation, seem to belong to the more expensive Blackfriars rather than to the Globe, but in spite of this the Globe could contain it almost as easily as it did *Cymbeline*, *The Winter's Tale*, and *Henry VIII*. Despite wide differences in the audience and the atmosphere (for we must remember that the

1. "The performances must have been of a semi-private nature" (J. Q. Adams: *Shakespearean Playhouses* [1917], p. 393).

Blackfriars was an indoor theatre with a brightly lit stage, much smaller than the Globe and capable of more subtle effects) the play could easily have been acted at both theatres; the Globe had the three-level tiring-house[1] which seems indispensable (see below), as well as the necessary traps and machines to deal with the more spectacular episodes.

But the Blackfriars was the natural home of the play. For information about the kind of production achieved in this playhouse as a consequence of the irruption of the adult company into the sphere of the more refined boys' companies, see J. Isaacs, "Production and Stage Management at the Blackfriars Theatre" (*Shakespeare Assocn. Pamphlet*, 1933). Mr Isaacs emphasizes the new role of music in indoor production, and it may assist us in seeing the *Tempest* "masque" in perspective if we recall his remark that "when the Court Masque by inevitable process of grafting, was made a part of theatrical production, it lost its expensive settings and bulky and elaborate movable properties, but it retained that which was most suitable and welcome in the private theatre—its music" (p. 24). Indeed *The Tempest* is impregnated with atmospheric music, which would fare less well in the great yard of the Globe than in the small private theatre. Whether or no Shakespeare had been directed during his last years to produce work specially adapted for the Blackfriars, as G. E. Bentley argues (*Shakespeare Survey*, 1 (1948), pp. 38 ff) it is far easier to imagine it making its effect there, in a theatre affected by the learned Vitruvian revival which was penetrating the English theatre from Europe,[2] and before an audience with some pretensions to cultivated sensibility.[3]

The model for the Blackfriars was in fact that type of royal banqueting hall of which the short-lived state-apartment built at Whitehall in 1606–7 was a contemporary representative.[4] It was in

1. J. C. Adams: *The Globe Playhouse* (1943), p. 308. Although the third acting-level is conjectural, and some investigators would reject it together with much else in Adams's reconstruction (see, e.g., C. Walter Hodges, "Unworthy Scaffolds" in *Shakespeare Survey* 3 (1950), pp. 83 ff.) there seems to be no other satisfactory explanation of the direction *on the top*, which occurs in this play and also in the Blackfriars play *The Double Marriage* (Fletcher, 1620). And Adams is surely incontrovertible in his insistence on the importance of the Globe's mechanical apparatus.

2. See L. B. Campbell, *Scenes and Machines on the English Stage during the Renaissance*, Cambridge, 1923. Neo-Vitruvianism was a courtly import, and would therefore pass into the professional theatre very easily under conditions such as those provided by the Blackfriars.

3. The standard work on this subject is A. Harbage, *Shakespeare's Audience* (1941).

4. Details of this hall are not precisely known, but its great successor, the

this royal theatre, at Hallowmas, 1611, that the first recorded performance of *The Tempest* took place in the King's presence. I call it a theatre advisedly; there was nothing makeshift about it. It certainly had a large stage, with a proscenium arch (sometimes decorated with the title of the masque or play) and scenic resources far beyond those of the Globe. Costume also was very lavish at court, and this may have affected such productions as that of *The Tempest*.[1]

The most sustained attempt to visualize a court performance of the play is Sir E. Law's Shakespeare Association Pamphlet on "Shakespeare's *Tempest* as originally produced at Court" (1920). Law points out a similarity between the settings of *The Tempest* and several masques produced between 1610 and 1613, and attaches particular importance to Campion's description of the scenes for his masque of 1613, devised for the marriage of Carr and Lady Essex. Campion, deprived by a quarrel of the new setting he wanted, had to make do with what was already available. This included a scene enclosed by a triumphal arch, sky and clouds, a high promontory, on one side a rock in the sea, on the other a wood; "betweene them appeared a sea in perspective. . ." In apology for the shortcomings of this scenery, he writes "That our modern writers have rather transferred their fictions to the persons of Enchanters and Commanders of spirits" so that "in imitation of them he had founded his whole invention upon enchantments and severall transformations." It would be rash to suggest that this setting was an old one left over from *The Tempest*, but it will perhaps help the reader to envisage a Jacobean *Tempest* more spectacular in setting as well as in machinery than we are accustomed to contemplate. Law has many interesting conjectures concerning the presentation of the "masque" in the green-baize "short-grass'd green" of the inner stage, with its winding staircase down which the goddesses might walk to earth, and also concerning costume, which has nowhere else been so fully treated in connexion with this play. One might also refer to his salutary insistence on the observance of act-divisions, on the splendour of the lighting, and on the importance of the music. This short work is certainly not yet superseded. Miss Campbell describes many spectacular effects

work of Inigo Jones, is still to be seen in Whitehall, where it houses the United Services War Museum.

1. The players were given to finery themselves, but could scarcely rival the court with its traditions of spectacular extravagance—witness the practice of destroying the masque-furnishings when the performance ended (Chambers, *Eliz. Stage*, I. 206).

which could certainly be achieved at the Banqueting House, though beyond the scope of the Globe, where the main set of the play would very likely be a simple arrangement of property trees leading like an avenue to the cave (the "study" aperture) in the tiring-house wall.

It is not my intention to venture into the highly specialist and controversial field of inquiry wherein scholars attempt detailed accounts of the disposition of scenery, exploitation of the playhouses' physical characteristics, and use of machines, but a few notes on I. i and III. iii, where the main difficulties of presentation arise, may not come amiss, though I depend entirely upon the work of the scholars mentioned.

Sea-scenes were not uncommon in Elizabethan drama, and were often enacted at theatres like the Red Bull, which seems to have been if anything less well equipped than the Globe. Theatrical machinery existed for realistic ship- and sea-scenes, and even for real rolling billows,[1] but it seems unlikely that anything of this sort was used in *The Tempest*, where we do not need to see the labouring ship *ab extra*. L. B. Wright (in *Anglia*, LI (1927), 104 ff) has made a study of sea-scenes on the Elizabethan stage. The primary means of creating the illusion of action on shipboard was, of course, suggestive noise and terminology. Nautical noises off, the blowing of whistles—"here let them make a noise as if they were mariners" runs one stage-direction—were sometimes augmented by a direct request to the audience to use their imagination, on the lines of the choric appeals in *Henry V*. This latter device Shakespeare abjures in *The Tempest*, as he abjures all choric comment in that play, but in both *Pericles* and *The Tempest* there are plenty of suggestive noises and language. Wright finds, as against Chambers, that the possibility of exploiting the higher levels of the tiring-house façade was not ignored and he produces evidence that the tarrass or balcony was used to represent the poop. We may be reasonably certain that the Master speaks from the tarrass. In claiming that ropes and rigging might have been used for sailors to climb from one level to another, Wright incurs the criticism of G. F. Reynolds (*The Staging of Elizabethan Plays* (1940), pp. 179–81). In *The Double Marriage* (1620), a Blackfriars play, a boy appears "a-top" which, if J. C. Adams is right, means on the platform of the music gallery, the third level of the tiring-house. If this part of the structure was used as an acting area at all one can well believe that it would be allowed to represent a crow's nest. There is of course no call for this in *The Tempest*. I have heard the sugges-

1. Campbell, *op. cit.* p. 156.

tion that symbolic rigging or a mast might have been constructed at the chamber-level. It is, of course, hard to define the point at which symbolism breaks down and becomes frankly absurd, but anyway a mast would look strange on the "poop". Nevertheless, the idea of rope-ladders on the façade is attractive; in this play the mariners, running to their stations, and impeded by the gentlemen, might well have been hurrying aloft as well as across the stage.

III. iii is Shakespeare's most elaborate experiment in stage-spectacle. On this scene Mr J. C. Adams has expended a vast amount of ingenuity, considering it for the most part as it might have been staged at the Globe. Here the words "on the top", which many editors in the past altered to "above", take on a new import-ance.[1] Prospero's appearance is not, says Adams, essential to the action, and he is there merely to co-ordinate the complex display going on below him by transmitting cues to the musicians behind him who in turn provide cues for stage-hands and the prompter. For the details of this theory the reader must be referred to *R.E.S.* XIV (1938), 404–19, and *The Globe Playhouse*, pp. 319–22. Adams conjectures, with plausible support from his knowledge of the powers and conventions of theatrical mechanists, that the table which rises does so on a trap upon which, concealed by the hangings of the table, there lurks a stage-hand. Ariel descends from the heavens on a machine which must have been improved from that used in *Cymbeline* to make possible single flights without a car; he covers the banquet on the table with his harpy's wings; whereupon the stage-hand removes a panel in the table top and whisks the banquet (usually a light refreshment) out of sight. Ariel then lifts his wings, and by a quaint device the banquet has indeed vanished. Mr Adams makes all this seem very plausible and works out all the trap-, music-, and thunder-signals necessary in accordance with normal Elizabethan stage usage. This very attractive theory may in the end perish by reason of its own inclusiveness; if anything goes wrong with any part of it, the whole structure is endangered. But we may be sure that at the Blackfriars and at Court, this scene was performed with the aid of some ingenious mechanist, whose devices, if not exactly those of Adams, would rival them in effec-tiveness.

---

1. The direction occurs also in *1 H 6*, III. ii. 26 (S.D.); this was, of course, not a Globe play.

Appendix F

THE MUSIC OF *THE TEMPEST*

Music is of great importance in *The Tempest*, which contains more songs than any other play, and which often demands instrumental music also. Fortunately a little of the original music survives.

The songs, "Where the bee sucks", and "Full fadom five", were printed in Dr John Wilson's collection of *Cheerfull Ayres or Ballads* (1659) in versions attributed to Robert Johnson.[1] Of this composer much that has been written is confused or erroneous. In 1596 he was apprenticed to Sir George Carey, later Lord Hunsdon, for seven years. Carey held the office of Lord Chamberlain, and lived in Blackfriars, very near the private theatre. When he had served his apprenticeship Johnson was sworn in as a lutenist in the service of the King, and he retained this office until his death in September, 1633. It is quite clear that he was often employed in the composition of masques and other entertainments. It is also clear that his music was used not only at court but in the theatres of the King's Men, partly in the antimasques which the players conveyed into their normal productions, partly in original compositions. Thus, the music he wrote for Beaumont's wedding masque of 1613 was probably used in *Two Noble Kinsmen*—this exemplifies a frequent practice. On the other hand the music for Beaumont and Fletcher's *Valentinian*[2] and Webster's *The Duchess of Malfi*[3] appears to have been specially composed for the play. He wrote a good deal of music for the great celebrations of 1612–13, and Richmond Noble thinks that the *Tempest* songs must date from this period, in view of Johnson's failure to follow exactly the text of "Full fadom five" (*Shakespeare's Use of Song*, p. 107). But even if there were a revision, which seems unlikely, there is some inconsequence in Noble's argument. We cannot be certain that Wilson printed the music exactly as he found it, or at any rate exactly as Johnson wrote it. On the other hand, Noble has justly appraised these songs as of a kind written by Shakespeare only at the end of his career—"set songs so deeply embedded in the text as dialogue that it is unnecessary to stop the action to permit them to be performed, for they are essentially a part of it" (pp. 150–1).

In 1922 W. J. Lawrence drew attention to B.M. Add. MS. 10444,

1. Excellent versions for voice and piano were arranged by Anthony Lewis and published in 1936 by the Lyrebird Press (Paris).
2. "Care-charming sleep"; see Lewis, *op. cit.*
3. In B.M. Add. MS. 29481.

"Full fadom five" J. Wilson, <u>Cheerfull Ayres</u>

Full fadom five thy fa~ther lies;   of his   bones are cor~al made; those are pearls that were his eyes

no-thing of him that doth fade, but doth suf~fer a   sea ~ change In~to some~thing rich and strange Sea nymphs hourly

ring his knell; Harke, now I hear them, Harke ~ now I hear them, Ding, Dong   Bell

Ding Dong   Ding Dong   Bell   Ding Dong Ding Dong Bell   Ding Dong Ding Dong Bell

"Where the bee sucks" J. Wilson, Chearfull Ayres

Where the bee sucks there suck I — In a cowslip's bell I lie; There I couch when

owls do cry, on the bat's back I do fly, af-ter sum-mer mer-ri—ly Mer-ri-ly Mer-ri-ly

Shall I live now un-der the blo-ssom that hangs on the bough. Mer-ri-ly, Mer-ri-ly shall I live now,

un-der the blossom that hangs on the bough.

"The Tempest" B.M. Add. M S 10444, № 62

which contains a remarkable collection of masque music,[1] and made an admirable, though not always accurate, attempt to identify the several pieces. He conjectured that one item, labelled simply "The Tempest", and attributed by the B.M. Catalogue to Robert Johnson, was "the Reapers' Dance in Shakespeare's play". But he was extremely cautious about this. The music certainly suggests a lively dance rather than Winds dancing in "a horrid storm", an antimasque in *Chloridia* (1631) which is chiefly responsible for Lawrence's uncertainty, and it could be either the Reapers' dance or the dance of the Shapes in III. iii. At any rate it seemed worth printing the music here. Add. MS. 10444 is a badly copied manuscript which separates the two parts and makes mistakes which, in the absence of bar-lines, can be very bewildering.[2] In this same manuscript there is a dance entitled "They [sic] Hay-makers Masque", which could conceivably be music from the entertainment in Act IV. Lawrence, however, seems not to have thought so; he makes no attempt at an attribution. The evidence is indeed meagre, and I therefore do not give this item.[3]

1. *Music and Letters*, III (1922), 49–58.

2. The version here printed owes much to Dr D. P. Walker.

3. "The Tempest," with other dramatic music attributable to Johnson, was performed in an arrangement by Dr R. Woodham in the University of Reading, 22 March 1952.

Additional note

John P. Cutts writes elaborately of the music as related to contemporary theories of *musica mundana* in "Music in *The Tempest*", *Music and Letters*, XXXIX (1958), 347–58.

Appendix G

LINEATION

Note. Here are recorded all points at which the lineation of this edition differs from that of the Folio, and a few cases where the present text follows F, but where other editors, or the later Folios, have not done so. The practice of the Arden edition is to set out the second part of a line divided between two speakers in such a way as to make evident its relationship to the first part of the line, e.g., III. iii. 103:

> *I'll fight their legions o'er.*
>
> *I'll be thy second.*

This, however, is not the practice of the Folio, where the second part of the line is almost always started afresh at the left-hand margin. The normal and unambiguous setting of the second parts of divided lines in this way in F is not here recorded.

The decision between verse and prose in this edition is conventional. My text does not greatly differ in this respect from those of Pope and Johnson.

I. i. 54. *For ... patience*] *for ... theirs.* | *I'am ... patience* F.

56–7. *This . . . drowning* | *The . . . yet*] *This . . . drow-* | *ning the . . . Tides.* | *Hee'l . . . yet* F.

59. *him.* | *. . . "Mercy*] *him.* A confused noyse within. | *Mercy* F.

I. ii. 1–2. *If ... have* | *Put*] F; *If ... you* | *Have put* Seymour.

252–3. *Thou ... the ooze* | *Of*] *Thou ... yͤ Ooze* | *Of* F; *Thou ... the* | *Ooze of* F4.

301–6. *Go . . . sea:* | *Be . . . to* | *No . . . invisible* | *To . . . shape,* | *And . . . hence* | *With diligence.*] *Goe . . . Sea,* | *Be . . . inuisible* | *To . . . shape* | *And . . . hence* | *With diligence.* F.[1]

311–12. *'Tis ... sir,* | *I ... 'tis*] *'Tis ... on.* | *But ... 'tis* F.

---

1. The arrangement in F cannot be the original one; nor can that in the present text, which seeks merely to preserve as many full lines as possible. Perhaps there is some mechanical confusion, indicated by the placing in F of Ariel's *Exit* in mid-column, and the repetition of the speech-heading *Pro.* (See textual note on p. 29.) But the emendation of F2 (see textual note on p. 28) together with the omission of *thine and* (which is pointless, and possibly the result of an imperfectly registered cancellation in MS.) leaves us with two regular lines at the start of the passage. Mr H. F. Brooks, independently and in the course of quite another argument, urges the redundancy of *go* in l. 305 (the printer possibly caught it from the previous line). It is just possible that the lines originally read thus: *Go make thyself like to a nymph o'th'sea:* | *Be subject to no sight but mine; invisible* | *To every eyeball else. Go take this shape,* | *And hither come in't: hence with diligence.*

363–4. *Deservedly ... rock,* / *Who ... prison.*]*Deseruedly ... hadst*/
   Deseru'd ... prison. F.

381–3. Foot ... there, / And ... bear] Foot ... there, / And,
   sweet sprites, the burthen bear Pope (following
   Dryden).

381–9. Foot ... there, / And ... bear / *The ... hark.* / *Burthen*
   ... Bow-wow. / *Ari. ... bark: / Burthen ... Bow-wow.* /
   Ari. ... hear / *The ... chanticleer* / *Cry ... dow.*]
   Foote ... beare / the ... dispersedly. / *Harke ... barke,* /
   bowgh-wawgh. / *Ar. ... Chanticlere / cry cockadidle-*
   dowe. F.

II. i.   12–13. *Look ... strike*] *Looke ... wit,* / *By ... strike* F.

16–17. *When ... offer'd,* / *Comes ... entertainer—*] *When ...*
   entertaind, / *That's ... entertainer.* F.

27–8. *Which ... crow?*] *Which ... wager,* / *First ... crow?* F.

51. *How ... green!*] *How ... lookes?* / *How greene?* F.

76–7. *What ... it!*] *What ... too?* / *Good ... it?* F.

187–93. *Would ... find* / *They ... sir,* / *Do ... it:* / *It ... doth,* / *It*
   ... lord, / *Will ... rest,* / *And ... heavy.*] *Would ...*
   thoughts, / *I ... so.* / *Please ... Sir,* / *Do ... it:* / *It ...*
   Comforter. / *We ... person,* / *While ... safety:* / *Thanke*
   ... heauy. F.

196–7. *Doth ... not* / *Myself*] *Doth ... finde* / *Not my selfe* F.

239–40. *That ... me,* / *Who's ... Claribel.*] *That ... drown'd.* /
   He's gone. / *Then ... Naples?* / *Claribell.* F.

270–5. *But ... conscience.* / *Ay ... kibe,* / *'Twould ... not* / *This*
   ... consciences, / *That ... they,* / *And ... brother,*] F
   (substantially); *But ... that?* / *If ... slipper:* / *But ...*
   bosom: / *Twenty ... Milan,* / *candied ... molest!* / *Here*
   ... brother Pope.

II. ii. 43–4. *I ... sea,* / *Here ... ashore,—*] *I ... ashore.* F.

45–6. *This ... comfort.*] *This ... mans* / *Funerall ... comfort.* F
   (neither line full).

56. *This ... comfort.*] *This ... too:* / *But ... comfort.* F
   (neither line full).

58. *What's ... Do you*] *What's ... matter?* / *Haue ... here?* /
   Doe you F (neither line full).

73–4.] As verse, divided *prithee;* / *I'll* Steevens.

81–4.] As verse, divided *wilt*/*Anon ... trembling;* / *Now*
   Steevens.

89–90. *I ... me!*] *I ... voyce:* / *It ... be,* / *But ... de- / fend me.* F.[1]

1. The condition of F rather strongly suggests that the object of the
printer was to lose space (see *Intro.*, p. xiv, n. 1), as he makes four lines of a
speech that would go comfortably into two, and even has to space out the

117–19. *These ... sprites. | That's ... liquor : | I ... him.*] *These
... sprights : | that's ... will | kneele ... him.* F.

120. *How ... hither?*] *How ... scape? | How ... hither?* F
(neither line full).

126–7.] As verse, divided *thy | True* Steevens.

131–2. *Here ... goose.*] *Here ... Booke. | Though ... made | like
... Goose.* F (first line not full).

134–6. *The ... ague?*] *The ... rocke | by ... hid : | How ...
Ague?* F (last two lines not full).[1]

144–7. *By ... sooth!*] *By ... Mon- | ster ... Monster : | The ...
Moone? | A ... Monster : | Well ... sooth.* F (last four
lines not full).

148–9.] As verse, divided *island; | And* Johnson.

158–9. *But ... monster!*] *But ... drinke : | An ... Monster.* F
(neither line full).

160–4. *I'll ... berries; | I'll ... enough. | A ... serve! | I'll ...
thee, | Thou ... man.*] *I'le ... thee | Berries ... enough. | A
... serue; | I'le ... thou | wondrous man.* F (third line
not full).

167–72. *I ... grow; | And ... pig-nuts; | Show ... how | To ...
thee | To ... thee | Young ... me?*] *I ... grow; | and ...
pig-nuts; | show ... snare | the ... clustring | Philbirts ...
Scamels | from ... me?* F.

181–2. *Nor ... firing | At requiring;*] *Nor ... requiring;* F
(one line).

III. ii. 22–3. *How ... valiant.*] *How ... shooe : | Ile ... valiant.* F.

36–7. *I ... thee?*] *I ... pleas'd | to ... thee?* F; *I ... pleas'd | To
... again the suit I made thee?* Steevens.[2]

38–9. *Marry ... Trinculo.*] *Marry ... it, | I ... Trinculo.* F
(neither line full).

40–2. *As ... island.*] *As ... Tirant, | A ... me | Of ... Island.* F;
As ... to | A ... cunning | Hath ... island Nicholson conj.[3]

47–8. *Trinculo ... teeth.*] *Trinculo ... tale, | By ... teeth.* F.

57–8. *How ... party?*] *How ... compast? | Canst ... party?* F
(neither line full).

---

line *But ... de-* in a noticeable and abnormal manner.

1. F starts a new line at *How* because Stephano begins to address a different
person.

2. F may have intended this as verse (it does not invariably capitalize the
initial letter of the first word). The omission of each *to* in l. 37, as by Steevens,
leaves two regular lines.

3. If the passage is really verse, the first line should probably remain as it is in
F. F's division of the second and third lines may need to be corrected thus : *hath |
Cheated.*

67–70. *Trinculo ... thee.*] Trinculo ... *danger : | Interrupt ...*
this | hand ... a | Stockfish ... thee. F (first line not full).[1]

71. *Why ... off.*] *Why ... nothing : | Ile ... off.* F (neither
line full).[2]

74–5. *Do ... time.*] *Do ... that, | As ... time.* F (first line not
full).

76–9. *I ... fingers!*] *I ... and | hearing too? | A pox ... doo : |
A murren ... your | fingers.* F (second line not full).[3]

104–7. *Monster ... Trinculo.*] *Monster ... and | I ... Trin- |
culo ... Vice-royes : | Dost ... Trinculo?* F (third line
not full).[4]

109–10. *Give ... head.*] *Giue ... thee : | But ... head.* F.

117–18. *At ... sing.*] *At ... reason, | Any ... sing.* F.

119–21. Flout ... 'em, / And ... 'em; / Thought is free.] Flout
... and flout 'em, / Thought is free. F.

126–7. *If ... list.*] *If ... likenes : | If ... list.* F.

129–30. *He ... us!*] *He ... thee; | Mercy ... vs.* F.

142–3. *This ... nothing.*] *This ... me, | Where ... nothing.* F.

145. *That ... story.*] *That ... by and by : | I ... storie.* F
(neither line full).

146–7. *The ... work.*] *The ... away, | Lets ... worke.* F
(neither line full).

148–9. *Lead ... on.*] *Leade Monster, | Wee'l ... Taborer, | He ...
on.* F (first line not full).

150. *Wilt ... Stephano.*] *Wilt come? | Ile ... Stephano.* F
(neither line full).

III.iii. 13–14. *That ... advantage | Will ... tonight;*] *That ... t'effect.*
The ... throughly. | Let ... to night, F.

IV. i. 165–6. *Thy ... Spirit, | We ... Caliban.*] *Thy ... pleasure? |*
Spirit ... Caliban. F.

194–5. *Pray ... not | Hear ... cell.*] *Pray ... may | not ... Cell.* F.

196–8. *Monster ... us.*] *Monster ... harmles Fairy, | Has ... vs.* F.

199–200. *Monster ... indignation.*] *Monster ... which | My ...*
indignation. F.

201–2. *So ... you,—*] *So ... should | Take ... you.* F.

211–12. *That's ... monster.*] *That's ... wetting : | Yet ... Monster.*
F (first line not full).

1. The spacing in F is abnormally lavish.
2. There is no question here of F setting the speech as verse; the compositor
(B) is anxious to make the scene fill the whole of p. 12.
3. See note on p. 80, and *Intro.*, p. xvi.
4. F starts a new line when the speaker addresses a different person. Cf.
II. ii. 134–6.

213–14. *I . . . labour.*] *I . . . bottle, | Though . . . labour.* F (first line not full).

220–1. *Give . . . thoughts.*] *Giue . . . hand, | I . . . thoughts.* F (first line not full).

222–3. *O King . . . thee!*] *O King . . . worthy* Stephano, | *Looke . . . thee.* F.[1]

v. i. 95–6. *miss thee; | But*] Ff; *misse | Thee, but* F.

199–200. *Let . . . with | A*] *Let . . . remembrances | With a* Malone.

220. *Hast . . . news?*] *Hast . . . land? | What . . . newes?* F.

256–8. *Every . . . coragio!*] *Euery . . . let | No . . . is | But . . .* Corasio. F (lines not full).

278. *He . . . wine?*] *He . . . now; | Where . . . wine?* F (neither line full).

282–4. *I . . . fly-blowing.*] *I . . . last, | That . . . bones: | I . . . fly-blowing.* F (second line not full).

---

1. The remainder of this scene is free of variants. From l. 227 the F text begins a new page (16). The change can be explained only in terms of casting-off. I suspect (against Willoughby) that the latter part of 15b was set by B, A reuming at the end of the column.

ADDITIONAL NOTES

INTRODUCTION

p. xlvi, n. 1: *Melior natura.* The unidentified poet cited by Phillips is not at all obscure; this expression is borrowed from Ovid, *Metamorphoses*, i. 21: *Hanc deus et melior litem natura diremit;* which Sandys translates as follows: But God the better Nature, this [conflict] decides (*op. cit.* p. 1). The context in Ovid is the regulation of Chaos by God, or the Stoic principle of divine order in the universe—a nature higher than that represented by disorganized chaos. Sandys comments: "[God] he also calleth the *Better Nature*; so named by the Stoicke" (p. 19). The idea as used by Shakespeare and Phillips incorporates the notion of the element of divine reason which distinguishes the nature of man from that of brute; Prospero's Art involves a union with the divine principle, and all the civilized partake of it, in contrast to Caliban who, like Chaos, does not.

p. lxxii, l. 1: *Thorndike.* A. H. Thorndike, *The Influence of Beaumont and Fletcher on Shakespeare* (1901).

COMMENTARY

p. 5, I. i. 22: The reading *presence* supposes a *c* : *t* error, on the evidence of the Hand D ection of *Sir Thomas More*, a very probable one in Shakespeare. The spelling *presenc* in foul papers must have been copied as *present* by Crane or, more probably, an earlier transcriber; *presenc* occurs in the *More* passage (l. 62). The Boatswain is ironically asking Gonzalo to exercise his authority as a court official ("you are a counsellor") and enforce the peace appropriate to the king's presence, or his presence-chamber. "The peace of the presence" sounds like a set phrase, but so far I have not encountered it elsewhere.

p. 7, I. i. 49: *Lay her a-hold*] Very common in nautical writings, and metaphorically; cf. Donne, *Essayes in Divinity* (1651), p. 20: "to ly hulling upon the face of the waters . . ."; and Florio, *Montaigne*, II. i: "now gliding gently, now hulling violently..."

p. 8, I. i. 57: *The washing of ten tides*] Cf. Cooke's *Green's Tu Quoque* (Dodsley, III. 10) (of a gallant who says he will turn pirate): "O master! have the grace of Wapping before your eyes, remember a high tide!"

p. 16, I. ii. 107: *To have no screen*] It has been suggested that my comment is unnecessarily complicated, and the relative simplicity of Kittredge preferred to it. I disagree; but here is Kittredge's paraphrase: "He was playing the part of the Duke, but he was playing it *for me*, as my representative. There was, then, a screen or distinction between the Duke's part he played and the real Duke. By making himself Duke, he would remove that screen, since he would then be identical with the part he played—would be playing it for himself."

p. 27, I. ii. 269: W. J. Craig noticed in Hakluyt a reference to native women "marked in the face with blewe strekes . . . round about the eyes." (Glasgow ed., VII, 209; see Rich, *Apolonius & Silla*, ed. Morton Luce (1912), p. 4, n. 2.) C. J. Sisson (*New Readings in Shakespeare*, 1956) cites evidence to support the interpretation "tearstained, livid".

p. 27, I. ii. 281: *strike*] The comparison may be more difficult than I suggest; Kittredge says it refers "to the clapper, i.e. 'the contrivance for striking or shaking the hopper so as to make the grain move down to the millstones' (N.E.D.)".

p. 30, I. ii. 318: *when?*] Cf. Middleton, *The Witch* (Malone Soc., 1949), l. 1989.

p. 32, I. ii. 355: *capable of*] Cf. *1 Return from Parnassus* (ed. Leishman, 1949), l. 273, and note *ad loc.*

p. 34, I. ii. 383: The incidence of textual corruption is abnormally high in the songs; possibly the copy was sometimes a MS. song book, either as a transcript corrupt in itself, or because of arrangement baffling to compositors. The existence of versions of "It was a lover" superior to that of the F *AYL.* lends colour to the hypothesis that the compositor sometimes set songs from debased texts.

p. 37, I. ii. 424: One should perhaps also refer to Chaucer, *Knights Tale*, ll. 1101–2, where Palamon cannot tell whether Emilye is woman or goddess. And see *Paradise Regained*, II, 156–7. And the following: Boccaccio, *Filostrate*, I. 38; Chaucer, *Troilus*, I. 425; Politian, *Giostra*, I. 49; *O qual che tu sia, vergin sovrana, / O ninfa o dea (ma dea m'assembri certo)* . . . ; and Marino, *Adone*, Canto iii: *Ed o qual tu ti sia ch'a me ti mostri / Tutta amor, tutta grazia, o Donna o Diva, / Diva certo immortal.* . .

p. 45, II. i. 35–6: Dr H. Brooks suggests that a copyist has been confused by the irruption of *Adr.* into a run of *Ant.* and *Seb.* speech-headings; after setting that for l. 34, he momentarily thought of *Adr.* as *Ant.*, and followed it with *Seb.*

p. 51, II. i. 164: '*Save*] Mr J. C. Maxwell doubts whether "God save" could ever have been regarded as an oath, or profane. But no one was sure how the statute of 1606 was to be interpreted, and there is evidence of extreme caution. Jonson, in revising *Every Man In His Humour*, altered "God save" to "'Save" in I. ii. 1. We may say that the statute encouraged a preference for "'Save" in both these cases.

p. 53, II. i. 191: *It is a comforter*] J. E. Hankins (*Shakespeare's Derived Imagery*, [1953], p. 118) suggests a debt to Palingenius, *Zodiacus Vitae*: "But vnto troubled minds it is, a comfort great in deede" (Googe's translation, [1576], p. 39).

p. 54, II. i. 216: *Trebles*] C. J. Sisson (*New Readings in Shakespeare*, 1956) says this is a metaphor from draughts. "At a stroke Seb. will overleap three superiors, Antonio, Ferdinand and Alonso, and become King, in one move."

p. 57, II. i. 261: *A chough...*] A foolish talker; cf. Erasmus, *Praise of Folly*, trans. J. Wilson (1688), ed. Mrs P. S. Allen (1913), p. 164: "lest those Choughs should chatter at me . . ." In *2 Return from Parnassus*, l. 226 (ed. Leishman, 1949), the word "chuffes" means "churls".

p. 61, II. ii. 3: *By inch-meal*] Cf. Donne, *Letters to Severall Persons of Honour* (1651): "God loves your soul, if he be loth to let it go inch-meal. . ."

p. 78, III. ii. 15: *standard*] In support of the N.S. gloss: jokes of this kind about the Standard, a conduit in Cheapside, were current. Middleton uses them more than once, e.g. *Michaelmas Term*, II. i. 109 (ed. Bullen, I. 240).

p. 79, III. ii. 25: *debosh'd*] Cf. Scott, *Redgauntlet*, Cap. III: "deboshed with brandy". *O.E.D.* says Scott revived the form.

p. 83, III. ii. 124–5: Mr J. B. Trapp has generously provided me with an historical account of Nobody. The literary history begins in *Odyssey* ix, where Odysseus tricks Polyphemus by giving his name as οὖτις. Widely diffused in folklore (see Stith Thompson, *Motive Index of Folklore*, IV, 344), Nobody re-emerges as a considerable literary theme in the Middle Ages. An Angevin cleric called Radulphus dedicated to the future Pope Boniface VIII a *Sermo Neminis* (c. 1290), which consists of a collection of biblical, patristic, and liturgical references to Nemo, making up a sort of biography (*Nemo ascendit in coelum*, John, iii. 13; *Deum Nemo vidit*, John, i. 18 etc.). This sermon, which may or may not have been seriously intended, was elaborately refuted by Stephano de Sancto Giorgio in a work which condemns this new heresy of Neminianism. Upon the seriousness of this work opinion is also divided. Whatever the truth, many later examples of such sermons, some English, survive. The German and French humanists established Nobody as a satirical theme, a sort of universal scapegoat (Q: Who broke this cup? A: Nobody), and as the antitype of Somebody. The Nobody-Somebody theme was popular in England.

As for "the picture of Nobody", he was first represented in a cut of c. 1500, illustrating a *Sermo de Sancto Nemine*, as an empty rectangle, "since nobody is depicted therein". Later a conventional pictorial type emerged: Nobody was a ragged, bespectacled figure, often with a padlocked mouth to indicate enforced silence, and surrounded with a heap of broken objects. This type is seen in English broadsheets, but in England Nobody is also depicted as a head placed immediately above a vast pair of trunk hose, and this type is common in the early seventeenth century. The best-known illustrations are on the title-page of the 1606 *Nobody and Somebody*, and in George Baron's *Nobody his Complaint*, 1652.

p. 84, III. ii. 126–7: Stephano "confuses his phrases. . . He should have said . . . 'If thou beest a devil, show thyself in thy likeness [thy true shape]. If thou beest a man, take't as thou list,' i.e. 'take my defiance as it may please thee, either with or without resentment—a form of challenge' " (Kittredge).

p. 88, III. iii. 46: *Wallets*] Kittredge sees an allusion to the goitres suffered by Swiss mountaineers.

p. 88, III. iii. 48: *Each putter-out of five for one*] Mr J. C. Maxwell disputes the last part of the note, arguing that "of" could loosely mean "at the rate of"—the explanation of Symons in the Irving Shakespeare.

p. 89, III. iii. 53: J. E. Hankins (*Shakespeare's Derived Imagery*, [1953], pp. 261–2) finds here a debt to Palingenius, *Zodiacus Vitae*: see Googe's translation of 1576, ed. R. Tuve, [1947], pp. 49, 158. The whole passage is based on *Aeneid* III. 225–66, especially perhaps on the speech of Celaeno. The habitual allegorization of Virgil would make it easy to interpret the Harpies as emblematic of pride, guilt, and avarice: see, e.g. Coluccio Salutati, *De Laboribus Herculis* (ed. B. L. Ullman, Zurich, [1947]), III. xiv (I. 233 ff., esp. 240).

p. 90, III. iii. 73: *delaying, not forgetting*] Kittredge cites Plutarch's *De Sera Vindicta Numinis*.

p. 94, IV. i. 13: *gift*] Prof. T. M. Parrott in a review of this edition (*J.E.G.P.*, LV [1956], 149–56) points out that F, in l. 8 above, reads *guift*; if the copy had *guift* here also the compositor's error is easily understood.

p. 94, IV. i. 15: *virgin-knot*] Probably Catullus, III. 27: *Zonam soluere virgineam.*

p. 94, IV. i. 23: *lamps*] There is also an allusion to the clear or smoky burning of the torch, which was regarded as an omen (Kittredge).

p. 97, IV. i. 64: pioned] For the "flower" interpretation, it may be added that peonies seem to have been cultivated and their seeds used as a spice or medicine. "I haue peper and piones, quod she, and a pound of garlike" (*Piers Plowman* (B), v. 312).

p. 98, IV. i. 72 (S.D.): *Juno descends*] In MSS. known to be Crane's (e.g. Middleton, *The Witch*) S.D.s are often marked early, an indication of his using prompt-copy. This is not generally true of *Tp.*, but this S.D. looks like a survival in Crane's transcript of some prompter's note: here, perhaps, an actor needed warning that it was time to go to some remote place (perhaps the house on top) to prepare his entrance, or descent.

p. 100, IV. i. 96: bed-right] As C. J. Sisson says (*New Readings in Shakespeare*, 1956), this is not the same as "bed-rite"; a "right" is paid, a "rite" is celebrated. But in this connexion the notions of tribute and ceremony were doubtless confused or amalgamated.

p. 104, IV. i. 150: *thin air*] Cf. *Cym.*, I. iii. 20–1: "till he had melted from / The smallness of a gnat to air."

p. 105, IV. i. 164: *Come ... Ariel*] C. J. Sisson (*ibid.*) takes "Come" to be a past participle, and "I thank thee" to be addressed to Ariel.

p. 114, V. i. 27: *rarer*] not merely, of course, "less common", but also "finer".

p. 114, V. i. 27–8: See also Cato, *Disticha*, I. 38 (known to Elizabethan schoolboys); Chaucer, *Franklin's Tale*, ll. 743–5 and *Troil.*, IV. 1584. "The idea—*vincit qui patitur*—is a commonplace" (Robinson, *Poetical Works of Chaucer*, n.d., p. 827, with more references). See also Jonson, *Case is Altered*, I. vii. 71–3: "the property of the wretch is, he would hurt and cannot; of the man, he can hurt and will not".

p. 114, V. i. 36: *demi-*] *O.E.D.* does not give the sense "quasi-", but it is implicit in some of the examples, like Jewel's "his Dimi Communion, his Priuate Masse" (1565) and the expression "demi-male" for "eunuch". Possibly there was confusion with the Greek δημι, as in *demiurge*, which carries the idea of a substitute.

p. 120, v. i. 124: *subtleties*] Mr E. Schanzer challenges my note, allowing the "confectionery sense" only as secondary. But *taste* in l.123 suggests otherwise. The metaphor implies that the wonders they have so far seen are mere frivolities or trifles to the banquet of wonder yet to come.

p. 123, v. i. 174: *wrangle*] In support of the meaning "cheat, deceive", cf. "My love and I for kisses play'd, / Shee would keep stake, I was content. / But when I wonne shee would be paid; / This made me aske her what she meant. / Pray, since I see (quoth shee) your wrangling vayne, / Take your owne kisses, give me myne againe." (*Poetical Works of William Strode*, ed. B. Dobell, [1907], p. 47.) Strode's dates are 1602–45. "Wrangling" could still mean "quarrelling" here; but "cheating" suits the sense well.

Swift's "Furniture of a woman's mind" has something very close to the required sense:

> Improving hourly in her Skill,
> To cheat and wrangle at Quadrille ...

(*The Poems of Jonathan Swift*, ed. H. Williams, 2nd ed., 1958, II, 416.

p. 128, v. i. 249: *probable*] Mrs W. M. T. Nowottny, reviewing this edition in *M.L.R.*, L (1955), 327–30, says that the sense here is "rather that of *requiring* proof or examination". This is preferable, but I can find no support for it. Another *O.E.D.* meaning, "worthy of acceptance or belief" (cf. *2 H 6*, III. ii. 178) is possible.

SIXTH EDITION

Introduction

p. xx, n. 2: (See also notes on IV. i. 37 and IV. i. 167.) Some support for Gray is offered in Irwin Smith, "Ariel as Ceres", *Shakespeare Quarterly*, IX (1958), 430–2, where it is argued that certain inconsistencies in IV. i are the result of alterations made to give Ariel time to change into the Ceres costume and back again. Prospero's order (37) is at once modified: he tells Ariel to act "presently" (42) but then orders him not to come till called (49–50). He then repeats the sermon on continence he has just given (14 ff., 50 ff.). Iris, not Ariel, then appears. After the masque Prospero's "Our revels now are ended" (148 ff.) is an insertion just long enough to enable Ariel to change out of his Ceres costume. But even if one accepts this, it is unnecessary to suppose that the alterations were made later for a special performance. The need for Ariel to double Ceres could equally well have been discovered before the first performance, and the adjustments made in rehearsal. Smith also assumes that "presented" (167) means "acted". And the question of what occupied the place of the masque in the original play remains unanswered.

p. xxviii, n. 1: E. P. Kuhl, "Shakespeare and the Founders of America: *The Tempest*" (*P.Q.* XLI [1962], 133–46), surveys the facts and argues, unconvincingly, for much closer connexions between the play and the Virginia Council; holding, for example, that Caliban represents the enemies of the venture, especially Cecil.

p. xxxix, n. 2: Additional information on earlier English dramatic "wild men" appears in R. H. Goldsmith, "The Wild Man on the English Stage", *M.L.R.* LIII (1958), 481–91.

p. xli, n. 5: C. J. Sisson, "The Magic of Prospero", *Shakespeare Survey*, XI (1958), 70–7, argues that the notoriety of such conjurors as Forman and Savory would make it necessary for Shakespeare to disassociate Prospero's art "from the evil manifestations" of such black magic. Prospero performs none of their tricks; like Rosalind's magician he is "most profound in his art yet not damnable" (*A.Y.L.*, v. i. 55). But Sisson thinks that Shakespeare slipped in attributing to Prospero Medea's power *manes ... exire sepulchris*. See pp. 149–50.

p. lxxi, l. 15: An interesting new conjecture as to the source of *The Tempest* is that of Carol Gesner ("*The Tempest* as a Pastoral Romance", *Shakespeare Quarterly*, x [1959], 531–9). Observing that *Temp.*, like *A.Y.L.*, *Cymb.*, and *Wint.*, fulfils Greenlaw's rules of pastoral plots deriving from *Daphnis and Chloe* (*S.P.* XIII [1916], 122–54), Miss Gesner holds that "*Temp.* embodies elements of the Longus romance which were the typical pastoral material of the Renaissance," but proceeds to assert that Shakespeare used Longus directly, pointing out parallels between characters (Prospero and Philetas, Miranda and Chloe, Caliban and Dorco); parallels of plot and incident (Chloe's education, her seeing Daphnis for the first time, the incursion of foreigners into an island, etc.); and verbal parallels. Shakespeare could have read Longus in Day's version (1587) or Amyot's (1559 and later edd.). This would help to account for the element of pastoral romance in the play, and strikes me as a probable conjecture.

pp. lxxiv–lxxvi: paragraph *Miss Welsford's theory ... regulations*. For a dissentient view of the five-act structure see C. Leech, "The

Structure of the Last Plays", *Shakespeare Survey* II (1958), 25–127.

Commentary

p. 67, II. ii. 160–1: *I'll . . . enough.*] R. H. Goldsmith, *M.L.R.* LIII (1958), 481–91, compares Bremo's lines in *Mucedorus*: "Thou shalt be fed with quailes and partridges, / With blacke birds, larkes, thrushes and nightingales. / Thy drink shall bee goates milke and christal water, / Distilled from the fountaines & the clearest springs. / And all the dainties that the woods affords / Ile freely giue thee . . ."

p. 78, III. ii. 12–14: *for my part . . . and on.*] That this part of Stephano's speech belongs properly to Trinculo (cf. II. ii. 129–30) is the suggestion of M. Weidhorn, *N. & Q.*, n.s. IV (1957), 335. The reasons given for this change, principally that Stephano is made to lie unnecessarily, do not seem potent.

p. 80, III. ii. 62: *pied*] This, according to Hilda Hulme ("Shakespearian Glosses", *R.E.S.*, n.s. VI [1955], 133–4), refers not to Trinculo's costume but to his "mindless mischievous chattering", as in dialect "chatter-pie".

p. 90, III. iii. 65: *dowle*] A Stratford inventory of 1600 includes four instances of the word, e.g. of "dowle pillows". In pointing this out, Hilda Hulme, "Shakespeare of Stratford", *R.E.S.* X (1959), 21–2, supports the conjecture of *O.E.D.* that *dowl* is etymologically related to *down*.

p. 97, IV. i. 64: pioned and twilled brims] C. O. Fox in *N. & Q.*, n.s. IV (1957), 515–16, produces what is in effect Harrison's view but without assuming that "banks" refers to river-banks. *Pioned* means "excavated", *twilled* means "intertwined". The allusion is to a type of Warwickshire hedge—"raised banks topped by layered hedges which enclose the meadows".

p. 115, V. I. 41: *masters*] M. K. Flint and E. J. Dobson ("Weak Masters", *R.E.S.*, n.s. X [1959], 58–60) compare *Mac.*, IV. i. 163 and argue for the meaning "instruments". "Master" is a disguised form of obsolete *mister* from O. Fr. *mestier* (Mod. F. *métier*) <*misterium*<*ministerium*, in the sense of instrument or tool employed in the exercise of a craft. The semantic connexion with "minister" is evident in *Temp.*, I. ii. 275 and III. iii. 87, and possibly in I. ii. 162–3 Gonzalo is "master" in the sense of "instrument".

Appendix B

p. 145, l. 22: Stacy Johnson, "The Genesis of Ariel", *Shakespeare*

Quarterly, II (1951), 206, suggests that Shakespeare got the name from the *Steganographia* of Trimethius, in which Ariel appears as one of the twenty-eight planetary angels. R. R. Reed, Jr, "The Probable Origin of Ariel", *Shakespeare Quarterly*, XI (1960), 61–5, thinks Shakespeare was remembering Shrimp in Munday's *John a Kent & John a Cumber* (1589?) —a familiar spirit with some of Ariel's powers. There are some parallels of incident and language.